HOW TO PRACTICE
VEDIC
ASTROLOGY

HOW TO PRACTICE
VEDIC
ASTROLOGY

A Beginner's Guide to Casting Your
Horoscope and Predicting Your Future

ANDREW BLOOMFIELD

Destiny Books
Rochester, Vermont

Destiny Books
One Park Street
Rochester, Vermont 05767
www.InnerTraditions.com

Destiny Books is a division of Inner Traditions International

Library of Congress Cataloging-in-Publication Data

Bloomfield, Andrew, 1960-
    How to practice Vedic astrology : a beginner's guide to casting
your horoscope and predicting your future / Andrew Bloomfield.
        p. cm.
Includes bibliographical references and index.
    ISBN 0-89281-085-8
    1. Hindu astrology. I. Title.
    BF1714.H5B585 2003
    133.5'9445--dc21

                                            2003010311

Printed and bound in the United States at Capital City Press

10 9 8 7 6 5 4 3 2 1

Text design and layout by Priscilla Baker
This book was typeset in Sabon, with Agenda as a display typeface

ACKNOWLEDGMENTS

I would like to thank my parents Nathaniel and Suzanne for their love and enthusiastic support, and for making every opportunity available to me.

This book would not have been possible without the kindness of a remarkable Los Angeles–based Vedic astrologer and his family, who welcomed me into their home and treated me as one of their own.

Thanks also to Sandy Lee for her wisdom, encouragement, playfulness, and inspiration.

I would like to acknowledge Gareth Esersky at the Carol Mann Agency. Also, Ehud Sperling at Inner Traditions, who has championed so many vital and important books over the years.

I'm deeply appreciative of the whole team at Inner Traditions • Bear & Company, particularly managing editor Jeanie Levitan and my editor Laura Schlivek, for helping in innumerable ways. It's been a pleasure working with you two.

Finally, a special thanks to Michiel Boender, Svetlana, and the team at GeoVision software for producing the finest Vedic astrology software currently on the market, and so graciously customizing a version to complement this book.

DISCLAIMER

How to Practice Vedic Astrology is intended as an introduction to the practice of Vedic astrological interpretation. The author and publisher disclaim any responsibility or liability for actions taken on any reader's part based on interpretation of astrological information obtained from this book or from the accompanying software CD. It is the author's hope that any reader who wishes to delve further into the art of Vedic astrological interpretation will seek the services of a professional Vedic astrologer.

Note: Apart from well-known public personalities, the names of people whose charts are analyzed in this book have been altered so as not to reveal their true identities or jeopardize their privacy.

CONTENTS

◈

Part I—The Basics

Part II—Reading Charts

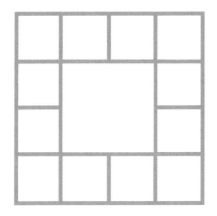

INTRODUCTION

Many centuries ago in India, a great king was told by his Vedic astrologer that his son was destined to be killed by a boar on a certain date, at a certain hour. Luckily, the king had enough time to secure his castle, to make sure his son wouldn't wander outside. He even enlisted his most trusted aide to track his son at every moment.

As the appointed time neared, the king met with the astrologer again, and stated it was now impossible for his son to be killed by a boar, as the castle was now impenetrable. The astrologer reminded the king that it wasn't yet the appointed hour. While the king's son was playing with a ball upstairs on a small balcony under the watchful eye of the king's aide, the king paced the floors. Convinced they had averted the danger, the aide decided to peek in on the king, who yelled, "Where's the boy?!" Turning, the king and his aide watched as the Vedic astrologer slowly entered the courtyard and approached the boy's dead body. A rock column lay next to the fallen child. Horrified,

the king and his aide ran outside and discovered that the column had been knocked loose by the boy's ball and hit the boy on the head. As they examined the column, they saw an image of a boar had been inscribed on its top.

Fast-forward several hundred years to Hollywood, California. An aspiring screenwriter has completed what he thinks is a terrific screenplay. He consults a Vedic astrologer who tells him even though the script is finished, if he brings the project out now, there is little chance for success. However, if he waits and follows the timing the astrologer lays out for him, he is told his project will gross a certain amount of money, and the astrologer writes that amount on the back of this man's chart. Although the writer is anxious to put the project in motion, he heeds the astrologer's advice. And in doing so, the movie makes almost the exact amount predicted by the astrologer, and goes on to win an Academy Award.

An ancient, 5000-year-old system of astrology from India is sweeping the country, attracting people from all walks of life, including Wall Street power brokers and Hollywood's most prominent actors and directors. The phenomenon is Vedic astrology.

In the sacred ancient language of India, Vedic astrology is called *jyotish,* pronounced jo-tish, meaning "the science of light." An encounter with Vedic astrology has the power to transform your life by shedding light on the dark recesses that contain the primal, unconscious, driving forces behind your thoughts and actions.

Yet even so, Vedic astrology, unlike some forms of astrology, is concerned less with psychological issues than the more practical concerns of work, relationships, health, success, wealth, and children. More importantly, it can answer with great precision, sometimes to the day, when significant events are likely to occur, whether it's meeting a life partner or getting a new job.

Further, when the chart indicates that good things are heading your way, this system provides you with methods to enhance those positive indications, helping to bring even better results. When challenging situations are indicated, remedial measures are recommended that will diminish, or help you avoid their full impact.

Can planets in the sky really influence events on Earth? Of course. What better example is there than of the moon affecting the tides? And because your body is made primarily of water, other celestial bodies affect you, as well as the moon, with staggering ramifications. Perhaps this is the reason that J. P. Morgan is said to have proclaimed, "Millionaires consult advisors; billionaires consult astrologers."

The planets do not really control us, however. Planets only exert influence. The ocean's waves may not have a choice in how they respond to this influence, but we do. Having free will, a person who uses it in alignment with divine purpose can generate more energy than the strongest planet. But in order to know where to focus this power, you have to understand the tendencies of the planets through Vedic astrology. Otherwise, you are operating blindly and are at the whim of the planets. As it is said, "If you don't change your direction, you'll get where you're headed."

CAUSE AND EFFECT

I once heard an Indian saint say, "Just because you're a vegetarian doesn't mean a charging bull is going to stop when you stand in its path." In other words, just because you consider yourself a good person doesn't mean that life is going to be fair. According to Vedic astrology (and physics), there is a strong link between cause and effect. For every action there is an equal and opposite reaction.

The problem for most of us is that we can't remember what we have already put into motion. Most of us can't even remember what we ate for dinner last week, let alone what we did years or, as Hindu thought would take into account, lifetimes ago. When the seeds of those actions ripen and come back to us, they bring either uplifting or challenging results. These results are made infinitely complex, too, by the effects they have had on countless others' lives and by others' reactions to our original actions. Because we can't remember what we did to deserve the good or bad results of these actions, we sometimes become incredulous. "How unfair!" we say, or "Why me?" or, if it's something good, "I always knew I was blessed." This cosmic action and reaction over multiple lifetimes explains why some people get all the breaks, and everything they touch turns to gold.

And it explains why innocent children can experience terrible violence and disease. Why some people live lives of deceit and never get caught, while others get blamed for things they didn't even do. Why catastrophic events will take the lives of many people, but leave a few survivors. Why some win the lottery and others never will.

From a Vedic astrological standpoint, when bad things happen to good people, it's because at some point in time they acted out of alignment with the natural flow of the universe, and the reaction has come back to them. What befalls us is not necessarily the same ill that we performed in the past, but what happens to us is always something that we had a hand in setting in motion.

A distinction should be made between individual and universal will. When you act according to individual will, the results don't bring true satisfaction or fulfillment. Even though you may succeed at getting what you want, you experience no peace of mind or contentment. Instead you want more, or better, or you say, "wouldn't it be nicer if it was yellow instead of red." On the other hand, when you act from a place of divine purpose, you serve universal will and your actions will be in harmony with your true life's purpose.

How do you know the difference between selfish and universal actions? For most people, it's the little voice inside that says, "I know I can make this happen (or get away with this), even though I know it's wrong." "Wrong" is not a moral or ethical determination. It's an inner barometer that informs us whether we're manipulating a situation for selfish ends or for the greater good. That is not to say that every action a person performs must be nice and pretty.

In the classic Indian text *Bhagavat Gita*, a warrior stands frozen on a battlefield, unable to pick up his weapon and fight because friends and family make up members of the other side. Krishna, the warrior's divine comrade and mentor, explains that everyone must engage in some sort of activity, and that actions can either bind a person or liberate him. The key is to perform actions but not be attached to their results. Krishna tells the warrior that everyone must play out his or her *dharma,* or duty, and the nature of a warrior is to fight. Krishna inspires the warrior to pick up his weapons and fight a courageous battle, since this is his life's purpose.

THE FOUR GOALS OF LIFE

Vedic astrology was first cognized by the ancient sages (*maharishis*) who "saw" the true interactions of the entire cosmos. They developed this system to help people actualize the four basic goals, or stages, of human existence. These four goals are shared by almost every living person regardless of nationality, religious orientation, or color. They are: *kama, artha, dharma,* and *moksha.*

- *Kama* means desire. More specifically, it pertains to the full enjoyment of the senses, whether good food, pleasant music, beautiful views, soft touches, or fragrant smells. Of course, in the cycle of life one's desires change. What begins as a desire for mother's milk soon becomes a desire to wear mascara, then a desire for early retirement.
- *Artha* means wealth, and relates to obtaining material comfort. When you are not stressed out about paying your bills every month, you have more ease, better health, and clearer thinking, which frees you to focus on things that you feel are more important.
- *Dharma* has many translations, one of which is purpose. Dharma here pertains to your life work, or vocation. It is your inborn drive to discover a vocational path that utilizes your innate talents and abilities so that your worldly work is a full expression of who you are.
- *Moksha* means liberation, alignment with a greater purpose, spiritual freedom.

Although moksha is one of the four aims of life, it is actually the bedrock upon which the other three sit. To realize our goals in the real world requires a greater purpose behind them. Otherwise, our achievements are useless and fleeting.

HOW I DISCOVERED VEDIC ASTROLOGY

Years ago I used to think astrology was a joke, and would laugh at people who lived their lives according to some unseen planetary forces. For several years, I owned a bookstore in Seattle, and didn't even stock books on astrology.

Then, one day in 1988, an astrologer from India came to my store, asked for my birth information, and told me that my bookstore, which I had created and in which I had invested enormous energy, would be sold within the year. The following year, I sold the store.

Intrigued, I followed the astrologer to his home in Los Angeles where he and his wife graciously invited me to live with them while I worked as his assistant. Over the years, I kept my ears open and listened to his readings. The astrologer didn't treat a famous CEO or an Oscar-winning actor any differently from a bum on the street. He simply gave them all advice to the best of his ability based on their planets.

I gained a great respect for the system of Vedic astrology, especially its predictive ability, which lets us know both *that* something is likely to happen, and *when* it is likely to occur. When the chart indicates a later marriage, it frees you to focus on your career now. When it indicates an earlier marriage, it's alerting you to keep your eyes open now for that special person.

I came to learn that Vedic astrology simply shows the planetary influences on your life and that the specific outcomes that these influences commonly manifest can be influenced by your own actions. Remember that every living person has the ability to overcome the influence of the planets by exercising his or her free will. Good fortune can be augmented and great challenges mitigated by appropriate measures.

For example, famous people often came into the Indian astrologer's office. In some cases these people's planets did not clearly indicate fame or greatness. The astrologer explained that these people's wills and actions were so strong that they made things happen for themselves. They created their own destiny, often by understanding the planetary influences that were at work in their lives and transcending them.

I came to realize that Vedic astrology is not deterministic, but its knowledge is power. It gives you information about yourself that enables you to activate your strengths (even if they're latent or unconscious) or learn ways to deal with your weaknesses. Also, since Vedic astrology can be extremely precise about the influence of planets and their likely outcome, it's important to remember that no matter what is indicated in the chart, you can take measures. Just as, in the martial arts, the prac-

titioner knows both how to damage his opponents and how to heal them, remedial measures offered in Vedic astrology help you to sidestep and perhaps avoid trouble, and sometimes even turn problematic indications into favorable ones.

Finally, I came to understand why Vedic astrology is frequently called predictive astrology. I once told a client that on June 21, 1986, his life had probably taken a dramatic turn. Dumbfounded, he said that was the day his true love married someone else and spun his life in a new direction forever. The date was etched in his memory. Although this may sound like pulling a date out of thin air, you will actually learn how to make predictions similar to this one by learning about the *dasha* system outlined in this book.

A GOOD PLACE TO START

For several years I lived in Nepal, where one day I met a Tibetan lama who told me the following story. When Tibetan lamas first began teaching Loving-Kindness meditation to large numbers of Westerners forty years ago, they had trouble getting the Westerners to develop as much compassion for others as they felt for themselves. It wasn't until much later that the lamas learned that many Westerners didn't feel love for themselves. This concept was incredible to the lamas, for the Tibetan language did not have a word to express lack of self-love. Now they saw the problem. If Westerners couldn't feel love on the inside, how could they express it for others?

Although the topic of cultivating self-love is beyond the scope of this material, it's important to be conscious of the messages we are giving ourselves on a moment-by-moment basis. Are they mostly positive or negative? Do they uplift, or batter down?

I once heard a Hindu saint say, "When people insult us we are so happy to agree with them, 'Yes, it's true what you say, I'm really terrible.' But when someone says they love us, suddenly we doubt it, 'Really? Are you sure?'"

So it's important to remember that as you learn about the planetary forces in Vedic astrology and become intentional with your goals and dreams, you also need to believe deep down inside that you deserve the best possible outcome. In that way you help to energize positive planetary influences and weaken negative ones.

This book presents a beginner's guide to Vedic astrology. Many variables and subtleties of chart interpretation cannot be covered in this volume, although I've given you enough concepts to work with as a student. In the back of the book are references to other materials, and to Vedic astrologers from whom you can seek more information, if you choose to keep learning this system.

Finally, and most importantly, since this is a very basic study, it's imperative that you *not* read something in this book and make immediate assumptions about your (or anyone else's) chart. Vedic astrology is a deep and profound body of knowledge. Practitioners can spend decades studying it, and even then have more to learn. Remember that sometimes a little bit of knowledge can be more dangerous than not having the knowledge at all.

Part I
THE BASICS

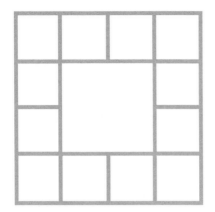

GETTING STARTED

We'll begin with some fundamentals of Vedic astrology. The first thing you'll want to do is create your chart.

You'll need:

- Your date of birth
- Your time of birth (if you don't know it, see Birth Time Adjustment below)
- Your place of birth

Because Vedic astrology involves many complex calculations, we've included a CD-ROM of Parashara's Light, currently the best Vedic astrological software available. Just type your name, date of birth, time of birth, and place of birth into the appropriate fields. Click on the Geovision Atlas so the computer can calculate your birth coordinates, and then click the OK button. In a matter of seconds you will be looking at your Vedic birth chart.*

*If you don't have access to a computer and would prefer that I send you your birth chart, please see the Appendix for information on ordering your chart.

BIRTH TIME ADJUSTMENT

The rising sign sets the tone for the entire chart, and is calculated using an accurate time of birth. If you are uncertain of your exact birth time, there will be some question about the accuracy of your rising sign, since the rising sign changes houses roughly every two hours. The easiest way to remedy this situation is to estimate the time of your birth, perhaps by relying on a relative's memory. If you don't have a surviving relative, note the time you usually wake up, or go to sleep. People who stay up late are usually born late at night, and those who naturally wake up early are often born in the morning.

Perhaps a more accurate technique is simply to locate the Moon in your chart, designated by "Mo," and use the house in which it is located as your rising sign. Using the Moon's house as a substitute rising sign gives extremely accurate results, which is why many Vedic astrologers read the chart from the position of the Moon even when they know the person's actual time of birth.

If you calculate your chart using an estimated time of birth (not the Moon technique just described) you may need to adjust the time a few hours ahead or back, until you find a description listed in Table A that best describes you:

For instance, let's say your estimated chart indicates that you have Aries rising, meaning that you tend to be bold, rash, and driven. Instead, you may be patient and easygoing, in which case you'll need to advance the time of your birth an hour or so for Taurus rising. Or, you may be the sacrificing sort who is deeply mystical and emotional, in which case you'll move the time back an hour or so for Pisces rising.

THE CHART

Once you calculate your chart, you will notice that Vedic astrology charts look quite different from those of Western astrology. But the houses go by the same names, are twelve in number, and have roughly the same meaning.

Two types of charts exist in Vedic astrology, one used mostly in Northern India, the other in the South. In this book we'll use the Southern Indian style, which you'll notice is square in shape, and fixed, meaning that the signs remain in the same place regardless of the person's birth date. Look at Chart 1 and notice how the signs in your own chart are in the same position as in this sample chart— Pisces is always in the top left, Gemini in the

Table A: The Characteristics of Each Rising Sign

RISING SIGN	CHARACTERISTICS
Aries	bold, rash, driven, passionate, selfish, may be short in stature
Taurus	patient, slow-moving, routine, materialistic, may have a thick neck and broad forehead
Gemini	curious, articulate, flexible, communicator, easy to let go of things and people
Cancer	home and family-oriented, emotional, wide-faced, finds it hard to let go of things or people
Leo	likes being the center of attention, dramatic, vain
Virgo	perfectionist, critical, communicator, interest in health, may be tall in stature
Libra	artistic, driven, tactful, diplomatic, indecisive, may be tall in stature
Scorpio	intuitive, penetrating, deeply emotional, secretive
Sagittarius	philosophical, fanatical, outspoken, impatient, blunt
Capricorn	cautious, businesslike, conservative, aloof
Aquarius	clever, witty, humanitarian, opinionated, independent, loner
Pisces	sacrificing, mystical, emotional, escapist, may be short in stature

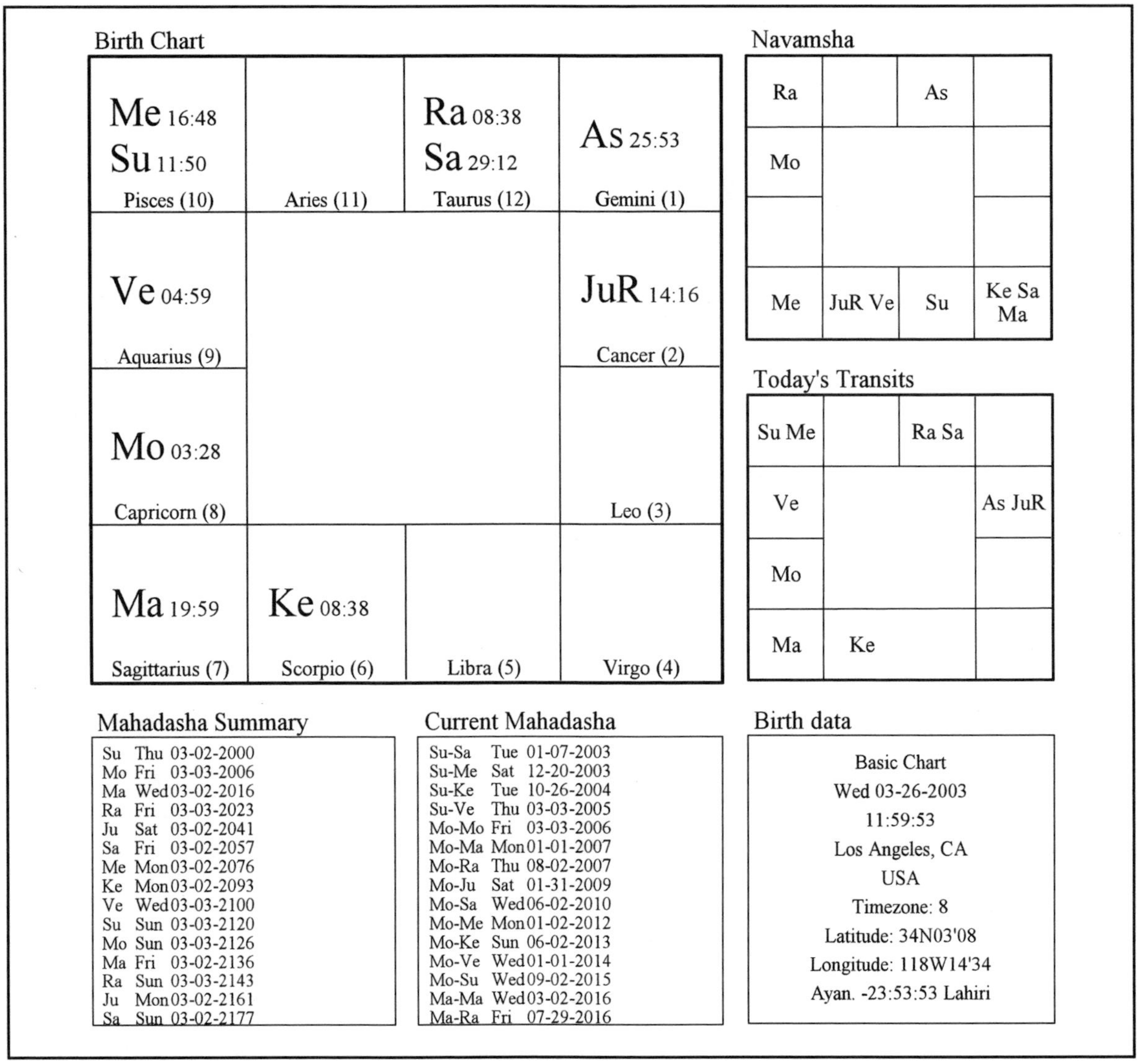

Birth Chart				Navamsha			
Me 16:48 **Su** 11:50 Pisces (10)	Aries (11)	**Ra** 08:38 **Sa** 29:12 Taurus (12)	**As** 25:53 Gemini (1)	Ra		As	
Ve 04:59 Aquarius (9)			**JuR** 14:16 Cancer (2)	Mo			
Mo 03:28 Capricorn (8)			Leo (3)	Me	JuR Ve	Su	Ke Sa Ma

Today's Transits

Su Me		Ra Sa	
Ve			As JuR
Mo			
Ma	Ke		

Ma 19:59 Sagittarius (7)	**Ke** 08:38 Scorpio (6)	Libra (5)	Virgo (4)

Mahadasha Summary

Su	Thu	03-02-2000
Mo	Fri	03-03-2006
Ma	Wed	03-02-2016
Ra	Fri	03-03-2023
Ju	Sat	03-02-2041
Sa	Fri	03-02-2057
Me	Mon	03-02-2076
Ke	Mon	03-02-2093
Ve	Wed	03-03-2100
Su	Sun	03-03-2120
Mo	Sun	03-03-2126
Ma	Fri	03-02-2136
Ra	Sun	03-03-2143
Ju	Mon	03-02-2161
Sa	Sun	03-02-2177

Current Mahadasha

Su-Sa	Tue	01-07-2003
Su-Me	Sat	12-20-2003
Su-Ke	Tue	10-26-2004
Su-Ve	Thu	03-03-2005
Mo-Mo	Fri	03-03-2006
Mo-Ma	Mon	01-01-2007
Mo-Ra	Thu	08-02-2007
Mo-Ju	Sat	01-31-2009
Mo-Sa	Wed	06-02-2010
Mo-Me	Mon	01-02-2012
Mo-Ke	Sun	06-02-2013
Mo-Ve	Wed	01-01-2014
Mo-Su	Wed	09-02-2015
Ma-Ma	Wed	03-02-2016
Ma-Ra	Fri	07-29-2016

Birth data

Basic Chart

Wed 03-26-2003

11:59:53

Los Angeles, CA

USA

Timezone: 8

Latitude: 34N03'08

Longitude: 118W14'34

Ayan. -23:53:53 Lahiri

Chart 1—The Basic Chart

top right, Virgo in the bottom right, and Sagittarius in the bottom left. What makes each chart unique is the play of the planetary positions over this fixed palette.

You may also notice that all of your planets have been moved back approximately 23 degrees from their Western astrological position. If you're used to your Sun being at 10 degrees Leo, you will see in the Vedic system that it is now around 17 degrees in Cancer. This difference is due to Vedic astrology being based on the constellations, in contrast with the Earth-based Western tropical system. The Western system is referred to as tropical because it uses solstices and equinoxes as reference points, as opposed to the fixed placement of constellations of the Vedic system. Being an Earth-based system, Western astrology encompasses Western sensibilities of imposing our will on our environment, through a certain amount of control, in order to succeed as an individuated, ego-based soul. The Vedic system is more concerned with how to work within a cosmology that incorporates every living being, so that we can bring into manifestation the full expression of our planets without causing any harm, or upsetting the natural universal flow.

While Western astrology looks to the relationship between our Earth and Sun, using the equinoxes as points of reference, the Vedic system of constellational astrology transcends our Sun-based environment, taking into account our entire galaxy. Western astrology focuses on how you'll react to the situation at hand; Vedic astrology explains how you arrived in the situation in the first place, and then provides *upayas,* or methods, for bringing things into balance. Though the two systems shared the same point of reference several thousand years ago, they have separated over time due to the precession of the equinoxes, and other variances that affect the earth's orbit. Technically speaking, then, Western astrology uses a symbolic zodiac, because it does not relate to the actual position of the stars, while Vedic astrology uses the actual zodiac.

The planets and their meanings in the Vedic system are more or less the same as their Western counterparts, except Rahu ("Ra" in your chart), the north lunar node, and Ketu ("Ke"), the south lunar node, which play highly significant roles in Vedic astrology. Rahu can indicate strong worldly desires, allergies, career success, events of mass destruction, or epidemics, while Ketu can indicate mysticism or psychic ability, hypersensitivity, wild imagination, or psychosis.

Also, you'll notice that none of the extra-Saturnian planets are indicated in the Vedic system, primarily because they weren't known about when Vedic astrology was first cognized, more than 5000 years ago. Even though Neptune, Uranus, and Pluto are not included in Vedic astrology, some say their influences are paralleled by certain combinations of planets and other indications in the Vedic system.

Another difference between Western and Vedic astrology is a principle basic to the art of Vedic astrology. The Sun, so important to the assessment of a chart in the Western system, has much less significance in the Vedic system. As a power of ego, the Sun has more to do with outward appearances and, to some degree, superficiality. The Moon is more important in Vedic astrology because it signifies the deep emotional motivations and aspirations of the human soul. Consider how it usually takes time for you to get to know and trust a new acquaintance. This trust-building period is necessary because you need to determine if what you're seeing (Sun) is really what you're getting (Moon). It's also true that you can know more about people by watching what they do (Moon), than by listening to what they say (Sun).

The birth chart that you have just generated is a diagram of the heavens that shows your tendencies, habits, likes, and dislikes, based on the past. Because Vedic astrology has Hindu philosophy as its foundation (a bedrock principle of which is *karma*), significant meaning is given to the past. Although the concepts of past lives and transmigration of the soul may be difficult to comprehend, ideas like "As you have sown so shall you reap" and Newton's third law of motion, "For every action there is an equal and opposite reaction," have meaning for most of us.

So, as you start to decipher your chart and find certain tendencies indicated you might not be so fond of, remember they are from the past and it is your choice whether to fuel these tendencies or change them.

We'll start at the beginning: the rising sign.

STEP 1—THE NATURE OF THE RISING SIGN (1st HOUSE)

Look at your chart and find your rising sign, indicated by "As" in one of the squares and the number "(1)" next to the zodiac name. In sample Chart 1, "As" is located in Gemini and indicated as the 1st house by "(1)". We start at the rising sign, or 1st house, because

Table B: Rising Signs and Their Ruling Planets

RISING SIGN	CHARACTERISTICS (POSITIVE/NEGATIVE)	RULING PLANET	ELEMENT	QUALITY
Aries	dynamic/domineering	Mars	fire	cardinal
Taurus	patient/stubborn	Venus	earth	fixed
Gemini	adaptable/restless	Mercury	air	mutable
Cancer	nurturing/moody	Moon	water	cardinal
Leo	dramatic/proud	Sun	fire	fixed
Virgo	exacting/critical	Mercury	earth	mutable
Libra	diplomatic/indecisive	Venus	air	cardinal
Scorpio	intense & secretive/perverse	Mars	water	fixed
Sagittarius	direct/hot-headed (& excessive)	Jupiter	fire	mutable
Capricorn	businesslike/inhibited	Saturn	earth	cardinal
Aquarius	independent/opinionated	Saturn	air	fixed
Pisces	introspective/ungrounded	Jupiter	water	mutable

your life started there. It's the constellation that was rising on the horizon at the moment of your birth. From the rising sign, the numbers of the other houses are determined by moving in a clockwise manner.

The "As" stands for ascendant (another name for the rising sign) and indicates the 1st house. The actual degree of the rising sign is indicated by the number next to it. In our sample chart, the ascendant is located at 25 degrees, 53 minutes. (If you're using the Moon as your rising sign because you don't know your time of birth, the Moon will represent your ascendant, and as such becomes your 1st house.)

What does the 1st house tell you? A lot! It indicates your entire character and life purpose, setting the tone for your entire personality. Table B is simplistic, but gives you a sense of how much influence the rising sign has on your life. Take time to jot information specific to your chart in a notebook so you'll be able to keep track of it as you read further.

Two categories in Table B may need more explanation: element and quality.

The element connected with a sign gives it its organic composition:

- Fire signs are just as they sound: dynamic, driven, impulsive, and action-oriented.
- Earth signs are grounded, slower moving, practical, and sometimes stubborn.
- Air signs are intellectual, visionary, insightful, detail-oriented, and sometimes self-centered and nervous.

- Water signs are intuitive, emotional, nurturing, and sometimes spacey and out of touch with reality.

The quality category addresses the activity-nature of the sign:

- Cardinal signs set things in motion, initiate projects, and are driven.
- Fixed signs are stabilizers, grounded, and slow moving.
- Mutable signs are malleable, flexible, multi-skilled, and talented.

Now that you've studied Table B and noted the element and quality of your rising sign, let's explore the planets.

STEP 2—PLANETS IN THE 1st HOUSE

Observing the planets enables us to fine-tune our chart analysis. As you examine your chart, you'll notice that some houses are occupied by planets, while others are not. Now, look at your 1st house and see if one or more planets are located there. If so, locate the planets below, and read their descriptions. If no planets are located in your 1st house, go to Step 3.

Sun (Su) in the 1st house can make a person proud, somewhat irritable, and driven. If the Sun is placed in Libra, however, where it is weakest, there is a noticeable lack of confidence, and you may struggle with self-acceptance or health complaints or difficulties with your father (or your father may have life challenges). If the Sun falls close to the actual degree of the rising sign, though, even if it *is* located in Libra, you may still express strong ego and self-confidence.

Moon (Mo) in the 1st house brings softness and beauty to the face, a certain inner radiance. Emotionally you will be intuitive and perhaps moody. If the Moon is placed in Scorpio, where it is weakest, there may be health problems, emotional disturbances, and sexual difficulties (often female).

Mars (Ma) in the 1st house produces fire, a warrior-like nature, passion, impulsiveness, and difficulty with monogamy. It may also help you look younger than your actual years, though you may have a ruddy complexion. A poorly placed Mars can bring accidents or injuries, especially when located in Cancer, where it is weakest. There might be injuries to the head or rashes on the face.

Mercury (Me) in the 1st house brings great communication skills, quick-wittedness, and a talkative nature. If Mercury is in Pisces, where it is weakest, there may be nervousness, mental instability, and a possible speech impediment.

Jupiter (Ju) in the 1st house can indicate a heavy or big-boned build, as Jupiter brings its expansiveness to the body. This placement is extremely fortunate and brings you many uplifting opportunities. However, if Jupiter is in Capricorn, where it is weakest, you may not be properly recognized for your efforts. In some cases Jupiter can bring overoptimism, which can lead to overcommitting or overextending yourself.

Venus (Ve) in the 1st house brings great physical beauty. Venus also brings you refinement, charm, and sensuality. If Venus is placed in Virgo, where it is weakest, your experiences in love may fall short of your expectations.

Saturn (Sa) in the 1st house is most fortuitous for service or humanitarian-oriented endeavors. It brings slow, steady progress by persevering over time. If Saturn is in Aries, where it is weakest, it can bring frustrations in your personal or professional progress, and you may encounter delays, obstacles, and the feeling of being restricted.

Rahu (Ra) in the 1st house brings an aggressive nature and worldly success. It can also indicate an unusual or unique person who may marry (possibly a foreigner) more than once. Although it is unclear in which house Rahu operates at its weakest, a problematic Rahu can affect health and confidence.

Ketu (Ke) in the 1st house brings a mystical nature and highly sensitive nervous system. Like Rahu in the 1st, Ketu can bring unhappiness in marriage and the possibility of more than one marriage. Although it is unclear in which house Ketu operates at its weakest, a problematic Ketu can make one highly susceptible to peer influences, deception, or other people's energy.

STEP 3—NO PLANETS IN THE 1st HOUSE

If you skipped Step 2 because you didn't find a planet in your 1st house, please don't feel that something is wrong with your chart. Look at this column taken from Table B on page 12:

RISING SIGN	RULING PLANET
Aries	Mars
Taurus	Venus
Gemini	Mercury
Cancer	Moon
Leo	Sun
Virgo	Mercury
Libra	Venus
Scorpio	Mars
Sagittarius	Jupiter
Capricorn	Saturn
Aquarius	Saturn
Pisces	Jupiter

Notice that every rising sign (1st house) has a ruling planet. Now look at your chart and do the following:

1. Find your 1st house.
2. Find the planet that rules that house (see table above).
3. Find where that planet is placed in your chart.

Now study the following table:

Table C: Horoscope Houses and Their Indications

HOROSCOPE HOUSES	INDICATIONS
1st house (rising sign)	character and life purpose
2nd house	wealth through career, childhood
3rd house	creativity, courage, younger sibling
4th house	mother, vehicles, property
5th house	children, higher education, speculation
6th house	health, enemies
7th house	love, marriage, partnerships, opponents
8th house	longevity, sensuality, mysticism, inheritance
9th house	father, luck, religion/spirituality, travel
10th house	career, fame
11th house	opportunity, older sibling, friends
12th house	foreign travel, loss, confinement, emancipation

Notice that every house has a specific indication. Now that you have located the ruler of your 1st house, recognize that it will be expressed through the nature of the house in which it is located.

For instance, because Table C shows that the 3rd house is connected with creativity, guess what the focus will be if your 1st house ruler is placed in the 3rd house? That's right. You've got the chart of an artist. If the 1st house ruler is in the 6th, which according to Table C is associated with health, you've got the chart of a healer. Of course, this is an oversimplification, but you get the idea.

So, with that in mind, locate your 1st house ruler and recognize where your strengths lie (or karmas play out). If your 1st house ruler is placed in the 7th house, for example, this indicates that in this lifetime you will work through a great deal of karma in the area of partnerships, committed intimate relationships, and marriage. This issue of house ruler placement is discussed in more length beginning on page 49, where we delve more deeply into 1st house issues. For now, however, let's go ahead and figure out how to interpret the houses. There are a number of ways to categorize them.

One way is to look at the 1st, 5th, and 9th houses as beneficial. The 3rd, 6th, 10th, and 11th houses are called improving (*upachaya*) houses because even if they are afflicted, they can improve over time through your commitment to change. The most challenging houses are the 8th and 12th. However, this does not mean that these houses only reflect life's worst possible scenarios—though they sometimes do. The 8th and 12th houses can also show positive transformation through deep personal exploration.

(If you don't know your time of birth and are using the placement of your Moon as your rising sign, simply count in a clockwise fashion, using the Moon's house as number one, in order to locate your other houses. For example, if your Moon is placed in Scorpio, your 5th house is Pisces. If your Moon is in Virgo, your 8th house is Aries.)

PLANETS AND THEIR MEANINGS

Now that we've looked at the signs and the meanings of the houses, let's look more closely at the planets, and some key words regarding what they represent.

Table D: Planets and Their Signifiers

PLANET	SIGNIFIERS (*KARAKAS*)
Sun	father, power, ego, the limelight
Moon	mother, emotions
Mars	brothers, energy
Mercury	the mind, communication
Jupiter	expansion, children, money, luck, wisdom
Venus	love, happiness, the arts
Saturn	restriction, discipline
Rahu	worldly desires, disasters
Ketu	psychic ability, mysticism

Some planets are considered benefic (positive), and others malefic (negative).

- Jupiter and Venus are benefics.
- Mars, Saturn, Rahu, and Ketu are malefics.
- Mercury is neutral, taking on the influence of planets that come in contact with it.
- The Sun has a malefic tendency (since it's so hot), but can accentuate the benefic quality of planets nearby (as long as those planets stay about 8 degrees from the Sun; otherwise they will become "combust" and lose power).
- The Moon tends to be benefic when waxing, and malefic when waning.

As mentioned above, houses that tend to be uplifting in nature, like the 5th and 9th, welcome benefic planets readily.

Houses that are challenging in nature, for instance the 8th and 12th, destroy the positive nature of benefics. However, malefic planets tend to thrive when located in these challenging houses.

Note the placement of planets in your chart. Are your benefic planets like Venus and Jupiter placed in uplifting houses like the 5th and 9th, or challenging ones, like the 6th and 8th? If you find that a benefic planet like Venus, for instance, is placed in a challenging house, though the natural energies of that planet may be restricted, the benefits of this placement can include charisma, passion, love of mysticism, and a long life. In other words, even challenging planetary placements have certain positive indications.

Also notice if the Moon is waxing or waning, and whether any planets are located too close (within 8 degrees or so) to the Sun. If so, they are weakened. In the case of Mercury being combust by the Sun, for instance, one can experience mental anguish and nervousness.

ASPECTS

One of the unique ways a Vedic astrologer can make predictions is by observing the interaction of the planets, called aspects (planetary influences). Unlike the Western astrological system, in which an aspect can only occur when two planets are a certain number of degrees from one another, Vedic astrology uses the entire house.

Here are five major aspects found in a chart:

1. Every planet influences any other planet it conjoins (is in the same house with).
2. Every planet influences any other planet it opposes (lies opposite to).
3. Mars aspects the house in which it's placed, along with the 4th, 7th, and 8th houses from itself.
4. Jupiter aspects the house in which it's placed, along with the 5th, 7th, and 9th houses from itself.
5. Saturn aspects the house in which it's placed, along with the 3rd, 7th, and 10th houses from itself.

When determining the Mars, Jupiter, and Saturn aspects, remember that the house you're starting from is counted as 1, and that you count in a clockwise manner. So, four houses from Virgo is Sagittarius, five houses from Taurus is Virgo, and so on.

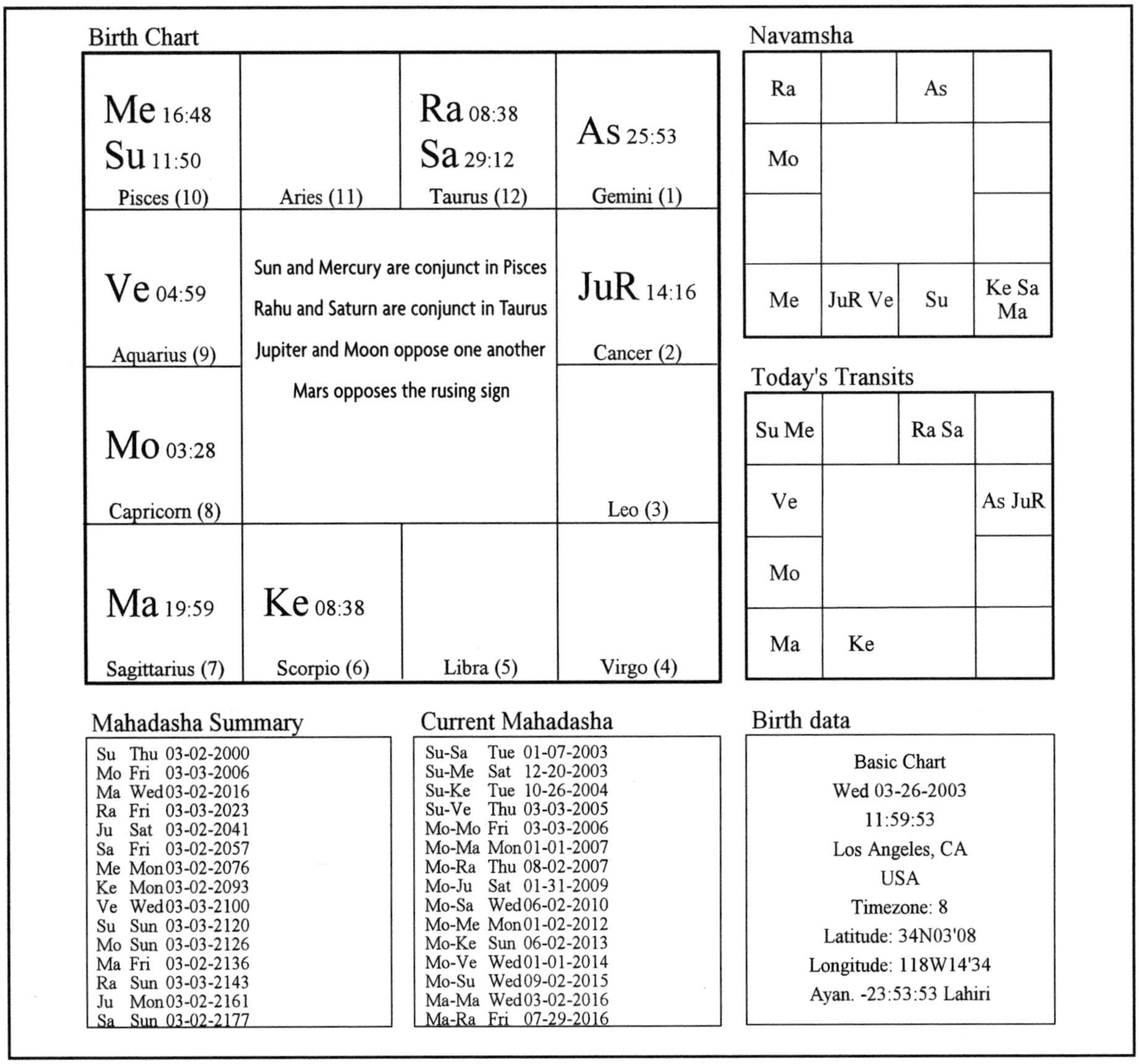

Birth Chart				Navamsha			
Me 16:48 **Su** 11:50 Pisces (10)	Aries (11)	**Ra** 08:38 **Sa** 29:12 Taurus (12)	**As** 25:53 Gemini (1)	Ra		As	
Ve 04:59 Aquarius (9)	Sun and Mercury are conjunct in Pisces Rahu and Saturn are conjunct in Taurus Jupiter and Moon oppose one another Mars opposes the rusing sign		**JuR** 14:16 Cancer (2)	Mo			
Mo 03:28 Capricorn (8)			Leo (3)				
Ma 19:59 Sagittarius (7)	**Ke** 08:38 Scorpio (6)	Libra (5)	Virgo (4)	Me	JuR Ve	Su	Ke Sa Ma

Today's Transits

Su Me		Ra Sa	
Ve			As JuR
Mo			
Ma	Ke		

Mahadasha Summary

Su	Thu	03-02-2000
Mo	Fri	03-03-2006
Ma	Wed	03-02-2016
Ra	Fri	03-03-2023
Ju	Sat	03-02-2041
Sa	Fri	03-02-2057
Me	Mon	03-02-2076
Ke	Mon	03-02-2093
Ve	Wed	03-03-2100
Su	Sun	03-03-2120
Mo	Sun	03-03-2126
Ma	Fri	03-02-2136
Ra	Sun	03-03-2143
Ju	Mon	03-02-2161
Sa	Sun	03-02-2177

Current Mahadasha

Su-Sa	Tue	01-07-2003
Su-Me	Sat	12-20-2003
Su-Ke	Tue	10-26-2004
Su-Ve	Thu	03-03-2005
Mo-Mo	Fri	03-03-2006
Mo-Ma	Mon	01-01-2007
Mo-Ra	Thu	08-02-2007
Mo-Ju	Sat	01-31-2009
Mo-Sa	Wed	06-02-2010
Mo-Me	Mon	01-02-2012
Mo-Ke	Sun	06-02-2013
Mo-Ve	Wed	01-01-2014
Mo-Su	Wed	09-02-2015
Ma-Ma	Wed	03-02-2016
Ma-Ra	Fri	07-29-2016

Birth data

Basic Chart
Wed 03-26-2003
11:59:53
Los Angeles, CA
USA
Timezone: 8
Latitude: 34N03'08
Longitude: 118W14'34
Ayan. -23:53:53 Lahiri

Chart 2—Conjunctions and Oppositions

What do these aspects mean? Generally speaking:

- The aspects of Mars are fiery and dynamic.
- Saturn's aspects are contracting and persevering.
- Jupiter's aspects are expansive and beneficent.

Look at your chart now. Find your Mars. Remember that Mars influences the house it's in, the 4th house from itself, the 7th house from itself, and the 8th house from itself.

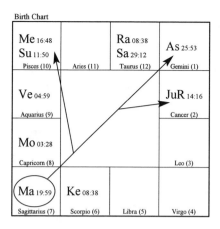

Chart 3—Mars's Aspects

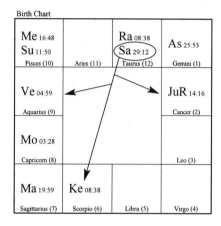

Chart 4—Saturn's Aspects

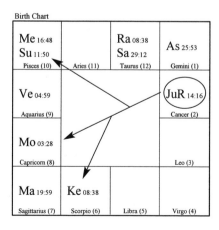

Chart 5—Jupiter's Aspects

First, recognize that Mars brings energy to the house in which it is located. Now, starting with the house in which Mars is placed, count four houses from that house in a clockwise fashion. Mars influences that house, too. Now count three more houses clockwise to the 7th house from your Mars placement. It influences that house, too. Now count one more house to the 8th house beyond Mars. It influences that house, as well.

Do the same thing for your Saturn. It influences the house it's in, as well as the 3rd, 7th, and 10th houses from itself.

Do the same thing for Jupiter. It influences the house it's in, as well as the 5th, 7th, and 9th houses from itself.

If you can't remember what the houses or planets indicate, refer back to Tables C and D. Does Jupiter hit your 2nd house? Because Jupiter brings expansion (Table D), and the 2nd house indicates money (Table C), you may be wealthy, or will come into money at some point in your life. Does Saturn aspect the 2nd house? As Saturn is a contracting influence, you may have the opposite experience of not having enough money.

You will notice when looking at your chart that next to each planet is a number. This number is the actual position of the planet in the zodiac, and is described in degrees (the first number), followed by minutes (the second number). Each astrological sign is defined by 30 degrees, because each sign represents 30 degrees of arc, with 360 degrees of arc making up the complete circle. The numbers you will see, then, range anywhere from 0 to 30 within any one sign. Again, luckily we have computers that can calculate these exact positions for us.

When you look at the association of planets, whether a conjunction (two planets together in the same house), an opposition (two planets sitting in houses 180 degrees from one another), or the aspects that Mars, Jupiter, and Saturn throw on the chart, it's important to pay attention to the number of degrees that separate the planets. Although two planets placed in the same house are said to be conjunct, if they sit close to the exact degree of each other the power of conjunction is exceedingly strong. However, if they are 25 degrees away from each other, although the aspect still technically exists, its effect is weaker.

PLANETARY EXALTATION AND DEBILITATION

In certain locations planets give their strongest results, and in others their weakest. Planets placed in the houses they rule are considered strong, so long as they are not negatively aspected (explained below in Planetary Friends and Enemies). There are also places in the chart where planets operate at their best, and other places where they are quite weak. These are called exaltation and debilitation points. Exaltation points are not always as good as they sound. For instance, a woman client of mine has an exalted Jupiter and an exalted Mars opposing each other. That sounds great, but these particular planets drive her in extremely selfish directions, and she is entirely self-absorbed. Likewise, debilitated planets are not as bad as they sound. They enable a person to have experiences that bring wisdom, understanding, compassion, and intuition.

In addition to the descriptions above, planets in very early or very late degrees of a house tend to be quite weak.

RETROGRADE PLANETS

Of course, planets don't really travel in reverse direction. It only appears that they do

Table E: Exaltation and Debilitation of Planets

PLANET	PLACE OF EXALTATION	PLACE OF DEBILITATION
Sun	10 degrees Aries	10 degrees Libra
Moon	3 degrees Taurus	3 degrees Scorpio
Mars	28 degrees Capricorn	28 degrees Cancer
Mercury	15 degrees Virgo	15 degrees Pisces
Jupiter	5 degrees Cancer	5 degrees Capricorn
Venus	27 degrees Pisces	27 degrees Virgo
Saturn	20 degrees Libra	20 degrees Aries

from our perspective on Earth. On occasion, a planet will be in retrograde motion at the time of a person's birth. Depending on what planet that is, and where it is placed, it may have a significant impact on the chart.

Also, since the planets continue to transit over our fixed birth planets, when transiting planets turn retrograde they can also affect our lives. For instance, several times a year Mercury turns retrograde for about three weeks at a time. Whenever that occurs, there are usually minor problems with things whose functions or processes are ruled by Mercury, such as communication and transportation. Cars and planes may break down or be delayed, phones and computers may malfunction, people may

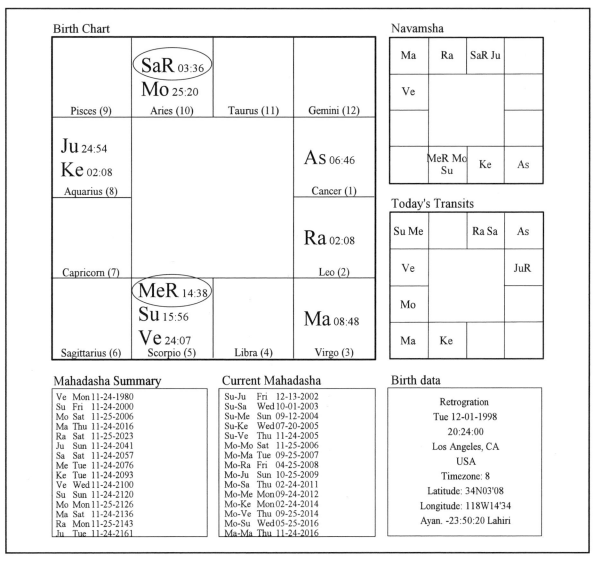

Chart 6—Retrogration

misunderstand one another, appointments may be missed, or addresses may be jotted down incorrectly.

If a planet is retrograde in a birth chart, it will create some developmental delays, introspective tendencies, or unconventionality in that person, depending on the planet, and where it is placed. A Saturn placed in the 3rd house, for instance, will delay the time it takes a person to develop his or her courage, or recognize artistic abilities. A retrograde Venus can indicate unusual sexual desires, an unconventional marriage, or unique aesthetic tastes.

Usually this retrograde motion will redirect the natural energy of the planet inward. Saturn in retrograde can make a person introspective. Mars in retrograde can internalize what are usually outwardly manifest passions. Retrograde Jupiter can lead to lethargy and laziness.

In Chart 6, notice the "R" located next to Saturn (Sa), and Mercury (Me). This indicates that both Saturn and Mercury are retrograde. Because Aries is the 10th house (career) in this chart, retrograde Saturn shows that the per-

Table F: Planetary Friends and Enemies

PLANET	FRIENDS	ENEMIES	NEUTRAL
Sun	Moon Mars Jupiter	Venus Saturn	Mercury
Moon	Sun Mercury	None	Mars Jupiter Venus Saturn
Mars	Sun Moon Jupiter	Mercury	Venus Saturn
Mercury	Sun Venus	Moon	Mars Jupiter Saturn
Jupiter	Sun Moon Mars	Mercury Venus	Saturn
Venus	Mercury Saturn	Sun Moon	Mars Jupiter
Saturn	Mercury Venus	Sun Moon Mars	Jupiter

son may experience delays in finding his or her vocational path, or be extremely vigilant and detail-oriented in his or her current career.

The retrograde Mercury in Scorpio in this chart sits too close to the Sun (within two degrees), which creates combustion. Mercury being combust and retrograde brings nervousness and a lack of confidence, which in this chart example could also describe the person's child, because Scorpio represents the 5th house (children).

PLANETARY FRIENDS AND ENEMIES

Just as you get along with some people and do not get along with others, so some planets work well together, while others do not. This empathy or antipathy is not just between planets (Table F), but can also be seen when the planets are located in certain signs (Table G). Rahu and Ketu are not included, since there exists no decisive opinion as to where the lunar nodes operate at their best, or worst.

Table G: Planetary Relationships by Sign

HOUSE	FRIENDS	ENEMIES	NEUTRAL
Aries	Jupiter Sun Mars	Saturn Venus Mercury	Moon
Taurus	Mercury Saturn Sun Venus	Jupiter Moon Mars	
Gemini	Saturn Venus Mercury	Jupiter Mars Sun	Moon
Cancer	Jupiter Mars Moon	Saturn Mercury Venus	Sun
Leo	Jupiter Mars Sun	Saturn Mercury Venus	Moon
Virgo	Venus Mercury	Jupiter Mars Moon	Saturn Sun
Libra	Mercury Saturn Venus	Jupiter Sun Mars	Moon

Table G: Planetary Relationships by Sign (continued)

HOUSE	FRIENDS	ENEMIES	NEUTRAL
Scorpio	Jupiter Sun Moon Mars	Saturn Mercury Venus	
Sagittarius	Mars Sun Jupiter	Saturn Venus	Moon Mercury
Capricorn	Venus Mercury Saturn	Moon Mars Jupiter Sun	
Aquarius	Venus Saturn Jupiter	Moon Mars Sun	Mercury
Pisces	Mars Moon Jupiter	Saturn Venus Mercury Sun	

A practical example of the interaction between two planets can be seen in Paul Newman's chart (Chart 7). His rising sign planets Mercury, Venus, and Jupiter brought him beauty and success; they made him a star. But if you look at the planet Jupiter in Table F, you'll see that Venus is one of its enemies. How can this be, when these are the very planets that brought him success and beauty?

This is an example of one of the more subtle issues in Vedic astrology. Venus and Jupiter are both beneficent, magnanimous planets. And as such, you'd think they'd get along. But instead, they vie for attention like two beautiful women in one room, both of whom want to be noticed. So even though they brought him beauty, that beauty was at times uncomfortable for Paul. Rumor has it that as a "pretty boy," he had to work harder at his acting to prove that he was more than just good looking.

Another example can be seen between the planets Saturn and Mars, described in Table F as enemies. In the spring of 1999 Saturn was

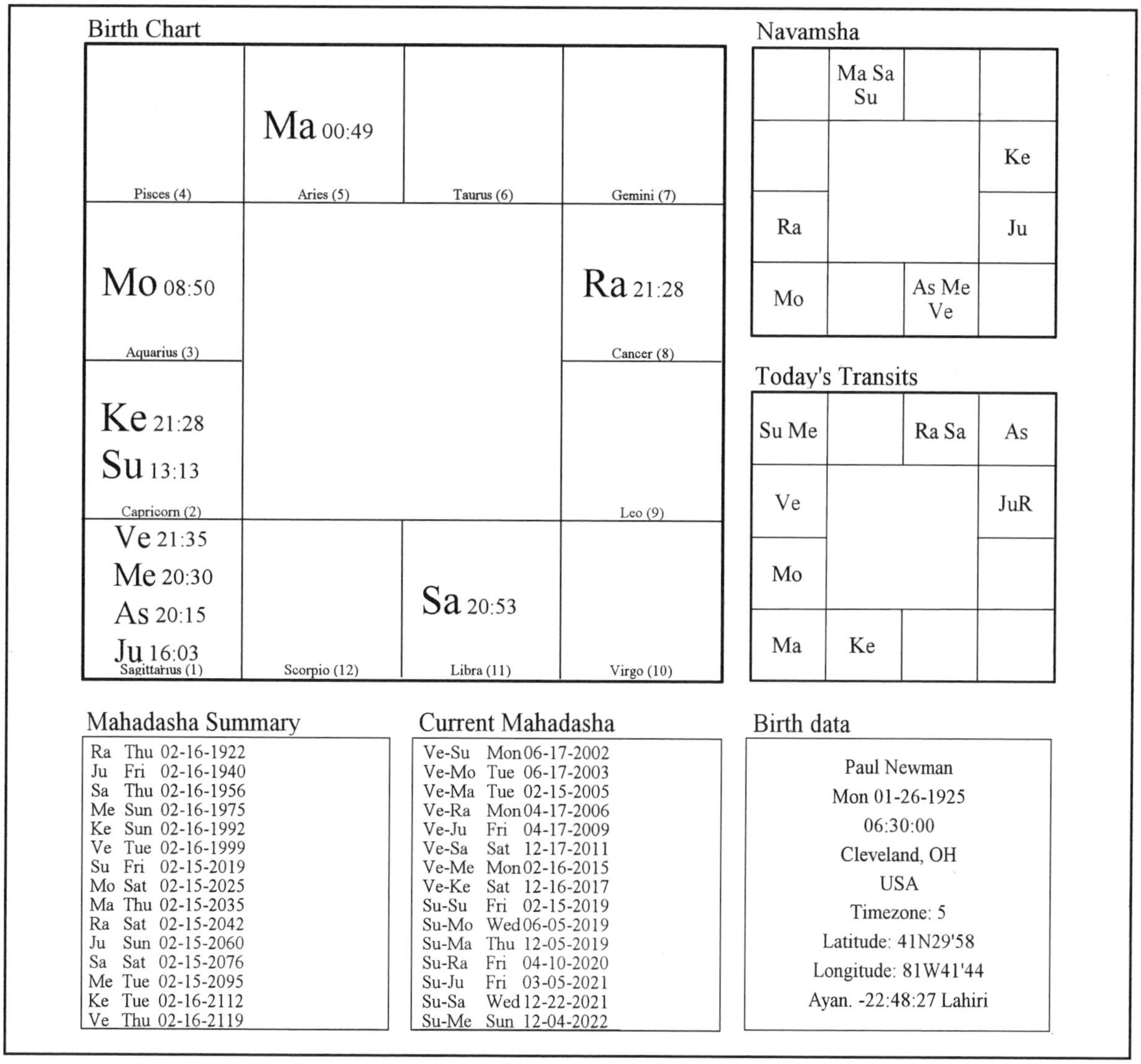

Birth Chart

	Ma 00:49		
Pisces (4)	Aries (5)	Taurus (6)	Gemini (7)
Mo 08:50			Ra 21:28
Aquarius (3)			Cancer (8)
Ke 21:28 Su 13:13			
Capricorn (2)			Leo (9)
Ve 21:35 Me 20:30 As 20:15 Ju 16:03		Sa 20:53	
Sagittarius (1)	Scorpio (12)	Libra (11)	Virgo (10)

Navamsha

	Ma Sa Su		
			Ke
Ra			Ju
Mo		As Me Ve	

Today's Transits

Su Me		Ra Sa	As
Ve			JuR
Mo			
Ma	Ke		

Mahadasha Summary

Ra	Thu	02-16-1922
Ju	Fri	02-16-1940
Sa	Thu	02-16-1956
Me	Sun	02-16-1975
Ke	Sun	02-16-1992
Ve	Tue	02-16-1999
Su	Fri	02-16-2019
Mo	Sat	02-15-2025
Ma	Thu	02-15-2035
Ra	Sat	02-15-2042
Ju	Sun	02-15-2060
Sa	Sat	02-15-2076
Me	Tue	02-15-2095
Ke	Tue	02-16-2112
Ve	Thu	02-16-2119

Current Mahadasha

Ve-Su	Mon	06-17-2002
Ve-Mo	Tue	06-17-2003
Ve-Ma	Tue	02-15-2005
Ve-Ra	Mon	04-17-2006
Ve-Ju	Fri	04-17-2009
Ve-Sa	Sat	12-17-2011
Ve-Me	Mon	02-16-2015
Ve-Ke	Sat	12-16-2017
Su-Su	Fri	02-15-2019
Su-Mo	Wed	06-05-2019
Su-Ma	Thu	12-05-2019
Su-Ra	Fri	04-10-2020
Su-Ju	Fri	03-05-2021
Su-Sa	Wed	12-22-2021
Su-Me	Sun	12-04-2022

Birth data

Paul Newman
Mon 01-26-1925
06:30:00
Cleveland, OH
USA
Timezone: 5
Latitude: 41N29'58
Longitude: 81W41'44
Ayan. -22:48:27 Lahiri

Chart 7—Paul Newman

transiting Aries, its enemy's house, according to Table G, and opposed transiting Mars in Libra, its enemy planet. We all felt the intensity, for just as Mars went retrograde that spring, the bombing in Kosovo began (Chart 8).

And when Saturn and Mars moved even closer together in opposition, the school mas-sacre in Littleton, Colorado, occurred (Chart 9). Notice that Mars and Saturn are both positioned at almost exactly the same degree in opposition.

Remember to consider these planetary relationships when studying your own chart, not only when two or more planets occupy

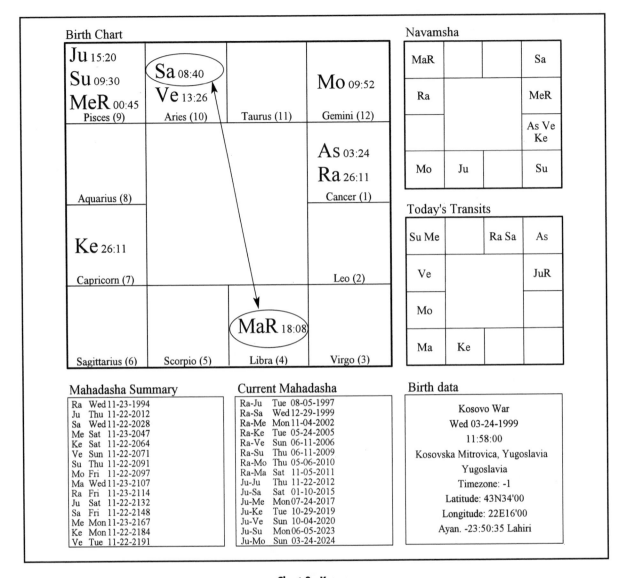

Birth Chart

Ju 15:20 Su 09:30 MeR 00:45 Pisces (9)	Sa 08:40 Ve 13:26 Aries (10)	Taurus (11)	Mo 09:52 Gemini (12)
			As 03:24 Ra 26:11 Cancer (1)
Aquarius (8)			
Ke 26:11 Capricorn (7)			Leo (2)
Sagittarius (6)	Scorpio (5)	MaR 18:08 Libra (4)	Virgo (3)

Navamsha

MaR			Sa
Ra			MeR
			As Ve Ke
Mo	Ju		Su

Today's Transits

Su Me		Ra Sa	As
Ve			JuR
Mo			
Ma	Ke		

Mahadasha Summary

Ra	Wed	11-23-1994
Ju	Thu	11-22-2012
Sa	Wed	11-22-2028
Me	Sat	11-23-2047
Ke	Sat	11-22-2064
Ve	Sun	11-22-2071
Su	Thu	11-22-2091
Mo	Fri	11-22-2097
Ma	Wed	11-23-2107
Ra	Fri	11-23-2114
Ju	Sat	11-22-2132
Sa	Fri	11-22-2148
Me	Mon	11-23-2167
Ke	Mon	11-22-2184
Ve	Tue	11-22-2191

Current Mahadasha

Ra-Ju	Tue	08-05-1997
Ra-Sa	Wed	12-29-1999
Ra-Me	Mon	11-04-2002
Ra-Ke	Tue	05-24-2005
Ra-Ve	Sun	06-11-2006
Ra-Su	Thu	06-11-2009
Ra-Mo	Thu	05-06-2010
Ra-Ma	Sat	11-05-2011
Ju-Ju	Thu	11-22-2012
Ju-Sa	Sat	01-10-2015
Ju-Me	Mon	07-24-2017
Ju-Ke	Tue	10-29-2019
Ju-Ve	Sun	10-04-2020
Ju-Su	Mon	06-05-2023
Ju-Mo	Sun	03-24-2024

Birth data

Kosovo War

Wed 03-24-1999

11:58:00

Kosovska Mitrovica, Yugoslavia

Yugoslavia

Timezone: -1

Latitude: 43N34'00

Longitude: 22E16'00

Ayan. -23:50:35 Lahiri

Chart 8—Kosovo

one house, but when planets align by aspect (see Aspects on page 17). For instance, let's say you are Taurus rising and Saturn is located in Sagittarius, your 8th house, and your Sun is in Aquarius, your 10th house. We know that Saturn influences (or aspects) the 3rd house from itself, so in this case it strikes your Sun in the 10th house, the house of career. While Sun in the career house is ordinarily a wonderful placement, Saturn aspecting that house, and its enemy Sun, can bring delays in career success and power struggles, especially with any type of authority figure, like a boss.

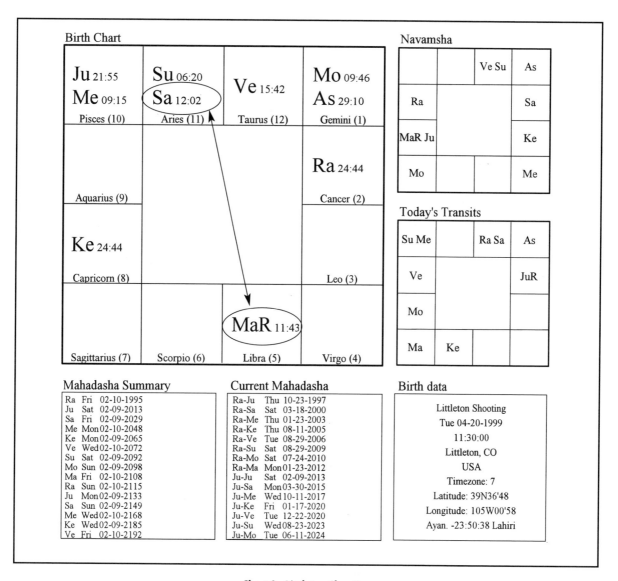

Birth Chart

Ju 21:55 / Me 09:15 — Pisces (10)	Su 06:20 / Sa 12:02 — Aries (11)	Ve 15:42 — Taurus (12)	Mo 09:46 / As 29:10 — Gemini (1)
Aquarius (9)			Ra 24:44 — Cancer (2)
Ke 24:44 — Capricorn (8)			Leo (3)
Sagittarius (7)	Scorpio (6)	MaR 11:43 — Libra (5)	Virgo (4)

Navamsha

		Ve Su	As
Ra			Sa
MaR Ju			Ke
Mo			Me

Today's Transits

Su Me		Ra Sa	As
Ve			JuR
Mo			
Ma	Ke		

Mahadasha Summary

Ra	Fri	02-10-1995
Ju	Sat	02-09-2013
Sa	Fri	02-09-2029
Me	Mon	02-10-2048
Ke	Mon	02-09-2065
Ve	Wed	02-10-2072
Su	Sat	02-09-2092
Mo	Sun	02-09-2098
Ma	Fri	02-10-2108
Ra	Sun	02-10-2115
Ju	Mon	02-09-2133
Sa	Sun	02-09-2149
Me	Wed	02-10-2168
Ke	Wed	02-09-2185
Ve	Fri	02-10-2192

Current Mahadasha

Ra-Ju	Thu	10-23-1997
Ra-Sa	Sat	03-18-2000
Ra-Me	Thu	01-23-2003
Ra-Ke	Thu	08-11-2005
Ra-Ve	Tue	08-29-2006
Ra-Su	Sat	08-29-2009
Ra-Mo	Sat	07-24-2010
Ra-Ma	Mon	01-23-2012
Ju-Ju	Sat	02-09-2013
Ju-Sa	Mon	03-30-2015
Ju-Me	Wed	10-11-2017
Ju-Ke	Fri	01-17-2020
Ju-Ve	Tue	12-22-2020
Ju-Su	Wed	08-23-2023
Ju-Mo	Tue	06-11-2024

Birth data

Littleton Shooting
Tue 04-20-1999
11:30:00
Littleton, CO
USA
Timezone: 7
Latitude: 39N36'48
Longitude: 105W00'58
Ayan. -23:50:38 Lahiri

Chart 9—Littleton Shooting

MAHADASHA—THE MAJOR CYCLE OF THE PLANETS

A unique system in Vedic astrology, the *mahadasha* system enables you to determine with great accuracy when an event is likely to occur in your life. Although there are several types of dasha systems, the one used in this book is called *Vimshottari*.

The mahadasha system determines when a particular planet will come into power, and for how long. If that planet is well placed in your chart, it will bring good results during its mahadasha. If the planet is not well placed, the cycle may be more conflicted.

In an ideal world, the natural life span of a person is 120 years. The mahadasha system breaks up those 120 years into major planetary periods. They cycle in the following fixed order:

Sun	6 years
Moon	10 years
Mars	7 years
Rahu	18 years
Jupiter	16 years
Saturn	19 years
Mercury	17 years
Ketu	7 years
Venus	20 years
Total:	120 years

That does not mean that everyone starts with the Sun mahadasha at the same time. Since the mahadasha system is set in motion at the moment of your birth (based on the placement of your natal Moon), everyone's mahadasha system is unique to him or her.

For instance, you may be born halfway through your Venus mahadasha. Because the Venus mahadasha is 20 years in length, you will experience 10 more years of Venus, followed by 6 years of the Sun, and so on. Now look at your own chart and check the Mahadasha Summary table located at the bottom left of the page to see which mahadasha was in effect when you were born.

Even though people do not share the exact planetary cycles, the order with which these mahadasha occur is the same for everyone.

Table H: Mahadasha Placements

PLANET	LENGTH	IF WELL PLACED	IF AFFLICTED
Sun	6 years	fame, good for father	lacking confidence, difficult for father
Moon	10 years	emotional balance, good for mother	emotional turmoil, difficult for mother
Mars	7 years	passion, power, energy	accidents, arguments
Rahu	18 years	worldly success	losses, downfall
Jupiter	16 years	prosperity, good for children, spirituality	no luck, difficulties with children
Saturn	19 years	honor (over time)	poverty, delays
Mercury	17 years	writing, speaking enhanced	nervousness, poor self-esteem
Ketu	7 years	mystical, spiritual	deluded, hypersensitive
Venus	20 years	love, money, comforts	love challenges, loss of money

Everyone's 7-year Ketu mahadasha will be followed by his or her 20-year Venus mahadasha, followed by the 6-year Sun mahadasha, and so on.

Each cycle brings to the forefront certain latent tendencies in the chart. In the most general terms, during the 6-year Sun mahadasha you might experience exposure or prominence; the 20-year Venus cycle might bring experiences of love and material comfort. The 19-year Saturn mahadasha may bring you focus and discipline (perhaps burden), whereas the 17-year Mercury mahadasha may make you a writer, communicator, or teacher. The specific effects of these major cycles on an individual depend on the uniqueness of his or her chart.

Remember, in assessing the nature of the mahadasha, you must take into account the house that planet occupies. In the example of the Mercury mahadasha referred to in the previous paragraph, if that Mercury were placed in the 12th house, then the mahadasha would more likely find you poring over deeply religious texts in an ashram, than being on the lecture circuit. Or, if we're referring to a child's chart with a 12th house Mercury mahadasha just beginning, the child might suffer during this period from shyness, a lack of confidence, or a speech impediment.

Though the power expressed during the mahadasha is always present in your natal planets (the planets you were born with), this energy is often latent and only expresses itself fully when the major cycle of that planet starts. The mahadasha activates that planet's energies, amplifying its effect.

Bhukti—The Minor Cycle of the Planets

Within mahadashas, there are smaller divisions of time called *bhuktis*, during which a particular planet casts its particular influence on the mahadasha. Within the context of the mahadasha, or larger cycle of the planet, these minor periods give you information about smaller increments of time within the larger cycles.

The relationship between mahadasha and bhukti can be seen in the example of education. Many people attend school between the ages six and eighteen. So if we look at that time in terms of a mahadasha, we would say the mahadasha—or the overall quality of your life at that time—is about learning.

Then within that mahadasha, we would see distinctions, or bhuktis. One distinction is that you were in elementary school for six years. Another is that there were four years to your high school education. So even though the mahadasha, or major theme of your life, is learning, the bhukti indicates the type of learning, what you might be studying, when you are likely to fall in love with a classmate, and so on.

Using another example, let's say you were born with Jupiter in your 10th house, the house of career. During your 16-year Jupiter mahadasha, then, the focus in your life will be your career. However, within your Jupiter mahadasha, you will experience the Venus bhukti. So within that career-oriented period of time, when the Venus bhukti cycle begins, you may find that you fall in love or get married. The overall quality of the time is career-oriented (your Jupiter mahadasha), but within that major cycle Venus casts her inflection and brings love, or at the very least will spin your career in more artistic directions.

Creating the Mahadasha Summary for a chart is complicated and time-consuming. Thankfully, we have computers that can make the calculations for us. Please take a look at your own chart, and determine your current mahadasha. You will see on your chart a Mahadasha Summary that looks something like this:

Mahadasha Summary

Ve: Aug 15, 1948

Su: Aug 15, 1968

Mo: Aug 15, 1974

Ma: Aug 15, 1984

Ra: Aug 16, 1991

Ju: Aug 15, 2009

Sa: Aug 15, 2025

Me: Aug 15, 2044

Ke: Aug 16, 2061

Then, you will see the current mahadasha broken up into bhuktis:

Current Mahadasha

Ra-Ra: Aug 16, 1991

Ra-Ju: Apr 28, 1994

Ra-Sa: Sep 20, 1996

Ra-Me: Jul 28, 1999

Ra-Ke: Feb 14, 2002

Ra-Ve: Mar 4, 2003

Ra-Su: Mar 4, 2006

Ra-Mo: Jan 27, 2007

Ra-Ma: Jul 28, 2008

Notice that both the mahadasha and bhukti order of planets is the same. Moon always follows Sun, Mercury always follows Saturn, Venus always follows Ketu, and so on.

Mahadasha Predictions

Now that you've located your current mahadasha and bhukti, as you follow along, ask yourself the same questions about your chart that we're asking about Chart 10.

Pretend that you don't know whose chart this is and ask yourself the following sequence of questions: What is the rising sign?

Aries, which Table B tells us brings a dynamic, domineering nature, is the rising sign. Table B also indicates that Aries is associated with the element fire and is a cardinal sign, indicating a person who sets things in motion and is driven. We also discover that Aries is ruled by Mars, the planet of war. How will this person make money? Money is indicated by the 2nd house (Table C), which in this case is Taurus. What planet rules Taurus? Table B tells us it's Venus. Where is Venus placed in this chart? In the 7th house, Libra. What does the 7th house indicate? Table C tells us it's partnership or opponents. So this person will make money through dynamic interaction with another.

Can we tell more specifically how this might occur? Look at the 10th house, the house of career, which is Capricorn, ruled by Saturn (Table B). That ruling planet Saturn is located in Serena's 6th house, the house of enemies (Table C), and conjunct its enemy Sun (Table F), and lucky Jupiter. So this person

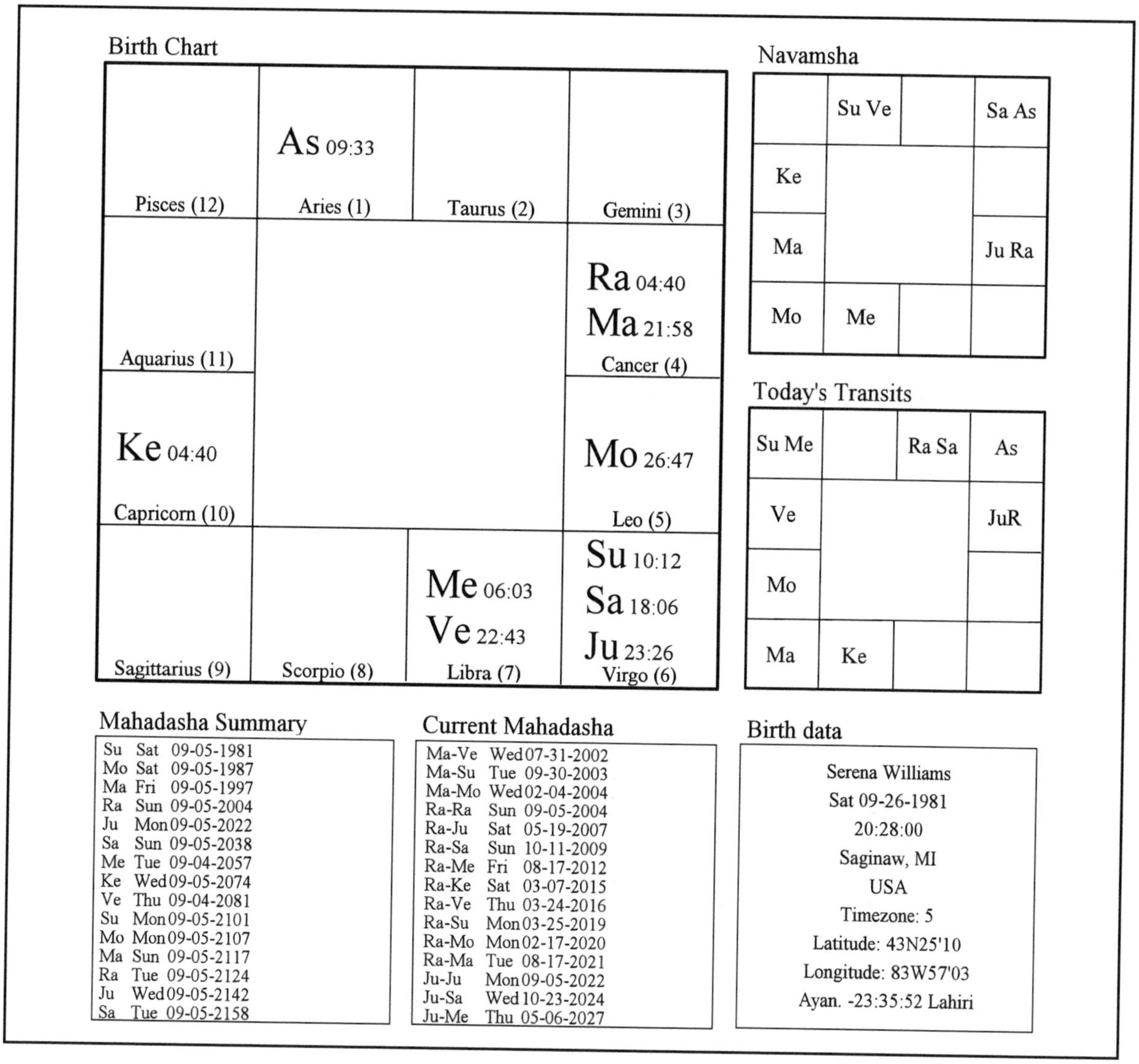

GETTING STARTED 31

Chart 10—Serena Williams

essentially gets paid to fight! Sound like a professional athlete?

Now that we know generally how this person will work, can we tell when any success might occur? Look at the Mahadasha Summary. Since we determined that Mars is the planet of war, we would anticipate that when the Mars mahadasha began, success and attention would begin to occur.

According to the Mahadasha Summary, Serena's Mars mahadasha started in September 1997 and remains in power until September 2004. It was right when the Mars came into power that Serena broke into the top 50 professional women's tennis players. Within months she signed a $12 million contract to represent Puma sporting gear. The following year she became the first African-American woman to win the U.S. Open since Althea Gibson in 1958. And since then she has gone on to win Wimbledon, the French Open, and a second U.S. Open in 2002, defeating her sister in the final of each—ironic, since her 7th house ruling planet signifying opponents is also the name of the sister she needed to overcome to get on top: Venus.

ANOTHER METHOD OF PREDICTION—TRANSITS

Predicting when events are most likely to happen in a person's life can be accomplished by:

- Analyzing the Mahadasha Summary, which we've just discussed.
- Noting what *houses* are being impacted by transiting planets.
- Noting what *planets* are being affected by transiting planets.

It's important to understand that while our natal planets are determined by the moment of our birth, all the planets continue to revolve around us, constantly throwing their aspects onto our birth houses and planets. Planets move at different speeds, so whereas the Moon crosses a house every two and a half days or so, Mercury takes about three weeks, Venus about three and a half weeks, Mars six weeks, Jupiter one year, Rahu and Ketu about one and a half years, and Saturn two and a half years. Generally, the longer the period of transit, the greater the impact on your life. While a three-week Venus transit over your 2nd house may find you going to restaurants and enjoying fine dining, a one-year Jupiter transit over that same house could bring you a windfall of money that would let you quit your job!

When a well-placed Jupiter transits a person's 5th house, for instance, it can mean the birth of a child, or the start of an advanced-degree program because the 5th house relates to children and higher education. (Table D tells us that Jupiter signifies children and wisdom.) Rahu transiting the 2nd house can bring tremendous wealth. Why? The 2nd house represents money, and Table D tells us that Rahu signifies worldly desires. Venus or Jupiter transiting the 4th house can bring a new car or house. Saturn transiting the 4th house can bring a change of residence. If you know what the particular influence is likely to bring, you can anticipate the results and make appropriate adjustments.

For example, when Ketu entered my house of career, I was approached by two filmmakers who asked me to write a script for them. Knowing that Ketu was influencing my career house, an influence that often brings deception, I realized ahead of time that this project would probably not pan out, and the money that was promised me would probably never be seen.

But since I wanted to hone my skills as a writer, I decided to get involved in the project.

Since I knew deception was in the air, I registered my ideas and script with the copyright office in Washington, D.C. As the Ketu indicated, the men did try to steal my ideas without paying me . . . until they found out about the copyright.

You can also satisfy transits by taking a proactive approach to life. I recently had a difficult transit over my 4th house and since one of the 4th house indications is vehicles, I decided to have preventive maintenance done on my car during this time, since it was already having a few problems. I used the transit to my advantage rather than risk having my car break down during that transit, which might have happened had I not taken measures.

The third form of prediction involves transiting planets aspecting your natal planets. In this case, you'll need to determine what type of influence a transiting planet is having on your natal planet. For instance, are they friends or enemies? Then, you must consider the planet itself being impacted by the transit, as well as the house that planet rules.

For instance, let's say Jupiter is transiting a house that is occupied by your 4th house ruler. Even though Jupiter is not actually crossing your 4th house, by making contact with the ruler of the 4th, all of that house's issues tend to flourish.

Look again at Chart 10, Serena's chart. This time we will focus on the table titled "Today's Transits," particularly on the slower-moving planets of Jupiter, Saturn, and Rahu, and see how they impact her natal

chart. Remember, Jupiter brings expansion, Saturn brings restriction, and Rahu acts as a malefic (Table D).

When this book went to press, Jupiter was transiting Cancer, Serena's 4th house, thus automatically throwing an aspect onto the house it opposes, her 10th house of career, Capricorn. Could you have anticipated the results? Recall that Jupiter is exalted in Cancer (Table E), where it's able to give its finest results. The 4th house being indicative of property and cars, it won't surprise you to learn that during this transit Serena and her sister built themselves a multimillion-dollar mansion at Palm Beach Gardens, and purchased another nearby for their parents. Also, since Jupiter throws such a powerful aspect onto her career house, during this transit Serena was able to win Wimbledon, the French Open, and the U.S. Open.

What would you expect when Saturn transited Serena's 2nd house, particularly when its enemy Mars and malefic Rahu all conjoined there in the spring of 2002? Yes, a conflict around money. In April she was sued by Women's Sports Zone, Inc. for $45 million for pulling out of an exhibition tennis tournament.

That Saturn transit was a challenging one for Serena, a time during which her dog was killed and she was the target of a persistent stalker. What would you expect to happen when Mars moved into opposition to its enemy Saturn during the spring of 2001? (Look back to Chart 8 and Chart 9 to remind yourself of the impact the Mars/Saturn opposition had on Kosovo and Littleton.) These planets lined up around the time of the tennis tournament at Indian Wells, and their alignment occurred shortly after rumors swirled that Richard Williams was forcing the two sisters to throw matches, deciding ahead of time who would win. When Serena went out to play for the championship at Indian Wells, she was booed, heckled, and subjected to the worst verbal cruelty. As she explained afterwards, "I can do this. I've been through worse. My ancestors were in slavery. I could be dying right now and I'm not. I've got to suck it up." When she got to match point she said, "Get me out of here, get me out of the worst day of my life."

What would you expect when Rahu transited Serena's 4th house? One of the 4th house indications is the mother, and Rahu is a powerful malefic. You would expect some difficulty for Serena's mother. In February of 1999, Serena's mother, Oracene, ended up in the hospital, accompanied by Serena and her sister Venus. Police reports state she'd suffered three broken ribs, and medical personnel suspected battery. After repeated questioning her mother finally admitted, "I know you know what happened, but I am fearful for my daughter's careers."

If Serena's Mars mahadasha is so wonderful, as we discussed earlier, why would she be subjected to these types of disappointments during the intervening transits of her planets? Look again at the placement of her Mars. Table E tells us that it is located at almost its fullest point of debilitation in Cancer. So it is

essentially a weak placement, particularly in the area of the heart (a 4th house indication). These issues we've discussed must have taken a heavy toll on Serena's heart. It's possible that radiant smile is masking deeper emotional issues that will need to be addressed at some point.

You can analyze your own transits in the same way we looked at Serena's: by studying the small transit chart called Today's Transits located to the right of your birth chart. Where are the transiting planets impacting your chart right now? Is Jupiter crossing your 5th house? Then you might consider getting further education, maybe night school. Jupiter in the 5th can also bring children into your life, so be vigilant if you don't want to conceive now. Is Saturn in your 2nd? You may be earning less than you're paying out, so you'll want to conserve your money.

Simply notice the indication of the house (Table C) and the nature of the planet transiting it (Table D).

NAVAMSHA

Vedic astrology uses many techniques to fine-tune a chart's prediction, many of which are extremely technical and beyond the scope of this book. One method we do use in the chapters ahead is the use of a harmonic chart. By splitting houses into smaller divisions, we can tell more about the nature of the chart, just as by splitting atoms we are able to see more deeply into the nature of physical reality. Although there are many possible divisional charts, the one employed in this book is the ninth harmonic, called the *navamsha*.

The navamsha chart looks exactly like the natal chart, using the same signs and planets. You will notice, however, that the position of the planets is usually different than in the natal chart. This is how you determine whether the planet is as strong as it is in the natal chart.

Let's say Venus is placed in Capricorn in the natal chart. If you want to see how strong that planet truly is, look at the navamsha. If Venus is located in Pisces—its place of exaltation—in the navamsha, your expectations for that Venus would increase. If Venus is found in Virgo in the navamsha, where it is debilitated, you would discover that that Venus is actually a bit weak. Similarly, if you find the navamsha Venus in friendly houses or aspected by friendly planets, it has more strength. And if it is found in an enemy house or aspected by its enemies, it is weakened.

If the natal placement of the planet and the navamsha position are one and the same, you have a condition called *vargottama*, indicating added strength for the planet. This means if the planet is well placed in the natal chart, vargottama increases its indicated positive nature, and if poorly placed in the natal chart, vargottama emphasizes its negativity.

In Chart 10, notice that Serena's navamsha chart has Gemini rising, indicated by the "As" located there. This position enables a person to juggle many different projects at the same time, telling us more about Serena than we could learn from her birth chart at first glance. As Gemini is ruled by Mercury, the planet of communication, it's not surprising to learn that Serena and her sister started a tennis newsletter four years ago called *The Tennis Monthly Recap*. She also has interests in music, design, and acting, all of which are Gemini traits.

Notice also that Saturn is located in the rising sign of her navamsha chart. Saturn is a controlling influence and indicates her father's impact and control over Serena's life. How do we know it's the father? Saturn rules the 9th house in the navamsha, and Table C tells us the 9th house represents the father.

REMEDIAL MEASURES

Vedic astrology is such a complete system that it shows not only the possibility of certain events, but also provides us ways to enhance the positive events and deflect the challenging ones. The three most common remedies are:

- Repeating planetary mantras
- Wearing gemstones
- Performing planetary fire rituals *(yagyas)*

While applying remedial measures can bring remarkable results, I want to emphasize that you don't really need to spend money to strengthen your planets. I mention them only because they are a part of the tradition of Vedic astrology. Understand that true change comes from within. It's a misconception to think that if you spend enough money on a gem or fire ritual, you'll suddenly have a new life. You won't. Instead, you need to identify your life challenges. Real transformation can occur when you commit to changing your problems and couple that commitment with action in that direction.

Mantras

Mantras are empowered syllables, words, or phrases. The mantras that Vedic astrology employs are specific incantations that send energy to planets that are well placed, and whose energies you want to further enhance, as well as to planets that are poorly placed and in need of empowerment.

Mantras are not necessarily religious. They are not just based on faith or belief, but also on simple physics. A vacuum will naturally fill if an opening into it is made. We are in the world to experience abundance in all areas; so whenever we recognize, name, and then appease whatever is missing in our life, we allow the universe to fill that void.

The Vedic mantras are in Sanskrit, which for most of us can be a difficult language to pronounce correctly. The sound, meter, and rhythm of these incantations need to be just right, so you may want to listen to recordings

Table I: Planetary Mantras and Seed Syllables

PLANET-DAY	MANTRA	SEED SYLLABLE (*BIJA*)
Sun-Sunday	Om Suryaya Namaha *aum sir-yah-yah nah-mah-hah*	Om Sum *aum soom*
Moon-Monday	Om Somaya Namaha *aum so-mah-yah nah-mah-hah*	Om Som *aum soam*
Mars-Tuesday	Om Angarakaya Namaha *aum ahn-garah-kah-yah nah-mah-hah*	Om Am *aum ang*
Mercury-Wednesday	Om Bhudaya Namaha *aum bhu-dah-yah nah-mah-hah*	Om Bum *aum buhm*
Jupiter-Thursday	Om Brihaspataye Namaha *aum bri-has-pah-tah-yeh nah-mah-hah*	Om Brahm *aum bruhm*
Venus-Friday	Om Shukraya Namaha *aum shu-krah-yah nah-mah-hah*	Om Shrim *aum shreem*
Saturn-Saturday	Om Shanaischarya Namaha *aum sha-nice-char-yah nah-mah-hah*	Om Sham *aum shum*
Rahu	Om Rahave Namaha *aum rah-hah-veh nah-mah-hah*	Om Ram *aum rahm*
Ketu	Om Ketave Namaha *aum keh-tah-veh nah-mah-hah*	Om Kem *aum came*

of the mantras sung by Vedic priests before you try chanting them. See the Appendix for the way to obtain such recordings, if interested.

In Table I, you will find simplified versions of the mantras to repeat. You can say them once with each incoming breath, and once with each outgoing breath, either aloud or silently. You can repeat either the mantra or the seed syllable. The essence of these mantric phrases is to offer obeisance to a particular planet, thereby encouraging its energies to manifest even more strongly in your life.

For overall well-being, chant the mantra for the ruling planet of your rising sign, or for any beneficent planet occupying your 1st house. Or, choose the area of your life you want to enliven, and chant the mantra for the planet that rules that house. If you need to energize material prosperity, chant for the planet that rules the 2nd house. To help smooth out a difficult intimate relationship or marriage, chant for the 7th house ruler, and so on.

Chant these mantras in two 10-minute meditations at the beginning and end of your day, every day for twenty-one days, or until the benefit you are seeking takes place. In addition, you can repeat the mantra silently to yourself—once on inhalation, once on exhalation—while you are doing other things like walking, showering, driving, running, and commuting throughout the day.

Gemstones

In Vedic astrology, a gemstone corresponds to a specific planet, because its vibratory quality resonates with that planet. You can enhance the energy of any planet in your chart by wearing a gemstone that relates to that particular planet.

I've seen some remarkable results with gemstones. Clients with speech impediments or shyness have become more articulate and confident by wearing stones for Mercury. Clients who hadn't had a date for years suddenly became swamped with attention by wearing stones for Venus. Some of my spiritual clients' lives have been enhanced by Ketu stones, and clients have luck conceiving by wearing stones for the 5th house, or for Jupiter.

Stones used should be natural, in order to assure their molecular integrity, and should not be dyed, heat treated, or color enhanced. Gems that are sold in jewelry stores are *not* the types of stones you will want to use for Vedic purposes. Instead, I recommend you consider contacting a jeweler skilled in the art of choosing gemstones for Vedic purposes (see Appendix).

Prescribing gemstones is tricky, and you may find three Vedic astrologers give you three different opinions of what stone would work best for you. The best thing to do is take the stone on approval and sit with it a few days. You should immediately feel the positive effects of the stone, or things should run more smoothly for you, or dreams should be pleasant. If the opposite is true, the stone may not be the best choice. The decision-making process should be between you and the Vedic jeweler.

The stones should be 2–3 carats in size for primary stones, and 4–5 carats or more for

Table J: Planets and Their Gemstones

PLANET	GEMSTONE	SECONDARY STONE	FINGER	DAY
Sun	ruby	red spinel	ring	Sunday
Moon	pearl	moonstone	index	Monday
Mars	red coral	carnelian	index	Tuesday
Mercury	emerald	green tourmaline	pinkie	Wednesday
Jupiter	yellow sapphire yellow zircon	yellow topaz or	index	Thursday
Venus	diamond white zircon	white sapphire or	middle	Friday
Saturn	blue sapphire	tanzanite	middle	Saturday
Rahu	hessonite	orange zircon	middle	Saturday
Ketu	chrysoberyl (cat's eye)	—	middle	Saturday

secondary stones. If you can't afford the primary gemstone, the secondary stone can work just as well as long as it is of good quality and of sufficient size. Given that the quality of stone the average person in India can afford is not high, and that they seem to do fine with the stones they can afford, you do not need to overspend for these stones. However, the stone should be attractive and bring joy to you when you see it. It should enliven something inside when you look at it.

Fingers on the hand correspond to the planets. So you will want to wear the stone of a particular planet on the finger associated with it. Also, when you wear the stone for the first time, you'll want to do so on the day associated with the planet, either at daybreak, or at high noon when the sun is at its strongest, ideally when the Moon is waxing. The setting should either be in yellow gold to bring energetic vibrations to the stone, or white gold or platinum to bring balancing energy to the stone.

The gem can also be set as a pendant. In either case, the back of the setting should be open so that the stone is exposed to the skin. You can also find *navaratna* rings or pendants in which every planet, including the Moon's nodes, is represented by a small gemstone. These are particularly useful for empowering the entire chart, and bringing positive energy to every planet.

Yagyas (Fire Rituals)

Fire rituals should only be performed by Vedic priests well versed in the practice. By offering precious scents, seasonings, fruit, and flowers, these priests appease the planets on your behalf. Remarkably, you don't even need to be in attendance. The priests will create a fire offering based on your planets and whatever issue you are confronting.

Fire rituals can be performed to enhance wealth and prosperity, to remove obstacles in your life, to help find a marriage partner, or help to conceive. Also, ceremonies can be performed for all of the planets for overall toning and balancing of the energies in your life.

In the case of serious situations, extensive yagyas are performed. Although many issues can be appeased with a one-day yagya, these longer rituals can last a week or more. To contact a Hindu temple to arrange a yagya, see the Appendix.

ASTRO-LOCALITY

Although not a part of Vedic astrology in the traditional sense, I mention this system of chart interpretation because, frankly, there are just some places around the world that enhance the positive nature of your planets, and others that amplify the stresses.

You can actually locate cities, states, and countries around the world where you will be likely to make a lot of money, find love, or have great professional success. You can also choose places—or you may discover that you are currently living in such a place—that

holds you back, is the worst possible place for love, or where you will have nothing but dead-end jobs.

This system is uncanny, and I highly recommend that you at least look at your astro-locality chart along with your Vedic chart in order to see how the city in which you are living helps or hinders your progress. A great example of the specific effects of astro-locality is the chart of Grace Kelly, whose planets operated wonderfully in Hollywood and tragically in Monaco. See the Appendix for more information.

SUMMARY

We have discussed but a few of the simpler principles of the Vedic system of astrology. Remember, even experts who have studied this system for decades still continue to learn; it is a vast body of knowledge. Some of its more technical aspects, such as determining planetary strengths (*shad bala*), planetary combinations (*yogas*), and the lunar mansions (*nakshatras*) are beyond the scope of this book, but this doesn't subtract from you having a good working knowledge of the basics, and the ability to interpret a great deal from any chart. (I do suggest you familiarize yourself with the all-important nakshatras by studying the book *Nakshatras* by Dennis Harness.)

In the chapters ahead, don't be frustrated if information is contradictory. One indication in your chart might show that your relationship with your mother is great; another might say that it is terrible. This is one of the complexities of chart interpretation. You must learn to consider the chart as a whole, and you can start by analyzing your own chart, since only you know if you and your mother's relationship is good or not.

And remember, your chart shows the results of who you've been in the past. Your future does not have to be the same as your past. The present moment, and the next, and the next are completely fresh, clean, unmarked slates. You can make of them what you want. Vedic astrology is not deterministic,

no matter how accurate it may be. You can pull negative aspects from your past into the present and repeat your failures and disappointments, or you can realize that you're making the choice to do so, and re-create yourself . . . if you really want to.

As you enter the next chapter, remember you can always refer back to the tables for clarification. They give you the basics, and ultimately will help you analyze and obtain some real insight about your own chart, and thus your own life.

Part II
READING CHARTS

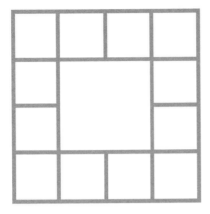

THE 1st HOUSE

The Body

Perhaps the greatest cause of discomfort, ill health, and unhappiness is trying to be someone you're not. The persistent influences of parents and family, of peer pressure, of societal norms and cultural trends can present monumental obstacles to finding your place in the world. However, it is in the 1st house that your true character, personality, body, and behavior are reflected.

For this reason, the 1st house is extremely important. Parents, especially, can use it to gain insight about their child and prevent themselves from directing the child against his or her nature. Knowing your child's 1st house enables you to understand how best to raise the child in accordance with his or her planets.

If upon analyzing your chart, you find out you've been living a life that others created for you, the 1st house also reveals ways to make the necessary adjustments to bring yourself into more alignment with who you really are. Sometimes these changes are very small, and at other times more dramatic.

Usually when we are very young and impressionable, we absorb attitudes and beliefs about ourselves and others that might have been true at one moment but have no bearing later in life. Remember that you empower any self-limiting thoughts by giving them energy. You're the only reason they're still here. Otherwise, they'd have fallen away a long time ago.

This means that your "program" plays a certain way and if you believe and empower the program, you will attract the people, energy, and experience that substantiate your sense of yourself, positive and negative. For instance, the idea "Nobody likes me" attracts the experience of nobody liking me. The idea "I'm always at the right place at the right time" attracts a natural ease and calm. Vedic astrology encourages people to break from their negative "program" by connecting with their true spirit. By changing your inner state, you also shift your worldview. The Vedic sages believe this maxim: "Change your mind, change your life."

Although the change may be simple, for some people it becomes a major challenge, since they discover it's easier to be bound by the comfort of a "program" with which they are familiar. They would rather feel certain of self-limiting identity than have the trouble of going through a change.

Ultimately, however, it is essential that we align ourselves with our true purpose. Paraphrasing from the Gospel According to Thomas, "If you bring forth what is within you, what you bring forth will save you. If you do not bring forth what is within you, what you do not bring forth will destroy you."

As an example, a client of mine, a lawyer, had been extremely unhappy in her career, and felt something was severely lacking in her life. She had Saturn in the house of the rising sign, and one thing that Saturn in someone's 1st house suggests is a natural orientation toward service. At my suggestion, she shifted from focusing on the fast life of litigation and making a name for herself to representing more underprivileged clients and doing a fair amount of pro bono work. The results have been rewarding and positive. For the first time in her life, she feels happy and in alignment with who she is.

If you have Venus in your 1st house, and are not expressing yourself artistically in life, or have the communicative planet of Mercury in the 1st house, but are not writing or speaking, or have a strong emotional planet like Mars there, but hold your emotions in all the time, it's time to make a change.

The 1st house also explains why some people are tall (Virgo rising) while others are short (Aries rising); some are heavier (Jupiter in the 1st house) while others are skinny (Saturn in the 1st house); why some are prone to acne (Mars in the 1st house) while others are unblemished (Moon in the 1st house); why some are treated with respect (Jupiter) while others are shunned (Ketu); some given the benefit of the doubt (Venus) while others are the first to be blamed (Rahu); some are high-powered (Sun) while others are languid (Ketu); some are health conscious (Mercury) while others are fast-food freaks (Mars).

THE NATURE OF YOUR 1st HOUSE

Look again at your chart, and locate your rising sign. Though we touched on the nature of the rising sign in the introduction, we can now explore it in greater depth. Read the description below that pertains to your sign.

Aries

The symbol of the Ram for Aries is apt, since Aries rising people tend to go headfirst into things. You are driven and ambitious, an initiator with courage and strength. Sometimes you are impulsive. If you look at Table B, you'll see that this energy comes from the fiery planet Mars, which rules Aries. This sign is also associated with the element fire, and its activity is cardinal.

Balance for Aries: Be aware that at times Aries can be brusque and selfish. As long as someone is talking about you and your interests, you are amiable, but if the focus shifts to someone else you may be thinking, "Are we *still* talking about you?" It's important that you strive to be tolerant of other people's issues and ideas. Also, think through the possible ramifications of your actions before doing or saying something.

Taurus

Symbolized by the Bull, Taureans tend to be patient, persevering, artistically inclined, close to nature, and materially oriented. You enjoy the comforts of living and routines. Ruled by Venus, you respond to sensuality and the arts. As a fixed sign, you stand firm for what you believe in. The earth element makes you practical and tactile oriented.

Balance for Taurus: Although being firm in your beliefs is your nature, you can sometimes become stubborn and unyielding. When you're being inflexible, your energy is not circulating, and you may feel stuck or stagnant. What feels like strength is actually a weakness. Remember a stiff reed is easily broken but a supple blade of grass can bend and sway. To help yourself identify the places and emotions in which you're stuck, it's important to express your frustrations, if even just to yourself. You need to vent so that your emotions don't build up and become explosive for lack of having an outlet.

Gemini

Symbolized by the Twins, Gemini people tend to be multitalented. You can perform many duties or be involved in many projects at the same time. Ruled by Mercury, Geminis generally find themselves involved in some sort of communication, whether as speakers, writers, actors, or teachers. You're highly creative (the air element), innovative, and charming, with a mutable nature that makes you malleable and flexible mentally, physically, and emotionally.

Balance for Gemini: Though you may be multitalented, and it's easy for you to engage in many projects simultaneously, you may find it difficult to finish any one of them. This ability to flit between projects also operates in your relationships. You can hurt people by bonding quickly and then pulling away just as quickly. Even if your mind is off to the next thing, make an effort to bring closure to everything and with everyone with whom you have a relationship.

Cancer

The Crab is tenacious. This attribute can express itself in holding strongly to domestic values of family and home, or nesting tendencies. Intuitive and expressive (Cancer is a water element), Cancer is ruled by the Moon, the planet of the emotions. Since it is a cardinal sign, Cancer people can be most effective in their careers by coupling their dynamic cardinal energy with their deep emotional intuition.

Balance for Cancer: At times you can be hypersensitive or moody, influenced by other people's opinions of you and susceptible to peer or environmental pressure. It's important to recognize that what you're feeling may not be your own emotion. Because you are intuitive, you pick up on a lot of energy and influence from your surroundings. You need to remember that self-worth comes from within, and shouldn't be gauged by how other people react to you.

Leo

The Lion is proud, dramatic, and ambitious, wanting to be the center of attention—just as a lion in the jungle attracts the attention of all the other animals. Fiery like Aries, Leo is a fixed sign, so even though you possess dynamic action, you also have the balancing force of perseverance. You want to be at the helm, issuing orders, running the show, while being in the spotlight.

Balance for Leo: Recognize that your need to be in the spotlight can alienate others. You need to become conscious of your voltage output and control it so that it suits every different situation. You have an innate dignity that people notice whether you are "on stage" or not, so relax. Humility is a useful characteristic for Leos to cultivate, since the appearance Leos give of being confident and capable can mask deep insecurities and conflicting personality traits. These challenges can be glossed over unless Leos look within and admit to their dysfunctions.

Virgo

Strongly connected with health and healing, Virgos can be fanatical about exercise or health products. As an earth sign ruled by Mercury, Virgos tend to possess good communication skills, and to be perfectionists and detail oriented. You like order and cleanliness, and have a very good memory for facts, figures, and even history. Virgos tend to excel as physicians or healers, as well as teachers, lecturers, writers, scientists, and therapists.

Balance for Virgo: Recognize that your need for perfection can bring you frustration and anxiety. You ought to guard against being highly critical of others. There is a natural perfection to the universe, one that is not influenced in the least by whether you perceive it as perfect or not. You must loosen your grip on your expectations—the "ideal" mate or perfect job, for instance—so that you can see all the opportunities available to you that you wouldn't otherwise consider.

Libra

Ruled by Venus, Libra is an aesthetically oriented sign. You tend to enjoy the arts, dance, literature, and music. As a cardinal sign, Libra has a momentum and a dynamic expression of energy that is aesthetic in nature and diplomatic, always tending toward balance and justice. As an air sign, your mind stays active, constantly coming up with new ideas, plans, and projects. As champions of justice, Libras can become overzealous in their enthusiasm, or unwavering in their opinions, making them either wonderful leaders or fanatics.

Balance for Libra: The sign of Libra is symbolized by the scales and naturally searches for balance and harmony. From this natural tendency an indecisive quality may arise. Because you take into account the ramifications of every decision, it becomes hard for you to settle on one particular course of action. On the other hand, to take advantage of any positive outcome, you must take action. It's important to come to terms with what you really want or need, and act from that place, or you may find yourself living a life that is not a true expression of your own passions. Work at disassociating yourself from others' opinions.

Scorpio

The intensity of this sign can manifest in either highly uplifting or deeply destructive ways. As a fixed, watery sign ruled by Mars, Scorpios are somewhat secretive or private by nature, and can either utilize their probing nature and resourcefulness to encourage or inspire others, or get caught up in jealousy, lust, or vengeful activities. Perhaps more than any other sign, the consequences of a Scorpio's actions are more intense and potentially destructive, if used in a negative manner.

Balance for Scorpio: As a sign ruled by fiery Mars, Scorpio's energies and passions are best brought into balance through creative avenues (acting, for instance), health-oriented endeavors (science or medicine—particularly surgery or acupuncture), or physical activities (athletics). Otherwise, the intensity of this sign can be misused and its curling scorpion's tail can strike and hurt itself and others.

Sagittarius

Philosophically oriented, Sagittarius is ruled by expansive Jupiter, bringing you magnanimous enthusiasm. Since yours is a fire sign, you can be direct and sometimes brash, seeking independence while at the same time wanting to fit in with convention. With skill at critical thinking and the ability to communicate, you can be formidable. But since your sign is mutable, you are also flexible.

Balance for Sagittarius: Your ruling planet, Jupiter, can sometimes bring overconfidence, overoptimism, exaggeration, and fanaticism. You can tend to be selfish, especially with intimate partners. Recognize that the skill with which you can see others' faults can also help you bring greater clarity to your own life.

Capricorn

An earth-based sign ruled by stern, focused Saturn, Capricorn brings a traditional, disciplined approach to life. Things need to be practical and observable to be considered of value. Through steady, conservative, economical actions, you will eventually succeed in life, though perhaps not as early as you might have hoped. The cardinal nature of this sign brings a hardworking and driven nature. People may be surprised to find you have a great sense of humor (usually dry).

Balance for Capricorn: With the strong influence of Saturn, it's important to strive to balance your energies. You need to incorporate lightness, humor, and artistry into your life—if even just as an audience member. That doesn't mean you have to take up acting, but might mean it would do you good to go see a play. The discipline of a Capricorn can sometimes be severely constricting, and your cautiousness needs to be chipped away by playing a little more and having fun.

Aquarius

Intellectually oriented Aquarius is a humanitarian-based sign ruled by Saturn. Since your element is air, you possess great imagination and vision. You usually act with the greater good in mind. As a fixed sign, there is a tendency to be strongly independent, something of a loner, imaginative but somewhat aloof.

Balance for Aquarius: Aquarians can sometimes be too set in their ways and stuck in their opinions. This tendency becomes problematic if you have negative or self-deprecating feelings about yourself, which is not uncommon for Aquarius people. Aquarians do not change or adapt easily. You need to learn to be kind to yourself first; then you can truly benefit others.

Pisces

Intuitive, expansive Pisces is a deeply imaginative sign, ruled by magnanimous Jupiter, and somewhat dreamy due to its watery mutable qualities. Often self-sacrificing and mystically oriented, you relate well with others because, chameleon-like, you can easily become the type of person that people would most want to be around. This tendency enables creative types to adjust their output to meet the expectations of their audience, and, thus, can reap both admiration and remuneration.

Balance for Pisces: Your challenge is to ground yourself in practical activities to help bring your ideas into manifestation. Gardening, where your hands have direct contact with the earth, or any physical exercise can bring you the substantive energy, the emotional psycho-physiological bedrock on which you can build. Since you are naturally intuitive and have difficulty in setting boundaries, it's easy to mistake another person's mental state for your own. Using these tendencies to your advantage, you can excel as a therapist, mediator, intuitive counselor, or life coach.

IF A PLANET OCCUPIES THE 1st HOUSE

You will find the list of 1st house planets below familiar. I have repeated it from the section on the rising sign in Part I. To help fine-tune the descriptions below, you'll want to assess whether the planet is welcome in the house in which it is placed (Table G). If the planet is in the house of a friend, the positive nature of the following description is enhanced. If the planet is in the house of an enemy, more of the negative possibilities need to be considered. (The parenthetic letters next to each planet below refer to how the planet is notated in your chart.)

Sun (Su) in the 1st house can make a person proud, somewhat irritable, and driven. If the Sun is placed in Libra, however, where it is weakest, there may be a noticeable lack of confidence, and you might struggle with self-acceptance and/or health complaints, or difficulties with the father (or he may have problems on his own).

Moon (Mo) in the 1st house brings softness and beauty to the face, and a certain inner radiance. Emotionally you will be intuitive and perhaps moody. If the Moon is placed in Scorpio, where it is weakest, there may be health problems, emotional disturbances, and sexual difficulties (often female).

Mars (Ma) in the 1st house produces fire, which can translate as passion, impulsiveness, and difficulty with monogamy. It may also help you look younger than your actual years, though you may have a ruddy complexion. If Mars is in Cancer, where it is weakest, you might experience injuries to the head or rashes on the face.

Mercury (Me) in the 1st house brings great communication skills, quick-wittedness, and a talkative nature. If Mercury is in Pisces, where it is weakest, there may be nervousness, mental instability, and a possible speech impediment.

Jupiter (Ju) in the 1st house can indicate a heavy or big-boned build, as Jupiter brings its expansiveness to the body. This placement is extremely fortunate and brings you many uplifting opportunities. However, if Jupiter is in Capricorn, where it is weakest, you may not be properly recognized for your efforts. In some cases Jupiter can make you overoptimistic, which can lead to overcommitting or to overextending yourself.

Venus (Ve) in the 1st house brings great physical beauty. Venus also brings you refinement, charm, and sensuality. If Venus is placed in Virgo, where it is weakest, your experiences in love can fall short of your expectations, or you may have difficulty in being able to receive love.

Saturn (Sa) in the 1st house is most fortuitous for service or humanitarian-oriented endeavors. It brings slow, steady progress by perseverance over time. If Saturn is in Aries, where it is weakest, it can bring frustration with your personal or professional progress, and you may encounter delays, obstacles, and the feeling of being restricted.

Rahu (Ra) in the 1st house brings an aggressive nature and worldly success. It can also indicate an unusual or unique person who may marry (possibly a foreigner) more than once. Although it is unclear in which house Rahu operates at its weakest, a problematic Rahu can affect health and confidence.

Ketu (Ke) in the 1st house brings a mystical nature and highly sensitive nervous system. Like Rahu in the 1st, Ketu can bring unhappiness in marriage and the possibility of more than one marriage. Although it is unclear in which house Ketu operates at its weakest, a problematic Ketu can make one highly susceptible to peer influence and other people's energy.

HOW THE SIGN EXPRESSES ITSELF

Locate the planet that rules your rising sign (see Table B), and find where it's placed in your chart. Then read the description below that pertains to this placement. Remember to check whether the planet is placed in a friend's or enemy's house (Table G), and whether any other planet aspects it, either positively or negatively.

1st House Ruler placed in the 1st house brings natural strength of character, good health, and leadership ability. Focus on the body or personal character for your success. If afflicted by house placement or aspect, or if you have Scorpio, Gemini, or Virgo rising, having the ruler of the 1st house placed in the 1st house can indicate more than one marriage.

1st House Ruler placed in the 2nd house indicates a self-made person. Money is generated through some expression of the person's physicality, whether through an active, verbal, or communicative medium (such as a professional sport or acting). In some cases, as with Aries, Scorpio, and Aquarius rising, having the ruler of the 1st house appear in the 2nd house can indicate shyness or an eating disorder.

1st House Ruler placed in the 3rd house indicates strong abilities in the arts, whether dance, literature, or music. Ordinarily an adventurous type of person with a great deal of courage, with Capricorn or Aquarius rising, this power comes later in life (around the thirty-sixth year), making a person a late bloomer. This position also favors siblings, and can show the positive influence of a brother or sister in your life.

1st House Ruler placed in the 4th house can indicate both material and spiritual progress. It shows luck with fixed assets like homes and cars, but can also indicate an interest in spirituality. Maternal influences are also indicated by the 4th house, so if the ruler is well placed, the mother can have a positive influence in your life. Otherwise, the opposite would be true.

1st House Ruler placed in the 5th house favors a fine moral character if well placed, and you will be driven by the sense of having a strong destiny. It's also a good position for achieving higher education and for having children (or for influencing young people), as well as luck with speculation, love affairs, and learning spiritual techniques.

1st House Ruler placed in the 6th house either indicates skill in the healing arts, or that you may suffer from health complaints. Sometimes you may have both. If so, you can minimize your own physical challenges by helping others with theirs. As the 6th house also indicates enemies, you may find that you encounter people in your life who try to discredit you or bring you down out of jealousy or a feeling of inadequacy. Or, if the planet is well placed you will be impervious to these types of challenges.

1st House Ruler placed in the 7th house indicates benefits from a marriage or business partner. An intimate or professional partnership complements you in such a way that you feel more whole. The other person brings out and supports your best qualities. You learn many of life's lessons through intimate relationships.

1st House Ruler placed in the 8th house indicates that you may cultivate skills in secret, work behind the scenes, or have an interest in mysticism. You may also be lucky in gaining unearned money, whether through games of chance or an inheritance. However, this position can adversely affect the health or indicate accidents, perhaps to the head.

1st House Ruler placed in the 9th house is an extremely favorable position. Opportunities abound, and doors are constantly opening for you. You may feel as if you're riding a wave of grace, as this position shows accumulated merit from past lives. You may benefit from your father and have luck with spiritual pursuits. In afflicted cases, just the opposite is true.

1st House Ruler placed in the 10th house indicates that your physical characteristics or talents can be used as a career path. This is a good position for actors, comedians, or athletes and it shows a person is self-made, independent, and career-oriented.

1st House Ruler placed in the 11th house favors speculative investments or entrepreneurial pursuits. It can also indicate benefits from friends, the gender of whom can be shown by the nature of the planet placed there: Venus and the Moon show that one benefits from women friends, and Jupiter and Mars indicate male friends.

1st House Ruler placed in the 12th house indicates harm to one's confidence or health (possibly a head injury), so that inner resources must be called upon for solace. It also indicates a deeply transformative and spiritual orientation, and can also point to a lot of foreign travel. Since the 12th house is associated with confinement, a poorly placed planetary combination here can show physical restriction, but usually just indicates being a prisoner to your own negative thoughts. This is a wonderful placement for anyone seeking the most profound spiritual truths.

OTHER CONSIDERATIONS

- Note the element associated with your 1st house (see Table B). Remember that fire signs are driven, earth signs are patient, air signs are creative, and water signs are emotional.
- Also note the quality of your 1st house (see Table B). Cardinal signs initiate; fixed signs stabilize; mutable signs seek change.

Now check any aspects to the 1st house:

- Are any planets located in the same house as, or opposing any planet in, your rising sign? If so, are those planets friendly, neutral, or enemies? (See Table F.) For instance, say your Sun is placed in the rising sign and its enemy Saturn is in the 7th opposing it. This aspect shows a person who resists authority, and thus becomes strongly independent by nature.

- Remember that Mars energizes the house it's in, as well as the 4th, 7th, and 8th houses from itself. This means if Mars is placed in the 6th, 7th, or 10th houses of your chart, it throws an aspect onto your rising sign, keeping you dynamic, driven, impulsive and passionate.

- Saturn restricts or brings discipline to the house it's in, as well as the 3rd, 7th, and 10th houses from itself. This means if Saturn is placed in the 4th, 7th, or 11th houses of your chart, it throws an aspect onto your rising sign, making you practical, introspective, and perhaps shy.

- Jupiter expands or brings optimism to the house it's in, as well as the 5th, 7th, and 9th houses from itself. This means if Jupiter is placed in the 5th, 7th, or 9th houses of your chart, it throws an aspect onto your rising sign, making you optimistic, gregarious, and jovial.

- If you want to find out when your chart's 1st house energies will be enlivened, look to the 1st house ruler, or any planet located in the 1st house. Examine the Mahadasha Summary of your chart to see when that planet will come into power, and that will give you your answer. To find shorter periods when 1st house issues will be highlighted look to the 1st house ruler or any planet located in the 1st house, and find the time its bhukti will run.

For instance, let's say Mars occupies or rules your 1st house. Look at your Mahadasha Summary to see when the Mars cycle is due. If it's some time off, or has already passed, then look at your current mahadasha to determine when the Mars bhukti (minor cycle) is due. Otherwise, remember transiting planets can also enliven the rising sign.

- You'll also want to consider the nature of the planet when analyzing transiting planets. Though a transiting Mars over your rising sign may enliven qualities of the 1st house, it may also push you into an exercise regime. Jupiter, when transiting your rising sign, though it enhances the sign, may cause you to be lazier or to eat richer foods. You can always chant to the planet that is transiting your rising sign on the appropriate day for that planet to enhance its affects.

CHART EXAMPLES

It's due to the 1st house that Robert De Niro has an edgy disposition, Paul Newman has beautiful eyes, and Bruce Lee was so driven. It gives Winona Ryder her dark sensuality, Meg Ryan her fiery enthusiasm, and Meryl Streep her warm, nurturing energy. The 1st house defines the total makeup of a person, on a physical as well as energetic level.

If the rising sign is Cancer, for instance, as it is for Meryl Streep, you will notice the appearance of an expressive, emotional person.

What planet rules Cancer? Table B tells us it's the Moon. Because the rising sign indicates one's appearance, we would say that Meryl's appearance is strongly influenced by the Moon. And isn't it so? Her face has many lunar qualities: softness, wide like the full moon, lighter in color, smooth in appearance, luminescent, glowing as if by reflection.

Birth Chart

Ra 29:09 Pisces (9)	Mo 21:14 Aries (10)	Ma 15:40 Me 17:08 Taurus (11)	Su 07:34 Ve 25:16 Gemini (12)
Aquarius (8)			As 09:36 Cancer (1)
JuR 07:22 Capricorn (7)			Sa 08:25 Leo (2)
Sagittarius (6)	Scorpio (5)	Ke 29:09 Libra (4)	Virgo (3)

Navamsha

JuR Ra		Ve Ma	Me Sa
Su		Mo	Ke As

Today's Transits

Su Me		Ra Sa	As
Ve			JuR
Mo			
Ma	Ke		

Mahadasha Summary

Ve	Tue	08-10-1937
Su	Sat	08-10-1957
Mo	Sat	08-10-1963
Ma	Fri	08-10-1973
Ra	Sun	08-10-1980
Ju	Mon	08-10-1998
Sa	Sun	08-10-2014
Me	Tue	08-09-2033
Ke	Tue	08-09-2050
Ve	Thu	08-09-2057
Su	Mon	08-09-2077
Mo	Mon	08-09-2083
Ma	Sun	08-09-2093
Ra	Tue	08-10-2100
Ju	Wed	08-10-2118

Current Mahadasha

Ju-Sa	Wed	09-27-2000
Ju-Me	Thu	04-10-2003
Ju-Ke	Sat	07-16-2005
Ju-Ve	Thu	06-22-2006
Ju-Su	Fri	02-20-2009
Ju-Mo	Wed	12-09-2009
Ju-Ma	Sun	04-10-2011
Ju-Ra	Fri	03-16-2012
Sa-Sa	Sun	08-10-2014
Sa-Me	Sun	08-13-2017
Sa-Ke	Wed	04-22-2020
Sa-Ve	Mon	05-31-2021
Sa-Su	Wed	07-31-2024
Sa-Mo	Sun	07-13-2025
Sa-Ma	Thu	02-11-2027

Birth data

Meryl Streep

Wed 06-22-1949

08:05:00

Summit, NJ

USA

Timezone: 5

Latitude: 40N44'29

Longitude: 74W21'36

Ayan. -23:08:58 Lahiri

Chart 11—Meryl Streep

Notice that Jupiter opposes Streep's rising sign, increasing her expansive nature. In addition, her 1st house ruler, the Moon, is placed in her 10th house of career. This house ruler placement makes her strongly career-driven.

Let's look now at the renowned martial artist Bruce Lee, who like Streep was highly ambitious, but manifested that ambition in different ways.

His rising sign is Scorpio, which according to Table A shows that he was intense, dark, and secretive by nature. Mars rules Scorpio, which is the planet of war. It brought him great intensity, passion, and a fiery nature. All of these qualities can be seen just by looking

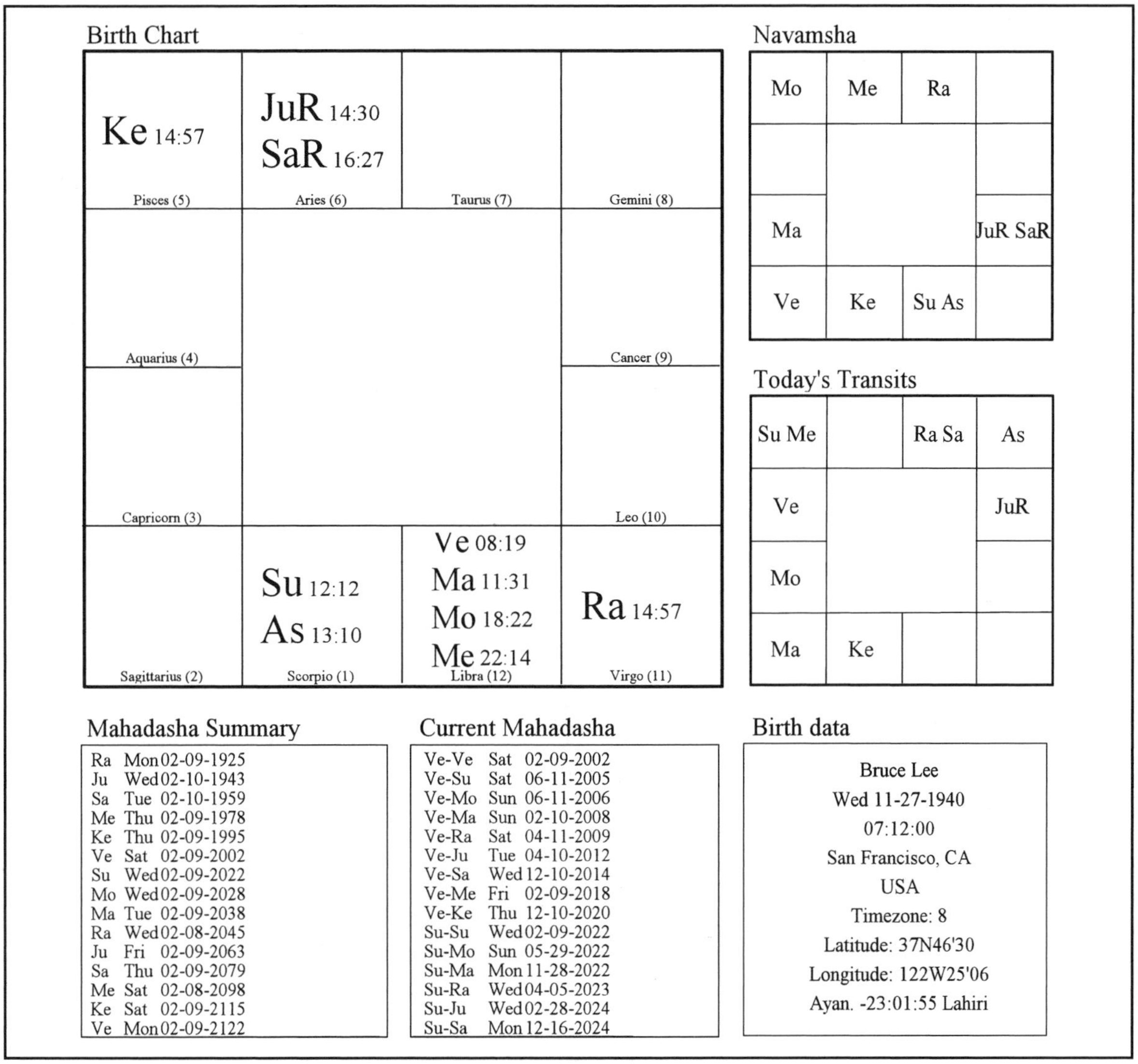

Birth Chart

Ke 14:57 Pisces (5)	JuR 14:30 SaR 16:27 Aries (6)	Taurus (7)	Gemini (8)
Aquarius (4)			Cancer (9)
Capricorn (3)			Leo (10)
Su 12:12 As 13:10 Sagittarius (2)	Scorpio (1)	Ve 08:19 Ma 11:31 Mo 18:22 Me 22:14 Libra (12)	Ra 14:57 Virgo (11)

Navamsha

Mo	Me	Ra	
Ma			JuR SaR
Ve	Ke	Su As	

Today's Transits

Su Me		Ra Sa	As
Ve			JuR
Mo			
Ma	Ke		

Mahadasha Summary

Ra	Mon	02-09-1925
Ju	Wed	02-10-1943
Sa	Tue	02-10-1959
Me	Thu	02-09-1978
Ke	Thu	02-09-1995
Ve	Sat	02-09-2002
Su	Wed	02-09-2022
Mo	Wed	02-09-2028
Ma	Tue	02-09-2038
Ra	Wed	02-08-2045
Ju	Fri	02-09-2063
Sa	Thu	02-09-2079
Me	Sat	02-08-2098
Ke	Sat	02-09-2115
Ve	Mon	02-09-2122

Current Mahadasha

Ve-Ve	Sat	02-09-2002
Ve-Su	Sat	06-11-2005
Ve-Mo	Sun	06-11-2006
Ve-Ma	Sun	02-10-2008
Ve-Ra	Sat	04-11-2009
Ve-Ju	Tue	04-10-2012
Ve-Sa	Wed	12-10-2014
Ve-Me	Fri	02-09-2018
Ve-Ke	Thu	12-10-2020
Su-Su	Wed	02-09-2022
Su-Mo	Sun	05-29-2022
Su-Ma	Mon	11-28-2022
Su-Ra	Wed	04-05-2023
Su-Ju	Wed	02-28-2024
Su-Sa	Mon	12-16-2024

Birth data

Bruce Lee
Wed 11-27-1940
07:12:00
San Francisco, CA
USA
Timezone: 8
Latitude: 37N46'30
Longitude: 122W25'06
Ayan. -23:01:55 Lahiri

Chart 12—Bruce Lee

at his face. This is the nature of his rising sign. The ruler of his rising sign is Mars, and it is located in the malefic 12th house, conjunct with Venus, Moon, and Mercury. That much power in the 12th house creates a powerful mystique, and explains why his legend has survived him. It also shows why his life was cut short at such an early age.

Sometimes the rising sign planets are not well placed, or the house itself is poorly aspected. When Sun and Rahu are together in the rising sign, there can be allergies. When a strong Mars predominates, there can be acne or other rashes on the skin. Also, Saturn, Mars, Rahu, or Ketu in various combinations in the 1st house can bring head injuries, addic-

Birth Chart

Ra 08:53 Pisces (7)	Mo 22:59 Aries (8)	Ve 21:24 Taurus (9)	Me 22:08 Su 23:48 Gemini (10)
JuR 14:01 Aquarius (6)			Cancer (11)
Capricorn (5)			Sa 21:54 Leo (12)
Sagittarius (4)	Scorpio (3)	Libra (2)	Ke 08:53 As 10:07 Ma 19:07 Virgo (1)

Navamsha

Ke	As Me	Su	Ma
JuR			Ve
		Sa Mo	Ra

Today's Transits

Su Me		Ra Sa	As
Ve			JuR
Mo			
Ma	Ke		

Mahadasha Summary

Ve	Fri	01-17-1936
Su	Tue	01-17-1956
Mo	Tue	01-16-1962
Ma	Mon	01-17-1972
Ra	Tue	01-16-1979
Ju	Thu	01-16-1997
Sa	Wed	01-16-2013
Me	Fri	01-16-2032
Ke	Fri	01-15-2049
Ve	Sun	01-16-2056
Su	Thu	01-16-2076
Mo	Thu	01-15-2082
Ma	Wed	01-16-2092
Ra	Thu	01-15-2099
Ju	Sat	01-16-2117

Current Mahadasha

Ju-Me	Sun	09-16-2001
Ju-Ke	Tue	12-23-2003
Ju-Ve	Sun	11-28-2004
Ju-Su	Mon	07-30-2007
Ju-Mo	Sat	05-17-2008
Ju-Ma	Wed	09-16-2009
Ju-Ra	Mon	08-23-2010
Sa-Sa	Wed	01-16-2013
Sa-Me	Tue	01-19-2016
Sa-Ke	Fri	09-28-2018
Sa-Ve	Thu	11-07-2019
Sa-Su	Sat	01-07-2023
Sa-Mo	Wed	12-20-2023
Sa-Ma	Sun	07-20-2025
Sa-Ra	Sat	08-29-2026

Birth data

Sam
Sun 07-09-1950
12:00:00
Los Angeles, CA
USA
Timezone: 8
Latitude: 34N03'08
Longitude: 118W14'34
Ayan. -23:09:57 Lahiri

Chart 13—Sam

tive tendencies, even brash or vulgar speech.

For instance, consider the following client history. Sam was once full of energy and a terrific athlete. But the Mars in his rising sign, in the sign of an enemy (see Table F) and conjunct Ketu, brought about a problem.

At the young age of twenty-five, he suffered a debilitating stroke. The source of the problem was in his head, shown by Mars affecting the head area by malefic aspect.

What role did Ketu play? It indicates a strange and unusual occurrence, as Ketu is the influence of things mysterious and uncharacteristic. So Mars and Ketu in a rising sign where Mars is the enemy showed that at some point in time Sam was going to suffer some type of unusual head injury. And when planets of this type are placed in Virgo—the sign of health—there are bound to be health problems.

Virgo, being a sign of health, often works two ways. Either the ruler of the sign and planets contained within the sign are well placed, whereby the person becomes interested in health, fitness, vitamins, health food—and enjoys good health—or the sign is ill placed and health becomes a problem.

Because Mars is the planet indicating trouble in this chart, we can speculate that when his Mars mahadasha began, Sam would have had the problem. Looking at his Mahadasha Summary, we see that Mars came into power on January 17, 1972. His stroke occurred later that spring.

Let's look at another chart with 1st house issues (Chart 14).

Kevin is tall and dark due to Saturn being placed in the rising sign, which is conjunct Rahu. Since Rahu is a worldly influence, and Saturn is a reserved one, there is a push-pull in a chart like this. Saturn in the rising sign can turn a person inward, (this influence is even more pronounced when retrograde, as it is in Kevin's chart) and make him introspective—a person who does best by being of service. Rahu is an influence that favors material accumulation.

If the Rahu influence becomes strong and Kevin tries to amass great wealth and assets for his own pleasure, Saturn will probably take them away. The general tone of this chart is altruistic, so a certain amount of energy must go in that direction. Kevin is a healer, and strongly committed to being of service, while at the same time he lives an opulent life, satisfying the Rahu qualities.

As mentioned earlier, the rising sign also has much to say about a person's physical appearance. In Kevin's chart, we saw Saturn give him his dark looks. Venus in the rising sign, on the other hand, would have occasioned beauty in the face and hair, and Jupiter would have brought heaviness and a broad forehead.

In the same vein, Mercury brings beauty and youth, as well as nervousness, a quick wit, or an articulate nature. Mars in the rising sign indicates a person who will always appear younger than he or she is, with a strong, well-proportioned body, and an energetic, impulsive nature. Mars in the rising sign also brings what is known in Vedic astrology as *kuja dosha*. Kuja dosha is a disturbance to the peaceful enjoyment of married life. It can indicate more than one marriage if a person marries early, or isn't careful about whom he or she marries. We will speak in more depth about kuja dosha when we explore the 7th house, the house of marriage.

The Sun in the rising sign indicates a person who stands out, is the center of attention—or wants to be—with a broad face and wide bones. A good example of this would be Julie Andrews, who has Virgo rising with Sun in her rising sign.

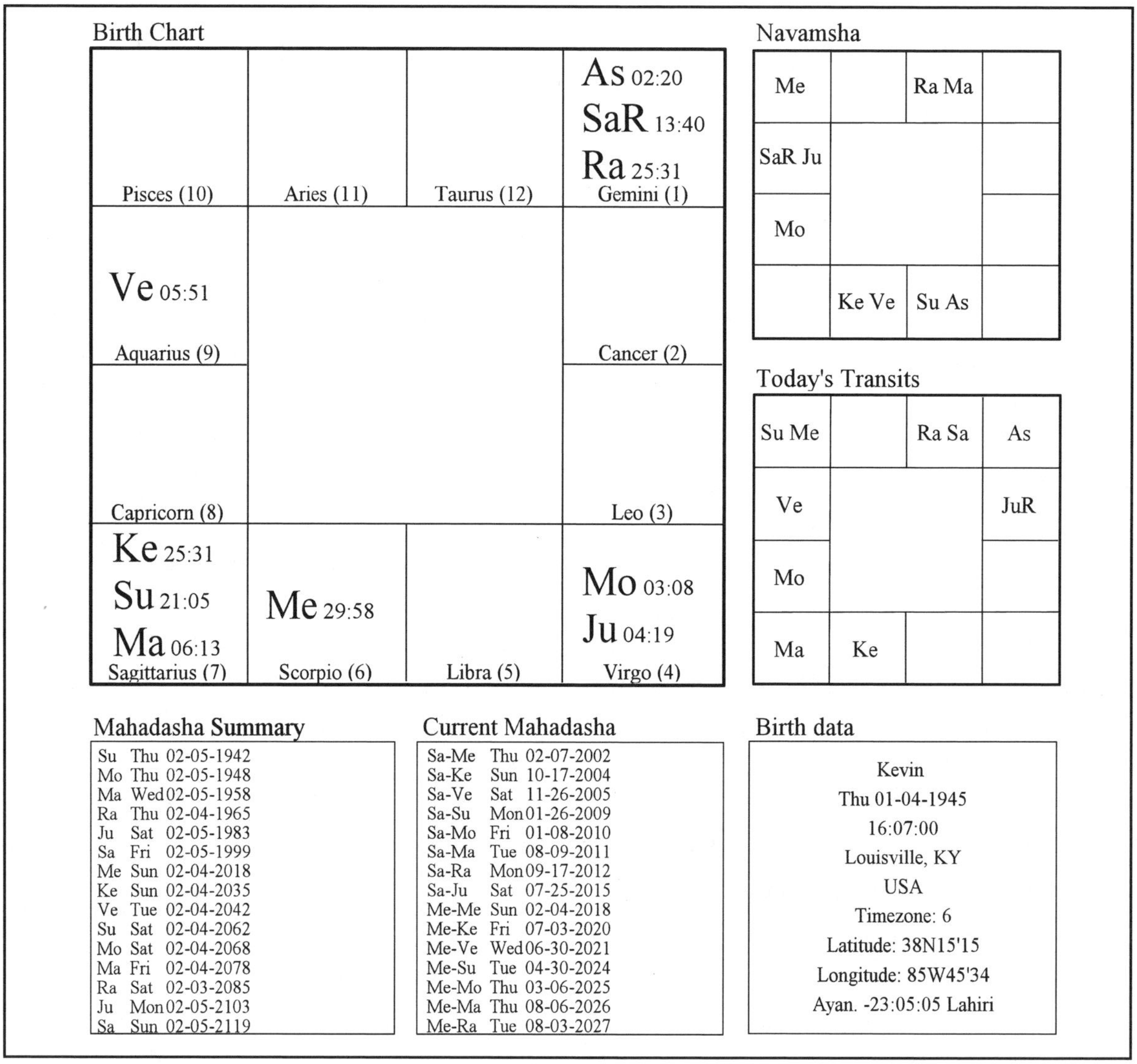

Birth Chart

			As 02:20 SaR 13:40 Ra 25:31
Pisces (10)	Aries (11)	Taurus (12)	Gemini (1)
Ve 05:51 Aquarius (9)			Cancer (2)
Capricorn (8)			Leo (3)
Ke 25:31 Su 21:05 Ma 06:13 Sagittarius (7)	Me 29:58 Scorpio (6)	Libra (5)	Mo 03:08 Ju 04:19 Virgo (4)

Navamsha

Me		Ra Ma	
SaR Ju			
Mo			
	Ke Ve	Su As	

Today's Transits

Su Me		Ra Sa	As
Ve			JuR
Mo			
Ma	Ke		

Mahadasha Summary

Su	Thu	02-05-1942
Mo	Thu	02-05-1948
Ma	Wed	02-05-1958
Ra	Thu	02-04-1965
Ju	Sat	02-05-1983
Sa	Fri	02-05-1999
Me	Sun	02-04-2018
Ke	Sun	02-04-2035
Ve	Tue	02-04-2042
Su	Sat	02-04-2062
Mo	Sat	02-04-2068
Ma	Fri	02-04-2078
Ra	Sat	02-03-2085
Ju	Mon	02-05-2103
Sa	Sun	02-05-2119

Current Mahadasha

Sa-Me	Thu	02-07-2002
Sa-Ke	Sun	10-17-2004
Sa-Ve	Sat	11-26-2005
Sa-Su	Mon	01-26-2009
Sa-Mo	Fri	01-08-2010
Sa-Ma	Tue	08-09-2011
Sa-Ra	Mon	09-17-2012
Sa-Ju	Sat	07-25-2015
Me-Me	Sun	02-04-2018
Me-Ke	Fri	07-03-2020
Me-Ve	Wed	06-30-2021
Me-Su	Tue	04-30-2024
Me-Mo	Thu	03-06-2025
Me-Ma	Thu	08-06-2026
Me-Ra	Tue	08-03-2027

Birth data

Kevin

Thu 01-04-1945

16:07:00

Louisville, KY

USA

Timezone: 6

Latitude: 38N15'15

Longitude: 85W45'34

Ayan. -23:05:05 Lahiri

Chart 14—Kevin

REMEDIES

Look again at Meryl Streep's chart on page 52, with Cancer rising—a sign ruled by the Moon. As we have already determined, her Moon is located in her 10th house, the house of career. She would not only bring energy to her emotional and physical well-being by strengthening the Moon, but would enhance her career prospects as well. To do this, she can wear a 3-carat pearl on her index finger, or a moonstone pendant of between 10 and 25 carats beginning on a Monday. She can also chant the Moon mantra, particularly on Mondays, and eat less on that day.

Now that she has entered the Jupiter mahadasha, she can wear a yellow sapphire on her index finger and chant the Jupiter mantra. However, because the Jupiter aspects her rising sign, she may find that during the 16-year Jupiter mahadasha she will be prone to put on weight.

She would do well to strengthen her Sun and Venus. Since both planets occupy her 12th house, they would benefit from increased energy. By enhancing these planets she could increase the degree to which she receives emotional nourishment. Unfortunately these planets are poorly placed, signifying the possible loss of a loved one (Venus is the planet of love, Sun indicates a man, and the 12th house signifies loss). She did, in fact, lose her lover in 1978, which, though tragic, fueled her to produce some of her most memorable work on screen.

Remedial measures are chart specific. What might work for Meryl Streep would certainly not be appropriate for Serena Williams. Let's explore some choices Serena might want to consider. She would benefit by wearing red coral. Though the stone's energy would especially help her during her current Mars mahadasha, I would recommend she wear the stone for life because Mars is her ruling planet and is natally weak. Also, she should have a Vedic fire ritual performed for her upcoming Rahu mahadasha to help smooth the transition between these major cycles. Since the Rahu is due in September, 2004, she should have the yagya done that summer.

Rahu mahadashas can be a bit tricky. Usually the Rahu takes away something or someone dear to you when it first begins (first bhukti). Then it can be very uplifting during the bulk of its cycle. But during the last part of the cycle (last bhukti), it can take something away again. Along with having yagyas performed, Serena might want to consider wearing a stone for Rahu or chanting the Rahu mantra.

STRENGTHENING YOUR 1st HOUSE

Now that you've familiarized yourself with your rising sign, you can bring strength to it by chanting the mantra for its ruler as many times a day as you like (see Table I). It's best to complete one repetition with each in-breath, and another with each out-breath. For some, it might be easier to use the shorter bija mantra (seed syllables) than the whole mantra in this way.

In addition, you may want to experiment with eating less food than usual on the day associated with the planet you want to strengthen. According to Vedic lore, by making a small sacrifice to the planet, the deity of the planet becomes pleased and showers its grace upon you.

If a planet occupies the 1st house, you can also chant its mantra as long as you do so carefully. That planet may be causing you some hardship that you will intensify with mantra repetition. For instance, if you have a weight problem and Jupiter sits in your rising sign, it's probably due to the Jupiter that you have weight issues. Jupiter is a jovial, expansive planet, and in the rising sign it brings expansion to the body. By chanting to Jupiter you would bring more of its influence into your life. Instead, you might consider chanting to Saturn in order to stimulate self-control and regularity in eating, or to the ruler of your 1st house.

If *two* planets should occupy your 1st house, say Venus and Saturn, then you need to pay attention to what planet you want to strengthen, and why. If you experience disappointment in love, chant the Venus mantra on Fridays and leave the Saturn alone. If you lack discipline in your life, chant for Saturn on Saturdays and leave the Venus alone.

If on the other hand Mars, or any malefic for that matter, occupies the rising sign, its influence may not be one you'll want to intensify. Strengthening Mars, for instance, can increase aggression and anger. The safest way to empower this type of chart is by chanting to the ruler of your rising sign, or to Venus—so enhancing the feminine nature of the chart to offset warlike Mars—or to Jupiter, to bring expansion and broad-mindedness. Chanting to the ruler of 5th and 9th house rulers may also help, as they are the most beneficent houses.

With regard to wearing gemstones, you'll also want to avoid enhancing the energy of a planet that will cause you more hardship. But generally speaking, you will be okay if you wear a stone for the ruler of your rising sign, the ruler of the 5th or 9th houses, or the current mahadasha.

Generally, it's best to wear the gemstone that corresponds to the ruler of your rising sign for your entire life, and then wear specific stones for the current mahadasha for only as long as the mahadasha lasts. Again, it's best to try out a stone first before purchasing it, in order to make sure the results you get are the ones you want.

SUMMARY

According to Hindu philosophy, you are already perfect. When you come into the world, this understanding can become distorted, so that you might feel that you are somehow flawed, or missing something. This is called *lila*, the divine play, where people appear to be in ignorance, but in fact, deep down inside, they are not.

Understand that the unique path your rising sign has set for you, providing you with skills and tools at your disposal, points the direction you must travel in order to rediscover yourself. But don't take the journey too seriously, since ultimately everything you are searching for has already been attained.

The 1st house indicates the body. We are born. What happens next? We think, conceptualize, have ideas, and in doing so move toward the 2nd house, because the 2nd house represents imagination. We must support our ideas by meeting our basic needs of food and shelter. That is why the 2nd house is primarily identified with wealth. There is a natural progression from the qualities you have discovered in your 1st house to their expression in the 2nd house. Let's find out how . . .

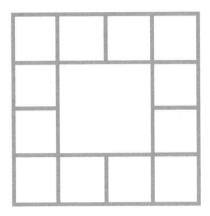

THE 2nd HOUSE

Wealth

The 2nd house is the house of wealth. This wealth is usually earned, as opposed to wealth gained from lottery, inheritance, or speculative investment. The 2nd house also indicates the mouth, and so refinement in articulation, or conversely problems with speech can be seen here. As an extension of this, it can also indicate the power to influence people with your speech.

It is a house that also indicates the right eye, imagination (and thus poetry), memory, and the lower face and neck area.

The 2nd house also shows the condition of a person's early life, as well as his or her eating patterns and habits of consumption. Addictive tendencies can be seen from the 2nd house: Mars or Rahu in the 2nd house can indicate a tendency toward alcohol, drug, or eating disorders, as well as toward the use of foul language.

Your family life is indicated by the 2nd house, especially your early years growing up. Whether you had a supportive, caring upbringing or one that was filled with challenges will be reflected in the 2nd house. The 2nd house also relates to longevity, as does the 7th house.

THE NATURE OF THE 2nd HOUSE

Find the 2nd house in your chart. If you are Leo rising, your 2nd house is Virgo. If you are Pisces rising, Aries is your 2nd house. Pay close attention to the zodiac sign of the 2nd house because the nature of that sign gives you a hint as to how your 2nd house issues will function.

For instance, if Virgo is your 2nd house, then you're precise in the words you choose and the way you express yourself. If your 2nd house is Gemini, then you may be multilingual, or make money from a number of projects simultaneously.

HOW THE 2nd HOUSE EXPRESSES ITSELF

Locate the planet that rules your 2nd house (Table B), and find where it's placed in your chart. Then read the description below that pertains to this placement.

The 2nd House Ruler placed in the 1st house indicates a strong focus on earning money, which you may accrue through forms of articulation (speaking, acting, teaching). Your sense of accomplishment is money based.

The 2nd House Ruler placed in the 2nd house shows great earning ability. When the ruler of a house is in its own house, it generally brings smoothness to that house's indications. In the case of the 2nd house, this indicates wealth, persuasive speaking ability, and the eating of fine foods.

The 2nd House Ruler placed in the 3rd house is associated with creativity, indicating that you can generate income through dance, literature, music, or acting. By hard work and courageous choices, you can enhance your finances. A sibling (usually younger) may help you in this regard. Indicates a challenging childhood.

The 2nd House Ruler placed in the 4th house indicates that you can generate money through dealings in real estate or other fixed assets, such as automobiles. You may also receive financial benefits from your mother.

Of course, if the ruler is not well placed or is aspected in a detrimental way, you can also lose money in dealing with homes or property, or due to the mother. Indicates a happy childhood.

The 2nd House Ruler placed in the 5th house indicates financial magnetism. Friends will look at you and wonder why money comes so easily to you. This is a position that favors luck with money. It also indicates money generated through entrepreneurial pursuits or gambling, or that your children will make a lot of money. This position suggests a happy childhood.

The 2nd House Ruler placed in the 6th house indicates several things. As you can see in Table C, the 6th house is associated with health and enemies. So this position shows you can generate income through the healing arts, whether through conventional or alternative medicines. It can also indicate making money by overcoming enemies, in the way that a boxer or professional athlete does. But this placement shows great unhappiness growing up.

The 2nd House Ruler placed in the 7th house shows that you may generate money through the help of your spouse, or that your spouse may be wealthy and generous so that you benefit from his or her wealth. This position also indicates associations with others, and combining efforts in order to make money, as in a partnership.

The 2nd House Ruler placed in the 8th house indicates that money may come from inheritance or winning the lottery, or in some unexpected, unearned way. I have also seen ghostwriters with this position, since they make money by working behind the scenes. However, more often than not, this placement indicates debt and the loss of money. It also indicates an unhappy childhood.

The 2nd House Ruler placed in the 9th house is a strong wealth indicator because the 9th house indicates luck. Spiritual teachers can have this placement, as money is generated by instructing about higher truths. Your father may be wealthy and generous with his wealth. This placement also indicates a happy childhood.

The 2nd House Ruler placed in the 10th house shows the ability to have a successful career and make money from it. The 2nd house ruler in the 10th shows that a career may involve some expression of the mouth, whether it's speaking (acting, singing, teaching) or eating (catering or restaurant business).

The 2nd House Ruler placed in the 11th house favors the flow of money (as with the 2nd house ruler in the 9th house). It can seem to come without effort. Friends or an older sibling may be responsible for your ability to make money, or the money can come through speculation or entrepreneurial pursuits.

The 2nd House Ruler placed in the 12th house usually indicates that it's difficult for you to hold on to money. Either you spend it faster than you can make it, or you are robbed of it (especially when traveling abroad). It may also indicate addictive tendencies, a speech impediment, difficulty speaking, or shyness.

PLANETS IN THE 2nd HOUSE

To help fine-tune the descriptions below, you'll want to assess whether the planet is welcome in the house in which it is placed (Table G). If the planet is in the house of a friend, the positive nature of the following description is enhanced. If the planet is in the house of an enemy, more of the negative possibilities need to be considered.

Sun (Su) in the 2nd house brings passion and energy to the voice. Though you can earn money, you can also spend it quickly. Can make a person seem vocally harsh. This is a good position for making money from the government.

Moon (Mo) in the 2nd house indicates a beautiful face and voice. You will speak sweetly and have a fertile imagination. An afflicted Moon may not affect the vocal smoothness, but can indicate that a person is deceptive through words.

Mars (Ma) in the 2nd house shows good strength in earning ability and a commanding vocal presence. There may also be addictions of the mouth, such as food, drugs, or alcohol. You might speak in a critical, brash manner, or have a scar on the mouth or neck area, or dental problems.

Mercury (Me) in the 2nd house brings extreme skill in oration and persuasion. You have a keen memory and are deeply imaginative. An afflicted Mercury produces the opposite effects, indicating problems with speech, either due to shyness or a physical anomaly.

Jupiter (Ju) in the 2nd house is one of the strongest indicators for accumulating great wealth. However, you may have a tendency to exaggerate, and can also gain weight from enjoying too much rich food.

Venus (Ve) in the 2nd house brings great beauty to the face and voice. This is a strong position for wealth. An afflicted 2nd house Venus, however, brings feelings of nothing being good enough. There is difficulty in feeling fully satisfied by anything.

Saturn (Sa) in the 2nd house indicates a difficult childhood, usually where love is hard to come by. It can also make a person shy and reserved. This position may favor the accumulation of wealth, but only slowly and steadily over time.

Rahu (Ra) in the 2nd house harms the 2nd house. There can be diseased teeth or gums, a scar on the mouth area, or the habitual use of

vulgarity when speaking. Not a good position for childhood happiness nor for smooth, delicate speech. However, earning ability can be phenomenal.

Ketu (Ke) in the 2nd house brings knowledge of the mystical or spiritual, and enables you to speak about these subjects with fluidity. There can be difficulty with addictive tendencies and deception until you develop discernment and discrimination later in life.

OTHER CONSIDERATIONS

- Note the element associated with your 2nd house (Table B). Remember that fire signs are driven; earth signs are patient; air signs are creative; and water signs are emotional.
- Also note the quality of your 2nd house. Cardinal signs initiate; fixed signs stabilize; and mutable signs seek change.

Now check any aspects to the 2nd house:

- Are any planets located in the same house as, or opposing any planet in, the 2nd house? If so, are those planets friendly, neutral, or enemies? (See Table F.) For instance, say Saturn is placed in the 2nd house and its enemy Mars is in the 8th house opposing it. This aspect indicates a conflict within a person where one part wants to be financially conservative (Saturn) while the other part wants to be impulsive with money (Mars). So the person will save for a while, then go on a spending spree!

- Remember that Mars energizes the house it's in, as well as the 4th, 7th, and 8th houses from itself. This means if Mars is placed in the 7th, 8th, or 11th houses of your chart, it throws an aspect onto your 2nd house, keeping it dynamic and driven, perhaps enabling you to jump at a favorable financial opportunity before anyone else can or, in afflicted cases, causing you to spend money too impulsively.

- Saturn restricts or brings discipline to the house it's in, as well as the 3rd, 7th, and 10th houses from itself. This means if Saturn is placed in the 5th, 8th, or 12th houses of your chart, it throws an aspect onto your 2nd house, making it more difficult to earn money or verbally express yourself. On the positive side, it helps regulate impulsive speaking or spending.

- Jupiter expands or brings optimism to the house it's in, as well as the 5th, 7th, and 9th houses from itself. This means if Jupiter is placed in the 6th, 8th, or 10th houses of your chart, it throws an aspect onto your 2nd house, increasing your ability to earn money as well as your verbosity.

- If you want to find out when your chart's 2nd house energies will be enlivened, look to the 2nd house ruler, or any planet located in the 2nd house. Examine the Mahadasha Summary of your chart to see when that planet will come into power, and that will give you your answer. To find shorter periods when 2nd house issues will be highlighted, look to the 2nd house ruler or any planet located in the 2nd house, and find the time its bhukti will run.

- Notice any influence transiting planets are having on your 2nd house or your 2nd house ruler. A Mars transit may cause you to be impulsive with your money. Jupiter will bring you luck with money. Saturn can either cause you to lose money, or teach you how to save it. You can chant to the planet that is favorably transiting your rising sign, on the appropriate day for that planet, to enhance its effects.

EXAMPLE CHARTS

To see how 2nd house principles can be applied, let's look at the chart of Julie Andrews.

We'll combine all of what we've discussed thus far in looking at her chart. Since we've already spoken about the 1st house, let's take another look at hers. Virgo rising shows that she is very exacting and precise, and the Sun in the rising sign shows that she likes to be the center of attention. Sun in the rising also indicates that she would have a broad face and features, and not a great deal of hair, which is true. In what way will she be the center of attention? Virgo is ruled by Mercury, so it's in some form of communication.

Now look where that Mercury is placed— in her 2nd house. So she expresses her character through voice and poetry (lyrics). The Moon and Jupiter also occupy the 2nd house, which is Libra. Remember that Libra is ruled by Venus—the planet of arts. So, even though

Julie Andrews didn't want to be typecast as a "goody-goody," those flowery 2nd house planets made it difficult for her not to be.

That she has three beneficent planets in the 2nd shows that she has more than one skill in this area. But because we are just looking at the 2nd house indications, we will focus on her singing ability, to which she brings pre-cision and training due to her Virgo rising qualities and to the expansive nature of the planets in the 2nd house.

Consider the other indications of the 2nd house. Would you say her childhood was wonderful? No, not really. Although powerful, beneficial planets occupy the house, look at Libra's ruler. Table B tells us it is Venus.

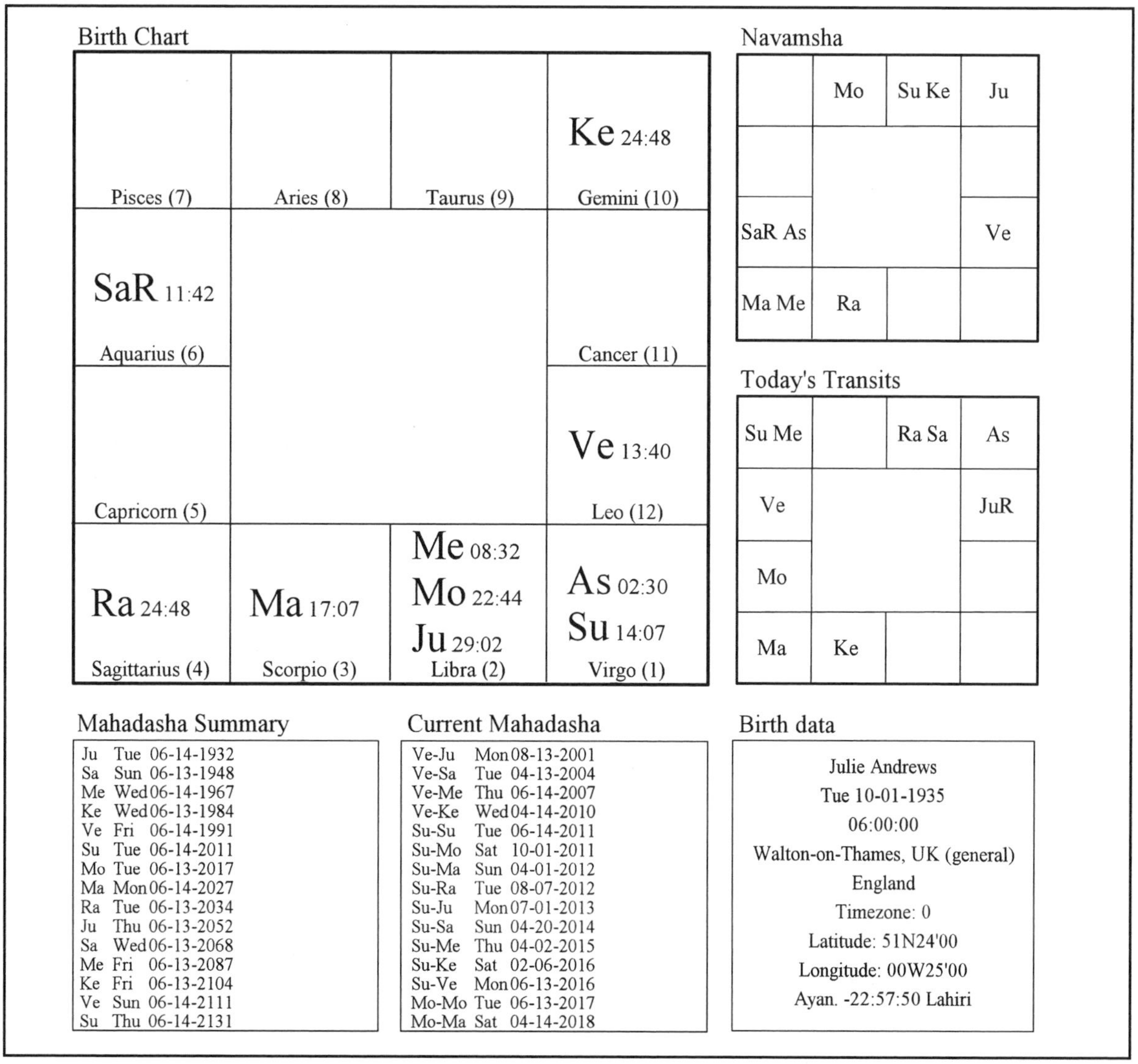

Birth Chart

Pisces (7)	Aries (8)	Taurus (9)	**Ke** 24:48 Gemini (10)
SaR 11:42 Aquarius (6)			Cancer (11)
Capricorn (5)			**Ve** 13:40 Leo (12)
Ra 24:48 Sagittarius (4)	**Ma** 17:07 Scorpio (3)	**Me** 08:32 **Mo** 22:44 **Ju** 29:02 Libra (2)	**As** 02:30 **Su** 14:07 Virgo (1)

Navamsha

	Mo	Su Ke	Ju
SaR As			Ve
Ma Me	Ra		

Today's Transits

Su Me		Ra Sa	As
Ve			JuR
Mo			
Ma	Ke		

Mahadasha Summary

Ju	Tue	06-14-1932
Sa	Sun	06-13-1948
Me	Wed	06-14-1967
Ke	Wed	06-13-1984
Ve	Fri	06-14-1991
Su	Tue	06-14-2011
Mo	Tue	06-13-2017
Ma	Mon	06-14-2027
Ra	Tue	06-13-2034
Ju	Thu	06-13-2052
Sa	Wed	06-13-2068
Me	Fri	06-13-2087
Ke	Fri	06-13-2104
Ve	Sun	06-14-2111
Su	Thu	06-14-2131

Current Mahadasha

Ve-Ju	Mon	08-13-2001
Ve-Sa	Tue	04-13-2004
Ve-Me	Thu	06-14-2007
Ve-Ke	Wed	04-14-2010
Su-Su	Tue	06-14-2011
Su-Mo	Sat	10-01-2011
Su-Ma	Sun	04-01-2012
Su-Ra	Tue	08-07-2012
Su-Ju	Mon	07-01-2013
Su-Sa	Sun	04-20-2014
Su-Me	Thu	04-02-2015
Su-Ke	Sat	02-06-2016
Su-Ve	Mon	06-13-2016
Mo-Mo	Tue	06-13-2017
Mo-Ma	Sat	04-14-2018

Birth data

Julie Andrews
Tue 10-01-1935
06:00:00
Walton-on-Thames, UK (general)
England
Timezone: 0
Latitude: 51N24'00
Longitude: 00W25'00
Ayan. -22:57:50 Lahiri

Chart 15—Julie Andrews

Where is the Venus in her chart? It falls in the 12th house, the house of loss. So her childhood was not altogether pleasant. Biographical notes mention that she dodged the bombs of the Nazis' blitzkriegs in England while performing with her artistic family during WW II.

Just as powerful beneficent planets in the 1st house of appearance gave Paul Newman beautiful facial features, those same planets in Julie Andrews's 2nd house brought her a beautiful voice.

But during the 1996–97 run of *Victor/Victoria* on Broadway, she began to have trouble with her voice, which eventually led to throat surgery to remove nodules on her vocal cords. Could this have been anticipated in the chart? First, look at her current mahadasha. It's Venus. And her Venus is in the 12th house, the house of loss. The 2nd house is her voice, and the ruler of that house is in the house of loss.

Since the Venus mahadasha runs a long time, 20 years, is it possible to see within that period more precisely when she might have voice problems? Yes. In March 1997, retrograde Mars was transiting her rising sign, opposed by Ketu and its enemy, Saturn. We've already seen the damage that can occur when Mars and Saturn oppose one another. When that same opposition hits a person's rising sign in this way, it must have some sort of an impact upon a person's head and neck region.

As the Saturn moved across her rising sign in opposition, it entered her 8th house, the house of longevity. The nature of Saturn is restriction. So when Saturn opposed Julie's

2nd house, the house of speech, it created a restriction to her voice. Due to a botched surgery, it seems that Julie will not recover her singing voice at all. Her husband Blake Edwards said, "I don't think she'll ever sing again . . . it's an absolute tragedy."

Could this loss of voice have been prevented? To some degree, perhaps. With knowledge of Vedic astrology, she would never have organized a long-running performance in 1996–97, the worst possible time to organize such an event. She pushed when her system was weakest, especially in the area of her 2nd house. She should have holed up and written her memoirs between 1996 and 2000, and given singing a rest. As it turns out, she is working on her autobiography now.

What about the 2nd house indications for addictive tendencies? Drew Barrymore is a wonderful example of Vedic astrology's predictive abilities in this area.

First, we see that Drew has Taurus rising. Table B tells us that Taurus rising is a fixed sign, which indicates that when a person falls into a certain pattern of behavior, he or she finds a certain comfort in it, even if it's destructive behavior. People with Taurus rising can sometimes be stubborn. Taurus's symbol is a bull, and Taurus people can have a tendency to dig their heels in and refuse to budge.

Drew has both Saturn and Moon in her 2nd house. Because the Moon is an expressive planet and Saturn has a restrictive influence, when combined they can create a speech impediment, the slight lisp that made Drew so endearing in the movie *E.T.* The Moon also

Birth Chart

Ve 05:45 Ju 00:46 Pisces (11)	Aries (12)	Ke 12:16 As 25:32 Taurus (1)	SaR 18:46 Mo 24:36 Gemini (2)
Su 10:03 Aquarius (10)			Cancer (3)
Me 16:40 Ma 00:11 Capricorn (9)			Leo (4)
Sagittarius (8)	Ra 12:16 Scorpio (7)	Libra (6)	Virgo (5)

Navamsha

SaR	Ke	Mo	Me
			Ju
Su Ma			As Ve
		Ra	

Today's Transits

Su Me		Ra Sa	As
Ve			JuR
Mo			
Ma	Ke		

Mahadasha Summary

Ju	Thu	08-14-1969
Sa	Wed	08-14-1985
Me	Sat	08-14-2004
Ke	Sat	08-14-2021
Ve	Sun	08-13-2028
Su	Thu	08-13-2048
Mo	Fri	08-14-2054
Ma	Wed	08-13-2064
Ra	Fri	08-14-2071
Ju	Sat	08-13-2089
Sa	Fri	08-14-2105
Me	Mon	08-14-2124
Ke	Mon	08-14-2141
Ve	Tue	08-13-2148
Su	Sat	08-13-2168

Current Mahadasha

Sa-Ju	Thu	01-31-2002
Me-Me	Sat	08-14-2004
Me-Ke	Wed	01-10-2007
Me-Ve	Mon	01-07-2008
Me-Su	Sun	11-07-2010
Me-Mo	Wed	09-14-2011
Me-Ma	Tue	02-12-2013
Me-Ra	Sun	02-09-2014
Me-Ju	Mon	08-29-2016
Me-Sa	Wed	12-05-2018
Ke-Ke	Sat	08-14-2021
Ke-Ve	Mon	01-10-2022
Ke-Su	Sun	03-12-2023
Ke-Mo	Tue	07-18-2023
Ke-Ma	Fri	02-16-2024

Birth data

Drew Barrymore
Sat 02-22-1975
11:51:00
Culver City, CA
USA
Timezone: 8
Latitude: 34N01'16
Longitude: 118W23'44
Ayan. -23:30:53 Lahiri

Chart 16—Drew Barrymore

indicates the emotions, and because the 2nd house also deals with happiness in one's childhood, we see that due to Saturn's influence, Drew could not have been very happy growing up.

The Saturn/Moon connection brings depression, heaviness in the mind, lack of optimism, and in the extreme, suicidal tendencies, which she had. Further, her Saturn is retrograde, so it drives her even further into isolation and creates mental unhappiness. A malefic influence like Saturn in the 2nd house also brings addictive tendencies, which she struggled with for years.

Could this have been predicted? Sure. Her Saturn mahadasha began in 1985, amplifying these tendencies, and it's been widely noted that she began drinking at the age of nine, which is exactly when this mahadasha started. The beauty of her chart, however, is that the planet that rules her rising sign is Venus. And look at where the Venus is in her chart: near its exaltation point in Pisces, conjoined with Jupiter. So this chart shows grace. With the ruler so well placed in her chart, she was bound to get through her trauma and shine again, which she has done. Because the 2nd house deals mostly with one's early years, the pressure of these planets has lifted slowly.

As is clear in Drew's case, the Moon is an

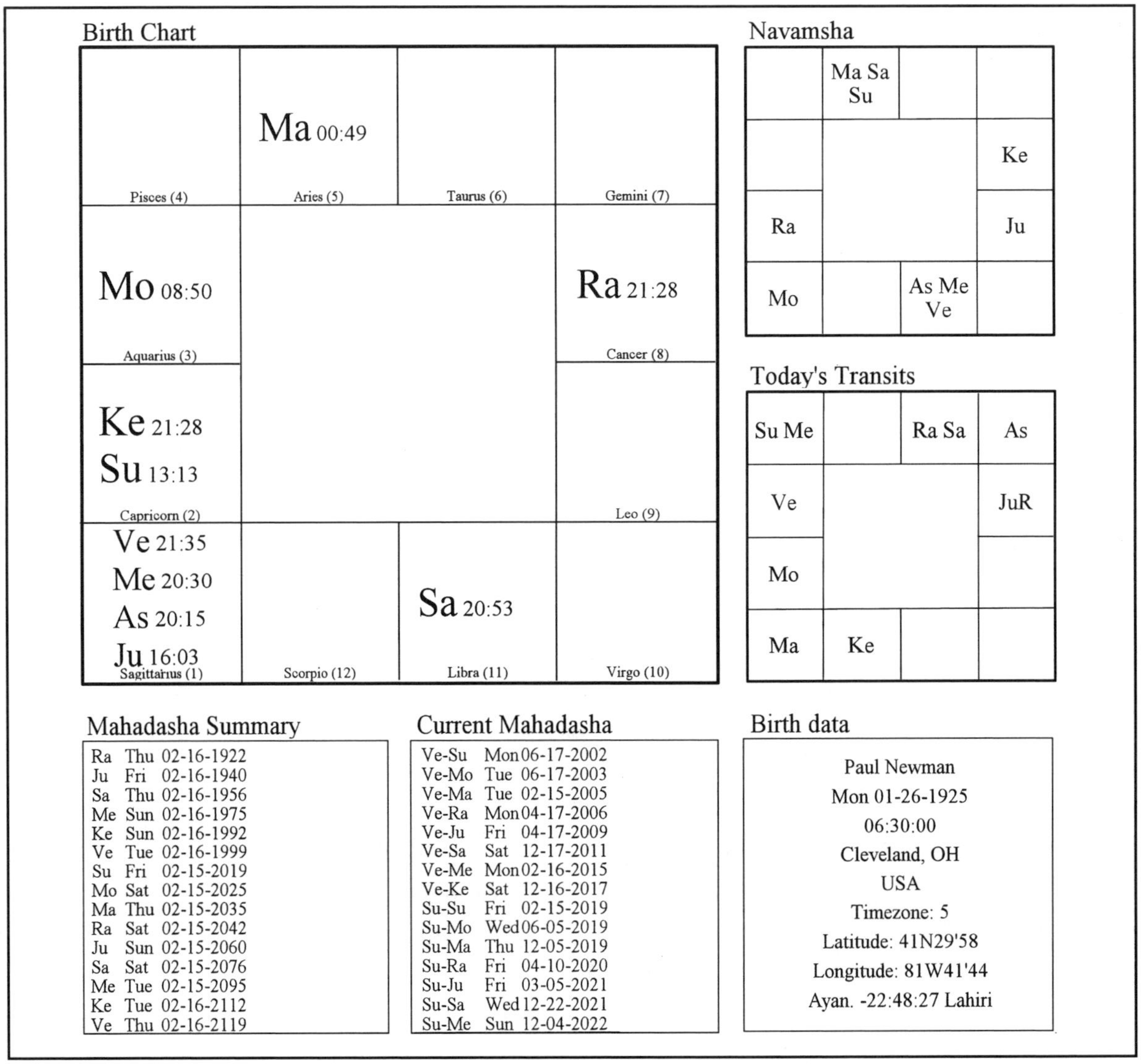

Birth Chart

Pisces (4)	Aries (5)	Taurus (6)	Gemini (7)
Ma 00:49 (Aries)			
Mo 08:50 — Aquarius (3)			Ra 21:28 — Cancer (8)
Ke 21:28 Su 13:13 — Capricorn (2)			Leo (9)
Ve 21:35 Me 20:30 As 20:15 Ju 16:03 — Sagittarius (1)	Scorpio (12)	Sa 20:53 — Libra (11)	Virgo (10)

Navamsha

	Ma Sa Su		
			Ke
Ra			Ju
Mo		As Me Ve	

Today's Transits

Su Me		Ra Sa	As
Ve			JuR
Mo			
Ma	Ke		

Mahadasha Summary

Ra	Thu	02-16-1922
Ju	Fri	02-16-1940
Sa	Thu	02-16-1956
Me	Sun	02-16-1975
Ke	Sun	02-16-1992
Ve	Tue	02-16-1999
Su	Fri	02-15-2019
Mo	Sat	02-15-2025
Ma	Thu	02-15-2035
Ra	Sat	02-15-2042
Ju	Sun	02-15-2060
Sa	Sat	02-15-2076
Me	Tue	02-15-2095
Ke	Tue	02-16-2112
Ve	Thu	02-16-2119

Current Mahadasha

Ve-Su	Mon	06-17-2002
Ve-Mo	Tue	06-17-2003
Ve-Ma	Tue	02-15-2005
Ve-Ra	Mon	04-17-2006
Ve-Ju	Fri	04-17-2009
Ve-Sa	Sat	12-17-2011
Ve-Me	Mon	02-16-2015
Ve-Ke	Sat	12-16-2017
Su-Su	Fri	02-15-2019
Su-Mo	Wed	06-05-2019
Su-Ma	Thu	12-05-2019
Su-Ra	Fri	04-10-2020
Su-Ju	Fri	03-05-2021
Su-Sa	Wed	12-22-2021
Su-Me	Sun	12-04-2022

Birth data

Paul Newman
Mon 01-26-1925
06:30:00
Cleveland, OH
USA
Timezone: 5
Latitude: 41N29'58
Longitude: 81W41'44
Ayan. -22:48:27 Lahiri

Chart 17—Paul Newman

all-important indication of one's emotional stability. It must be well placed for there to be fulfillment.

Let's look at the power of the Moon by comparing Paul Newman and John Belushi's charts.

Notice that both Paul and John have Jupiter and Venus in the same rising sign,

Sagittarius. Now notice their Moons. Paul's Moon is well placed in his 3rd house, which is Aquarius, giving him skill in the creative arts. Further, because of the humanitarian influence of Aquarius, he has done tremendous work with philanthropic activities.

Now look at John Belushi's Moon. It's in the weakest possible position, the 12th house,

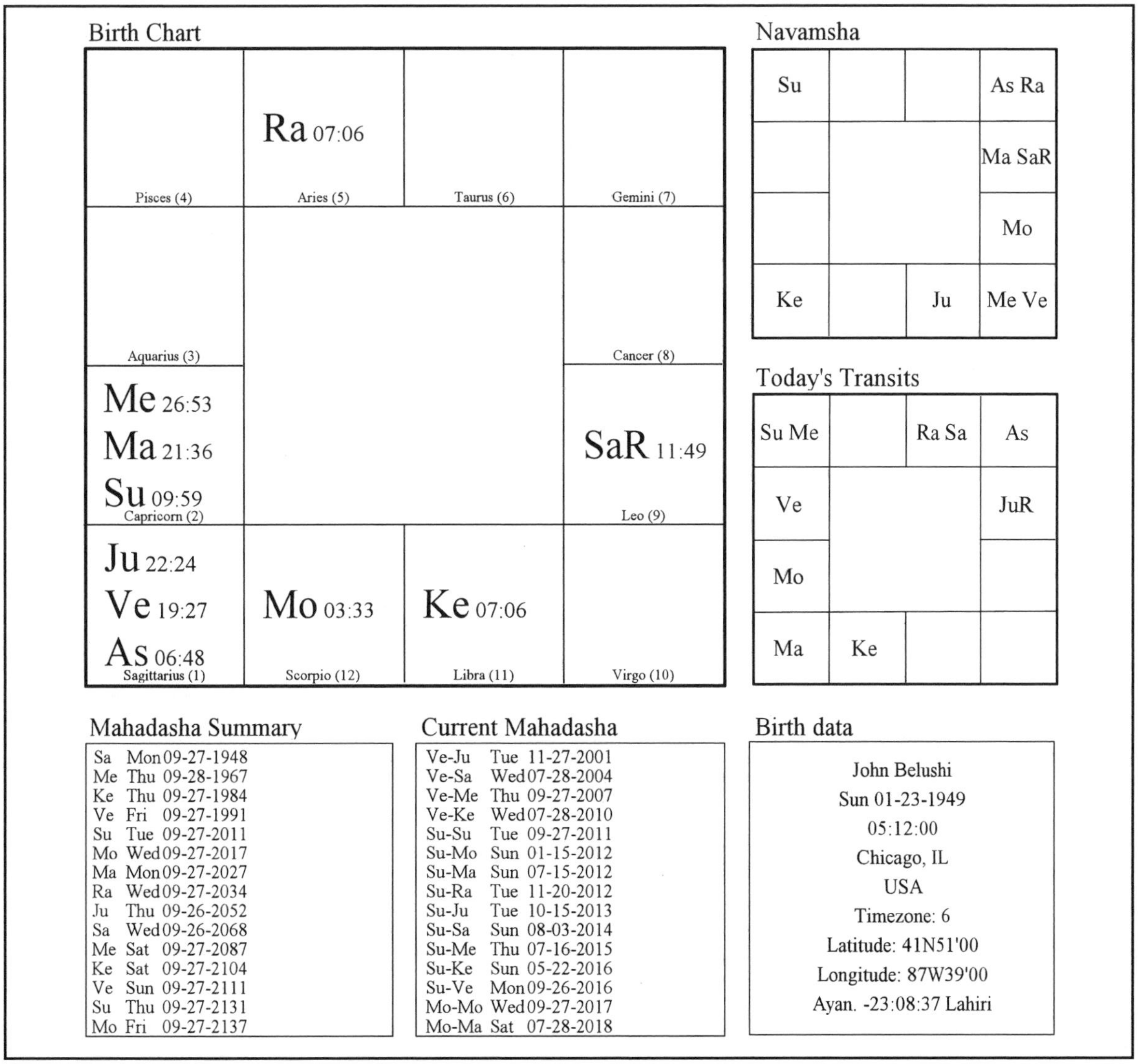

Birth Chart

	Ra 07:06		
Pisces (4)	Aries (5)	Taurus (6)	Gemini (7)
			Cancer (8)
Aquarius (3)			
Me 26:53 Ma 21:36 Su 09:59 Capricorn (2)			SaR 11:49 Leo (9)
Ju 22:24 Ve 19:27 As 06:48 Sagittarius (1)	Mo 03:33 Scorpio (12)	Ke 07:06 Libra (11)	Virgo (10)

Navamsha

Su			As Ra
			Ma SaR
			Mo
Ke		Ju	Me Ve

Today's Transits

Su Me		Ra Sa	As
Ve			JuR
Mo			
Ma	Ke		

Mahadasha Summary

Sa	Mon 09-27-1948
Me	Thu 09-28-1967
Ke	Thu 09-27-1984
Ve	Fri 09-27-1991
Su	Tue 09-27-2011
Mo	Wed 09-27-2017
Ma	Mon 09-27-2027
Ra	Wed 09-27-2034
Ju	Thu 09-26-2052
Sa	Wed 09-26-2068
Me	Sat 09-27-2087
Ke	Sat 09-27-2104
Ve	Sun 09-27-2111
Su	Thu 09-27-2131
Mo	Fri 09-27-2137

Current Mahadasha

Ve-Ju	Tue 11-27-2001
Ve-Sa	Wed 07-28-2004
Ve-Me	Thu 09-27-2007
Ve-Ke	Wed 07-28-2010
Su-Su	Tue 09-27-2011
Su-Mo	Sun 01-15-2012
Su-Ma	Sun 07-15-2012
Su-Ra	Tue 11-20-2012
Su-Ju	Tue 10-15-2013
Su-Sa	Sun 08-03-2014
Su-Me	Thu 07-16-2015
Su-Ke	Sun 05-22-2016
Su-Ve	Mon 09-26-2016
Mo-Mo	Wed 09-27-2017
Mo-Ma	Sat 07-28-2018

Birth data

John Belushi
Sun 01-23-1949
05:12:00
Chicago, IL
USA
Timezone: 6
Latitude: 41N51'00
Longitude: 87W39'00
Ayan. -23:08:37 Lahiri

Chart 18—John Belushi

debilitated in Scorpio, a dark, moody, destructive sign. While Paul's Moon brought him altruism, John's brought narcissism. Two rising signs with a great deal in common, but two very different results, all due to the differing Moon placements.

In another example, as we mentioned in the introduction, Rahu (the north node of the Moon) and Ketu (the south node of the Moon) create very strange and sometimes difficult-to-anticipate results on a chart. Look at Chart 19.

Greg's rising sign is Cancer, an intuitive sign, ruled by the Moon. The Moon is placed in the 5th house of Scorpio, its house of debilitation. What does this tell us?

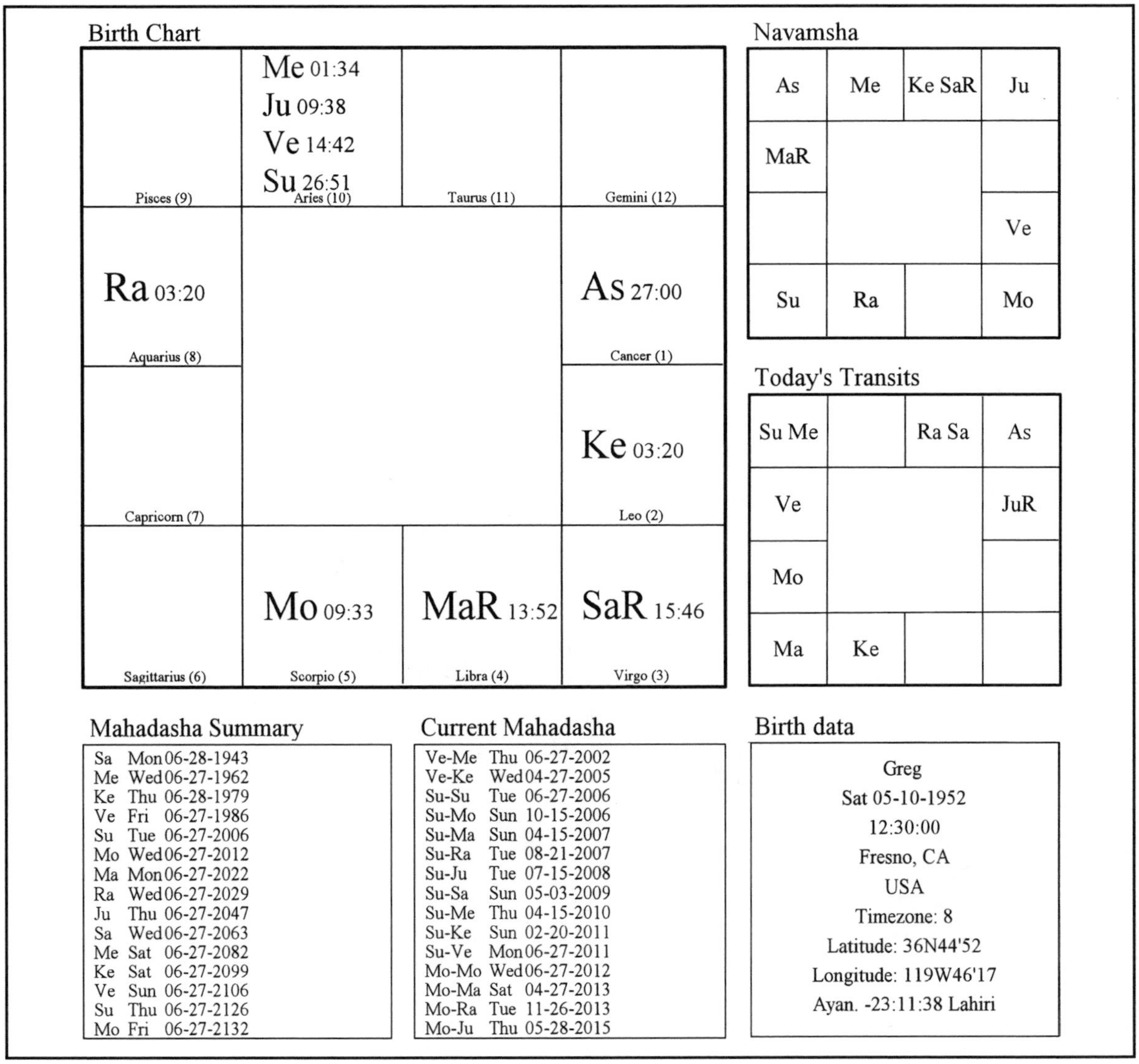

Birth Chart			
Pisces (9)	Me 01:34 Ju 09:38 Ve 14:42 Su 26:51 Aries (10)	Taurus (11)	Gemini (12)
Ra 03:20 Aquarius (8)			As 27:00 Cancer (1)
Capricorn (7)			Ke 03:20 Leo (2)
Sagittarius (6)	Mo 09:33 Scorpio (5)	MaR 13:52 Libra (4)	SaR 15:46 Virgo (3)

Navamsha			
As	Me	Ke SaR	Ju
MaR			
			Ve
Su	Ra		Mo

Today's Transits			
Su Me		Ra Sa	As
Ve			JuR
Mo			
Ma	Ke		

Mahadasha Summary

Sa	Mon	06-28-1943
Me	Wed	06-27-1962
Ke	Thu	06-28-1979
Ve	Fri	06-27-1986
Su	Tue	06-27-2006
Mo	Wed	06-27-2012
Ma	Mon	06-27-2022
Ra	Wed	06-27-2029
Ju	Thu	06-27-2047
Sa	Wed	06-27-2063
Me	Sat	06-27-2082
Ke	Sat	06-27-2099
Ve	Sun	06-27-2106
Su	Thu	06-27-2126
Mo	Fri	06-27-2132

Current Mahadasha

Ve-Me	Thu	06-27-2002
Ve-Ke	Wed	04-27-2005
Su-Su	Tue	06-27-2006
Su-Mo	Sun	10-15-2006
Su-Ma	Sun	04-15-2007
Su-Ra	Tue	08-21-2007
Su-Ju	Tue	07-15-2008
Su-Sa	Sun	05-03-2009
Su-Me	Thu	04-15-2010
Su-Ke	Sun	02-20-2011
Su-Ve	Mon	06-27-2011
Mo-Mo	Wed	06-27-2012
Mo-Ma	Sat	04-27-2013
Mo-Ra	Tue	11-26-2013
Mo-Ju	Thu	05-28-2015

Birth data

Greg
Sat 05-10-1952
12:30:00
Fresno, CA
USA
Timezone: 8
Latitude: 36N44'52
Longitude: 119W46'17
Ayan. -23:11:38 Lahiri

Chart 19—Greg

One of the indications of the 5th house is higher education, and the nature of Scorpio is secrecy—even more so because the Moon is in debilitation. So Greg learned about something that was highly educational, secretive, and intense. Now look at his 2nd house, the house of wealth. Ketu in the 2nd house indicates mystery, so its position shows an unusual or mysterious way to make money.

Greg was a drug smuggler. Was he successful? Where is the ruler of the 2nd house? Table B tells us the ruler of Leo, his 2nd house, is the Sun. The Sun is in its house of exaltation, Aries, along with Mercury, Jupiter, and Venus. And look how Jupiter throws a 5th house aspect on his 2nd house, fortifying it even more. You bet he was successful.

Can you tell when Greg was most successful? Look at the Mahadasha Summary. Yes, during the Ketu mahadasha that ran between the years 1979 and 1986. He made many millions during that period. Did he ever indulge in his product? Ketu in the 2nd house shows that yes, he had a tendency to use drugs.

It's interesting to note that celebrities who have strong 2nd houses not only have the power of speech and communication, but have strong money houses too. By the way, since the 2nd house also rules the teeth, celebrities generally have good-looking teeth (even if capped or whitened)! Let's see how wealth is indicated in some of their charts.

Brad Pitt has five planets in the 2nd; Julia Roberts has a Moon, Jupiter, and Venus conjunction in the 2nd; Whitney Houston has a Jupiter and Moon conjunction in the 2nd

(Jupiter's tendency toward overindulgence also led to her problems with addiction).

Wealth can also be seen by noting where the ruler of the 2nd house is placed. Harrison Ford has no planet in his 2nd house, but the 2nd house ruler is placed in his 9th house, one of the best positions for wealth.

What about Oprah Winfrey? She is considered the world's most highly paid entertainer, so we would expect her 2nd house, or its ruler, to be well fortified.

What we find in Chart 20 is that her 2nd house ruler, Mercury, is in her 6th house, conjoined by Venus and the Sun, and aspected by Jupiter. Why the 6th house? The 6th house indicates healers. And though most of us see her as a talk show host and entrepreneur, she is actually healing people, by delving into deep, sometimes painful stories or emotions, by donating millions to charities, and by starring in film roles that purge deep, painful issues. These are all methods of healing that reach people worldwide.

REMEDIES

In the fall of 1994, Julie Andrews should have had a large fire ritual performed for her Venus. In addition, she should have worn a diamond or white sapphire to bring energy to the ruler of her 2nd house located in the 12th house in her chart. Every day she should have chanted the Venus mantra. These measures, coupled with not scheduling any demanding performances during the worst period of her Venus mahadasha, would have helped preserve her voice.

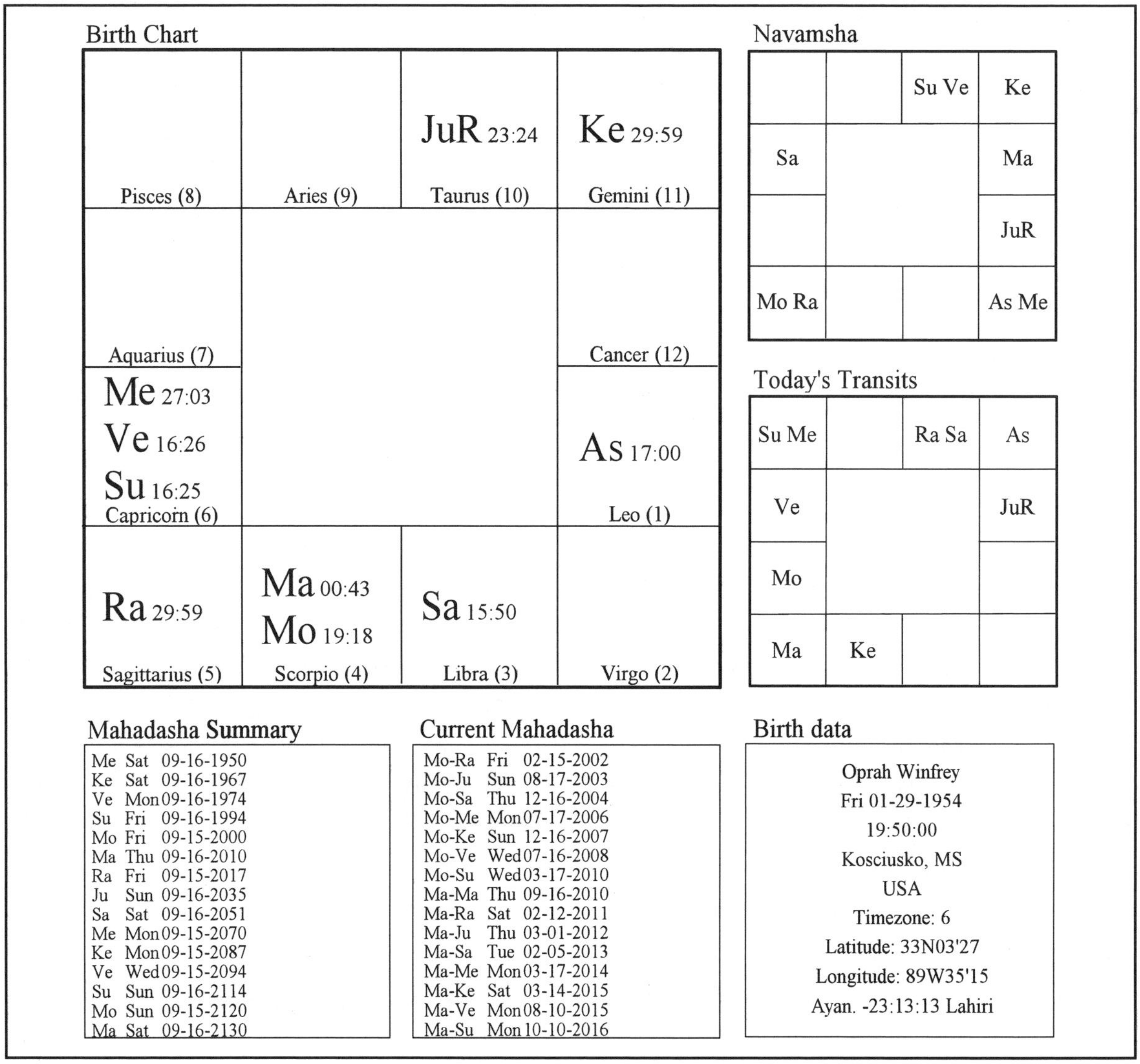

Birth Chart

		JuR 23:24	Ke 29:59
Pisces (8)	Aries (9)	Taurus (10)	Gemini (11)
Aquarius (7)			Cancer (12)
Me 27:03 Ve 16:26 Su 16:25 Capricorn (6)			As 17:00 Leo (1)
Ra 29:59 Sagittarius (5)	Ma 00:43 Mo 19:18 Scorpio (4)	Sa 15:50 Libra (3)	Virgo (2)

Navamsha

		Su Ve	Ke
	Sa		Ma
			JuR
Mo Ra			As Me

Today's Transits

Su Me		Ra Sa	As
Ve			JuR
Mo			
Ma	Ke		

Mahadasha Summary

Me	Sat	09-16-1950
Ke	Sat	09-16-1967
Ve	Mon	09-16-1974
Su	Fri	09-16-1994
Mo	Fri	09-15-2000
Ma	Thu	09-16-2010
Ra	Fri	09-15-2017
Ju	Sun	09-16-2035
Sa	Sat	09-16-2051
Me	Mon	09-15-2070
Ke	Mon	09-15-2087
Ve	Wed	09-15-2094
Su	Sun	09-16-2114
Mo	Sun	09-15-2120
Ma	Sat	09-16-2130

Current Mahadasha

Mo-Ra	Fri	02-15-2002
Mo-Ju	Sun	08-17-2003
Mo-Sa	Thu	12-16-2004
Mo-Me	Mon	07-17-2006
Mo-Ke	Sun	12-16-2007
Mo-Ve	Wed	07-16-2008
Mo-Su	Wed	03-17-2010
Ma-Ma	Thu	09-16-2010
Ma-Ra	Sat	02-12-2011
Ma-Ju	Thu	03-01-2012
Ma-Sa	Tue	02-05-2013
Ma-Me	Mon	03-17-2014
Ma-Ke	Sat	03-14-2015
Ma-Ve	Mon	08-10-2015
Ma-Su	Mon	10-10-2016

Birth data

Oprah Winfrey
Fri 01-29-1954
19:50:00
Kosciusko, MS
USA
Timezone: 6
Latitude: 33N03'27
Longitude: 89W35'15
Ayan. -23:13:13 Lahiri

Chart 20—Oprah Winfrey

Drew Barrymore would have felt quite a bit of relief if a Saturn fire ritual had been performed when Saturn came into power. She also would have benefited from experimenting with the blue sapphire, but because stones for Saturn are the most tricky (they can exacerbate the problem), you have to monitor the results closely. A stone for the Moon, or for Mercury, which rules her 2nd house and is placed in her 9th (the house of good luck and good fortune), could have helped minimize the impact of that Saturn mahadasha on her.

For powerful challenging planets that come into power during their mahadasha, it helps to have a fire ritual performed. These ceremonies can have tremendously uplifting results and blast through difficulties in a dramatic fashion.

Since Drew is still under the influence of Saturn, she would benefit by applying some of the remedies mentioned for Saturn. When Drew's Mercury mahadasha begins in 2004 she'll want to wear a 3-carat emerald or 5-carat green tourmaline, and chant the mantra for Mercury daily.

John Belushi's case is more difficult. His Jupiter and Venus in his rising sign must have given him the sense that he was indestructible. Those planets tend to bring overoptimism, and people who run on their energies rarely consider listening to others' opinions or advice.

However, when his Sun mahadasha began, he could have brought benefit to the energies of that planet through remedial measures. The challenge here is that the Sun in his 2nd house gave him his creativity, brashness, vulgarity, and an addictive nature, which in a sense was what made him famous.

To create a shift in those energies would have taken away from the qualities that brought him fame. He couldn't have strengthened his rising sign without fueling his optimism even more, and compounding his weight problem (Jupiter in the rising sign).

However, by strengthening the Moon in this chart, he could have brought himself more emotional stability without compromising his creative and bombastic nature. Because the moon is in a house of debilitation, a powerful series of fire rituals would have been recommended.

STRENGTHENING YOUR 2nd HOUSE

Again, the simplest way to empower the 2nd house is to chant the mantra on the appropriate day for the house's ruler. You can also chant for any planet located in the house, as long as you are certain you want the energies associated with that planet enhanced.

For instance, if your 2nd house is Leo, and no planet occupies your 2nd house, then you'll want to chant the mantra for the Sun, the ruler of Leo. The best day for Sun mantra repetition is Sunday. If Jupiter is placed in your 2nd house, you can bring money into your life by chanting the Jupiter mantra on Thursday, the day associated with Jupiter. Remember that by empowering a malefic planet in your 2nd house, you increase the risk of losing money, or impulsively saying something that you'll regret later. You can also perform a semi-fast on the day associated with the ruler of the 2nd house, or any planet placed there, in order to appease its deity.

Wearing a gemstone to strengthen a planet located in the 2nd house can also bring benefits (see Table J). However, remember that if the planet is malefic (Mars, Saturn, Rahu, or Ketu), you can amplify 2nd house difficulties by strengthening the malefic planet. A safer alternative is to strengthen the ruler of the 2nd house. That way, you enhance the natural characteristic of the 2nd house, without aggravating malefic tendencies. You can also strengthen any planet that favorably aspects the 2nd house. For instance, Jupiter in the

10th house of the chart throws an aspect onto the 2nd. So by bringing strength to the Jupiter you are automatically helping the 2nd house.

In an extreme 2nd house issue, like drug addiction, I would highly recommend Vedic fire rituals. Sometimes the energies are so thick in a person's life that it takes a bulldozer to blast through them. This, essentially, is what Vedic fire rituals can do.

SUMMARY

The 2nd house is primarily associated with wealth, specifically money generated through one's own actions in vocational pursuits. Material support comes when you have an idea, a vision, an aspiration, a creative impulse, and then the energy or courage to implement it. The 2nd house indicates the idea; the 3rd house gives you the courage to pursue it. From ideas come desires. When you become interested in something enough to move in its direction, you are crossing from the 2nd house into the 3rd.

As we begin to explore the 3rd house, remember that the houses of the zodiac are interwoven, so that each is a natural extension of the last. The 3rd house is where some people experience conflict, since they may try to accomplish or desire something that is beyond their natural inclination or ability. It's essential to be sensitive to the nature of your 1st and 2nd houses, in order to gauge the appropriate expression for the energetic pursuits and dreams indicated by your 3rd house. They should be natural expressions of who you really are, not a media-enhanced version of an "ideal you."

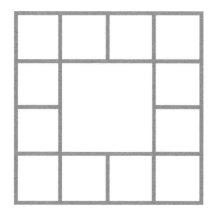

THE 3rd HOUSE

Creativity

The 3rd house indications include creative efforts such as dance, literature, drama, and music. It also signifies courage, the ears, arms, hands, and siblings (usually younger). The 3rd house is also called an upachaya house. This means that it is an improving house, and that if there are challenging indications for the 3rd house, they can improve over time, with effort. That's why most people who are artistic succeed only if they practice their skills diligently.

If the 3rd house is ruled by younger, faster moving planets, like Mercury or Venus, success can come earlier in life, whereas Saturn takes longer to bring results. Sometimes success is not realized until Saturn has fully matured, roughly around a person's thirty-sixth year.

Again, it is important to remember that the 3rd house is an upachaya (improving house). Whatever indications are there, they can be changed through sheer determination.

THE NATURE OF THE 3rd HOUSE

Find the 3rd house in your chart. If you are Sagittarius rising, your 3rd house is Aquarius. If you are Aries rising, Gemini is your 3rd house. Pay close attention to the zodiac sign of the 3rd house because the nature of that sign will show you the way 3rd house issues function.

For instance, if Libra is your 3rd house, then you're artistically creative. If your 3rd house is Capricorn, your passion is expressed in conservative and businesslike ways.

HOW THE 3rd HOUSE EXPRESSES ITSELF

Locate the planet that rules your 3rd house (see Table B), and find where it's placed in your chart. Then read the description below that pertains to this placement.

The 3rd House Ruler placed in the 1st house allows you to succeed through your own energy, without any outside help. Naturally courageous and adventurous, you also have innate talent in the arts, whether dance, music, or literature.

The 3rd House Ruler placed in the 2nd house indicates financial success only through significant effort because the 3rd house deals with discipline and courage. Success does not come easily, but it does come, if you maintain your vision of the big picture.

The 3rd House Ruler placed in the 3rd house fortifies all 3rd house indications. You have great skills in the arts, and you can pursue a career using those talents. Your enthusiasm can be contagious, and you are courageous and adventurous.

The 3rd House Ruler placed in the 4th house indicates efforts involving real estate or automobiles, or helping your mother. Since the 4th house is the place of the heart, it is also indicative of happiness. So usually this placement shows that you achieve personal comfort and satisfaction as a result of your creative efforts.

The 3rd House Ruler placed in the 5th house indicates that your aspirations might involve higher education, advanced degrees, and raising children. Entrepreneurial by nature, you might invest in speculative ventures. It's likely that you are driven by a sense of destiny.

The 3rd House Ruler placed in the 6th house is a common placement for people involved in the healing arts. It can also indicate that a sibling may have health problems. You may be talented in competitive sports as well as creative in the way you settle conflicts.

The 3rd House Ruler placed in the 7th house shows the possibility of entering into partnership with a sibling. Depending on other considerations, the partnership will be beneficial. Although you can enter into passionate love affairs, this position does not favor marriage.

The 3rd House Ruler placed in the 8th house indicates interests that might include mysticism, metaphysics, hidden teachings, or sensuality. Relationships with siblings may be strained. You must express or act on your desires carefully so that you do not deplete your energy.

The 3rd House Ruler placed in the 9th house suggests that your courage and adventurous spirit is expressed through long-distance travel and exploration. Your creative activities can involve the father or a spiritual teacher. This can also indicate that your decisions are made impulsively rather than from detailed planning.

The 3rd House Ruler placed in the 10th house indicates a career in the arts and strong career motivations. Since the 3rd house influences the arms and hands, these may be used in creative expression that is career-based. This placement also shows that a sibling may somehow be involved in your career.

The 3rd House Ruler placed in the 11th house indicates that energy will be directed toward entrepreneurial pursuits, and that there will be success with them. You may also strive to surround yourself with influential or helpful friends—people who can help you manifest your dreams and desires.

The 3rd House Ruler placed in the 12th house indicates several things. In this position, the 3rd house indications are harmed to some degree. Courage is lacking, and efforts meet with many obstacles. With this position, success takes an enormous amount of effort and an iron will. There may also be trouble with a sibling. However, the indications are quite positive if you are spiritually inclined, since efforts around spirituality and personal transformation are fully supported.

IF THERE ARE PLANETS IN THE 3rd HOUSE

To help fine-tune the descriptions below, you'll want to assess whether the planet is welcome in the house in which it is placed (Table G). If the planet is in the house of a friend, the positive nature of the following description is enhanced. If the planet is in the house of an enemy, more of the negative possibilities need to be considered.

Sun (Su) in the 3rd house brings power and courage. This position favors an artistic manager or agent. If afflicted, there can still appear to be power, but it's really covering up weakness.

Moon (Mo) in the 3rd house indicates strong interest and talent in the arts. Highly emotional, this position can make you fickle and perfection-oriented (depending on the sign it's in), but your enthusiasm is contagious.

Mars (Ma) in the 3rd house shows tremendous courage and an adventurous spirit. This position could indicate a leader of sorts in the artistic field. This is not a good placement for brothers, especially younger ones, who may have difficulty in life.

Mercury (Me) in the 3rd house, if unafflicted, is a strong indicator of artistic talent, particularly as an actor or writer. This placement also favors enthusiasm and passion for life. If afflicted, it can indicate mental instability and difficulty for a younger sibling.

Jupiter (Ju) in the 3rd house is a good position for directing or producing performance art, or films. It shows great skill in the arts, primarily in the role of visionary or creative conduit. If afflicted, though there may be enthusiasm and a certain amount of talent, artistic ventures tend to fail.

Venus (Ve) in the 3rd house brings a strong aesthetic taste, and perhaps an interest in women's fashion or art. Enthusiastic, fun-loving, and risk-taking, this Venus infuses you with charm and charisma. Afflicted, it brings difficulty in love, and disappointments from unfulfilled expectations.

Saturn (Sa) in the 3rd house restricts the indications of the 3rd house, showing a person who may be devoid of creative ability or who comes to experience their talents only after overcoming shyness and emotional contraction. Not a good position for a younger sibling.

Rahu (Ra) in the 3rd house is a powerful position. I have seen people with this placement, during their Rahu mahadasha, reach levels of success they never dreamed possible. However, it can make a person somewhat controversial and outspoken, and can indicate unhappiness for a younger sibling.

Ketu (Ke) in the 3rd house infuses creative inspirations with the mystical and mysterious. The wild imagination this position indicates is best channeled through some type of creative pursuit. Otherwise, there may be some mental imbalance.

OTHER CONSIDERATIONS

- Note the element associated with your 3rd house. Remember that fire signs are driven; earth signs are patient; air signs are creative; and water signs are emotional.
- Also note the quality of your 3rd house. Cardinal signs initiate; fixed signs stabilize; and mutable signs seek change.

Now check any aspects to the 3rd house:

- Are any planets located in the same house as, or opposing any planet in, the 3rd house? If so, are those planets friendly, neutral, or enemies? (See Table F.) For instance, say your Jupiter is placed in the 3rd house and opposed by Saturn. This planetary combination sometimes shows a person interested in law.
- Remember that Mars energizes the house it's in, as well as the 4th, 7th, and 8th houses from itself. This means if Mars is placed in the 8th, 9th, or 12th houses of your chart, it throws an aspect onto your 3rd house, keeping it dynamic and driven. This aspect keeps the momentum of creative efforts alive, enabling you to power your way through obstacles.
- Saturn restricts or brings discipline to the house it's in, as well as the 3rd, 7th, and 10th houses from itself. This means if Saturn is placed in the 6th, 9th, or 1st houses of your chart, it throws an aspect onto your 3rd house, bringing logic, discipline, and patience to your creative pursuits.
- Jupiter expands or brings optimism to the house it's in, as well as the 5th, 7th, and 9th houses from itself. This means if Jupiter is placed in the 7th, 9th, or 11th houses of your chart, it throws an aspect onto your 3rd house, expanding your artistic sensibilities. For instance, if you're a writer, maybe you'll consider directing.
- If you want to find out when your chart's 3rd house energies will be enlivened, look to the 3rd house ruler, or any planet located in the 3rd house. Examine the Mahadasha Summary of your chart to see when that planet will come into power,

and that will give you your answer. To find shorter periods when 3rd house issues will be highlighted, look to the 3rd house ruler or any planet located in the 3rd house, and find the time its bhukti will run.

- Notice any influence transiting planets are having on your 3rd house, or your 3rd house ruler. A Rahu transit will give you courage, and tend to shift your creative output from conservative to controversial. Or if you're already controversial you'll become more conservative. Saturn will cause you to become more research-oriented and Jupiter will inspire your creative endeavors. You can chant to the planet that is favorably transiting your rising sign, on the appropriate day for that planet, to enhance its effects.

EXAMPLE CHARTS

Eva Peron's chart is a wonderful chart to analyze in order to observe how the planets indicate certain potentialities and how they come to pass. First, look at her rising sign, Aries. Table A shows that Aries is a dynamic and domineering rising sign.

The Sun is in its house of exaltation, conjunct with powerful Mars. What planet rules Aries? Table B tells us it's Mars. So Mars is in its own sign—a very powerful placement. What does the Sun indicate? Table D tells us it indicates power and ego. Mars gives these indications even more energy. So we have a rising sign that indicates a powerful woman, and planets that further emphasize these qual-

ities. However, because Saturn aspects two enemies—Mars and the Sun—from her 4th house to within a few degrees, and because her Mars is combust, her life promised to be filled with a certain amount of struggle.

Obviously, due to an exalted Sun conjunct with Mars to the exact degree in its own house, this is the chart of a leader. But when might she have experienced difficulty? Remember that the 2nd house indicates, among other issues, happiness growing up (we saw that in Drew Barrymore's case). Malefic Ketu in Eva's 2nd house created unhappiness in childhood. When might it have happened? Remember, when you observe the latent energy of a planet, and then want to determine when its influence might most strongly be felt, look at the mahadashas.

According to the Mahadasha Summary, Eva's Ketu came into power in 1921. The cycle lasted seven years, until 1928. Shortly after her Ketu came into power, her father died, apparently one of the saddest times of her life. After his death, she and her remaining family suffered terribly, working at menial jobs. Eva was quoted as saying, "Suffering took on a new meaning every day." That's Ketu in the 2nd.

Now look at Eva's 3rd house, Gemini. Her Venus and Jupiter are in the 3rd house, and Mercury rules Gemini. Venus, the planet of the arts, and Jupiter, the planet of luck, conjoin in the 3rd house. What do you think happened when she entered her Venus mahadasha in 1928? She went into acting. By the end of her Venus mahadasha she was

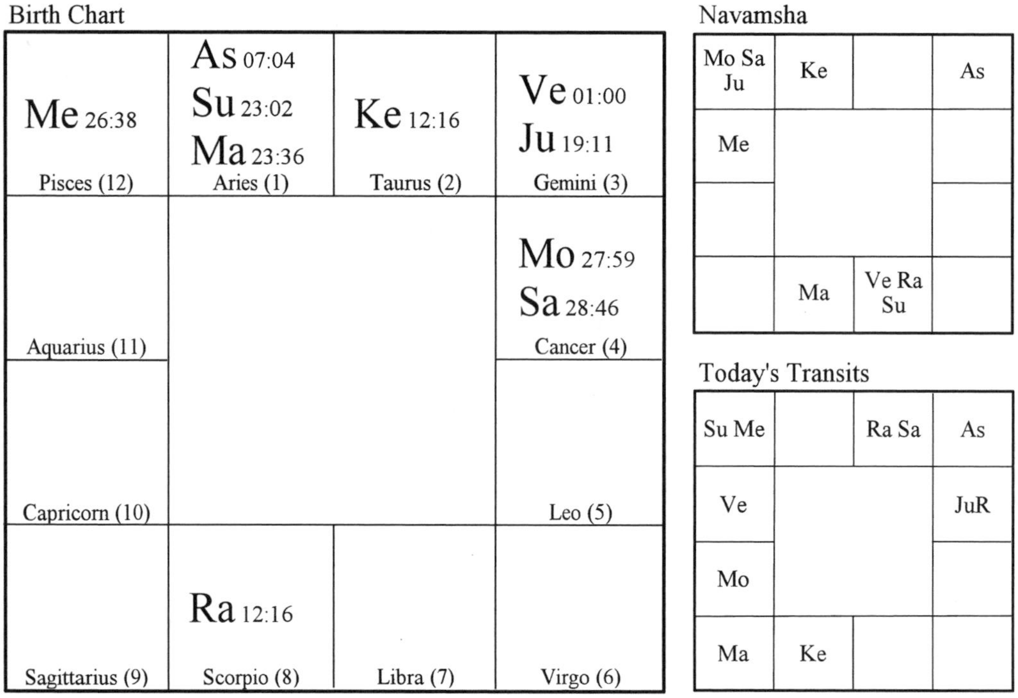

Birth Chart

Me 26:38 Pisces (12)	**As** 07:04 **Su** 23:02 **Ma** 23:36 Aries (1)	**Ke** 12:16 Taurus (2)	**Ve** 01:00 **Ju** 19:11 Gemini (3)
 Aquarius (11)			**Mo** 27:59 **Sa** 28:46 Cancer (4)
 Capricorn (10)			 Leo (5)
 Sagittarius (9)	**Ra** 12:16 Scorpio (8)	 Libra (7)	 Virgo (6)

Navamsha

Mo Sa Ju	Ke		As
Me			
	Ma	Ve Ra Su	

Today's Transits

Su Me		Ra Sa	As
Ve			JuR
Mo			
Ma	Ke		

Mahadasha Summary

Me	Sun	11-27-1904
Ke	Sun	11-27-1921
Ve	Mon	11-26-1928
Su	Fri	11-26-1948
Mo	Sat	11-27-1954
Ma	Thu	11-26-1964
Ra	Sat	11-27-1971
Ju	Sun	11-26-1989
Sa	Sat	11-26-2005
Me	Tue	11-26-2024
Ke	Tue	11-26-2041
Ve	Wed	11-25-2048
Su	Sun	11-25-2068
Mo	Mon	11-26-2074
Ma	Sat	11-25-2084

Current Mahadasha

Ju-Ma	Sun	07-28-2002
Ju-Ra	Thu	07-03-2003
Sa-Sa	Sat	11-26-2005
Sa-Me	Sat	11-29-2008
Sa-Ke	Tue	08-09-2011
Sa-Ve	Mon	09-17-2012
Sa-Su	Tue	11-17-2015
Sa-Mo	Sat	10-29-2016
Sa-Ma	Thu	05-31-2018
Sa-Ra	Tue	07-09-2019
Sa-Ju	Sun	05-15-2022
Me-Me	Tue	11-26-2024
Me-Ke	Sat	04-24-2027
Me-Ve	Thu	04-20-2028
Me-Su	Wed	02-19-2031

Birth data

Eva Peron

Wed 05-07-1919

05:14:00

Los Toldos, ARGENTINA (general)

Argentina

Timezone: 4:16:48

Latitude: 34S59'00

Longitude: 61W02'00

Ayan. -22:44:05 Lahiri

Chart 21—Eva Peron

considered a star. Do you think it came easily to her? She must have felt that she had latent talent in these areas, but the Ketu in the 2nd house brought a certain lack of refinement in speech.

Also, the ruler of the 3rd house, Mercury, is placed in debilitation in the 12th house of loss—one of the worst possible positions. How could we tell she'd overcome the limitations of the Mercury? In the navamsha, Mercury is placed in the 9th house of Aquarius, a much better position. This indicates there is more strength in Mercury than ordinarily seen in the natal position. But it was only after making tremendous effort that was she able to influence her 3rd house planets to bring the results she wanted.

What followed her Venus mahadasha? The Sun cycle. As mentioned earlier, her Sun, placed in exaltation, brings a leader. Her Sun mahadasha began in 1948, and by the early 1950s she was at the height of her political power, in an unprecedented position, given the strong patriarchal sensibilities of the place and time.

So beloved was Mrs. Peron, who died of cancer in 1952 (Rahu in the 8th house aspected by Mars, and the 8th house ruler combust), that the military leaders who overthrew her husband, Gen. Juan Domingo Peron, in 1955, confiscated her body to keep opposing political forces from using it to rally the masses.

Mother Teresa's chart (Chart 22) is another interesting one to consider with regard to the latent power of planets changing a person's destiny.

Mother Teresa's rising sign is Scorpio, a deeply private and secretive sign. Mystical Ketu sits in her 1st house, infusing her life with spirituality and a sense of higher purpose. Her 3rd house is Capricorn, an earth element sign. That means it's grounded in real-life situations, practical applications, pragmatic concerns. Many businessmen and bankers have Capricorn in their chart. Capricorn is ruled by Saturn, a persevering, disciplined influence in the chart.

As mentioned earlier, Saturn is also a planet that indicates the desire to be of service. Yet, it's a restricting influence on one's own self-expression. Where is the ruler of Mother Teresa's 3rd house? In the 6th, and it's retrograde. The 6th house indicates health and healing, exactly where she expressed her mission of caregiving. The retrograde Saturn shows even more introspection, a solitary life, and a certain detachment from the horrors she must have seen daily, so that she could continue to do her work.

Looking at Table E, notice that Saturn is debilitated in Aries. But debilitated planets when retrograde give exalted results. And malefic planets, as you learned, do well in challenging houses. Now look at the ruler of Aries, her 6th house, the house of healing. Table B tells us the ruler of Aries is Mars. Where is the Mars in her chart? In the 10th house, the house of career, conjoined by the ruler of that house, the Sun.

Ironically, her 10th house is Leo. So, even though Mother Teresa preferred to work behind the scenes, the Leo sign likes attention, the Sun indicates the limelight, and Mars gives these influences even more power, making it impossible that she would go unnoticed.

The 3rd house also indicates courage. Christa McAuliffe was chosen from 11,000 applicants to be the first teacher to fly in space on the Challenger Shuttle mission of 1986. Look at her chart.

Christa McAuliffe's rising sign is Taurus, which is ruled by Venus. Her Venus is placed in her 3rd house and is aspected by Jupiter from her 7th house (remember that Jupiter throws a 9th house aspect in a chart).

As the 3rd house represents courage, we see in this chart a great deal of courage because of the Venus. It seems appropriate that the mission was named Challenger. Jupiter, being an expansive, idealistic planet, brings the energy of the Venus into a visionary mode. And since we know Taurus to be a fixed, sometimes stubborn rising sign, I'm sure that once she set her goal, Christa wasn't easily deterred from it. Since the 1st house is the true expression of the person's character and life purpose, hers was to go on a great adventure.

Now look at the Saturn in her chart, placed in Leo. We know that Saturn makes a 3rd, 7th, and 10th house aspect on a chart. The 3rd house aspect hits her Mars in Libra to

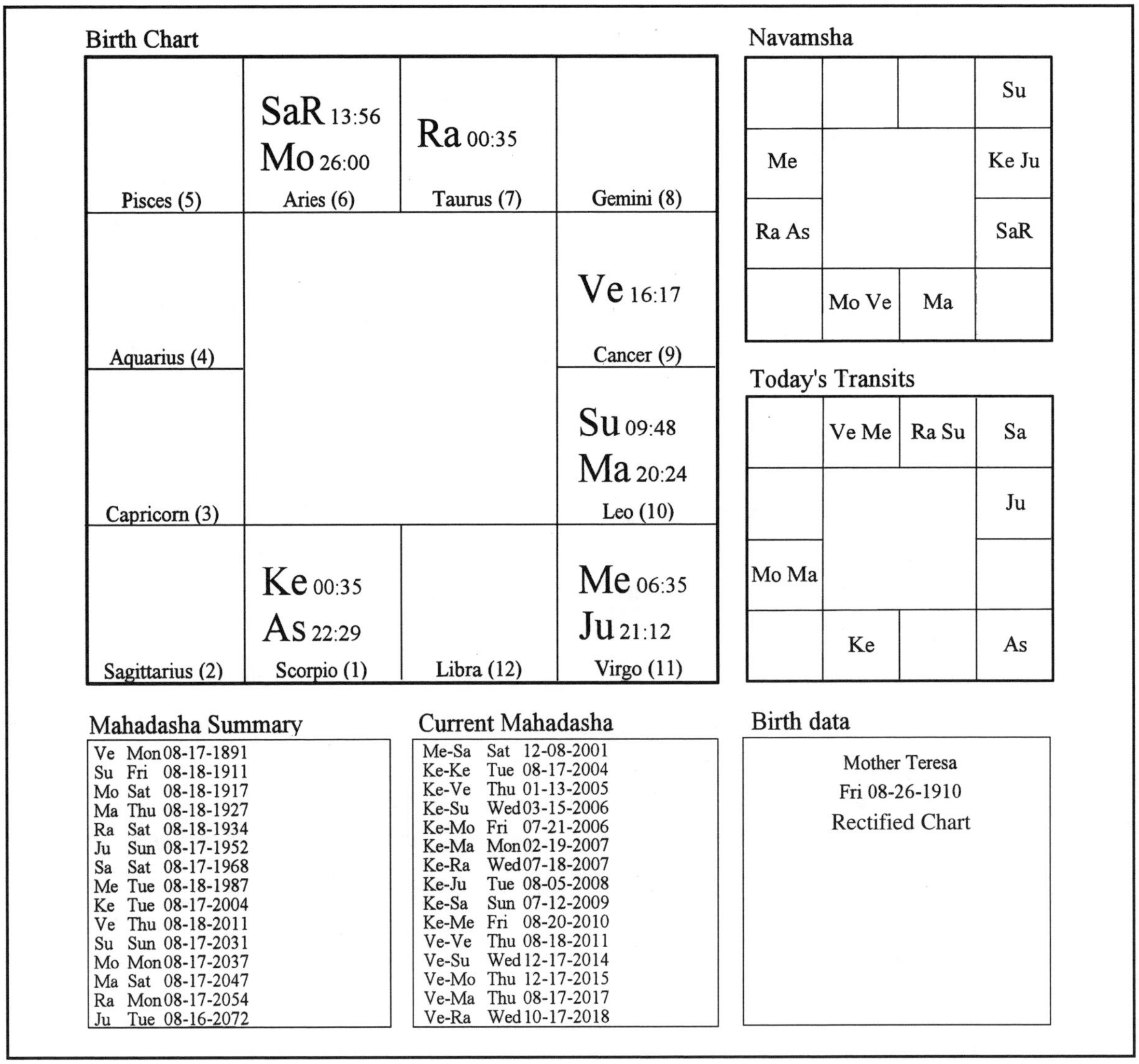

Birth Chart

Pisces (5)	SaR 13:56 Mo 26:00 Aries (6)	Ra 00:35 Taurus (7)	Gemini (8)
Aquarius (4)			Ve 16:17 Cancer (9)
Capricorn (3)			Su 09:48 Ma 20:24 Leo (10)
Sagittarius (2)	Ke 00:35 As 22:29 Scorpio (1)	Libra (12)	Me 06:35 Ju 21:12 Virgo (11)

Navamsha

			Su
Me			Ke Ju
Ra As			SaR
	Mo Ve	Ma	

Today's Transits

	Ve Me	Ra Su	Sa
			Ju
Mo Ma			
	Ke		As

Mahadasha Summary

Ve	Mon	08-17-1891
Su	Fri	08-18-1911
Mo	Sat	08-18-1917
Ma	Thu	08-18-1927
Ra	Sat	08-18-1934
Ju	Sun	08-17-1952
Sa	Sat	08-17-1968
Me	Tue	08-18-1987
Ke	Tue	08-17-2004
Ve	Thu	08-18-2011
Su	Sun	08-17-2031
Mo	Mon	08-17-2037
Ma	Sat	08-17-2047
Ra	Mon	08-17-2054
Ju	Tue	08-16-2072

Current Mahadasha

Me-Sa	Sat	12-08-2001
Ke-Ke	Tue	08-17-2004
Ke-Ve	Thu	01-13-2005
Ke-Su	Wed	03-15-2006
Ke-Mo	Fri	07-21-2006
Ke-Ma	Mon	02-19-2007
Ke-Ra	Wed	07-18-2007
Ke-Ju	Tue	08-05-2008
Ke-Sa	Sun	07-12-2009
Ke-Me	Fri	08-20-2010
Ve-Ve	Thu	08-18-2011
Ve-Su	Wed	12-17-2014
Ve-Mo	Thu	12-17-2015
Ve-Ma	Thu	08-17-2017
Ve-Ra	Wed	10-17-2018

Birth data

Mother Teresa
Fri 08-26-1910
Rectified Chart

Chart 22 – Mother Teresa

within 2 degrees, and its 10th house aspect hits her rising sign. Now look at the Mars in her chart, located in her 6th house. Remember that Mars throws a 4th, 7th, and 8th house aspect in a chart, and so Mars's 8th house aspect hits her rising sign, too.

So both Saturn and Mars conjoin by aspect to within several degrees of her ascendant. As mentioned earlier, when Mars and Saturn meet, there are generally explosive results. Now imagine what they do when they aspect a person's rising sign. When could you expect that she might have trouble from these planets? When the Mars mahadasha begins, which began in the summer of 1985.

Seven months later, she was killed in the

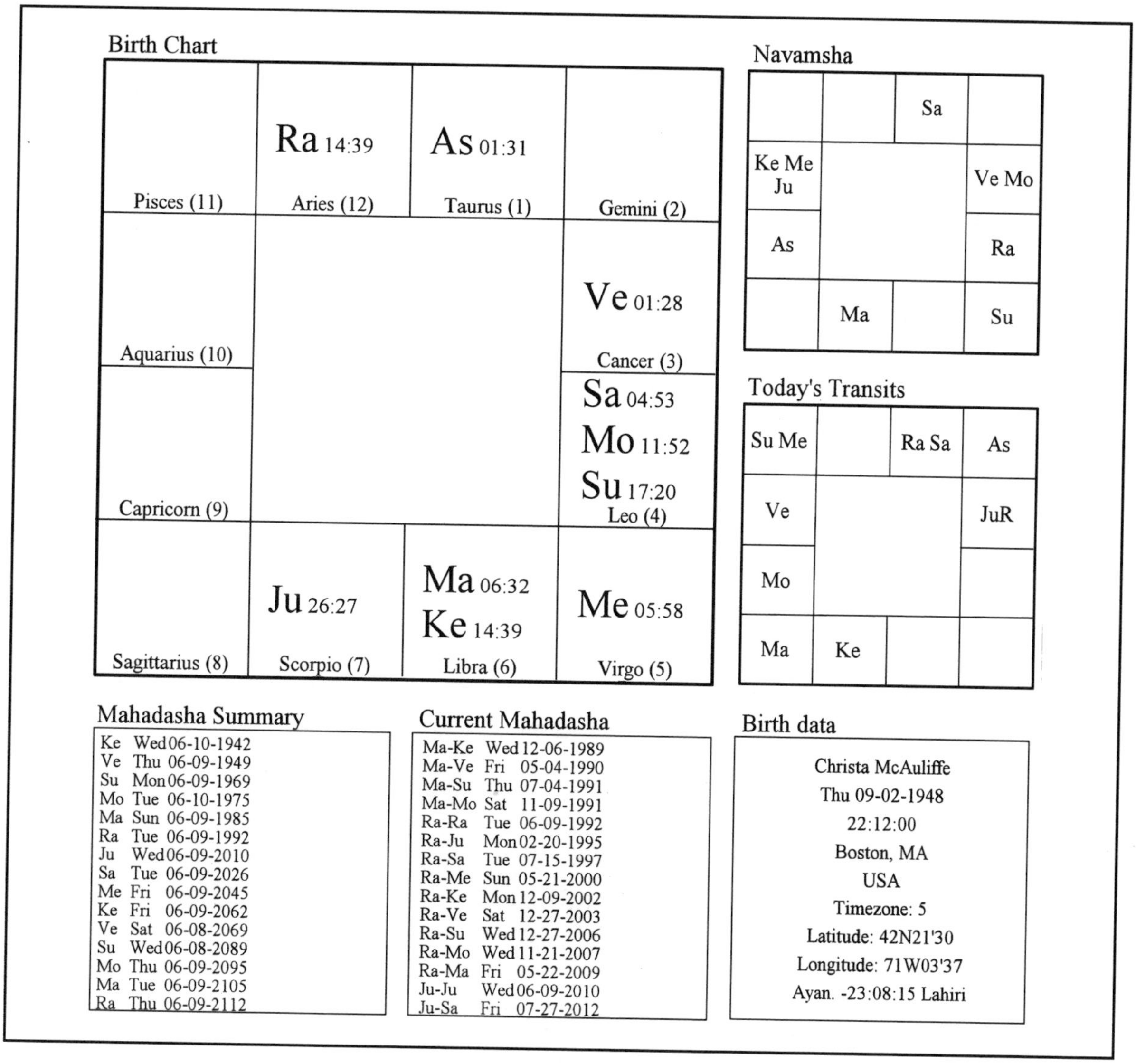

Birth Chart

Pisces (11)	Ra 14:39 Aries (12)	As 01:31 Taurus (1)	Gemini (2)
Aquarius (10)			Ve 01:28 Cancer (3)
Capricorn (9)			Sa 04:53 Mo 11:52 Su 17:20 Leo (4)
Sagittarius (8)	Ju 26:27 Scorpio (7)	Ma 06:32 Ke 14:39 Libra (6)	Me 05:58 Virgo (5)

Navamsha

		Sa	
Ke Me Ju			Ve Mo
As			Ra
	Ma		Su

Today's Transits

Su Me		Ra Sa	As
Ve			JuR
Mo			
Ma	Ke		

Mahadasha Summary

Ke	Wed	06-10-1942
Ve	Thu	06-09-1949
Su	Mon	06-09-1969
Mo	Tue	06-10-1975
Ma	Sun	06-09-1985
Ra	Tue	06-09-1992
Ju	Wed	06-09-2010
Sa	Tue	06-09-2026
Me	Fri	06-09-2045
Ke	Fri	06-09-2062
Ve	Sat	06-08-2069
Su	Wed	06-08-2089
Mo	Thu	06-09-2095
Ma	Tue	06-09-2105
Ra	Thu	06-09-2112

Current Mahadasha

Ma-Ke	Wed	12-06-1989
Ma-Ve	Fri	05-04-1990
Ma-Su	Thu	07-04-1991
Ma-Mo	Sat	11-09-1991
Ra-Ra	Tue	06-09-1992
Ra-Ju	Mon	02-20-1995
Ra-Sa	Tue	07-15-1997
Ra-Me	Sun	05-21-2000
Ra-Ke	Mon	12-09-2002
Ra-Ve	Sat	12-27-2003
Ra-Su	Wed	12-27-2006
Ra-Mo	Wed	11-21-2007
Ra-Ma	Fri	05-22-2009
Ju-Ju	Wed	06-09-2010
Ju-Sa	Fri	07-27-2012

Birth data

Christa McAuliffe

Thu 09-02-1948

22:12:00

Boston, MA

USA

Timezone: 5

Latitude: 42N21'30

Longitude: 71W03'37

Ayan. -23:08:15 Lahiri

Chart 23—Christa McAuliffe

tremendous explosion that rocked the entire world. Now look at the chart at the moment of launch, Chart 24. Remember, Mars aspecting Saturn in Christa's rising sign during the Mars mahadasha indicates the problem here. Now look at the planets sitting directly in opposition to her rising sign at the moment of launch: Mars and Saturn.

Another example of bravery is found in the chart of General Norman Schwarzkopf (Chart 25), who was best known for his decisive command of Allied Forces in Operations Desert Shield and Desert Storm.

With three planets in the rising, do you think he is powerful? Strong-willed? Absolutely. Having Jupiter in the 3rd house (Virgo)

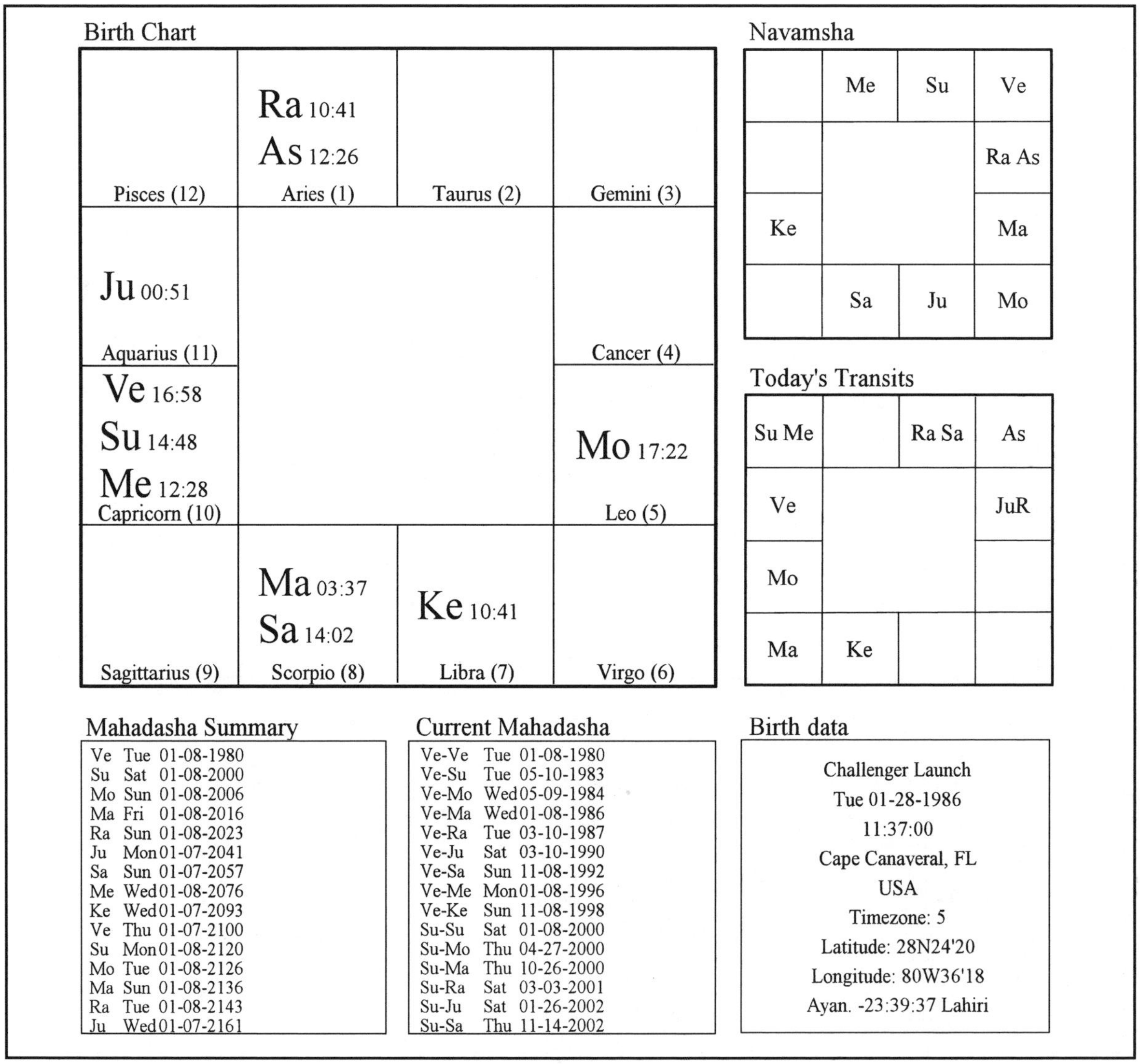

Birth Chart

	Ra 10:41 As 12:26		
Pisces (12)	Aries (1)	Taurus (2)	Gemini (3)
Ju 00:51 Aquarius (11)			Cancer (4)
Ve 16:58 Su 14:48 Me 12:28 Capricorn (10)			Mo 17:22 Leo (5)
Sagittarius (9)	Ma 03:37 Sa 14:02 Scorpio (8)	Ke 10:41 Libra (7)	Virgo (6)

Navamsha

	Me	Su	Ve
			Ra As
Ke			Ma
	Sa	Ju	Mo

Today's Transits

Su Me		Ra Sa	As
Ve			JuR
Mo			
Ma	Ke		

Mahadasha Summary

Ve	Tue	01-08-1980
Su	Sat	01-08-2000
Mo	Sun	01-08-2006
Ma	Fri	01-08-2016
Ra	Sun	01-08-2023
Ju	Mon	01-07-2041
Sa	Sun	01-07-2057
Me	Wed	01-08-2076
Ke	Wed	01-07-2093
Ve	Thu	01-07-2100
Su	Mon	01-08-2120
Mo	Tue	01-08-2126
Ma	Sun	01-08-2136
Ra	Tue	01-08-2143
Ju	Wed	01-07-2161

Current Mahadasha

Ve-Ve	Tue	01-08-1980
Ve-Su	Tue	05-10-1983
Ve-Mo	Wed	05-09-1984
Ve-Ma	Wed	01-08-1986
Ve-Ra	Tue	03-10-1987
Ve-Ju	Sat	03-10-1990
Ve-Sa	Sun	11-08-1992
Ve-Me	Mon	01-08-1996
Ve-Ke	Sun	11-08-1998
Su-Su	Sat	01-08-2000
Su-Mo	Thu	04-27-2000
Su-Ma	Thu	10-26-2000
Su-Ra	Sat	03-03-2001
Su-Ju	Sat	01-26-2002
Su-Sa	Thu	11-14-2002

Birth data

Challenger Launch
Tue 01-28-1986
11:37:00
Cape Canaveral, FL
USA
Timezone: 5
Latitude: 28N24'20
Longitude: 80W36'18
Ayan. -23:39:37 Lahiri

Chart 24—Challenger Launch Chart

brings with it knowledge of history and a visionary yet critical approach to leadership. First, it brings courage, and second, it brings the ability to articulate and amass support with an eye for detail (all Virgo traits), and to be practical in its execution.

Where is the ruler of Schwartzkopf's 3rd house? In the 2nd house, the house of oration, which gives him the breadth of vision and the ability to translate that vision into words and action. With the Sun in its own house of Leo, coupled with the ruler of his 3rd house Mercury (the planet of communication), he essentially roars like a lion and gets the respect a lion commands.

Now let's look at the effects of Rahu in the

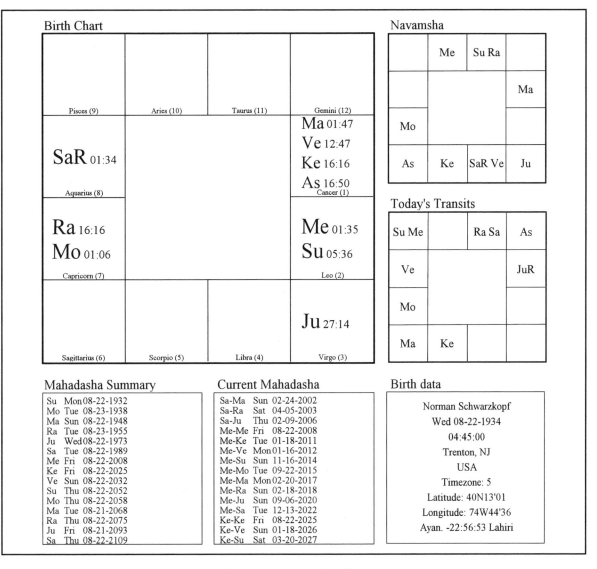

Chart 25—Norman Schwarzkopf

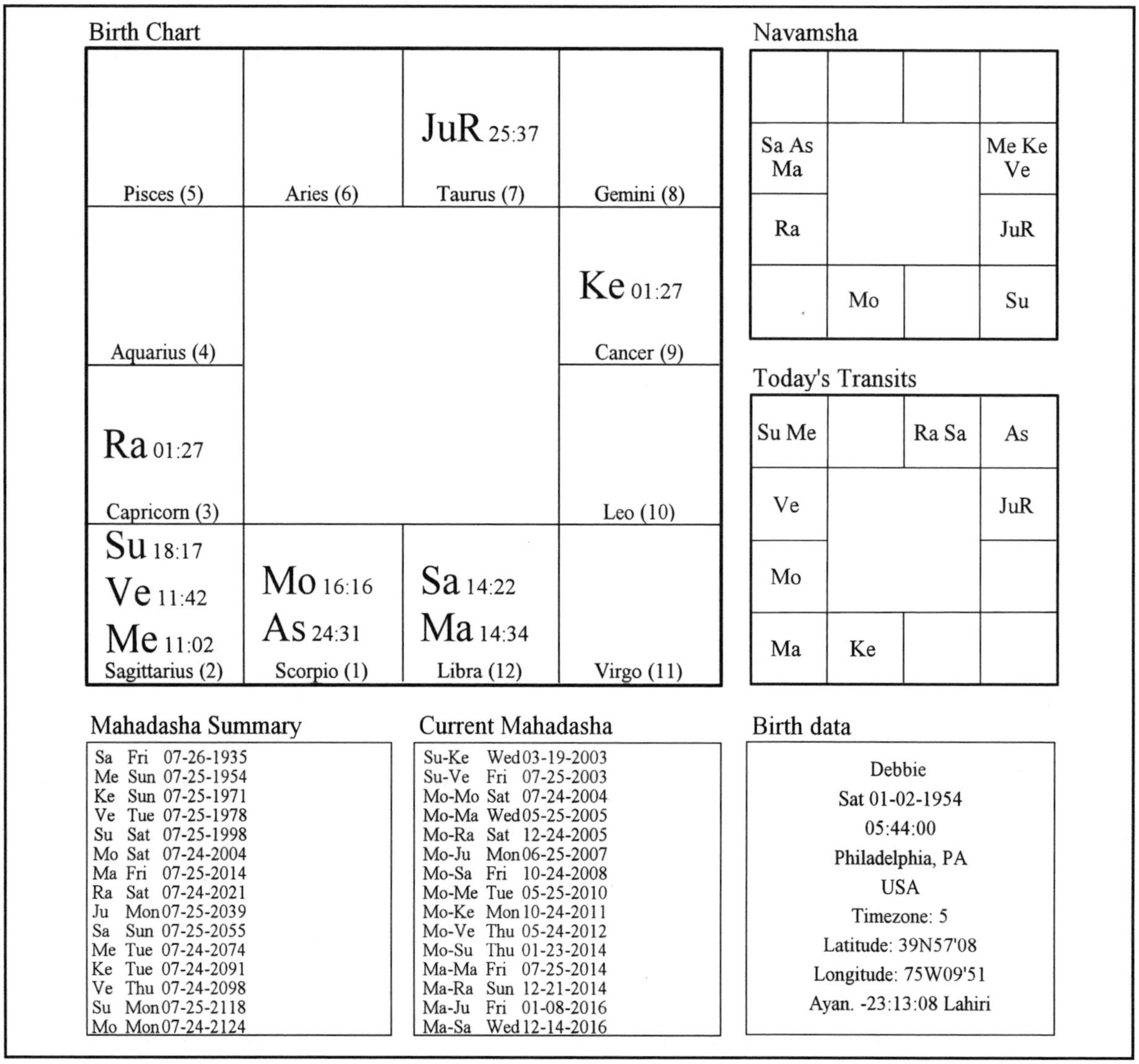

Birth Chart

Pisces (5)	Aries (6)	Taurus (7) JuR 25:37	Gemini (8)
Aquarius (4)			Cancer (9) Ke 01:27
Capricorn (3) Ra 01:27			Leo (10)
Sagittarius (2) Su 18:17 Ve 11:42 Me 11:02	Scorpio (1) Mo 16:16 As 24:31	Libra (12) Sa 14:22 Ma 14:34	Virgo (11)

Navamsha

Sa As Ma			Me Ke Ve
Ra			JuR
	Mo		Su

Today's Transits

Su Me		Ra Sa	As
Ve			JuR
Mo			
Ma	Ke		

Mahadasha Summary

Sa	Fri	07-26-1935
Me	Sun	07-25-1954
Ke	Sun	07-25-1971
Ve	Tue	07-25-1978
Su	Sat	07-25-1998
Mo	Sat	07-24-2004
Ma	Fri	07-25-2014
Ra	Sat	07-24-2021
Ju	Mon	07-25-2039
Sa	Sun	07-25-2055
Me	Tue	07-24-2074
Ke	Tue	07-24-2091
Ve	Thu	07-24-2098
Su	Mon	07-25-2118
Mo	Mon	07-24-2124

Current Mahadasha

Su-Ke	Wed	03-19-2003
Su-Ve	Fri	07-25-2003
Mo-Mo	Sat	07-24-2004
Mo-Ma	Wed	05-25-2005
Mo-Ra	Sat	12-24-2005
Mo-Ju	Mon	06-25-2007
Mo-Sa	Fri	10-24-2008
Mo-Me	Tue	05-25-2010
Mo-Ke	Mon	10-24-2011
Mo-Ve	Thu	05-24-2012
Mo-Su	Thu	01-23-2014
Ma-Ma	Fri	07-25-2014
Ma-Ra	Sun	12-21-2014
Ma-Ju	Fri	01-08-2016
Ma-Sa	Wed	12-14-2016

Birth data

Debbie

Sat 01-02-1954

05:44:00

Philadelphia, PA

USA

Timezone: 5

Latitude: 39N57'08

Longitude: 75W09'51

Ayan. -23:13:08 Lahiri

Chart 26—Debbie

third house by looking at Debbie's chart, Chart 26.

Debbie has Scorpio rising, with Rahu in the 3rd house.

Rahu is an unusual influence, creating situations that are out of the ordinary. When it is placed in the 3rd house, a person can show a certain impulsiveness, or brashness. However, Debbie doesn't exhibit any of those tendencies —her younger brother does. Remember that siblings (usually younger ones) are one of the 3rd house significations.

In Debbie's chart, the 3rd house ruler is placed in the 12th house, one of the poorest positions. To further compound this placement, her Saturn sits *to the exact degree* conjunct with its enemy Mars in the 12th house. Debbie's hotheaded brother got into a dispute, and ended up in jail.

Of course, this upset Debbie, until she learned from her Vedic chart that this combination of planets can also indicate the death of a younger sibling. She decided jail was better than death.

How could we predict that the brother would experience only jail and not death? Jupiter hits the 3rd house from Debbie's 7th, throwing a beneficent aspect onto the house, offering a certain amount of protection.

Shirley Maclaine's 3rd house (see Chart 27) shows greatness for a sibling: Shirley's 3rd house is ruled by Scorpio, which is ruled by Mars. This already tells us something about her brother, since the qualities of Scorpio include passion, resourcefulness, and drive. Obviously, he is a very motivated person. Notice that her 3rd house ruler, Mars, is located in the 8th house, showing her brother to be deeply sensual, and accomplished behind the scenes—both in sexual prowess (for which he has a reputation) and professional terms. Of course, her brother is Warren Beatty.

Because Shirley's 8th house is Aries, this gives an even greater indication that Warren will stop at nothing short of success. Mars, the indicator, further amplifies this for her brother, being conjunct in Aries with exalted Sun. Remember in Eva Peron's chart that her Aries, Mars, and Sun combination made her a commander.

Saturn in Shirley's chart throws an aspect onto Mars and the Sun in Aries. Whenever you see a Saturn/Sun connection, the person will have a strong independent streak. They will not want to work under, or be tied down by, anyone. Certainly this has been true (until recently) about Warren's love life, and professionally it elevated him from actor to Academy Award–winning director and producer.

Can we tell in Shirley's chart when Warren might expect success? Look at her Mahadasha Summary. Her Moon Mahadasha began in 1959, and her Moon is placed in Leo. If we see Shirley's 3rd house as indicative of Warren, then the Moon sits in the 10th house from the 3rd. Of course, the 10th house is career, and the Moon in the 10th house of Leo is the finest placement for career exposure. Sure enough, in 1961 Warren received rave reviews for his role in *Splendor in the Grass*, and his career was launched.

During Shirley's Moon mahadasha, Warren went on to star in a number of films, including *Bonnie and Clyde*. During her Mars mahadasha, beginning in 1969, Warren branched out into writing and producing, and by the time Shirley's Rahu came into power in 1976, Warren had moved into directing. Can we tell how well he would do as a director? Rahu occupies the 3rd house from the 3rd, so it magnifies any creative ability tremendously for Warren. Jupiter also aspects Rahu from Virgo almost to the exact degree, increasing his positive possibilities. Just after Shirley's Rahu came into power, Warren won the

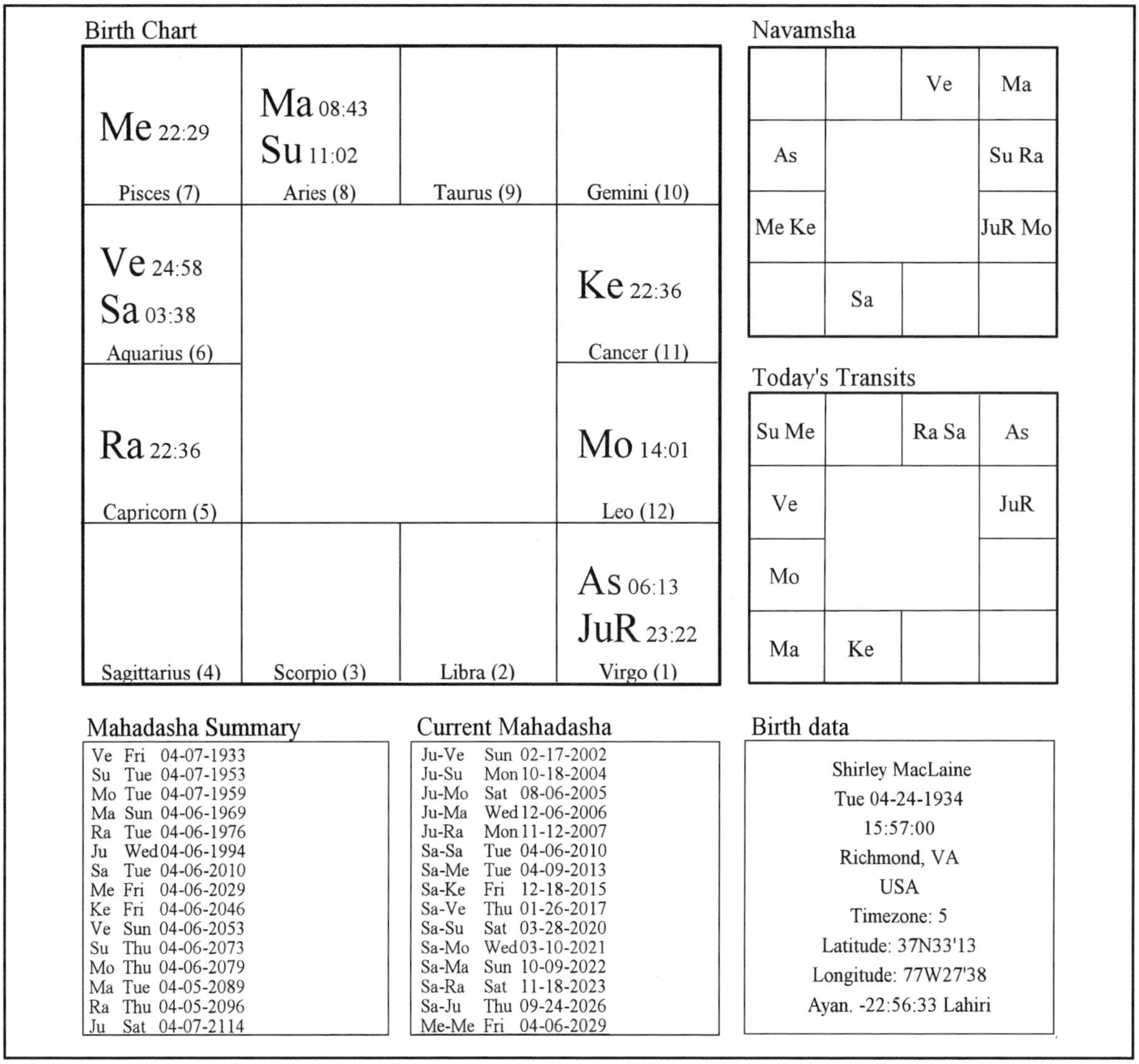

Birth Chart

Me 22:29 Pisces (7)	**Ma** 08:43 **Su** 11:02 Aries (8)	Taurus (9)	Gemini (10)
Ve 24:58 **Sa** 03:38 Aquarius (6)			**Ke** 22:36 Cancer (11)
Ra 22:36 Capricorn (5)			**Mo** 14:01 Leo (12)
Sagittarius (4)	Scorpio (3)	Libra (2)	**As** 06:13 **JuR** 23:22 Virgo (1)

Navamsha

		Ve	Ma
As			Su Ra
Me Ke			JuR Mo
	Sa		

Today's Transits

Su Me		Ra Sa	As
Ve			JuR
Mo			
Ma	Ke		

Mahadasha Summary

Ve	Fri	04-07-1933
Su	Tue	04-07-1953
Mo	Fri	04-07-1959
Ma	Sun	04-06-1969
Ra	Tue	04-06-1976
Ju	Wed	04-06-1994
Sa	Tue	04-06-2010
Me	Fri	04-06-2029
Ke	Fri	04-06-2046
Ve	Sun	04-06-2053
Su	Thu	04-06-2073
Mo	Thu	04-06-2079
Ma	Tue	04-05-2089
Ra	Thu	04-05-2096
Ju	Sat	04-07-2114

Current Mahadasha

Ju-Ve	Sun	02-17-2002
Ju-Su	Mon	10-18-2004
Ju-Mo	Sat	08-06-2005
Ju-Ma	Wed	12-06-2006
Ju-Ra	Mon	11-12-2007
Sa-Sa	Tue	04-06-2010
Sa-Me	Tue	04-09-2013
Sa-Ke	Fri	12-18-2015
Sa-Ve	Thu	01-26-2017
Sa-Su	Sat	03-28-2020
Sa-Mo	Wed	03-10-2021
Sa-Ma	Sun	10-09-2022
Sa-Ra	Sat	11-18-2023
Sa-Ju	Thu	09-24-2026
Me-Me	Fri	04-06-2029

Birth data

Shirley MacLaine

Tue 04-24-1934

15:57:00

Richmond, VA

USA

Timezone: 5

Latitude: 37N33'13

Longitude: 77W27'38

Ayan. -22:56:33 Lahiri

Chart 27—Shirley MacLaine

Academy Award for best director for the film *Reds*.

The above example illustrates how you can gather information about someone without even having their birth data. To find out about a person's younger sibling, study the person's 3rd house. For the mother, look to the 4th house. To find out about someone's children, study the 5th house, and for a second child, study the 3rd house from the 5th (younger sibling of the first child). To find out about a spouse, study the 7th house, and for the father, study the 9th house. For an older sibling, or a good friend, study the 11th.

REMEDIES

Though it sounds insensitive to admit, life sometimes hands you difficult challenges that help mold the person you become. These experiences might not be pleasant in the moment, but they deepen your soul and stretch the limits of your capacity. Such is the case with Eva Peron. Given her background, she would have been hard-pressed to come into contact with a Vedic astrologer, but if this were the chart of a client, I would recommend strong Vedic fire pujas at the beginning of each mahadasha.

There is risk involved with strengthening the fiery Sun and Mars in her rising sign. Because they are malefics, she would increase their destructive power by strengthening them. Better that she strengthen the Mercury and Jupiter with mantra repetition. I would also recommend she wear an emerald or green tourmaline to strengthen her debilitated Mercury. Jupiter is recommended because it rules her 9th house, Sagittarius. By enlivening the 9th house, she would bring grace into her chart, which would ease the conflict between her Sun, Mars, and Saturn. Whereas she had to fight for everything she got, a stronger Jupiter would have contributed more ease to her struggle.

Could Christa McAuliffe have avoided her disastrous end? It's not likely. Sometimes a person's destiny is designed that way. Her original launch date was actually not the date on which she flew. As the launch date changed a number of times, Mars drew ever nearer in degree to her ascendant. It's almost as if the universe designed it this way for some larger purpose.

Incidentally, I have noticed that every time NASA has planned a launch when Mercury is retrograde, they reschedule the launch at least two times. Each day's delay costs them about a million dollars. Also, there is tremendous risk to launching when Saturn and Mars interact, as was the case with Challenger. More recently a Saturn/Mars opposition was in effect when the Columbia crew perished trying to land their craft. Certainly NASA would benefit by consulting Vedic astrology.

What about Debbie's brother? He needs to make an internal change more than anything else. The situation in which he finds himself has less to do with her afflicted 3rd house and more with his own inner state. I can recommend any number of powerful remedial techniques, but if the person doesn't generate the change from within, there are still bound to be difficulties. I would recommend powerful Vedic fire rituals for this situation, and hope that they free up enough space in his situation or psyche that change is possible. We would need to look directly at his chart in order to know what best to prescribe.

STRENGTHENING YOUR 3rd HOUSE

You can strengthen your 3rd house by chanting the mantra for any planet found there, or for the ruler of the 3rd house itself. Fasting on the day associated with your 3rd house ruler can also bring benefit.

Because fear is the reason most people don't realize obtainable dreams, it's important to recognize that when you begin to strengthen the 3rd house, a great deal of energy will be released into your life. This energy is creative and courageous in nature and thus should be channeled through some form of artistic expression, or to fuel a new project or idea. Embracing this power can help you to make dramatic changes in your life.

If you don't use the newfound energy in a constructive manner, however, it will tend to create deeper ruts in your present situation that may be more difficult to extricate yourself from next time. It's important that you have a plan, or at least an outline, before you release 3rd house energy, so that you make the most of the opportunity.

SUMMARY

Using the analogy of a newborn child, we start with the body (1st house), then evolve to speaking and eating (2nd house), leading to desire (3rd house), the fulfillment of which satisfies the heart. The 4th house is the natural progression of the first three houses, and as such deals with nurturing, comfort, and fullness that hopefully comes as a result of 3rd house desires bringing us a certain level of satisfaction. The archetype of this nurturing presence is the mother, which is what the 4th house represents.

In order for desires to lead to fulfillment of the heart, the Vedas speak of the distinction between *shreyas* and *preyas*. Shreyas are impulses that capture our fancy and bring pleasure in the moment, but can lead to long-term disappointment. Preyas may not seem very enticing in the moment, but lead to tremendous growth and fulfillment in the long run. It's important to recognize the distinction between these two in order for your desires to manifest in such a way that they bring deep and lasting fulfillment, since that is what the 4th house represents.

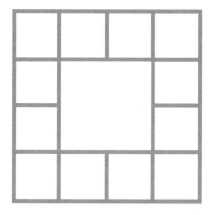

THE 4th HOUSE

The Mother

The 4th house has several significations: fixed assets like a home, car, land, and property; your mother; overall happiness; education; the quality of your heart (emotionally and physically); your lungs. Short journeys are also indicated by the 4th house.

Whenever you want to get a sense of a person quickly, look immediately to the 4th house. For instance, if Jupiter is well placed there, the person may have a magnanimous nature, and is probably kind and generous. Venus could show a person who is quite loving by nature. Mercury might indicate a nervous type of person.

Saturn in the 4th house, on the other hand, can indicate someone who is emotionally closed down or reserved. Monks and other renunciates typically have Saturn occupying or aspecting their 4th houses. Saturn restricts 4th house issues, which have to do with accumulation of worldly or material goods or attributes. Ketu and Rahu in the 4th house can indicate a tricky or deceptive nature, and Mars or the Sun in the 4th house can indicate a person who is irritable, driven, or fiery.

THE NATURE OF THE 4th HOUSE

Find the 4th house in your chart. If you are Taurus rising, Leo is your 4th house. If you are Capricorn rising, Aries is your 4th house. Pay close attention to the zodiac sign of the 4th house because the nature of that sign will show you the way 4th house issues function.

For instance, if Libra is your 4th house, you might want to decorate your home beautifully. If your 4th house is Capricorn, you tend to keep your emotions in check.

HOW THE 4th HOUSE EXPRESSES ITSELF

Locate the planet that rules your 4th house (see Table B), and find where it's placed in your chart. Then read the description below that pertains to this placement.

91

The 4th House Ruler placed in the 1st house shows that your natural inclination is toward creating a family environment. Home, family, and "nesting" are focal points for you. Your mother also plays a prominent role in your life.

The 4th House Ruler placed in the 2nd house indicates that money is accrued through real estate or automobiles. Your mother benefits you financially. You feel most happy and content when you have sufficient money.

The 4th House Ruler placed in the 3rd house indicates that you might purchase property or an automobile from a sibling. Fulfillment comes only through making intentional efforts to that end—it doesn't fall in your lap. Generally, 4th house attributes and influences are not strong in this position, and the relationship with the mother may be strained.

The 4th House Ruler placed in the 4th house is an extremely favorable position, and all 4th house indications are enhanced. This position indicates possession of the comforts of living, a warm, openhearted nature, and a good relationship with the mother.

The 4th House Ruler placed in the 5th house indicates that happiness comes from giving birth to and raising children, or simply being around children. Higher education is also fulfilling, as are spiritual pursuits and speculative ventures.

The 4th House Ruler placed in the 6th house has the positive indication that your mother could be a healer. Otherwise, this position is not generally favorable for 4th house matters. It can indicate problems with a house or car, and that the mother suffers from health complaints. It is also possible that you suffer from heart or lung ailments.

The 4th House Ruler placed in the 7th house indicates that you benefit from your spouse's property and real estate holdings. Emotional balance and fulfillment can be achieved by entering into partnership with another, in the context of either relationship or business.

The 4th House Ruler placed in the 8th house indicates that your mother may be mystical by nature or metaphysically oriented. You may also be interested in mysticism. However, there may be vehicular accidents in your life or difficulty in your living environment or with your mother.

The 4th House Ruler placed in the 9th house indicates that luck is enhanced by your mother's influence, which may be religious in nature. Also, the father is a powerful influence in your life. You may get a great deal of enjoyment from traveling, and being involved in spiritual pursuits, such as church, synagogue, or meditation.

The 4th House Ruler placed in the 10th house indicates that your mother may somehow be connected with your career, which can involve real estate, transportation, and even spiritual pursuits. This placement is extremely powerful, and can bring you fame.

The 4th House Ruler placed in the 11th house indicates that a great deal of property and revenue can be accrued. You find enjoyment in financial speculation, and in associating with friends. Your mother may be entrepreneurial.

The 4th House Ruler placed in the 12th house is a very powerful position for spiritual purists who want to live a spiritually oriented life. However, comforts of living are not favored with this placement, which may not be important if you live ascetically. Your mother may suffer from health issues and accidents, or be deeply spiritually inclined.

IF THERE ARE PLANETS IN THE 4th HOUSE

To help fine-tune the descriptions below, you'll want to assess whether the planet is welcome in the house in which it is placed (Table G). If the planet is in the house of a friend, the positive nature of the following description is enhanced. If the planet is in the house of an enemy, more of the negative possibilities need to be considered.

Sun (Su) in the 4th house brings power to the chart, but not much warmth of heart. An afflicted Sun can indicate weakness in the heart or lungs, and harms the indication for the mother or your relationship with her.

Moon (Mo) in the 4th house shows that you are content. This position brings luck with property, cars, and other fixed assets. Unafflicted, this position brings joy to the heart, but poorly placed shows problems for the mother and difficulty with other 4th house issues.

Mars (Ma) in the 4th house indicates you can accumulate many luxuries of life, but are not often happy even though you have them. You can be mean-spirited, and are likely to go through several marriages. This position is not at all favorable for the mother or vehicular travel.

Mercury (Me) in the 4th house, if unafflicted, is a strong indicator of a strong education and a knowledgeable mother. There is also the possibility of being a renowned teacher. If it *is* afflicted, however, it brings a wavering heart, nervousness, and problems for the mother.

Jupiter (Ju) in the 4th house brings great luck with homes, cars, and property. You are big-hearted and accepting of others without criticism. If afflicted, you may find it difficult to finish school or find yourself easily swayed by wayward mentors.

Venus (Ve) in the 4th house is similar to the indications of Jupiter there. In addition, association with women, as either friends or business partners, will bring benefit. If afflicted, there can be disappointments due to deceptive women or the mother.

Saturn (Sa) in the 4th house may keep your living situation sparse and monklike. If well placed, this position brings great discipline and perseverance. If afflicted, it can show weakness in the heart and lungs, and a mother who is aloof.

Rahu (Ra) in the 4th house can bring more luck with fixed assets than you thought imaginable. However, as unexpectedly as these possessions come, they can also go. This position can also indicate weakness to the lung or heart region.

Ketu (Ke) in the 4th house brings an unusual personality, one that is considered weird or unique. You may seek education in mystical arenas, and your mother may be mystically inclined. If this position is afflicted, it can indicate a sickly mother, or hard-to-diagnose ailments in the chest region.

OTHER CONSIDERATIONS

- Note the element associated with your 4th house. Remember that fire signs are driven; earth signs are patient; air signs are creative; and water signs are emotional.
- Also note the quality of your 4th house. Cardinal signs initiate; fixed signs stabilize; and mutable signs seek change.

Now check any aspects to the 4th house:

- Are any planets located in the same house as, or opposing any planet in, the 4th house? If so, are those planets friendly, neutral, or enemies? (See Table E.) For instance, say your Moon is placed in the 4th house, opposed by Jupiter. This planetary combination indicates luck with homes, property, and automobiles.
- Remember that Mars energizes the house it's in, as well as the 4th, 7th, and 8th houses from itself. This means if Mars is placed in the 9th, 10th, or 1st houses of your chart, it throws an aspect onto your 4th house, indicating you should be cautious when you drive and take care not to harm your lungs (give up smoking!).
- Saturn restricts or brings discipline to the house it's in, as well as the 3rd, 7th, and 10th houses from itself. This means if Saturn is placed in the 7th, 10th, or 2nd house of your chart, it throws an aspect onto your 4th house, bringing restriction to your living environment.
- Jupiter expands or brings optimism to the house it's in, as well as the 5th, 7th, and 9th houses from itself. This means if Jupiter is placed in the 8th, 10th, or 12th houses of your chart, it throws an aspect onto your 4th house, increasing your luck with fixed assets.
- If you want to find out when your chart's 4th house energies will be enlivened, look to the 4th house ruler, or any planet located in the 4th house. Examine the Mahadasha Summary of your chart to see when that planet will come into power, and that will give you your answer. To find shorter periods when 4th house issues

will be highlighted look to the 4th house ruler or any planet located in the 4th house and find the time its bhukti will run.

- Notice any influence transiting planets are having on your 4th house, or 4th house ruler. A Jupiter transit can bring you a new car or house. A Saturn transit can cause you to move from your current home. Pay attention to Mars crossing the 4th house, as you'll want to be more cautious when driving. You can chant to the planet that is favorably transiting your rising sign on the appropriate day for that planet to enhance its effects.

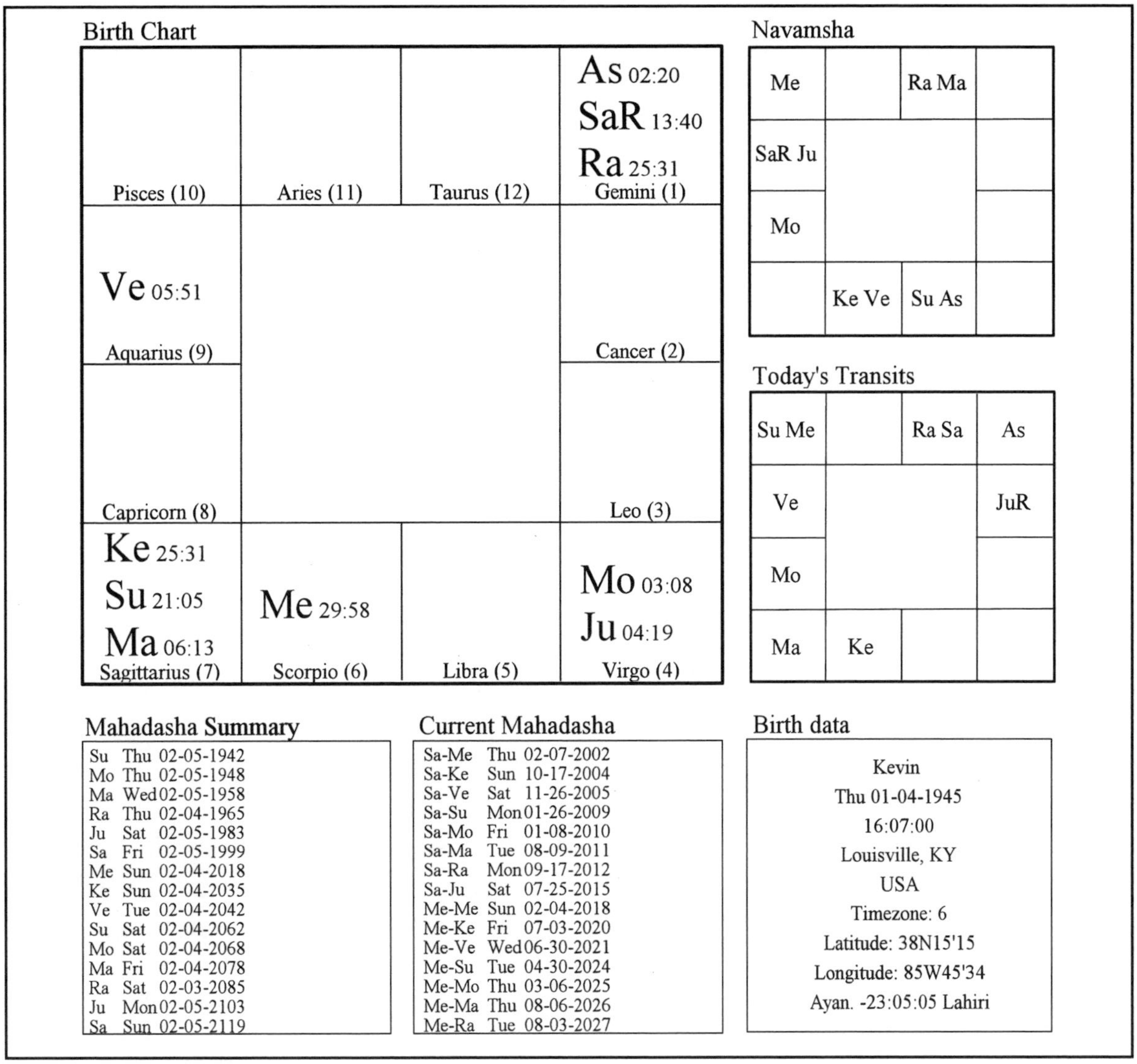

Birth Chart			
Pisces (10)	Aries (11)	Taurus (12)	As 02:20 SaR 13:40 Ra 25:31 Gemini (1)
Ve 05:51 Aquarius (9)			Cancer (2)
Capricorn (8)			Leo (3)
Ke 25:31 Su 21:05 Ma 06:13 Sagittarius (7)	Me 29:58 Scorpio (6)	Libra (5)	Mo 03:08 Ju 04:19 Virgo (4)

Navamsha		
Me		Ra Ma
SaR Ju		
Mo		
	Ke Ve	Su As

Today's Transits		
Su Me	Ra Sa	As
Ve		JuR
Mo		
Ma	Ke	

Mahadasha Summary

Su	Thu	02-05-1942
Mo	Thu	02-05-1948
Ma	Wed	02-05-1958
Ra	Thu	02-04-1965
Ju	Sat	02-05-1983
Sa	Fri	02-05-1999
Me	Sun	02-04-2018
Ke	Sun	02-04-2035
Ve	Tue	02-04-2042
Su	Sat	02-04-2062
Mo	Sat	02-04-2068
Ma	Fri	02-04-2078
Ra	Sat	02-03-2085
Ju	Mon	02-05-2103
Sa	Sun	02-05-2119

Current Mahadasha

Sa-Me	Thu	02-07-2002
Sa-Ke	Sun	10-17-2004
Sa-Ve	Sat	11-26-2005
Sa-Su	Mon	01-26-2009
Sa-Mo	Fri	01-08-2010
Sa-Ma	Tue	08-09-2011
Sa-Ra	Mon	09-17-2012
Sa-Ju	Sat	07-25-2015
Me-Me	Sun	02-04-2018
Me-Ke	Fri	07-03-2020
Me-Ve	Wed	06-30-2021
Me-Su	Tue	04-30-2024
Me-Mo	Thu	03-06-2025
Me-Ma	Thu	08-06-2026
Me-Ra	Tue	08-03-2027

Birth data

Kevin

Thu 01-04-1945

16:07:00

Louisville, KY

USA

Timezone: 6

Latitude: 38N15'15

Longitude: 85W45'34

Ayan. -23:05:05 Lahiri

Chart 28—Kevin

EXAMPLE CHARTS

Given that the 4th house indicates a person's home, what might you expect from Kevin's chart, which we looked at earlier?

His rising sign is Gemini, and his 4th house is Virgo. Jupiter and the Moon sit very powerfully in his 4th house. What does the Moon indicate? It indicates a person's emotional state, of course. The Moon, when it is conjoined with expansive, optimistic Jupiter, brings great happiness or luck with homes and property. Not surprisingly, Kevin considers his mother his best friend.

Kevin's home sits nestled at the base of a beautiful mountain, overlooking a pristine valley. This expansive vista is due to the placement of his Jupiter in the 4th house, since Jupiter brings expansiveness to any house it occupies, and often indicates a house built on a knoll, or up high. What else does Jupiter indicate? It indicates spirituality.

Kevin hosts spiritual teachers every time they visit the area. A veritable stream of teachers comes and goes from the magnificent house, which is filled with beautiful things from all over the world. It also has small indoor waterfalls, and every nook and cranny is filled with some wonderful thing. Kevin's eye for detail is due to Virgo being in his 4th house, which brings perfectionism, cleanliness, and an appreciation of intricacy and aesthetics.

Let's take a look now at a rather different 4th house.

Wendy (Chart 29) has Sagittarius rising, and her 4th house is Pisces. Saturn, which is a planet that brings restriction, sits in her 4th house. What would you imagine about her living situation? Yes, it is very simple. In fact, Wendy lived as a nun for many years, and now, though she no longer wears robes, she lives as simply as any nun would, even in the large urban center where she now resides.

THE ROLE OF THE MOTHER IN THE 4th HOUSE (APPLICABLE TO ANY FAMILY MEMBER)

To understand the role of the mother as designated by the 4th house, it's important to understand the concept of karma. It is believed that before birth, we choose (or are bound to) our parents and family in order to work out our karmic issues. Because the family system is the most intimate, the most intense karmas bring people together in family systems. Both positive and negative past life experiences influence the kind of relationship that brings you together again now. Karmas must play themselves out, which accounts for a lot of domestic violence. Statistics show that most murder victims are related to their assailants. Until a past-life situation is healed in present time, it will play itself out again and again.

So remember, your relationship with your mother can bring you great benefit, as well as great frustration or pain, and is a direct reflection of the type of karma you have with her. As hard as it is to accept, we feel the most resentment or anger or frustration with people or situations that mirror our own shortcom-

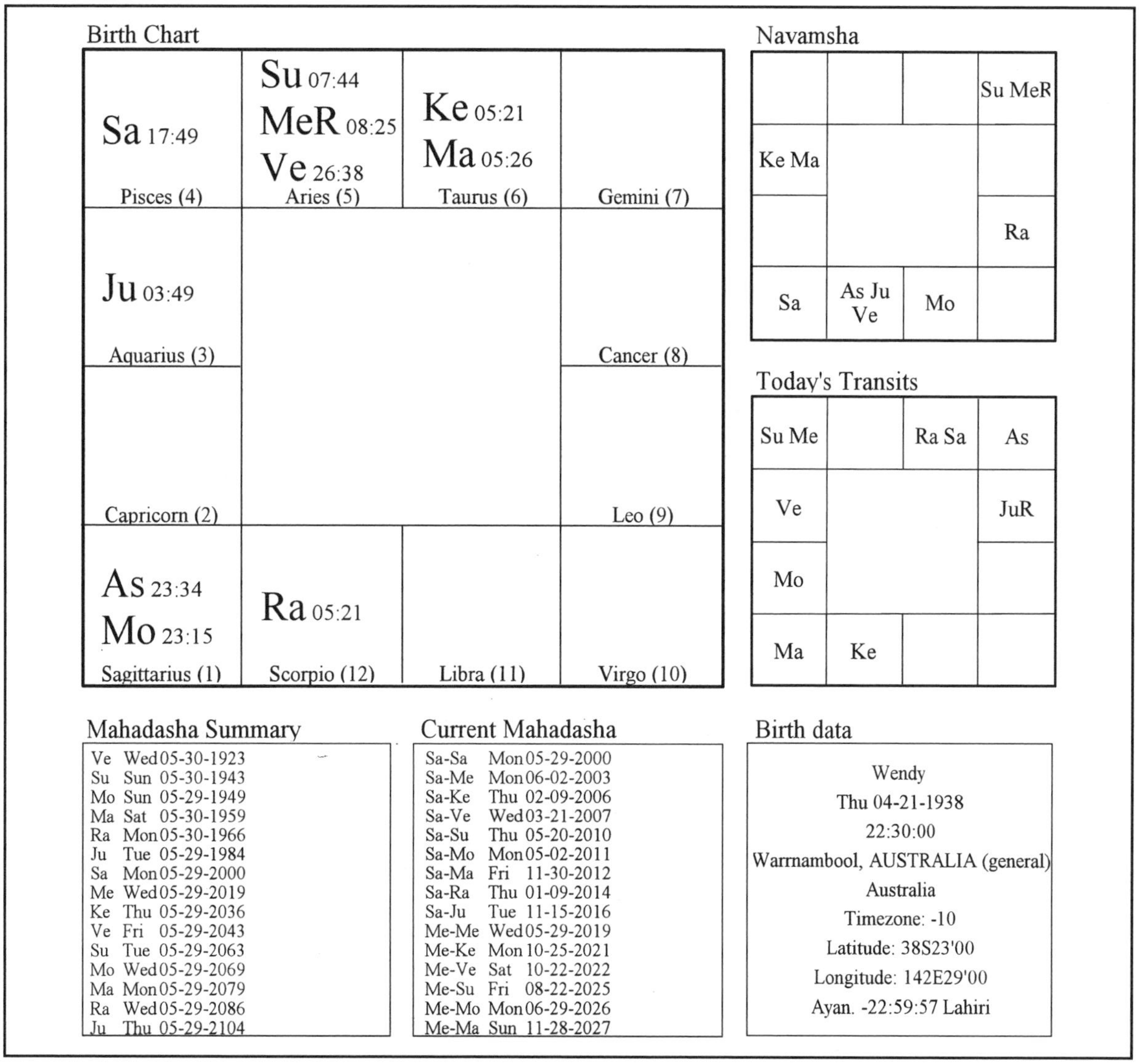

Birth Chart

Sa 17:49 Pisces (4)	**Su** 07:44 **MeR** 08:25 **Ve** 26:38 Aries (5)	**Ke** 05:21 **Ma** 05:26 Taurus (6)	Gemini (7)
Ju 03:49 Aquarius (3)			Cancer (8)
  Capricorn (2)			Leo (9)
As 23:34 **Mo** 23:15 Sagittarius (1)	**Ra** 05:21 Scorpio (12)	Libra (11)	Virgo (10)

Navamsha

			Su MeR
Ke Ma			
			Ra
Sa	As Ju Ve	Mo	

Today's Transits

Su Me		Ra Sa	As
Ve			JuR
Mo			
Ma	Ke		

Mahadasha Summary

Ve	Wed 05-30-1923
Su	Sun 05-30-1943
Mo	Sun 05-29-1949
Ma	Sat 05-30-1959
Ra	Mon 05-30-1966
Ju	Tue 05-29-1984
Sa	Mon 05-29-2000
Me	Wed 05-29-2019
Ke	Thu 05-29-2036
Ve	Fri 05-29-2043
Su	Tue 05-29-2063
Mo	Wed 05-29-2069
Ma	Mon 05-29-2079
Ra	Wed 05-29-2086
Ju	Thu 05-29-2104

Current Mahadasha

Sa-Sa	Mon 05-29-2000
Sa-Me	Mon 06-02-2003
Sa-Ke	Thu 02-09-2006
Sa-Ve	Wed 03-21-2007
Sa-Su	Thu 05-20-2010
Sa-Mo	Mon 05-02-2011
Sa-Ma	Fri 11-30-2012
Sa-Ra	Thu 01-09-2014
Sa-Ju	Tue 11-15-2016
Me-Me	Wed 05-29-2019
Me-Ke	Mon 10-25-2021
Me-Ve	Sat 10-22-2022
Me-Su	Fri 08-22-2025
Me-Mo	Mon 06-29-2026
Me-Ma	Sun 11-28-2027

Birth data

Wendy

Thu 04-21-1938

22:30:00

Warrnambool, AUSTRALIA (general)

Australia

Timezone: -10

Latitude: 38S23'00

Longitude: 142E29'00

Ayan. -22:59:57 Lahiri

Chart 29—Wendy

ings. Your life reflects your own issues. Want to see your mental state? Go outside. The way people react to you will give you a direct and immediate answer.

We've all thought that if we could just get rid of a certain person in our life, our happiness would improve. But what would really happen is that another person with the same annoying tendencies would come into our life to give us the very same problems. Just acknowledging this can be enough to give you some peace of mind and the ability to deal with the person or problem in an appropriate manner.

If your mother drives you crazy, try to see your relationship with her as a strength-building opportunity. If your experience with your mother causes you to separate from her, you have learned individuation. If your mother is rude and insensitive, you might decide to cultivate in yourself the opposite qualities of refinement and caring. In other words, what might seem like a terrible situation with your mother is actually a way that the cosmos is helping you to develop yourself. Carrie Fisher's chart is an excellent example of this.

Carrie was born with Sagittarius rising, and her 4th house is Pisces, ruled by Jupiter. Jupiter shows a powerful mother, no doubt, since it is placed in Carrie's 9th house con-

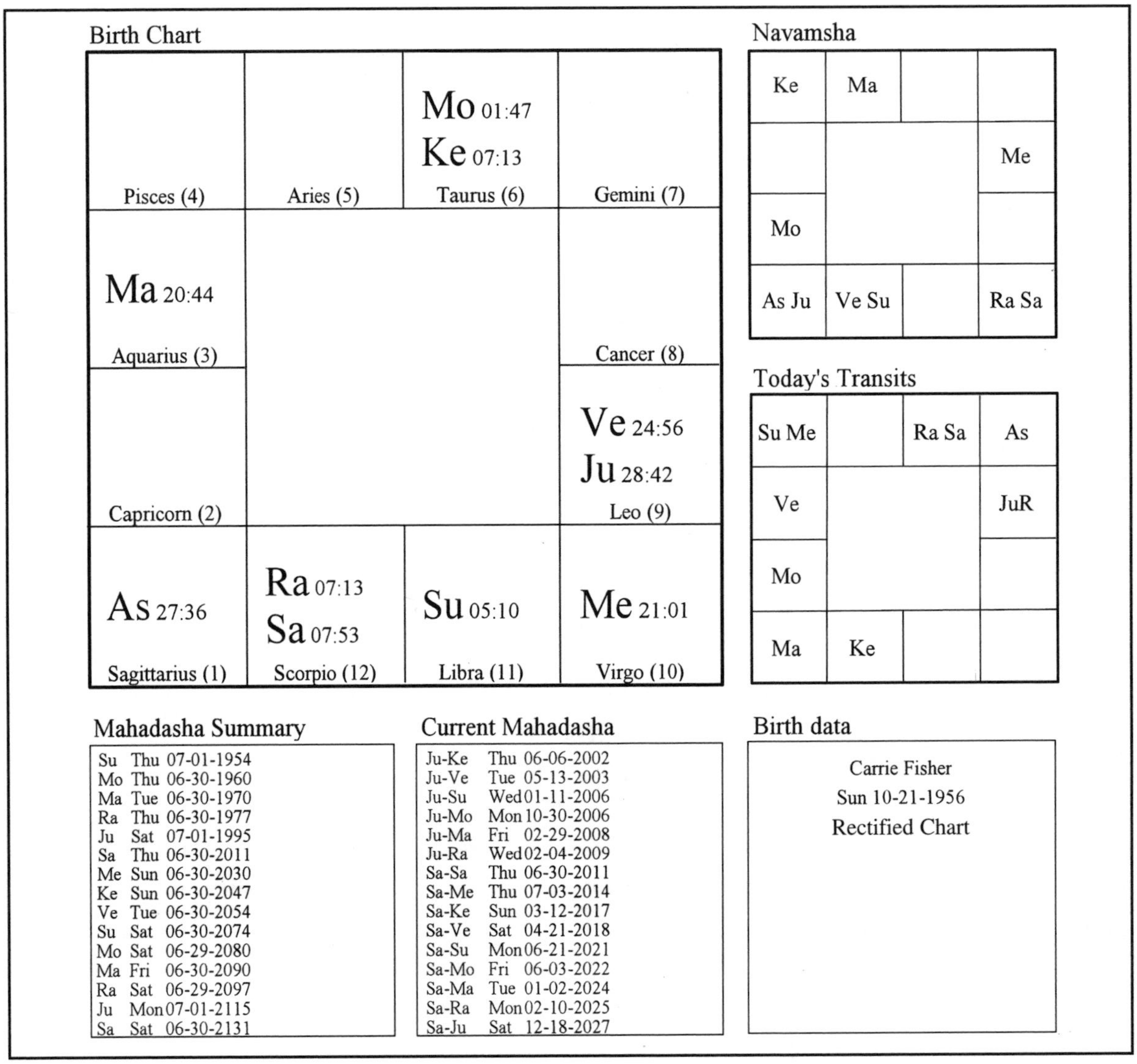

Birth Chart

Pisces (4)	Aries (5)	Mo 01:47 Ke 07:13 Taurus (6)	Gemini (7)
Ma 20:44 Aquarius (3)			Cancer (8)
Capricorn (2)		Ve 24:56 Ju 28:42 Leo (9)	
As 27:36 Sagittarius (1)	Ra 07:13 Sa 07:53 Scorpio (12)	Su 05:10 Libra (11)	Me 21:01 Virgo (10)

Navamsha

Ke	Ma		
			Me
Mo			
As Ju	Ve Su		Ra Sa

Today's Transits

Su Me		Ra Sa	As
Ve			JuR
Mo			
Ma	Ke		

Mahadasha Summary

Su	Thu	07-01-1954
Mo	Thu	06-30-1960
Ma	Tue	06-30-1970
Ra	Thu	06-30-1977
Ju	Sat	07-01-1995
Sa	Thu	06-30-2011
Me	Sun	06-30-2030
Ke	Sun	06-30-2047
Ve	Tue	06-30-2054
Su	Sat	06-30-2074
Mo	Sat	06-29-2080
Ma	Fri	06-30-2090
Ra	Sat	06-29-2097
Ju	Mon	07-01-2115
Sa	Sat	06-30-2131

Current Mahadasha

Ju-Ke	Thu	06-06-2002
Ju-Ve	Tue	05-13-2003
Ju-Su	Wed	01-11-2006
Ju-Mo	Mon	10-30-2006
Ju-Ma	Fri	02-29-2008
Ju-Ra	Wed	02-04-2009
Sa-Sa	Thu	06-30-2011
Sa-Me	Thu	07-03-2014
Sa-Ke	Sun	03-12-2017
Sa-Ve	Sat	04-21-2018
Sa-Su	Mon	06-21-2021
Sa-Mo	Fri	06-03-2022
Sa-Ma	Tue	01-02-2024
Sa-Ra	Mon	02-10-2025
Sa-Ju	Sat	12-18-2027

Birth data

Carrie Fisher
Sun 10-21-1956
Rectified Chart

Chart 30—Carrie Fisher

joined with Venus. Remember that Jupiter and Venus are not particularly friendly. In Paul Newman's chart we gave the analogy of two beautiful women in a room vying for attention. Essentially this is the type of relationship Carrie and her mother, Debbie Reynolds, have experienced, in which she and her mother have tried to outdo one another. This can be verified by looking at the Moon, the planet indicative of the mother (Table D), which sits conjunct with Carrie's Ketu and in her struggle-filled 6th house, the house of enemies (Table C).

Remember that the 2nd house reflects one's childhood. Carrie's 2nd house ruler, Saturn, is in the worst possible position: it is in the 12th house and conjunct to the exact degree with malefic Rahu. When might we expect her unhappiness to begin? Perhaps soon after she was born, since the Sun mahadasha was in power at the time of her birth. The Sun represents the father, and it is poorly placed in Carrie's chart (in debilitation). In fact, her father, Eddie Fisher, left the family to marry Elizabeth Taylor in 1959 when Carrie was just three years old. Carrie's Moon mahadasha didn't bring much relief when it began in 1960, since Carrie's Moon is poorly placed and indicates emotional disappointment.

You'll recall that the 2nd house indicates habits of the mouth. Not only does a marred 2nd house indicate an unhappy childhood, it shows the possibility of drug addiction.

Not surprisingly, Carrie's difficult childhood and family situation resulted in a best-selling confessional novel about a woman's struggle with drug addiction and mother-daughter rivalry, which was made into a very successful movie entitled *Postcards from the Edge*.

Another characteristic of the 4th house is that malefics are not well placed here. For instance, take a look at Terry's chart on page 100.

Terry's rising sign is Sagittarius, and Rahu is placed in the 4th house. Remember that the 4th house indicates the chest area of the body. Terry's chest is so severely caved in that it looks like a hole was taken out of his breastbone, a defect from birth. Otherwise, his body is normal and proportional.

Secondly, look at the Mars in his chart. It's placed in Virgo less than one degree away from that Rahu by opposition. This influences the 4th house negatively, particularly in terms of vehicular travel. In fact, some years ago Terry and a friend were driving along an urban street and crossed an unmarked railroad track just as a locomotive was barreling its way out of town. The impact threw the car 100 feet through the air and killed his friend instantly, although Terry escaped with only a scratch.

Now, look at Terry's navamsha. Remember, the navamsha is like getting a second opinion. The rising sign is Leo. Since we're analyzing the 4th house, we'll look at the 4th house in the navamsha. There we see Saturn conjunct with Rahu, and opposed by Mars and Ketu. So our concerns are compounded for Terry's 4th house indications because the navamsha's 4th house is so badly afflicted.

Now let's look at another chart that

Birth Chart

Ra 15:54 Pisces (4)	Aries (5)	Taurus (6)	**Mo** 11:18 Gemini (7)
Su 15:04 Aquarius (3)			Cancer (8)
Ju 26:50 **Me** 23:38 **Ve** 10:47 Capricorn (2)			**SaR** 23:30 Leo (9)
As 15:47 Sagittarius (1)	Scorpio (12)	Libra (11)	**Ke** 15:54 **MaR** 16:24 Virgo (10)

Navamsha

	Ve	Ke MaR	
Su			
Mo			Me As
	SaR Ra		Ju

Today's Transits

	Ve MeR Su	Ra	Sa
			Ju As
Ma			
	Ke	Mo	

Mahadasha Summary

Me	Fri	11-22-1996
Ke	Fri	11-22-2013
Ve	Sun	11-22-2020
Su	Thu	11-22-2040
Mo	Thu	11-22-2046
Ma	Wed	11-22-2056
Ra	Thu	11-22-2063
Ju	Sat	11-22-2081
Sa	Fri	11-22-2097
Me	Sun	11-22-2116
Ke	Sun	11-22-2133
Ve	Tue	11-22-2140
Su	Sat	11-22-2160
Mo	Sat	11-22-2166
Ma	Fri	11-22-2176

Current Mahadasha

Me-Su	Sun	02-16-2003
Me-Mo	Tue	12-23-2003
Me-Ma	Tue	05-24-2005
Me-Ra	Sun	05-21-2006
Me-Ju	Sun	12-07-2008
Me-Sa	Tue	03-15-2011
Ke-Ke	Fri	11-22-2013
Ke-Ve	Sun	04-20-2014
Ke-Su	Sat	06-20-2015
Ke-Mo	Mon	10-26-2015
Ke-Ma	Thu	05-26-2016
Ke-Ra	Sat	10-22-2016
Ke-Ju	Fri	11-10-2017
Ke-Sa	Wed	10-17-2018
Ke-Me	Tue	11-26-2019

Birth data

Terry

Mon 02-27-1950

03:33:00

Chicago, IL

USA

Timezone: 6

Latitude: 41N51'00

Longitude: 87W39'00

Ayan. -23:09:38 Lahiri

Chart 31—Terry

focuses on the mother. Gina's chart (Chart 32) has Gemini rising. Her 4th house is Virgo, occupied by Ketu and Mars conjunct with each other to the exact degree. Two malefics in perfect union in Virgo, the house of health, is bound to harm the mother. But what about the Moon, the planet that indicates the mother in the chart? It is also afflicted, being conjunct with retrograde Saturn. Look at the navamsha to see if things look any better there. The navamsha chart has Pisces rising and the same malefic Mars and Ketu conjunct with 4th house Gemini.

Gina's mother suffered from a long illness

Birth Chart			
Ra 17:09 Pisces (10)	Aries (11)	Taurus (12)	**As** 18:32 Gemini (1)
Aquarius (9) **Su** 21:22 **Ju** 21:17 **VeR** 15:26 Capricorn (8)			Cancer (2) **Mo** 04:25 **SaR** 25:09 Leo (3)
Me 26:45 Sagittarius (7)	Scorpio (6)	Libra (5)	**Ke** 17:09 **Ma** 17:28 Virgo (4)

Navamsha

As		Mo VeR	Ke Ma
			Ju Su
Me Ra	SaR		

Today's Transits

Su Me		Ra Sa	As
Ve			JuR
Mo			
Ma	Ke		

Mahadasha Summary

Ke	Thu	10-09-1947
Ve	Sat	10-09-1954
Su	Tue	10-08-1974
Mo	Wed	10-08-1980
Ma	Mon	10-08-1990
Ra	Wed	10-08-1997
Ju	Thu	10-08-2015
Sa	Wed	10-08-2031
Me	Sat	10-08-2050
Ke	Sat	10-08-2067
Ve	Mon	10-08-2074
Su	Fri	10-08-2094
Mo	Fri	10-08-2100
Ma	Wed	10-08-2110
Ra	Fri	10-08-2117

Current Mahadasha

Ra-Sa	Thu	11-14-2002
Ra-Me	Tue	09-20-2005
Ra-Ke	Tue	04-08-2008
Ra-Ve	Mon	04-27-2009
Ra-Su	Thu	04-26-2012
Ra-Mo	Thu	03-21-2013
Ra-Ma	Sat	09-20-2014
Ju-Ju	Thu	10-08-2015
Ju-Sa	Sun	11-26-2017
Ju-Me	Mon	06-08-2020
Ju-Ke	Wed	09-14-2022
Ju-Ve	Mon	08-21-2023
Ju-Su	Tue	04-21-2026
Ju-Mo	Sun	02-07-2027
Ju-Ma	Thu	06-08-2028

Birth data

Gina
Fri 02-03-1950
14:29:00
Salem, OR
USA
Timezone: 8
Latitude: 44N56'35
Longitude: 123W02'02
Ayan. -23:09:35 Lahiri

Chart 32—Gina

that completely debilitated her nervous system. This of course had an impact on Gina's childhood, which you can see by looking at the 2nd house ruler, the Moon, conjunct with its enemy Saturn.

Another interesting 4th house indication for the mother can be found in the life of Marie Sklodowska Curie (Madame Curie). She was one of the great scientists of this century, having won Nobel Prizes in Physics (1903) and Chemistry (1911) for performing pioneering studies with radium and contributing profoundly to the understanding of radioactivity.

Her oldest daughter, Irene Joliot-Curie, was

born in 1897. Let's look at the daughter's chart to see the indication of her famous mother in it.

Irene's rising sign is Taurus. Her 4th house is Leo, and the Sun is placed in its own sign in Leo, a powerful position, along with visionary and highly beneficent Jupiter. Sun and Jupiter together bring fame and success. It's interesting to note that the Sun indicates her mother in the house ruled by the Sun, and that she was involved in a science dealing with radiant heat and energy.

Irene was also home-schooled by her mother, again showing the strong influence of the 4th house on her chart. But we also see that Irene's Saturn aspects her 4th house from Scorpio, indicating a deep, hidden malevo-

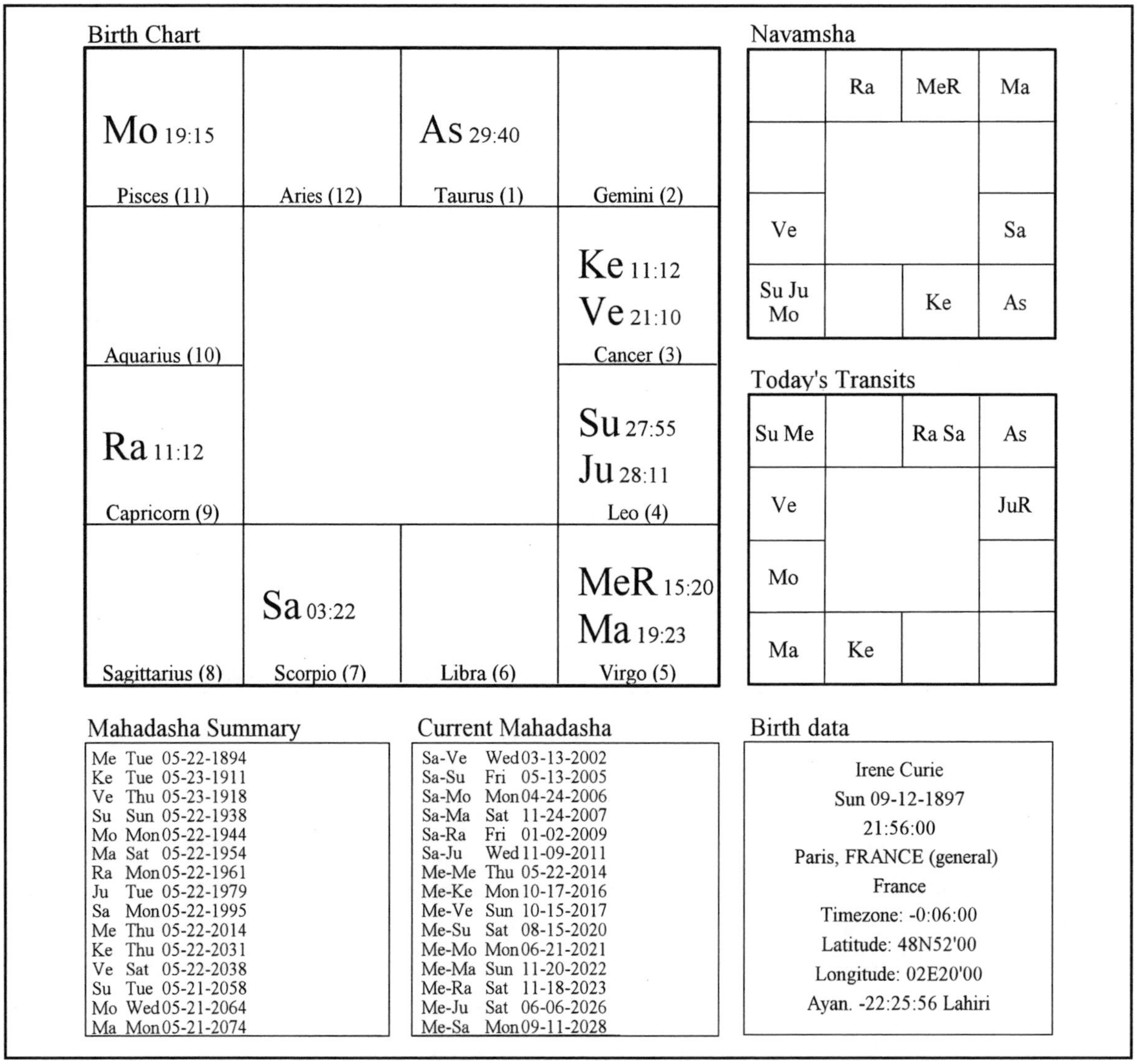

Birth Chart

Mo 19:15	**As** 29:40		
Pisces (11)	Aries (12)	Taurus (1)	Gemini (2)
			Ke 11:12 **Ve** 21:10
Aquarius (10)			Cancer (3)
Ra 11:12			**Su** 27:55 **Ju** 28:11
Capricorn (9)			Leo (4)
	Sa 03:22		**MeR** 15:20 **Ma** 19:23
Sagittarius (8)	Scorpio (7)	Libra (6)	Virgo (5)

Navamsha

	Ra	MeR	Ma
Ve			Sa
Su Ju Mo		Ke	As

Today's Transits

Su Me		Ra Sa	As
Ve			JuR
Mo			
Ma	Ke		

Mahadasha Summary

Me	Tue 05-22-1894
Ke	Tue 05-23-1911
Ve	Thu 05-23-1918
Su	Sun 05-22-1938
Mo	Mon 05-22-1944
Ma	Sat 05-22-1954
Ra	Mon 05-22-1961
Ju	Tue 05-22-1979
Sa	Mon 05-22-1995
Me	Thu 05-22-2014
Ke	Thu 05-22-2031
Ve	Sat 05-22-2038
Su	Tue 05-22-2058
Mo	Wed 05-21-2064
Ma	Mon 05-21-2074

Current Mahadasha

Sa-Ve	Wed 03-13-2002
Sa-Su	Fri 05-13-2005
Sa-Mo	Mon 04-24-2006
Sa-Ma	Sat 11-24-2007
Sa-Ra	Fri 01-02-2009
Sa-Ju	Wed 11-09-2011
Me-Me	Thu 05-22-2014
Me-Ke	Mon 10-17-2016
Me-Ve	Sun 10-15-2017
Me-Su	Sat 08-15-2020
Me-Mo	Mon 06-21-2021
Me-Ma	Sun 11-20-2022
Me-Ra	Sat 11-18-2023
Me-Ju	Sat 06-06-2026
Me-Sa	Mon 09-11-2028

Birth data

Irene Curie

Sun 09-12-1897

21:56:00

Paris, FRANCE (general)

France

Timezone: -0:06:00

Latitude: 48N52'00

Longitude: 02E20'00

Ayan. -22:25:56 Lahiri

Chart 33—Irene Joliot-Curie

lence that hits the 4th house by 10th house aspect. Slowly, Madame Curie's research was killing her by exposure to radioactive elements. Notice also that Irene's 4th house planets are in very late degrees, showing an inherent weakness in them. And because the Sun (her mother) is such a strong influence in Irene's chart, it's not strange to think that her mother pulled her into the same line of work.

Does the Sun in Irene's 4th house bring her success as well, or only indicate her mother's success? Let's look at the Mahadasha Summary, since we could best answer that question by looking to see what results came during the cycle of the Sun. Between the Venus and Sun cycles, Irene was awarded (along with her husband) the 1935 Nobel prize in chemistry for artificially induced radioactivity. And in 1940, she was awarded the Barnard Gold Medal for Meritorious Service to Science.

But because the 4th house also rules the heart and lung area, the same research that brought her fame began killing her, just as it did her mother, by affecting the lung area. In terms of analyzing her character, which as we mentioned can be seen from the 4th house, we see the Sun is in its own house, conjoined by expansive Jupiter, which shows a deeply caring woman.

Saturn, which aspects her Jupiter from the 7th house, also brings idealism, because of the Saturn/Jupiter connection. Look at the navamsha, with the Moon, Sun, and Jupiter in the 4th house, which also indicates fine character. In fact, in the mid-1930s when the Nazis were gaining in power, Irene broke with the scientific tradition of sharing research and making it available to everyone, and began to withhold her findings from publication. Irene and her fellow scientists sealed their definitive research on nuclear reactors late in 1939 and kept it secret until 1949. Both she and her husband were also active in anti-Nazi activities during World War II. In 1944, Irene fled to Switzerland with her two children. She eventually succumbed to leukemia, the same disease that killed her mother, at age fifty-nine.

Chart 34 is interesting with regard to the mother. It belongs to my Aunt Barbara, who was an Olympic athlete and grew up in Communist East Germany.

My Aunt Barbara's Virgo rising sign shows the great precision with which she performs. The ruler of her rising sign, Mercury, is located in her 8th house conjoined by the Sun in its house of exaltation, along with Venus. Notice how her Mercury is placed less than 1 degree from the Sun. As we saw with Eva Peron's chart, when a planet gets too close to the Sun, it is combust and becomes unable to fully express its power. The Sun symbolizes the father, or any other authoritative figure or situation. So this chart shows that some type of authoritative influence diminished Barbara's power and controlled her. This can also be seen in Saturn's opposition to her rising sign, on which it casts its restrictive influence.

Barbara's Moon is in her 4th house and is aspected by Saturn in Pisces (remember Saturn throws a 10th house aspect) and Mars

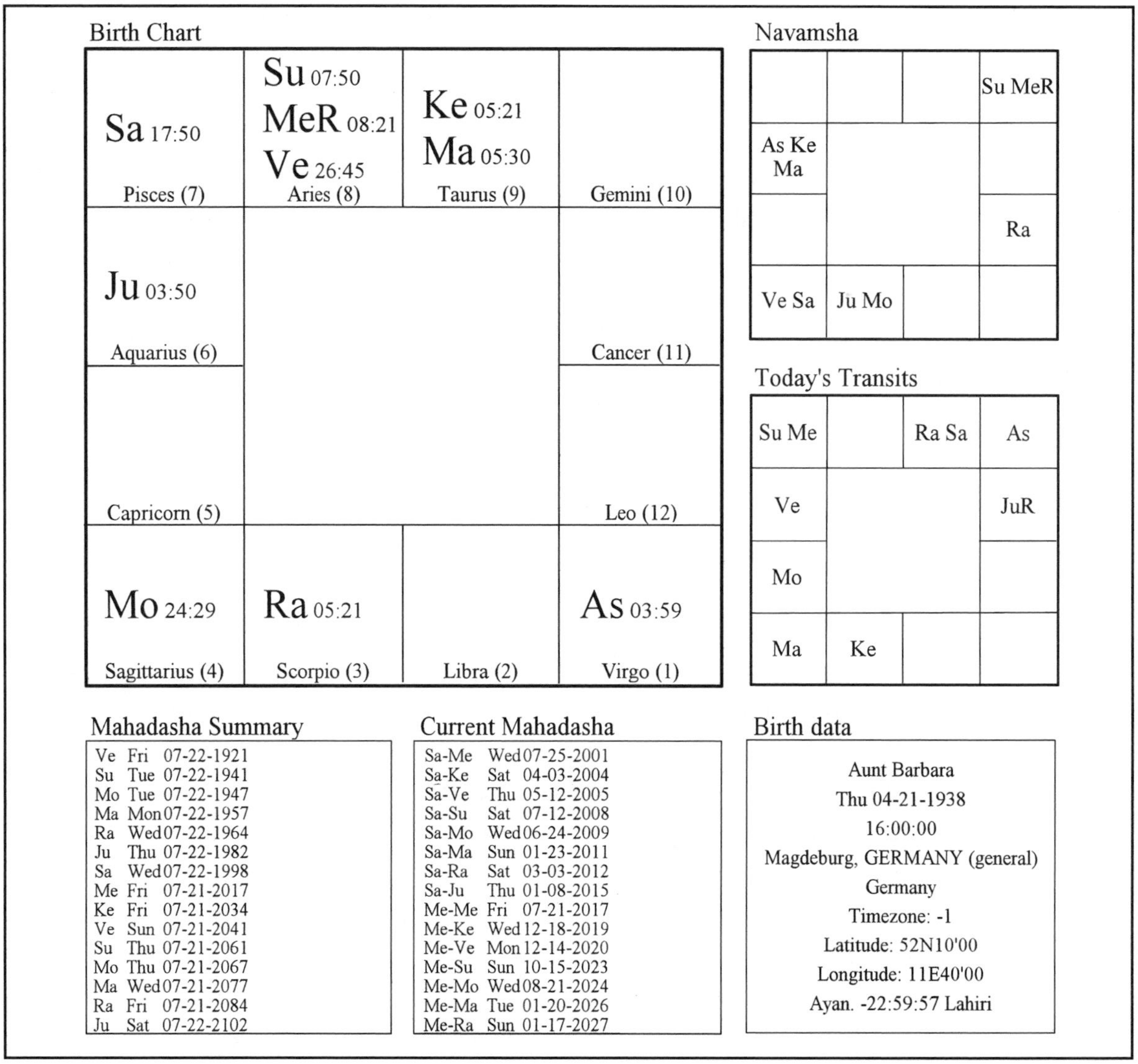

Birth Chart

Sa 17:50 Pisces (7)	**Su** 07:50 **MeR** 08:21 **Ve** 26:45 Aries (8)	**Ke** 05:21 **Ma** 05:30 Taurus (9)	 Gemini (10)
Ju 03:50 Aquarius (6)			 Cancer (11)
   Capricorn (5)			 Leo (12)
Mo 24:29 Sagittarius (4)	**Ra** 05:21 Scorpio (3)	 Libra (2)	**As** 03:59 Virgo (1)

Navamsha

			Su MeR
As Ke Ma			
			Ra
Ve Sa	Ju Mo		

Today's Transits

Su Me		Ra Sa	As
Ve			JuR
Mo			
Ma	Ke		

Mahadasha Summary

Ve	Fri	07-22-1921
Su	Tue	07-22-1941
Mo	Tue	07-22-1947
Ma	Mon	07-22-1957
Ra	Wed	07-22-1964
Ju	Thu	07-22-1982
Sa	Wed	07-22-1998
Me	Fri	07-21-2017
Ke	Fri	07-21-2034
Ve	Sun	07-21-2041
Su	Thu	07-21-2061
Mo	Thu	07-21-2067
Ma	Wed	07-21-2077
Ra	Fri	07-21-2084
Ju	Sat	07-22-2102

Current Mahadasha

Sa-Me	Wed	07-25-2001
Sa-Ke	Sat	04-03-2004
Sa-Ve	Thu	05-12-2005
Sa-Su	Sat	07-12-2008
Sa-Mo	Wed	06-24-2009
Sa-Ma	Sun	01-23-2011
Sa-Ra	Sat	03-03-2012
Sa-Ju	Thu	01-08-2015
Me-Me	Fri	07-21-2017
Me-Ke	Wed	12-18-2019
Me-Ve	Mon	12-14-2020
Me-Su	Sun	10-15-2023
Me-Mo	Wed	08-21-2024
Me-Ma	Tue	01-20-2026
Me-Ra	Sun	01-17-2027

Birth data

Aunt Barbara

Thu 04-21-1938

16:00:00

Magdeburg, GERMANY (general)

Germany

Timezone: -1

Latitude: 52N10'00

Longitude: 11E40'00

Ayan. -22:59:57 Lahiri

Chart 34—Barbara

(remember Mars throws an 8th house aspect). And the ruler of the 4th house, Jupiter, is in the 6th house, the house of enemies. So her 4th house is quite afflicted.

What do you suppose happened?

Barbara's mother was thrown into prison for black-marketing. Young Barbara was forced to give up her childhood to be groomed as an athlete, and if she refused, the East German government threatened to extend her mother's prison term indefinitely. You can see with an afflicted 4th house that *both* the mother and a person's happiness can suffer (remember the 4th house signifies the heart).

Her mother's arrest occurred during Barbara's Moon mahadasha, which began in 1947, when Barbara was only nine years old. It began a time of severe emotional stress and turmoil that lasted the entire ten-year Moon cycle. Even prior to that, things were not easy. Earlier in the decade Barbara's sister was sent to the forced labor camp Sachsenhausen for two years, and the KGB barged into the house at any time of the day or night for months.

Barbara's skill as an athlete—even under duress—is shown by her rising sign, which indicates an exacting nature, the powerful Mars/Moon connection in fiery Sagittarius, and the exalted Sun, Mercury, and Venus in fiery Aries. Those planets, placed in her 8th house, show hidden strength that can be explosive.

A great deal of my aunt's unhappiness, it turns out, came from having to sacrifice her childhood for a government agenda. Her mother was also anything but a positive influence, as is shown by the Moon/Saturn connection in Barbara's 4th house. As she says, "My mother was not a very nice person, but maybe she was sick. I loved her anyway." Her professional success will be discussed in the section on the 10th house.

REMEDIES

Should Wendy ever decide to give up her life of minimalism, rather than empowering her Saturn in the 4th house (which would only increase the ascetic nature of the house), she would strengthen the ruler of the 4th house, Jupiter. Chanting to Jupiter on Thursdays, eating a little bit less on that day, and wearing a yellow sapphire could bring expansion to her 4th house. As Jupiter rules not only her 4th house, but her rising sign as well, she would do well to befriend this planet.

Because Carrie's difficulties occurred so early in life, it wouldn't have been practical to have her chant planetary mantras. If this were a client's child, however, I would recommend the parents have Vedic fire ceremonies performed for the Sun before it came into power (at birth), and then for the Moon at the beginning of its mahadasha. Now, I would recommend that Carrie wear a navaratna pendant (a stone for every planet), which would strengthen her entire chart.

Terry's car accident, however, would have been about as difficult to remedy as the caved-in chest he was born with. These are strongly karmic situations that you can soften by appeasing Jupiter, the ruler of the 4th house, but that otherwise you may not have much impact upon. Because Jupiter rules both Terry's rising sign and 4th house, the recommendation would be the same as Wendy's above. However, I have seen remarkable results from Vedic fire rituals when a house of vehicular travel is afflicted.

Gina's mother's karma would have been difficult to overcome through remedial techniques. Because the 4th house also rules the heart, it's more important that Gina's experience with her mother doesn't have an impact on the way she feels about herself. In this regard, for her own stability I would recommend she strengthen the ruler of her 4th house, Mercury. This could be done by chanting the Mercury mantra on Wednesdays, by eating a little bit less that day, and perhaps by wearing an emerald or green tourmaline.

Irene's chart indicates a strong destiny, with Mercury and Mars in the 5th house. So to some degree there is not much to do with a chart that has its own terrific momentum. However, powerful health-restoring Vedic fire rituals could have mitigated to some degree the impact her research was having on her health.

Barbara's chart is similar to Irene's, in that her planets indicate a powerful destiny. The level of frustration she underwent fueled her athletic excellence and has enabled her to be a deeply compassionate human being. She could bring strength to the 4th house by appeasing Jupiter, the ruler of the 4th, as long as she didn't attract more conflict or liver problems. I sound this note of caution because although we're strengthening the ruler of the 4th house, her Jupiter, which is placed in the 6th house, will also affect her health.

Barbara *would* do well to bring strength to the Moon in order to increase feelings of joy and happiness in life. Chanting Jupiter and Moon mantras on Thursdays and Mondays would bring benefit, as would wearing a large moonstone and (if the Jupiter mantras were useful) a yellow sapphire.

STRENGTHENING YOUR 4th HOUSE

Chanting mantras for the 4th house ruler, or any benefic planet in the 4th house on the day associated with that planet, brings power to the 4th house. Eating less food on those planets' days also helps. You can also empower the 4th house from the 10th house (the house that opposes it) by strengthening any planet that favorably opposes the 4th house.

Since the indicator (karaka) of the 4th house is the Moon, you can also bring strength to the 4th house by chanting Moon mantras on Mondays and eating less on that day.

Remember, if your 4th house is afflicted, you'll want to be careful not to incite the malefic influence on the 4th house. Instead, work with the ruler of the house or any positive planet that aspects it.

If your mother herself has difficulty in life, it would be smart to have her chart assessed for the best remedial measures to employ. Although by bringing strength to your 4th house you may be able to heal mother issues in your own chart, this doesn't necessarily mean her life will become smoother.

SUMMARY

The easiest way to empower the 4th house is to pursue that which brings you the greatest joy. Since the 4th house relates to the heart, by gravitating to those activities and people who bring you fulfillment, you naturally strengthen the 4th house. This house indicates worldly as well as spiritual accumulation, and often functions to push people into spiritual pursuits when material wealth hasn't brought them the joy they expected.

Ideally, once a person finds a certain amount of satisfaction and contentment in life, he or she wants to share it. Just as a fully opened flower seeds others, so the 4th house leads to the 5th, the house of procreation.

Although the 5th house signifies children, the reference can also be symbolic. Giving birth to new ideas and undergoing a spiritual transformation (being reborn, if you will) are also 5th house expressions.

Hopefully by the time you are ready to bring new life into the world, whether in actuality or symbolically, you will have learned and gained wisdom from many of life's lessons and can uplift humanity with your 5th house contribution.

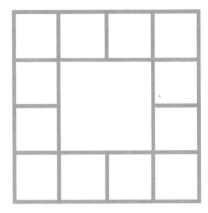

THE 5th HOUSE

Children

The 5th house is the house that signifies children, higher education, advanced degrees, and speculation such as entrepreneurial pursuits and gambling. The 5th house is strongly indicative of one's moral character and destiny, and someone with a powerful 5th house may have a sense from an early age that they are on Earth for a very specific reason. It also signifies discrimination, intelligence, and mantras.

The 5th house also rules the stomach area, so 5th house afflictions can include indigestion, ulcers, and other stomach ailments. Spirituality, in terms of ritual and liturgy, is also indicated by the 5th. Love affairs, though not with a spouse, are indicated by the 5th, as are experiences with government or legal organizations.

THE NATURE OF THE 5th HOUSE

Find the 5th house in your chart. If you are Scorpio rising, your 5th house is Pisces. If you are Cancer rising, Scorpio is your 5th house.

Pay close attention to the zodiac sign of the 5th house because the nature of that sign will show you the way 5th house issues function.

For instance, if Sagittarius is your 5th house, then you may give birth to a child who is philosophical by nature. If your 5th house is Aquarius, your destiny is oriented toward humanitarian goals.

HOW THE 5th HOUSE EXPRESSES ITSELF

Locate the planet that rules your 5th house (Table B), and find where it's placed in your chart. Then read the description below that pertains to this placement:

The 5th House Ruler placed in the 1st house indicates that the wisdom you have is beyond your chronological years, as if you were born with these gifts. You may be referred to as an "old soul." You may have a flair for speculation, like playing the stock market, and you benefit greatly from children.

The 5th House Ruler placed in the 2nd house indicates that you can earn a great deal of money through speculative ventures. It also signifies that intelligence born from educational pursuits can be easily communicated to others through the medium of speaking, teaching, and even poetry or writing.

The 5th House Ruler placed in the 3rd house indicates that you have a natural inclination to take risks, be courageous, and seek out adventure. You might have strong talents in the creative fields due to past life accomplishments in these arenas. A great deal of energy may be devoted to children, who could be the center of your life.

The 5th House Ruler placed in the 4th house shows that your happiness is associated with dealing with children, whether they are yours or not. Higher education and practicing spiritual techniques such as yoga and mantra repetition also bring fulfillment. Property and automobiles are abundant in your life, and you have a good relationship with your mother.

The 5th House Ruler placed in the 5th house indicates a strong destiny. You may announce what you will accomplish in life well before any of your peers have any clue. You also have a strong past-life connection to spiritual techniques and practices. This is a favorable position for children, higher education, and luck in speculative ventures.

The 5th House Ruler placed in the 6th house indicates that you have innate talents as a healer, although you may not be involved professionally in the healing arts. Your child may also have healing ability. However, this position can indicate that your child may have health complaints, or enemies, such as social problems with other kids.

The 5th House Ruler placed in the 7th house indicates that your luck in speculative ventures is enhanced through partnership or working with an associate. Your spouse may be well educated or spiritually oriented (or both). This is a good position for finding a destined marriage partner and happiness with children.

The 5th House Ruler placed in the 8th house shows that you may have knowledge of, or be interested in, the study of metaphysics and mysticism. This position can indicate the loss of money through speculation, so be careful. You may have difficulty in pursuing an advanced degree.

The 5th House Ruler placed in the 9th house is one of the finest placements of planetary rulers. You get tremendous grace from past-life merit. Things come easily to you, sometimes too easily. Your father may be well educated or a powerful spiritual presence. All 5th house indications are enhanced, and operate at their fullest potential.

The **5th House Ruler placed in the 10th house** favors fame in one's career. At the very least, you experience success in your career. You were destined for your vocational pursuits, so you might know far in advance that you would succeed in a certain area. Spiritual teachers, professional gamblers, and a career involving children can all have this placement.

The **5th House Ruler placed in the 11th house** is one of the best placements for success in speculation or entrepreneurial pursuits. Collaborating with friends can enhance your earning ability, as can associating with children. You may have powerful, influential friends.

The **5th House Ruler placed in the 12th house** indicates that you may lose money through speculation, and that getting an advanced degree may be challenging. You may decide not to have children, or your child may be somewhat reserved or withdrawn by nature. This is a fine position for pursuing the deepest spiritual truths.

IF THERE ARE PLANETS IN THE 5th HOUSE

To help fine-tune the descriptions below, you'll want to assess whether the planet is welcome in the house in which it is placed (Table G). If the planet is in the house of a friend, the positive nature of the following description is enhanced. If the planet is in the house of an enemy, more of the negative possibilities need to be considered.

Sun (Su) in the 5th house brings a powerful destiny that may not be based so much on fairness as accomplishment. You may feel that any means to an end is justified. This placement does not indicate many children—two at most.

Moon (Mo) in the 5th house shows that you may be involved in many romances, and benefit by your association with women, romantic or otherwise. If afflicted, you may be fickle, and make emotional decisions rather than logical ones, which can cause you to lose money.

Mars (Ma) in the 5th house indicates a warrior or fighter, someone who commands and takes action. This placement gives a pioneering intellect, but accompanies this with an inability to take advice. This position is not favorable for children, and may indicate an abortion or miscarriage. You may also have stomach troubles, like an ulcer.

Mercury (Me) in the 5th house, if unafflicted, brings brilliance and accomplishment in educational pursuits. This placement also favors giving birth to intelligent children. A poorly placed Mercury shows mental instability and difficulty with children.

Jupiter (Ju) in the 5th house brings governmental work or vocational pursuits that are political or law oriented. This is an extremely favorable position for children, both in terms of your enjoyment and their destiny. This placement enhances higher education, wisdom, and discrimination. If afflicted, this position shows the possibility of trouble with the government, such as having difficulty with the IRS, and of having children who will lead difficult lives.

Venus (Ve) in the 5th house is similar to the indications of Jupiter, but the focus is more on the artistic than on the governmental or legal. Women bring you luck, and your connection with these women is destined from past lives. If afflicted, you seek love in all the wrong places and are rarely satisfied.

Saturn (Sa) in the 5th house doesn't indicate many children, or problems with them if the planet is unafflicted. It may show separation from children or adoption of children. This placement does not show a great deal of luck, and forces you to become a self-made person. If afflicted, you may have problems with indigestion.

Rahu (Ra) in the 5th house brings a strong sense of destiny and somewhat insatiable desires. There is also the possibility of great success through speculation or entrepreneurial pursuits. The indications for children are like that of Mars, with the possibility of miscarriage or abortion.

Ketu (Ke) in the 5th house brings an interest in rituals that are mystical or spiritual in nature. It is said that these techniques come easily to you because you have cultivated them in a past life. Your children may also be strongly mystically inclined. If afflicted, you will experience deception.

OTHER CONSIDERATIONS

- Note the element associated with your 5th house. Remember that fire signs are driven; earth signs are patient; air signs are creative; and water signs are emotional.
- Also note the quality of your 5th house. Cardinal signs initiate; fixed signs stabilize; and mutable signs seek change.

Now check any aspects to the 5th house:

- Are any planets located in the same house as, or opposing any planet in, the 5th house? If so, are those planets friendly, neutral, or enemies (see Table F)? For instance, say your Moon is placed in the 5th house and opposed by its friend Jupiter. This planetary combination shows the possibility of many children.
- Remember that Mars energizes the house it's in, as well as the 4th, 7th, and 8th houses from itself. This means if Mars is placed in the 10th, 11th, or 2nd house of your chart, it throws an aspect onto your 5th house, indicating an athletic or passionate child, or one that might be accident prone.
- Saturn restricts or brings discipline to the house it's in, as well as to the 3rd, 7th, and 10th houses from itself. This means if Saturn is placed in the 8th, 11th, or 3rd house of your chart, it throws an aspect

onto your 5th house, bringing fewer children or speculative losses.

- Jupiter expands or brings optimism to the house it's in, as well as the 5th, 7th, and 9th houses from itself. This means if Jupiter is placed in the 9th, 11th, or 1st house of your chart, it throws an aspect onto your 5th house, enhancing issues around children and increasing your luck with speculation.

- If you want to find out when your chart's 5th house energies will be enlivened, look to the 5th house ruler, or any planet located in the 5th house. Examine the Mahadasha Summary of your chart to see when that planet will come into power, and that will give you your answer. To find shorter periods when 5th house issues will be highlighted, look to the 5th house ruler or any planet located in the 5th house, and find the time its bhukti will run.

- Notice any influence transiting planets are having on your 5th house, or 5th house ruler. A Jupiter transit of the 5th often brings children, so if you're trying to conceive, time it with this transit. Jupiter can also bring higher education, if you're considering going back to school or learning another skill. Faster moving Venus over the 5th can also bring you a short romantic fling. You can chant to the planet that is favorably transiting your rising sign, on the appropriate day for that planet, to enhance its effects.

CHART EXAMPLES

Let's look at a good example of a person with a strong destiny, John Travolta (Chart 35). His rising sign is Cancer, which is ruled by the Moon, and that planet is placed in his 2nd house, the house of wealth and power of speech. As you'll recall, the 1st house ruler in the 2nd house indicates a self-made person, whose physical characteristics and speaking ability bring him or her great wealth.

Now, let's look at John's 5th house, Scorpio. Mars rules Scorpio, and Mars is in his 5th house, so we find in this chart a strong destiny.

Though many remember him playing Vinnie Barbarino when he was nineteen years old in the 1975 sitcom *Welcome Back, Kotter*, in fact John Travolta joined a local actor's ensemble when he was just twelve years of age, and was soon starring in dinner theater performances. He took tap dancing lessons from Gene Kelly's brother Fred, and at the age of sixteen he dropped out of high school to pursue acting full time.

These types of choices indicate the pull of a strong destiny, a perfect example of someone with the 5th house ruler placed in the 5th house.

We can also see John's early career success in the mahadasha system. The Moon, which we mentioned earlier is so vital in his chart, came into power in 1973. It was just around that time that he made his Broadway debut, and his career took off. It was in the middle of the Moon's mahadasha that he made *Saturday Night Fever*.

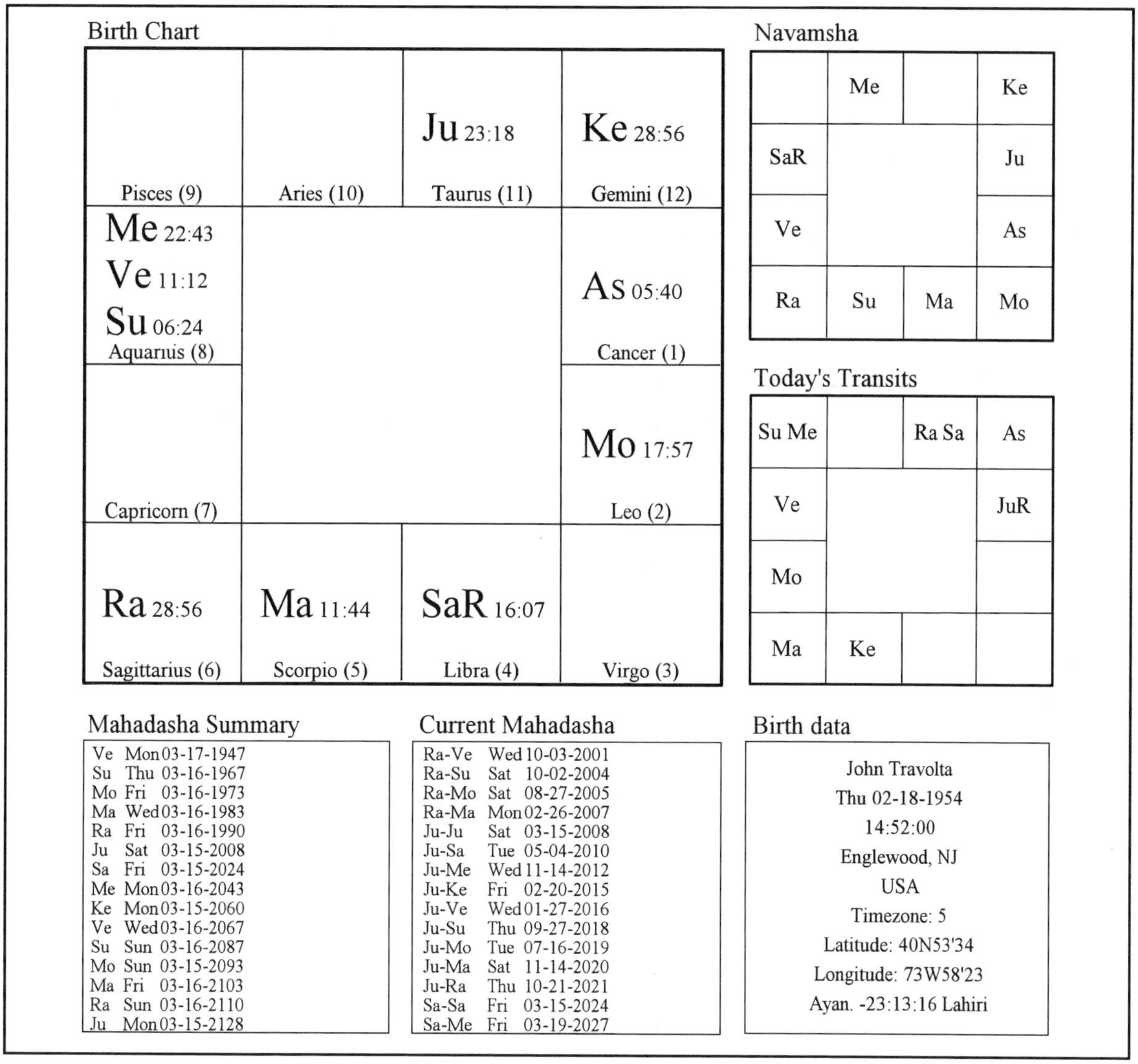

Birth Chart			
Pisces (9)	Aries (10)	Ju 23:18 Taurus (11)	Ke 28:56 Gemini (12)
Me 22:43 Ve 11:12 Su 06:24 Aquarius (8)			As 05:40 Cancer (1)
Capricorn (7)			Mo 17:57 Leo (2)
Ra 28:56 Sagittarius (6)	Ma 11:44 Scorpio (5)	SaR 16:07 Libra (4)	Virgo (3)

Navamsha

	Me		Ke
SaR			Ju
Ve			As
Ra	Su	Ma	Mo

Today's Transits

Su Me		Ra Sa	As
Ve			JuR
Mo			
Ma	Ke		

Mahadasha Summary

Ve	Mon	03-17-1947
Su	Thu	03-16-1967
Mo	Fri	03-16-1973
Ma	Wed	03-16-1983
Ra	Fri	03-16-1990
Ju	Sat	03-15-2008
Sa	Fri	03-15-2024
Me	Mon	03-16-2043
Ke	Mon	03-15-2060
Ve	Wed	03-16-2067
Su	Sun	03-16-2087
Mo	Sun	03-15-2093
Ma	Fri	03-16-2103
Ra	Sun	03-16-2110
Ju	Mon	03-15-2128

Current Mahadasha

Ra-Ve	Wed	10-03-2001
Ra-Su	Sat	10-02-2004
Ra-Mo	Sat	08-27-2005
Ra-Ma	Mon	02-26-2007
Ju-Ju	Sat	03-15-2008
Ju-Sa	Tue	05-04-2010
Ju-Me	Wed	11-14-2012
Ju-Ke	Fri	02-20-2015
Ju-Ve	Wed	01-27-2016
Ju-Su	Thu	09-27-2018
Ju-Mo	Tue	07-16-2019
Ju-Ma	Sat	11-14-2020
Ju-Ra	Thu	10-21-2021
Sa-Sa	Fri	03-15-2024
Sa-Me	Fri	03-19-2027

Birth data

John Travolta
Thu 02-18-1954
14:52:00
Englewood, NJ
USA
Timezone: 5
Latitude: 40N53'34
Longitude: 73W58'23
Ayan. -23:13:16 Lahiri

Chart 35—John Travolta

Over the next several years, John Travolta not only made movies, he became an American icon. His style of dress and his physical gestures became legend, in projects as diverse as '70s disco *Saturday Night Fever*, '50s doo-wop *Grease*, and '80s country *Urban Cowboy*.

Though the 5th house ruler placed in the 5th house shows powerful destiny, Mars in the 5th house placed in the house it rules (Scorpio) is even more powerful. It shows a warrior, a leader, and a trendsetter. Even a few years later, when John's planets were not as strong as they once were, he still made *Look*

Who's Talking, which grossed $150 million and spawned two sequels.

When Travolta made his career comeback film, *Pulp Fiction*, he quickly moved from the paltry $175,000 he made for that role to commanding $20 million per picture as an A-list actor. Mars in the 5th house, placed in its own sign, is impossible to keep down.

Although Mars in the 5th house indicates a position of leadership and power, it isn't the best placement for children. Mars is generally a malefic influence that harms the 5th house indications for children. Either the person will opt not to have children, or he or she may have difficulties with them. In an extreme case, you can lose a child with this placement.

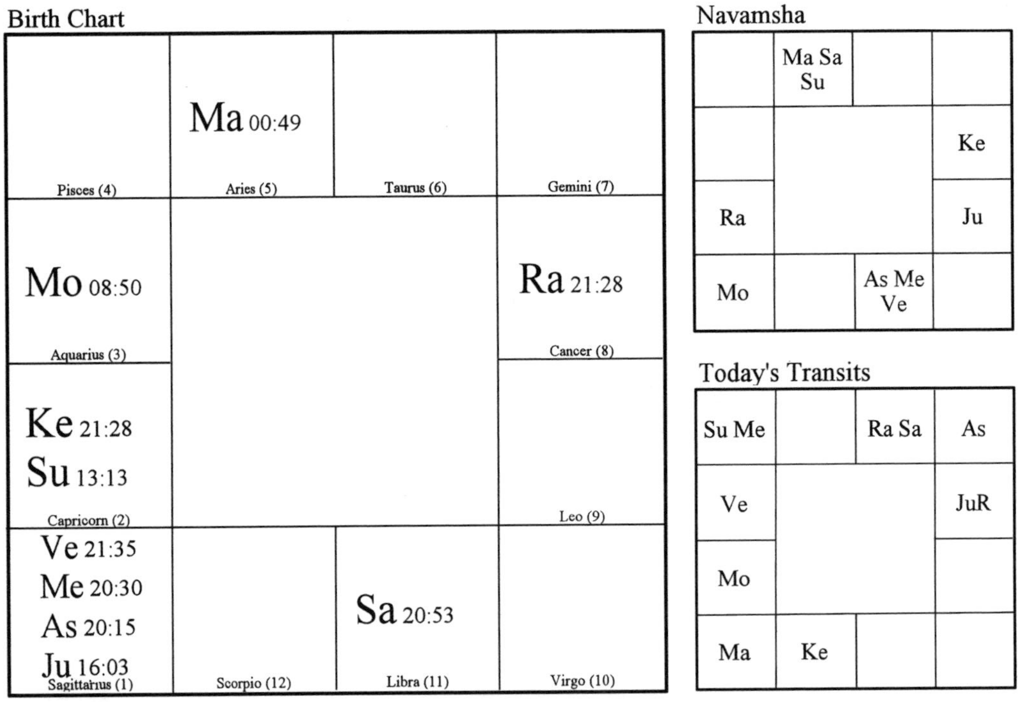

Birth Chart

Pisces (4)	Aries (5) Ma 00:49	Taurus (6)	Gemini (7)
Aquarius (3) Mo 08:50			Cancer (8) Ra 21:28
Capricorn (2) Ke 21:28 Su 13:13			Leo (9)
Sagittarius (1) Ve 21:35 Me 20:30 As 20:15 Ju 16:03	Scorpio (12)	Libra (11) Sa 20:53	Virgo (10)

Navamsha

	Ma Sa Su		
			Ke
Ra			Ju
Mo		As Me Ve	

Today's Transits

Su Me		Ra Sa	As
Ve			JuR
Mo			
Ma	Ke		

Mahadasha Summary

Ra	Thu	02-16-1922
Ju	Fri	02-16-1940
Sa	Thu	02-16-1956
Me	Sun	02-16-1975
Ke	Sun	02-16-1992
Ve	Tue	02-16-1999
Su	Fri	02-15-2019
Mo	Sat	02-15-2025
Ma	Thu	02-15-2035
Ra	Sat	02-15-2042
Ju	Sun	02-15-2060
Sa	Sat	02-15-2076
Me	Tue	02-15-2095
Ke	Tue	02-16-2112
Ve	Thu	02-16-2119

Current Mahadasha

Ve-Su	Mon	06-17-2002
Ve-Mo	Tue	06-17-2003
Ve-Ma	Tue	02-15-2005
Ve-Ra	Mon	04-17-2006
Ve-Ju	Fri	04-17-2009
Ve-Sa	Sat	12-17-2011
Ve-Me	Mon	02-16-2015
Ve-Ke	Sat	12-16-2017
Su-Su	Fri	02-15-2019
Su-Mo	Wed	06-05-2019
Su-Ma	Thu	12-05-2019
Su-Ra	Fri	04-10-2020
Su-Ju	Fri	03-05-2021
Su-Sa	Wed	12-22-2021
Su-Me	Sun	12-04-2022

Birth data

Paul Newman

Mon 01-26-1925

06:30:00

Cleveland, OH

USA

Timezone: 5

Latitude: 41N29'58

Longitude: 81W41'44

Ayan. -22:48:27 Lahiri

Chart 36—Paul Newman

Now let's look again at Paul Newman's chart.

Notice that Paul's 5th house ruler is placed in the 5th house, the same placement as John Travolta's. Aries is ruled by Mars, just as is Scorpio (Travolta's 5th house). This brought Newman the same type of powerful presence and charisma that Travolta has. Unfortunately, it is also a poor planetary position for children. Paul's only son died of a drug overdose in 1978. However, one of his daughters is close to Paul and helps him run his successful *Newman's Own* food business, whose profits go to charity.

Since Paul had six children, how would you know which child the afflicted 5th house would affect? Generally, when there are multiple children, you look at the 5th house as indicative of the first child, then the 3rd from the 5th (the 7th house) for the second child, and so on. In his case it becomes harder to track since he had children from two different wives (it would be useful to look at their charts). However, it is usually the case that once a malefic tendency has been expressed through a house, its poison is greatly diminished. This can be observed in family systems where one child may die, or be incapacitated in some way, and the surviving children live full, healthy lives.

Now let's take a look at the chart of the Artist Formerly Known as Prince (Chart 37).

Prince's rising sign is Libra, with Rahu in the rising sign. Looking at his 5th house, the benevolent Moon is sitting there, unaspected by any malevolent planet. A quick assessment of the chart shows that Prince would probably have healthy, handsome children, as the Moon brings beauty to the house in which it is placed. His 5th house is Aquarius, which we know from Table B is ruled by Saturn. When might you expect Prince would have a child? At quick glance, perhaps during his Saturn mahadasha, which began in the fall of 1989.

In fact, he did father a child during that time, just after his Venus bhukti (minor cycle within Saturn's major cycle) in 1996. But the child had major health difficulties and died soon thereafter. Why?

Look at the ruler of the 5th house, the house of children. It is placed in the 2nd house, in the very last degree of the house, and retrograde, in the fateful sandhi position mentioned earlier. Besides the ruler of the 5th house being placed in sandhi, the 2nd house is a difficult placement because the 2nd house and its ruler are known as *marakas* (killers). This is mentioned above in the description of the 2nd house as it relates to longevity.

In addition, Saturn's enemy the Sun (see Table F) sits opposing the Saturn with a powerful malefic aspect. And if you'll look at Table G you'll see that when Saturn is placed in Scorpio, it's in its enemy's house.

FINE-TUNING THE PREDICTION

As we already learned, each planet in the Vedic system, by its very nature, symbolizes a certain relationship in your life (see Table D). The Sun indicates the father, the Moon the mother, Venus the spouse, and so on. Jupiter is the indictor of children.

Where is the Jupiter placed in Prince's chart? It is placed in the fateful 12th house, the house of loss. And it's placed at a very late degree, is retrograde, and is opposed by Mars, which magnifies the unfortunate influence.

If you were to look at this chart and see the 5th house ruler placed in its enemy's house, in sandhi (the last degree of a sign) and retrograde, aspected by the malevolent Sun, you would want to see the degree to which the child is likely to suffer.

As mentioned earlier, the navamsha, or 9th harmonic chart, is used to fine-tune chart predictions.

Birth Chart

Ma 07:13 Pisces (6)	**Ke** 05:44 **Ve** 14:33 Aries (7)	**Me** 10:48 **Su** 23:23 Taurus (8)	Gemini (9)
Mo 08:42 Aquarius (5)			Cancer (10)
Capricorn (4)			Leo (11)
Sagittarius (3)	**SaR** 29:35 Scorpio (2)	**Ra** 05:44 **As** 23:25 Libra (1)	**JuR** 28:39 Virgo (12)

Navamsha

SaR	Me	As Ke	
			Su Ve
Mo	Ra		Ma JuR

Today's Transits

Su Me		Ra Sa	As
Ve			JuR
Mo			
Ma	Ke		

Mahadasha Summary

Ra	Mon	09-05-1955
Ju	Tue	09-04-1973
Sa	Mon	09-04-1989
Me	Thu	09-04-2008
Ke	Thu	09-04-2025
Ve	Sat	09-04-2032
Su	Tue	09-03-2052
Mo	Wed	09-04-2058
Ma	Mon	09-03-2068
Ra	Wed	09-04-2075
Ju	Thu	09-03-2093
Sa	Wed	09-04-2109
Me	Sat	09-04-2128
Ke	Sat	09-04-2145
Ve	Mon	09-04-2152

Current Mahadasha

Sa-Ma	Sat	03-09-2002
Sa-Ra	Fri	04-18-2003
Sa-Ju	Wed	02-22-2006
Me-Me	Thu	09-04-2008
Me-Ke	Mon	01-31-2011
Me-Ve	Sun	01-29-2012
Me-Su	Fri	11-28-2014
Me-Mo	Mon	10-05-2015
Me-Ma	Sun	03-05-2017
Me-Ra	Sat	03-03-2018
Me-Ju	Sat	09-19-2020
Me-Sa	Mon	12-26-2022
Ke-Ke	Thu	09-04-2025
Ke-Ve	Sat	01-31-2026
Ke-Su	Fri	04-02-2027

Birth data

Prince

Sat 06-07-1958

18:17:00

Minneapolis, MN

USA

Timezone: 6

Latitude: 44N58'48

Longitude: 93W15'49

Ayan. -23:16:44 Lahiri

Chart 37—Prince

As you already know, the navamsha chart is read just like the natal chart. Prince's navamsha chart shows Taurus rising, and we'll want to look at the 5th house to fine-tune the information about children. There we see retrograde Jupiter, the karaka (or indicator) for children, conjoined by malefic Mars in an enemy's house and opposed by its enemy,

retrograde Saturn. Saturn also aspects the Ketu in the rising sign. Finally, the ruler of the 5th house of children, Mercury, is located in the 12th house of loss. So this information compounds the seriousness of the situation as noted in the birth chart.

While we're on the subject of children, let's take a look at Madonna's chart.

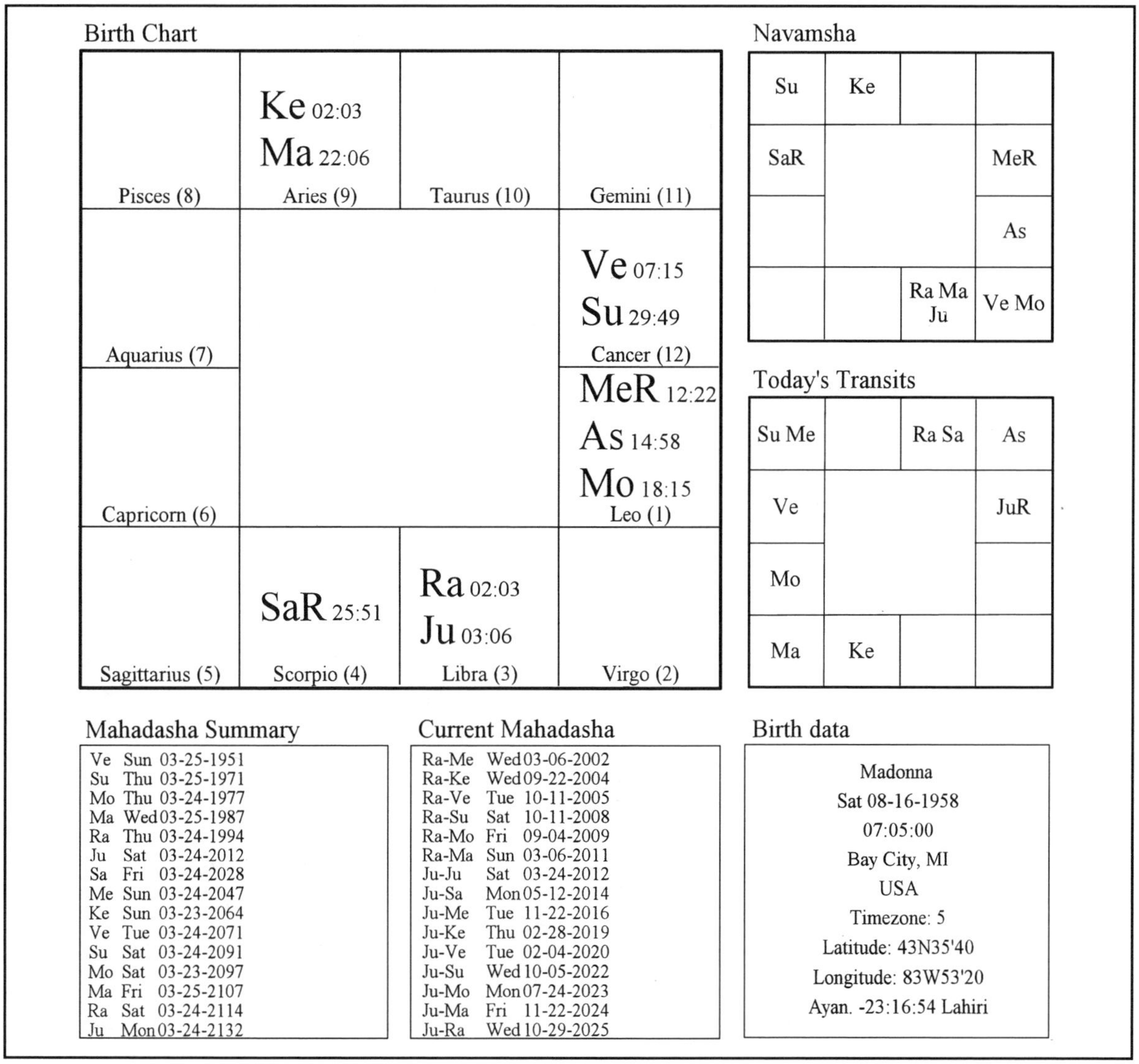

Birth Chart

	Ke 02:03 Ma 22:06		
Pisces (8)	Aries (9)	Taurus (10)	Gemini (11)
Aquarius (7)			Ve 07:15 Su 29:49 Cancer (12)
Capricorn (6)			MeR 12:22 As 14:58 Mo 18:15 Leo (1)
Sagittarius (5)	SaR 25:51 Scorpio (4)	Ra 02:03 Ju 03:06 Libra (3)	Virgo (2)

Navamsha

Su	Ke		
SaR			MeR
			As
		Ra Ma Ju	Ve Mo

Today's Transits

Su Me		Ra Sa	As
Ve			JuR
Mo			
Ma	Ke		

Mahadasha Summary

Ve	Sun	03-25-1951
Su	Thu	03-25-1971
Mo	Thu	03-24-1977
Ma	Wed	03-25-1987
Ra	Thu	03-24-1994
Ju	Sat	03-24-2012
Sa	Fri	03-24-2028
Me	Sun	03-24-2047
Ke	Sun	03-23-2064
Ve	Tue	03-24-2071
Su	Sat	03-24-2091
Mo	Sat	03-23-2097
Ma	Fri	03-25-2107
Ra	Sat	03-24-2114
Ju	Mon	03-24-2132

Current Mahadasha

Ra-Me	Wed	03-06-2002
Ra-Ke	Wed	09-22-2004
Ra-Ve	Tue	10-11-2005
Ra-Su	Sat	10-11-2008
Ra-Mo	Fri	09-04-2009
Ra-Ma	Sun	03-06-2011
Ju-Ju	Sat	03-24-2012
Ju-Sa	Mon	05-12-2014
Ju-Me	Tue	11-22-2016
Ju-Ke	Thu	02-28-2019
Ju-Ve	Tue	02-04-2020
Ju-Su	Wed	10-05-2022
Ju-Mo	Mon	07-24-2023
Ju-Ma	Fri	11-22-2024
Ju-Ra	Wed	10-29-2025

Birth data

Madonna

Sat 08-16-1958

07:05:00

Bay City, MI

USA

Timezone: 5

Latitude: 43N35'40

Longitude: 83W53'20

Ayan. -23:16:54 Lahiri

Chart 38—Madonna

This indication is seen more from the standpoint of the mahadashas. During the major cycle of her Mars, which lasted between the years 1987 and 1994, Madonna never would have settled down to have a child. Mars, being the planet of energy, pushes a person into the world with tremendous power.

In fact, the Madonna that most of us saw through the media was not the type of person who would likely make a commitment to motherhood. What happened?

Madonna entered her Rahu mahadasha in 1994, and it slowly grew in power. Longer mahadashas take longer to come into power than shorter ones. Since the Rahu mahadasha is an eighteen-year cycle, it takes several years to come up to speed.

The main point here is that although it is difficult to predict what the Rahu mahadasha will bring, one thing is certain: in ways that you are conventional you become alternative-minded, and in ways that you were alternative-minded, you become conventional. So when the Rahu came into power for Madonna, she approached the idea of motherhood from a surprisingly conventional perspective.

Now let's look at Sylvester Stallone's chart.

Although we'll analyze the 5th house shortly, first look at Stallone's 2nd house Capricorn, ruled by Saturn. As you'll remember, the 2nd house deals with the mouth area. Look where that Saturn is placed in Stallone's chart. In the challenging 8th house of an enemy, Cancer, conjoining Mercury and Venus,

which are also enemies for Cancer (Table G).

Why is this significant? A facial nerve was damaged when Stallone was being delivered with forceps, causing his characteristic facial droop and slightly slurred speech. Mercury is the planet of communication, and so his Saturn affected that planet detrimentally. The same Saturn also hits his Venus, the planet of beauty, making his facial features slightly askew.

Now, regarding the 5th house, let's see what we can tell about Stallone's children. He had two sons with his first wife, Sasha. We look to Stallone's 5th house to see the indications for his first child, which in this case is Aries, ruled by Mars. Where is Mars placed in Stallone's chart? In his 9th house. You'll remember from the description above that having the 5th house ruler placed in the 9th is one of the finest planetary placements. And indeed, his first child, Sage, born in 1976, has had award-winning success as an actor and wants to move into directing.

To analyze the indications for Stallone's second son, you simply use the 5th house as a starting point (indicating his first child) and look to his younger sibling. (Remember that one of the indications of the 3rd house is younger siblings.) So simply count three houses from the 5th (Stallone's 5th house Aries is the first house, his 6th house Taurus is the second house, and Gemini is the 3rd house). Here you arrive at Sage's younger brother.

Gemini now becomes the rising sign or 1st house for Stallone's second child, Seargeoh, born in 1979. Notice that the Sun is located in

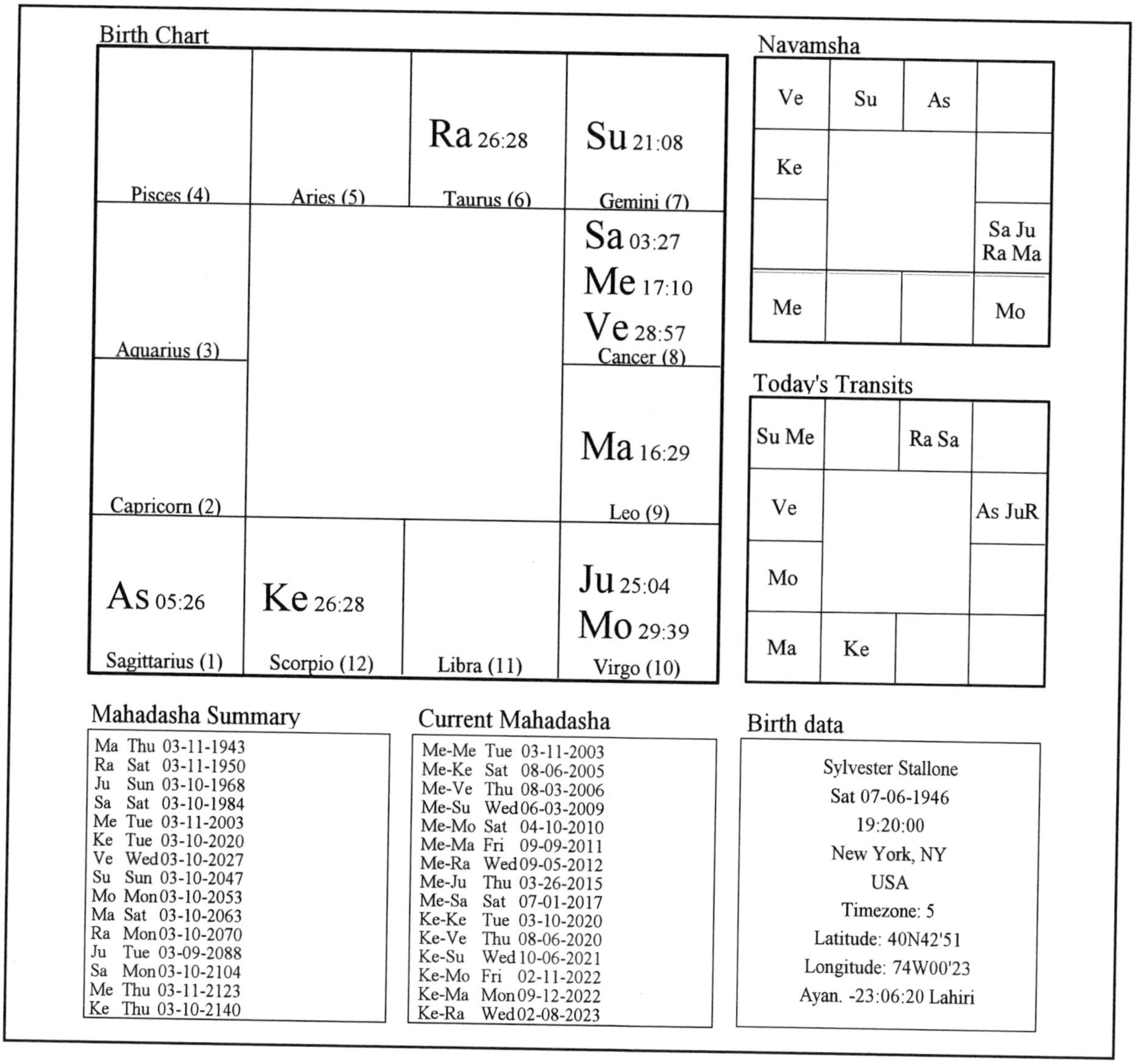

Birth Chart

		Ra 26:28	Su 21:08
Pisces (4)	Aries (5)	Taurus (6)	Gemini (7)
			Sa 03:27 Me 17:10 Ve 28:57
Aquarius (3)			Cancer (8)
			Ma 16:29
Capricorn (2)			Leo (9)
As 05:26	Ke 26:28		Ju 25:04 Mo 29:39
Sagittarius (1)	Scorpio (12)	Libra (11)	Virgo (10)

Navamsha

Ve	Su	As	
Ke			Sa Ju Ra Ma
			Mo
Me			

Today's Transits

Su Me		Ra Sa	
Ve			As JuR
Mo			
Ma	Ke		

Mahadasha Summary

```
Ma  Thu  03-11-1943
Ra  Sat  03-11-1950
Ju  Sun  03-10-1968
Sa  Sat  03-10-1984
Me  Tue  03-11-2003
Ke  Tue  03-10-2020
Ve  Wed  03-10-2027
Su  Sun  03-10-2047
Mo  Mon  03-10-2053
Ma  Sat  03-10-2063
Ra  Mon  03-10-2070
Ju  Tue  03-09-2088
Sa  Mon  03-10-2104
Me  Thu  03-11-2123
Ke  Thu  03-10-2140
```

Current Mahadasha

```
Me-Me  Tue  03-11-2003
Me-Ke  Sat  08-06-2005
Me-Ve  Thu  08-03-2006
Me-Su  Wed  06-03-2009
Me-Mo  Sat  04-10-2010
Me-Ma  Fri  09-09-2011
Me-Ra  Wed  09-05-2012
Me-Ju  Thu  03-26-2015
Me-Sa  Sat  07-01-2017
Ke-Ke  Tue  03-10-2020
Ke-Ve  Thu  08-06-2020
Ke-Su  Wed  10-06-2021
Ke-Mo  Fri  02-11-2022
Ke-Ma  Mon  09-12-2022
Ke-Ra  Wed  02-08-2023
```

Birth data

Sylvester Stallone
Sat 07-06-1946
19:20:00
New York, NY
USA
Timezone: 5
Latitude: 40N42'51
Longitude: 74W00'23
Ayan. -23:06:20 Lahiri

Chart 39—Sylvester Stallone

Gemini, an enemy's house. Being too hot an influence in a delicate sign that is ruled by Mercury, the Sun can harm confidence and the nervous system. To get a better sense of the damage, look at Gemini's ruler, Mercury. It is located in the second house of speech in an enemy's house, conjoined by Saturn and Venus, who both occupy an enemy's sign. Seargeoh was born autistic.

Although rumors had it that the child Janice Dickinson gave birth to in 1994 was Stallone's, DNA tests have since proved otherwise. So Stallone's true third child, Sophia Rose, was born in 1996. How do we see her through her father's chart? Again, you take the 3rd house from the 7th, signifying Seargeoh's younger sibling.

So the 3rd house from Gemini is Leo. And Stallone's Mars is placed there, one of the poorest placements for that planet, as it harms, and in some cases can indicate the death for, a child. Where might we find prob-

lems for Sophia? At first glance you'll want to check the head region due to Mars's placement in the rising sign, indicating the possibility of a head injury. But since Leo is a friendly house for Mars, you'll look to where Mars throws its aspects. In this case Mars hits malefic Ketu in the 4th, and the 4th house, as you now know, represents the heart and lung

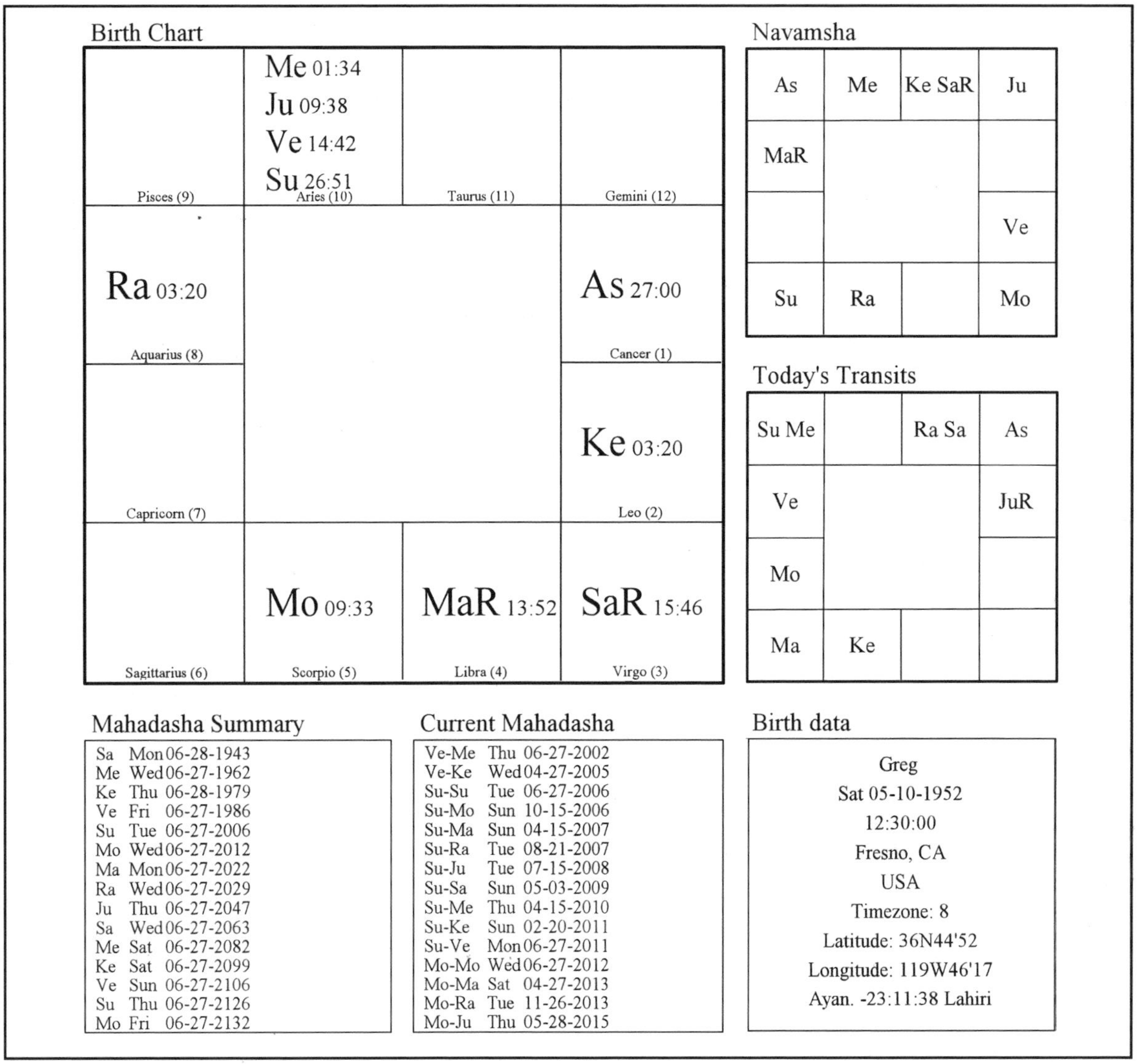

Birth Chart

Pisces (9)	Me 01:34 Ju 09:38 Ve 14:42 Su 26:51 Aries (10)	Taurus (11)	Gemini (12)
Ra 03:20 Aquarius (8)			As 27:00 Cancer (1)
Capricorn (7)			Ke 03:20 Leo (2)
Mo 09:33 Sagittarius (6)	MaR 13:52 Scorpio (5)	Libra (4)	SaR 15:46 Virgo (3)

Navamsha

As	Me	Ke SaR	Ju
MaR			
			Ve
Su	Ra		Mo

Today's Transits

Su Me		Ra Sa	As
Ve			JuR
Mo			
Ma	Ke		

Mahadasha Summary

Sa	Mon	06-28-1943
Me	Wed	06-27-1962
Ke	Thu	06-28-1979
Ve	Fri	06-27-1986
Su	Tue	06-27-2006
Mo	Wed	06-27-2012
Ma	Mon	06-27-2022
Ra	Wed	06-27-2029
Ju	Thu	06-27-2047
Sa	Wed	06-27-2063
Me	Sat	06-27-2082
Ke	Sat	06-27-2099
Ve	Sun	06-27-2106
Su	Thu	06-27-2126
Mo	Fri	06-27-2132

Current Mahadasha

Ve-Me	Thu	06-27-2002
Ve-Ke	Wed	04-27-2005
Su-Su	Tue	06-27-2006
Su-Mo	Sun	10-15-2006
Su-Ma	Sun	04-15-2007
Su-Ra	Tue	08-21-2007
Su-Ju	Tue	07-15-2008
Su-Sa	Sun	05-03-2009
Su-Me	Thu	04-15-2010
Su-Ke	Sun	02-20-2011
Su-Ve	Mon	06-27-2011
Mo-Mo	Wed	06-27-2012
Mo-Ma	Sat	04-27-2013
Mo-Ra	Tue	11-26-2013
Mo-Ju	Thu	05-28-2015

Birth data

Greg

Sat 05-10-1952

12:30:00

Fresno, CA

USA

Timezone: 8

Latitude: 36N44'52

Longitude: 119W46'17

Ayan. -23:11:38 Lahiri

Chart 40—Greg

region. We would anticipate a problem in that area for this child based on these planets, particularly an unusual or hard-to-diagnose problem due to the mysterious nature of Ketu. Two months after Sophia Rose's birth, she was diagnosed as having a hole in her heart. In November of 1996, three months after her birth, she underwent successful open-heart surgery.

Now let's look at another 5th house indication—higher education—in a slightly different light. The chart of Greg, the drug smuggler, (Chart 40), gives us a good example.

Greg's 5th house is Scorpio, with the Moon in Scorpio, bringing him advanced knowledge or higher education (a 5th house indicator) in covert activities. Since the Moon is in debilitation, the chart also indicates possible emotional or psychological disturbances.

The ruler of his 5th house is Mars, which is placed in his 4th house, and is retrograde. Remember that the 5th house ruler in the 4th house shows an abundance of homes and automobiles, and at the height of his success Greg owned several homes throughout the world and drove only the most exotic automobiles.

His retrograde Mars also indicates that since he purchased these properties through illegal means, he had to keep ownership of these homes and cars hidden. The retrogration of his Mars indicates the energy surrounding these assets was turned inward, and was unobservable to the common person.

So this is a chart of a high-stakes entrepreneur, a secret gambler, who made his livelihood through taking risks. This is what is indicated by his 5th house.

REMEDIES

In Vedic astrology, the 5th house is known as the house of *purva punya*, past-life merit. Often 5th house issues are strongly riveted in destiny, and remedial measures can do only so much. This explains why John Travolta would have a Jupiter opposing his 5th house Mars, bringing a benevolent aspect to that potentially dangerous placement, while Paul Newman would have malevolent Saturn opposing his 5th house Mars, increasing its negative nature.

Since the 5th house is associated with children, and a child's formative years are so important, the best remedial suggestion for the 5th house indication of children is to spend as much time as possible embracing and caring for your child during those years. In several of Paul Newman's biographies, it is noted that in the midst of trying to get his career on track and a dissolving marriage with his first wife, Paul felt he wasn't able to give his son the kind of attention he needed.

Here's where things get complicated. Had Newman been able to remedy the situation with his son, thousands of people might never have benefited from Newman's generosity. Over the last fifteen years, the *Newman's Own* line of food products has generated more than $100 million for charity, funded camps for sick children, and established the anti-drug *Scott Newman Foundation* in memory of his son.

A look at Prince's chart can bring an interesting element of Vedic astrology into better focus for us.

An accomplished Vedic astrologer has the ability to determine the most auspicious time a client should start an activity. This technique is called *muhurtha*, and it can apply as readily to starting a journey as to conceiving a child. In Prince's case, since he is in the Saturn mahadasha and his 5th house ruler is in the fateful last degrees, I would have highly recommended he have a muhurtha done to determine the best time to conceive. This might have helped balance some of the negative energy around his 5th house.

Otherwise, a Vedic fire puja can also help remove strong obstacles to the 5th house, as would chanting to Saturn and eating less food on Saturdays. I would recommend the very same thing for Stallone, since Saturn also rules his 5th house.

STRENGTHENING YOUR 5th HOUSE

It's important to understand what your motivation is for bringing new life into the world. Sometimes people decide to have children because they can't deal with their own issues and the easiest remedy is to stay busy with raising another life. The difficulty in this scenario is that such people usually give birth to children with the very issues they are trying to avoid in themselves, and then they have to see these dynamics played out 24/7.

This applies equally to giving birth to new ideas, projects, or businesses. Is the process of the creation of something a natural extension of your being, one that organically grows in that direction? Or are you trying to prove something to somebody? The care that goes into the design of a concept has *so* much to do with its ultimate outcome, and the way it impacts others.

Strengthening the 5th house ruler can be accomplished by chanting the mantra for the planet that rules the 5th on the day associated with that planet. It also helps to eat less food on that day. If the 5th house is afflicted, chant for any planet that aspects the 5th favorably. You can also chant for the indicator (karaka) of the 5th house, Jupiter, on Thursdays.

If your child is having difficulties, it is better to examine his or her chart in order to see specifically where to empower planets rather than to try to see it through yours. Also, recognize that transits generally have little impact on young children. Instead, you may feel the impact of those transits as if they were your own.

SUMMARY

When you bring new life into the world you have to protect it. A new child begins life by receiving immunizations and learning how to avoid life's hazards, whether avoiding a hot stove or looking both ways before crossing the street. Similarly, when you give birth to a new idea or inspiration, you need to protect and guard it until it gathers enough strength on its own. Sometimes your best well-wishers become your greatest critics when you start to come into your own and push in the direction of your destiny. Out of jealousy, they may try to discredit you or bring you back down to their level.

These are issues of enemies, which is what the 6th house is concerned with. The 6th house tests your resolve to really succeed at what you have set off to accomplish. Since the 5th house also deals with love affairs, moving into the 6th house forces you to come to terms with your level of commitment to that person, and whether you would consider the person a marriage partner (this is why the 7th house of marriage follows the 6th).

When you consider the 6th house, do so with courage and inspiration. The energy of the 6th will help strengthen your vision and fine-tune your dreams. But don't fall into the crab pot mentality. At seafood restaurants crabs are often thrown together into a large, open-topped aquarium. If you observe the crabs, you'll notice that on occasion, one of the crabs is able to latch a claw onto the side and pull itself up. In reaction, the other crabs reach out and grab the escaping crab, pulling it back down with the rest of them. As we explore the 6th house, embrace the opportunity to fight for what you believe in.

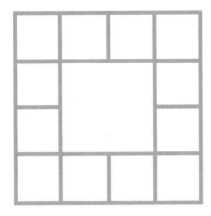

THE 6th HOUSE

Enemies

Considered the house of enemies, the 6th house is where you see the indication of people who become jealous of you, try to discredit you, try to intimidate you, try to bring you down. It is the house that tests your resolve and commitment to what you aspire to accomplish. It would seem to be one of the *dusthana* (malefic) houses, but technically it is an *upachaya* (improving) house, so it also shows that through effort you can overcome many of the negative indications here. By learning ways to deal with conflict skillfully, you can overcome any problems, enemies, or other challengers the world may bring you.

This house also indicates the healing professions, whether the practice of conventional or alternative medicine. It also signifies service-oriented, subservient, and even food-related activities, since the 6th house shows assimilation of food.

As this house indicates matters of health, any health problems can also be worked with advantageously, since the 6th house brings with it the possibility of improvement and correction. The focus for ill health may be on the liver, kidneys, or lower digestive tract. The 6th house also indicates your mother's natural brothers.

THE NATURE OF THE 6th HOUSE

Find the 6th house in your chart. If you are Libra rising, your 6th house is Pisces. If you are Virgo rising, Aquarius is your 6th house. Pay close attention to the zodiac sign of the 6th house because the nature of that sign will show you the way 6th house issues function.

For instance, if Pisces is your 6th house, you can be an intuitive healer. If your 6th house is Virgo, you might become obsessed with health and health supplements.

HOW THE 6th HOUSE EXPRESSES ITSELF

Locate the planet that rules your 6th house (see Table B), and find where it's placed in your chart. Then read the description below that pertains to this placement.

The 6th House Ruler placed in the 1st house indicates skills in the healing arts. Whether you are actually a healer or not does not diminish these talents, because people feel better just by being around you. You are service-oriented and persevering, and may support others. This placement may indicate bad health if the position is weak or afflicted.

The 6th House Ruler placed in the 2nd house indicates that you can earn your livelihood by healing, but that the money does not come easily. If you give up too soon, you will miss the financial opportunity that this placement promises. You can have speech difficulties or problems with the mouth, teeth, or eyes (usually the right eye).

The 6th House Ruler placed in the 3rd house is a position that can affect your siblings' health, or cause your sibling relationships to be strained. Efforts may be focused on maintaining good health. Courage and artistic abilities are not favored in this position, but if you feel strongly enough about something, and are committed to it no matter how long it takes to accomplish, this position can make it happen.

The 6th House Ruler placed in the 4th house indicates that your mother could suffer from health complaints, or that your relationship with her might be antagonistic. In some cases you embrace conflict, and get a great deal of satisfaction from entering into discord. This position can also indicate some weakness in the lungs or heart.

The 6th House Ruler placed in the 5th house affects children just as the 6th house ruler in the 4th affects the mother. Your child, then, could suffer from health issues, or your relationship with your child could be strained. You also have latent abilities in the healing arts.

The 6th House Ruler placed in the 6th house indicates that you are a warrior by nature, entering into combat and returning home victorious. Competitors, antagonists, and enemies cannot overcome your power even though they might try. People you employ to assist you bring you great benefit.

The 6th House Ruler placed in the 7th house relates to the spouse and indicates a marriage partner who may be unhealthy, or that your relationship with him or her may be strained. Otherwise, your spouse can be involved in the healing arts. This position also indicates the possibility of weakness in the sexual organs.

The 6th House Ruler placed in the 8th house can be especially beneficial for people involved in the healing profession of geriatrics, but it generally indicates a person with poor health. This placement is more indicative of chronic rather than acute problems. It can also show a person who regularly goes out of his or her way to cause problems for others.

The **6th House Ruler placed in the 9th house** might indicate a father in the healing arts, though it's more likely your relationship with him is strained, or that his health suffers. Generally speaking, you have a strong constitution and luck in overcoming competitors. You may express your spiritual tendencies through being of service to others.

The **6th House Ruler placed in the 10th house** is one of the strongest indications of a physician or healer, but you come into your power only after a certain amount of struggle and effort. Part of that struggle may be against people who try to hold you back or who are antagonistic toward your career choice.

The **6th House Ruler placed in the 11th house** indicates that people you thought were friends may actually turn out to be enemies. You may be deceived by others in entrepreneurial pursuits, and those "others" may include friends. However, after initial disappointment and refocusing, you can actually become successful in speculative ventures.

The **6th House Ruler placed in the 12th house** indicates difficulty with the lower digestive tract or sexual organs. Enemies can be encountered while traveling abroad. People hired to assist you turn out to cause you various kinds of losses. You have a tendency to work hard and not obtain the results equal to the amount of effort put forth.

IF THERE ARE PLANETS IN THE 6th HOUSE

To help fine-tune the descriptions below, you'll want to assess whether the planet is welcome in the house in which it is placed (Table G). If the planet is in the house of a friend, the positive nature of the following description is enhanced. If the planet is in the house of an enemy, more of the negative possibilities need to be considered.

Sun (Su) in the 6th house shows the chart of a healer or a person who is health conscious. You may also attract conflicts or jealousies, but are able to rise above them. If afflicted, you are held back by antagonists.

Moon (Mo) in the 6th house is the placement of humanitarians who tend to want to help others before helping themselves. If afflicted, this position indicates poor health for both you and (possibly) your mother.

Mars (Ma) in the 6th house indicates that you need to exercise restraint in your competitive nature and tendency to enter conflict because you have the potential of resorting to violence. Held in check, this placement empowers you and indicates great success.

Mercury (Me) in the 6th house, if unafflicted, shows skill in psychology and analytical reasoning. This position indicates that you would be able to overcome adversity through logical arguments. If afflicted, it brings weakness, nervousness, and poor eyesight.

Jupiter (Ju) in the 6th house shows that you use tact and diplomacy in dealing with conflict. You will want to get sufficient rest, more than your mind tells you is necessary. If afflicted, there could be difficulty with children, or you could be brought down by enemies.

Venus (Ve) in the 6th house indicates you may be in a service-oriented profession catering to women. Women as allies can also help you defeat antagonism. Afflicted, this position can bring health complaints related to sexual functioning.

Saturn (Sa) in the 6th house is a very good placement, as malefic planets do well in challenging houses. You slowly and steadily rise to the top of your field. If afflicted, you can suffer from health complaints that are circulatory in nature.

Rahu (Ra) in the 6th house indicates a person who employs alternative, unconventional methods of healing. This is a good placement, showing strength of spirit, but afflicted it can indicate a violent temper.

Ketu (Ke) in the 6th house shows your ability to work in secret to overcome antagonism instead of hitting it head-on. If afflicted it can show a tendency to use these same abilities for deceptive purposes.

OTHER CONSIDERATIONS

- Note the element associated with your 6th house. Remember that fire signs are driven; earth signs are patient; air signs are creative; and water signs are emotional.
- Also note the quality of your 6th house. Cardinal signs initiate; fixed signs stabilize; and mutable signs seek change.

Now check any aspects to the 6th house:

- Are any planets located in the same house as, or opposing any planet in, the 6th house? If so, are those planets friendly, neutral, or enemies? (See Table F.) For instance, say your Jupiter is placed in the 6th house and opposed by neutral Saturn. This planetary combination shows the possibility of legal disputes.
- Remember that Mars energizes the house it's in, as well as the 4th, 7th, and 8th houses from itself. This means if Mars is placed in the 11th, 12th, or 3rd houses of your chart, it throws an aspect onto your 6th house, giving you more strength to fend off antagonists. This position may also weaken your health somewhat.
- Saturn restricts or brings discipline to the house it's in, as well as the 3rd, 7th, and 10th houses from itself. This means if Saturn is placed in the 9th, 12th, or 4th houses of your chart, it throws an aspect onto your 6th house, bringing restrictive energy brought on by competitors or bosses.
- Jupiter expands or brings optimism to the

house it's in, as well as the 5th, 7th, and 9th houses from itself. This means if Jupiter is placed in the 10th, 12th, or 2nd houses of your chart, it throws an aspect onto your 6th house, bringing you tact in dealing with conflict.

- If you want to find out when your chart's 6th house energies will be enlivened, look to the 6th house ruler, or any planet located in the 6th house. Examine the Mahadasha Summary of your chart to see when that planet will come into power, and that will give you your answer. To find shorter periods when 6th house issues will be highlighted, look to the 6th house ruler or any planet located in the 6th house, and find the time its bhukti will run.

- Notice any influence transiting planets are having on your 6th house, or 6th house ruler. Mars can bring the possibility of accidents. The Rahu transit is especially good for detoxifying your system or beginning a healthy regime. Since malefics operate well in challenging houses (see page 17), Saturn transiting the 6th house can be favorable, giving you the strength, focus, and perseverance to overcome any obstacle. You can chant to the planet that is favorably transiting your rising sign, on the appropriate day for that planet, to enhance its effects.

CHART EXAMPLES

A good example of a chart displaying a strong 6th house is Michael Crichton's.

Crichton's 6th house ruler, Jupiter, is placed in his 1st house. This is the classic position for a healer. He graduated at the top of his class at Harvard Medical School and went on to write a number of books based on his medical knowledge.

But his planets pointed to a destiny far beyond the walls of a medical institution. Look at the overall potential of the chart. His rising sign is Cancer, and Jupiter is placed very close to its exact point of full exaltation in his rising sign (see Table E)—one of the finest, most powerful rising signs. Jupiter, the greatest benefic, at the acme of its power, sets the tone for his whole chart and life. The ruler of his rising sign, the Moon, is placed in the 10th house, showing that he is strongly career-oriented. The Sun, Mars, and Venus oppose the 10th house from the 4th house Libra, indicating an immensely powerful career potential, with most likely more than one talent (since multiple planets convene on the mid-heaven).

Rahu, the influence connected with material prosperity, is placed in his 2nd house, the house of wealth, virtually guaranteeing millions. Mercury, the planet of communication, sits powerfully in the 3rd house, the house of creativity and the arts.

Venus, Mars, and a weak Sun (perhaps indicating a desire to avoid the limelight) sit in Crichton's 4th house, indicating that he will live a life of luxury and material prosperity. His 5th house ruler is in the 4th, showing that he gets great happiness from higher education and learning. It's interesting to note that his 5th house of higher education is

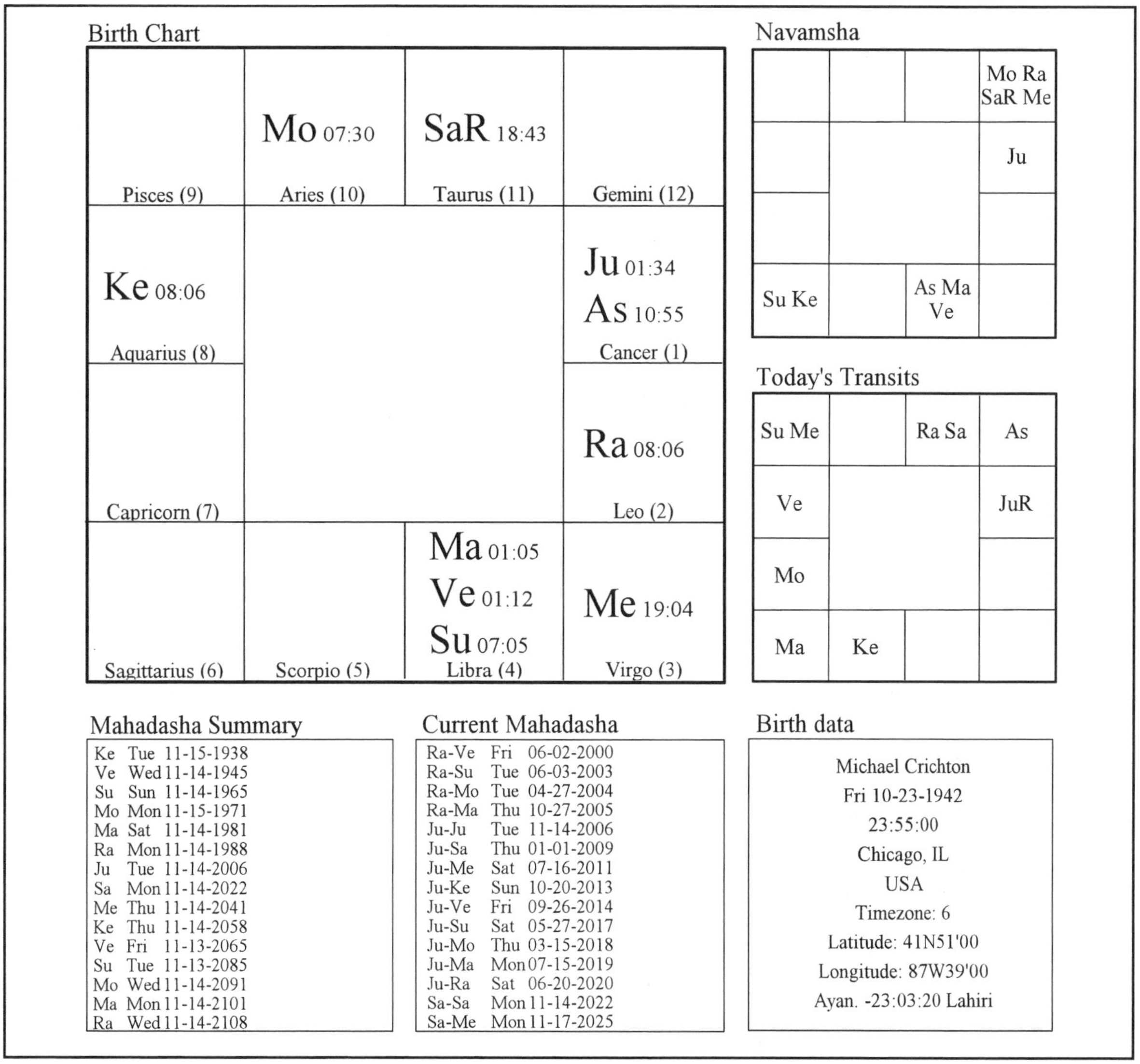

Birth Chart			Navamsha

Birth Chart

Pisces (9)	Aries (10) Mo 07:30	Taurus (11) SaR 18:43	Gemini (12)
Aquarius (8) Ke 08:06			Cancer (1) Ju 01:34 As 10:55
Capricorn (7)			Leo (2) Ra 08:06
Sagittarius (6)	Scorpio (5)	Libra (4) Ma 01:05 Ve 01:12 Su 07:05	Virgo (3) Me 19:04

Navamsha

			Mo Ra SaR Me
			Ju
Su Ke		As Ma Ve	

Today's Transits

Su Me		Ra Sa	As
Ve			JuR
Mo			
Ma	Ke		

Mahadasha Summary

Ke	Tue 11-15-1938
Ve	Wed 11-14-1945
Su	Sun 11-14-1965
Mo	Mon 11-15-1971
Ma	Sat 11-14-1981
Ra	Mon 11-14-1988
Ju	Tue 11-14-2006
Sa	Mon 11-14-2022
Me	Thu 11-14-2041
Ke	Thu 11-14-2058
Ve	Fri 11-13-2065
Su	Tue 11-13-2085
Mo	Wed 11-14-2091
Ma	Mon 11-14-2101
Ra	Wed 11-14-2108

Current Mahadasha

Ra-Ve	Fri 06-02-2000
Ra-Su	Tue 06-03-2003
Ra-Mo	Tue 04-27-2004
Ra-Ma	Thu 10-27-2005
Ju-Ju	Tue 11-14-2006
Ju-Sa	Thu 01-01-2009
Ju-Me	Sat 07-16-2011
Ju-Ke	Sun 10-20-2013
Ju-Ve	Fri 09-26-2014
Ju-Su	Sat 05-27-2017
Ju-Mo	Thu 03-15-2018
Ju-Ma	Mon 07-15-2019
Ju-Ra	Sat 06-20-2020
Sa-Sa	Mon 11-14-2022
Sa-Me	Mon 11-17-2025

Birth data

Michael Crichton

Fri 10-23-1942

23:55:00

Chicago, IL

USA

Timezone: 6

Latitude: 41N51'00

Longitude: 87W39'00

Ayan. -23:03:20 Lahiri

Chart 41—Michael Crichton

Scorpio, the house of deep, hidden things.

Of course, medical school requires knowledge of the body's hidden functions—of its anatomy and physiology—and Crichton's research for his suspenseful books likewise requires that he research details and develop a fine understanding of many different disci-plines. Most recently, in *Timeline*, he delved into quantum physics and medieval history.

Now let's look at a chart we glanced at earlier, one that shows the power to overcome obstacles—the chart of Oprah Winfrey. (See Chart 42.)

Oprah's rising sign is Leo, ruled by the

Sun. Among the characteristics of Leo is the desire to be in the limelight. The ruler of Leo is in her 6th house, conjoined by Venus and Mercury. Look at how close in degree her Venus is to her Sun. Planets must be at least 8 degrees from the Sun to give their full expression, or they are combust.

Venus is the planet of love. The Sun indicates a male influence. What can happen when the Sun burns Venus in the 6th house of conflict? Sexual abuse. Oprah was sexually molested several times by male relatives as a preteen.

The ruler of her 2nd house (Virgo) is Mercury, which is also in the 6th house. As you'll remember, the 2nd house, among other indications, deals with one's childhood. So

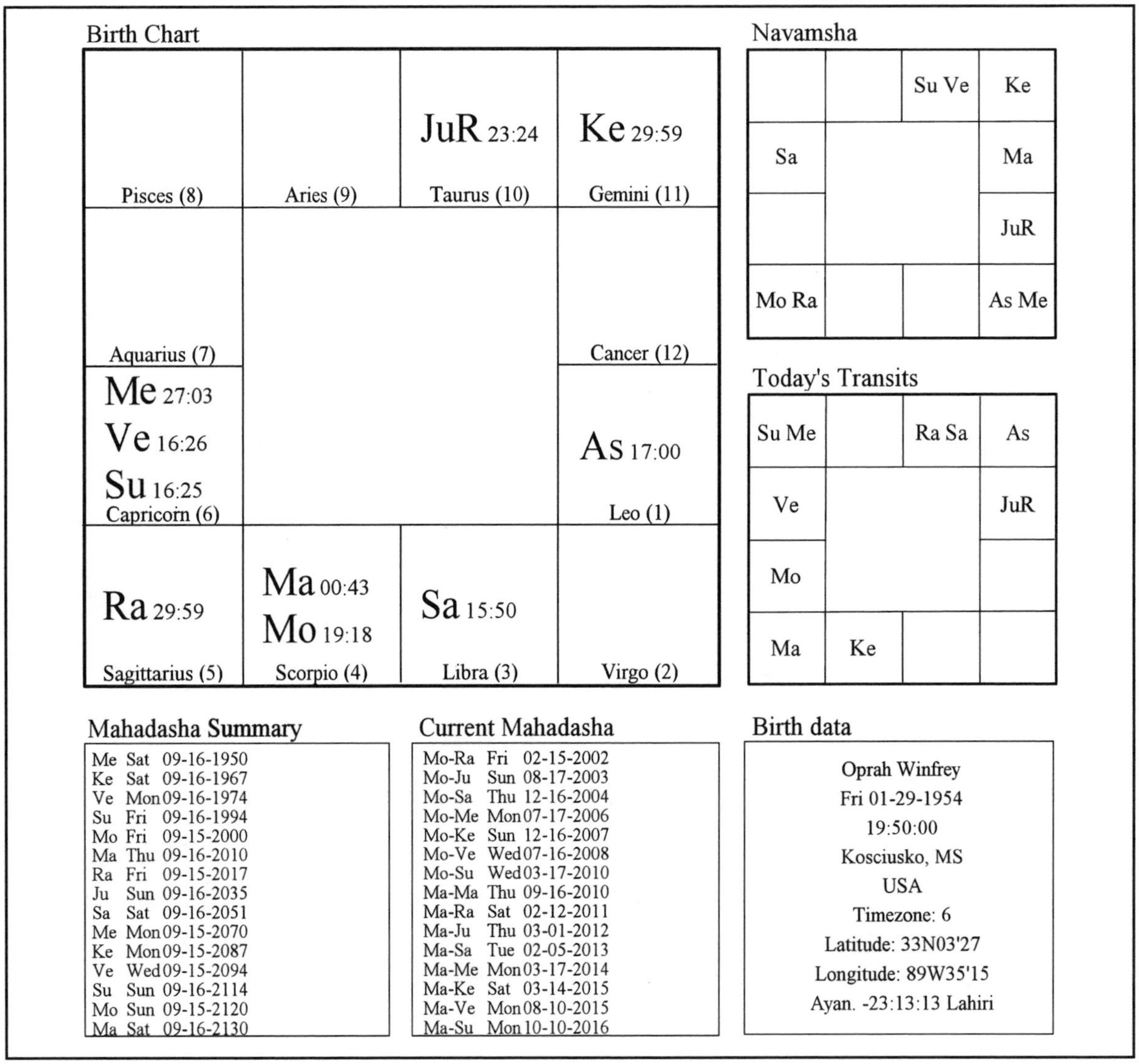

Birth Chart

		JuR 23:24	Ke 29:59
Pisces (8)	Aries (9)	Taurus (10)	Gemini (11)
Aquarius (7)			Cancer (12)
Me 27:03 Ve 16:26 Su 16:25 Capricorn (6)			As 17:00 Leo (1)
Ra 29:59 Sagittarius (5)	Ma 00:43 Mo 19:18 Scorpio (4)	Sa 15:50 Libra (3)	Virgo (2)

Navamsha

		Su Ve	Ke
Sa			Ma
			JuR
Mo Ra			As Me

Today's Transits

Su Me		Ra Sa	As
Ve			JuR
Mo			
Ma	Ke		

Mahadasha Summary

Me	Sat	09-16-1950
Ke	Sat	09-16-1967
Ve	Mon	09-16-1974
Su	Fri	09-16-1994
Mo	Fri	09-15-2000
Ma	Thu	09-16-2010
Ra	Fri	09-15-2017
Ju	Sun	09-16-2035
Sa	Sat	09-16-2051
Me	Mon	09-15-2070
Ke	Mon	09-15-2087
Ve	Wed	09-15-2094
Su	Sun	09-16-2114
Mo	Sun	09-15-2120
Ma	Sat	09-16-2130

Current Mahadasha

Mo-Ra	Fri	02-15-2002
Mo-Ju	Sun	08-17-2003
Mo-Sa	Thu	12-16-2004
Mo-Me	Mon	07-17-2006
Mo-Ke	Sun	12-16-2007
Mo-Ve	Wed	07-16-2008
Mo-Su	Wed	03-17-2010
Ma-Ma	Thu	09-16-2010
Ma-Ra	Sat	02-12-2011
Ma-Ju	Thu	03-01-2012
Ma-Sa	Tue	02-05-2013
Ma-Me	Mon	03-17-2014
Ma-Ke	Sat	03-14-2015
Ma-Ve	Mon	08-10-2015
Ma-Su	Mon	10-10-2016

Birth data

Oprah Winfrey
Fri 01-29-1954
19:50:00
Kosciusko, MS
USA
Timezone: 6
Latitude: 33N03'27
Longitude: 89W35'15
Ayan. -23:13:13 Lahiri

Chart 42—Oprah Winfrey

this position brings great unhappiness during one's formative years.

The ruler of her 3rd house (Libra) is Venus, and Venus is placed in her 6th house. So, early in life, her courage was shaky and love couldn't be found easily. However, because the 6th house is an upachaya (improving) house, she was able to overcome these stumbling blocks in her chart by sheer force of will and emerge victorious. If you know anything about Oprah's early life, you will know how many personal battles she had to overcome in order to get where she is today. Ironically, it was her willingness to share her struggles openly with her audience that allowed her to capture their hearts.

Mars, the ruler of her 4th house (Scorpio), is placed in the 4th house, conjoined by debilitated Moon. So a great deal of unhappiness was created by her mother, which makes sense when we consider that the sexual abuse occurred under her mother's roof.

Look also at Oprah's 5th house, Sagittarius, which is ruled by Jupiter. That Jupiter is located in her 10th house, indicating a career that could spread far and wide, since Jupiter is the most magnanimous and expansive planet. Coupled with this sense of destiny is exalted Saturn in her 3rd house (of desire), which gave Oprah the power to make it happen. As she herself has said, "All my life I have always known I was born to greatness."

On the challenging side of Oprah's chart, Rahu sits in the 5th house in sandhi, the fateful last degree. The 5th house represents children, and this Rahu cannot bring much benefit in the area of children. At the age of fourteen, Oprah gave birth to a premature baby, who died shortly thereafter.

Now consider the upachaya, or improving, quality of the 6th house. Everything in Oprah's life (relationships, family, and career) has improved dramatically. When she moved in with her father in Nashville he gave her support and a strict regimen of discipline and study, and within a few years she became the first African American anchor at Nashville's WTVF-TV. Of course the rest is history, with an Academy Award nomination (*The Color Purple*), her own studio (Harpo Productions), a net worth in the hundreds of millions of dollars, and tremendous generosity toward charities.

Now let's look at an example of what happens when the 6th house affects the health.

Mark has an interesting 6th house issue. Notice that he has Sagittarius rising. His 6th house, then, is Taurus, which is ruled by Venus. Where is that Venus placed? It is placed in Gemini, his 7th house.

Look again at the description above for the 6th house ruler placed in the 7th house. Sexuality is expressed through Venus, which also happens to be the ruler of his 6th house. The Venus in his chart is not only retrograde, but is hemmed in by very close degrees of the malefics Sun and Rahu, which indicates the possibility of a disease of the sexual organs. The 7th house deals with, among other issues, the sexual organs, and in this chart the 7th house ruler is placed in the house of health, which is a poor placement.

Mark had a testicle grow to the size of a

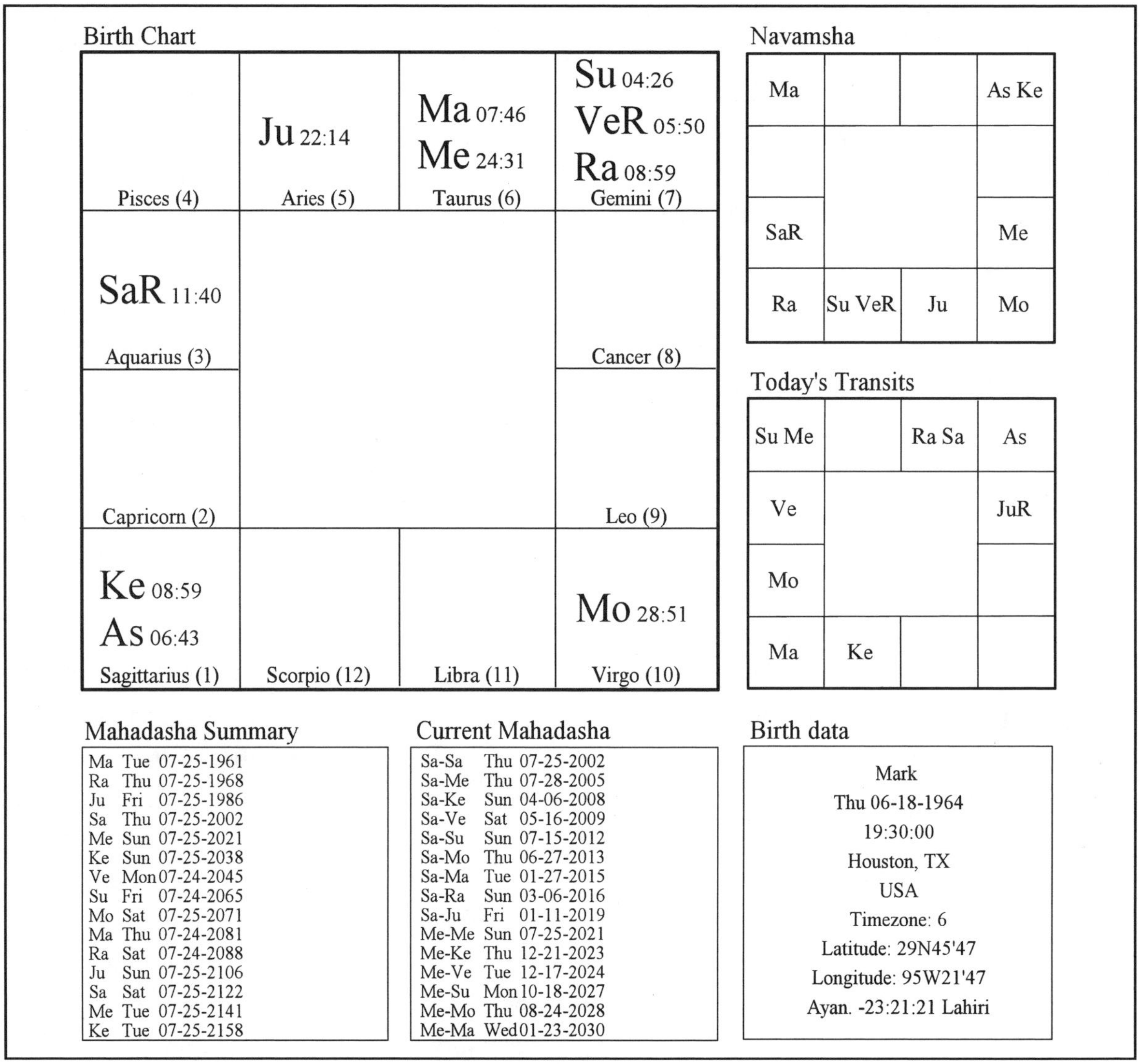

Birth Chart

Pisces (4)	Aries (5)	Taurus (6)	Gemini (7)
	Ju 22:14	Ma 07:46 Me 24:31	Su 04:26 VeR 05:50 Ra 08:59

SaR 11:40 Aquarius (3)		Cancer (8)

Capricorn (2)		Leo (9)

Sagittarius (1)	Scorpio (12)	Libra (11)	Virgo (10)
Ke 08:59 As 06:43			Mo 28:51

Navamsha

Ma			As Ke
SaR			Me
Ra	Su VeR	Ju	Mo

Today's Transits

Su Me		Ra Sa	As
Ve			JuR
Mo			
Ma	Ke		

Mahadasha Summary

Ma	Tue	07-25-1961
Ra	Thu	07-25-1968
Ju	Fri	07-25-1986
Sa	Thu	07-25-2002
Me	Sun	07-25-2021
Ke	Sun	07-25-2038
Ve	Mon	07-24-2045
Su	Fri	07-24-2065
Mo	Sat	07-25-2071
Ma	Thu	07-24-2081
Ra	Sat	07-24-2088
Ju	Sun	07-25-2106
Sa	Sat	07-25-2122
Me	Tue	07-25-2141
Ke	Tue	07-25-2158

Current Mahadasha

Sa-Sa	Thu	07-25-2002
Sa-Me	Thu	07-28-2005
Sa-Ke	Sun	04-06-2008
Sa-Ve	Sat	05-16-2009
Sa-Su	Sun	07-15-2012
Sa-Mo	Thu	06-27-2013
Sa-Ma	Tue	01-27-2015
Sa-Ra	Sun	03-06-2016
Sa-Ju	Fri	01-11-2019
Me-Me	Sun	07-25-2021
Me-Ke	Thu	12-21-2023
Me-Ve	Tue	12-17-2024
Me-Su	Mon	10-18-2027
Me-Mo	Thu	08-24-2028
Me-Ma	Wed	01-23-2030

Birth data

Mark
Thu 06-18-1964
19:30:00
Houston, TX
USA
Timezone: 6
Latitude: 29N45'47
Longitude: 95W21'47
Ayan. -23:21:21 Lahiri

Chart 43—Mark

grapefruit. His Rahu, which tends to bring about strange and unusual situations, sits a mere 3 degrees from the planet associated with the genitals, showing the strong possibility for this type of anomaly.

Another health-related 6th house issue can be observed in Steven Spielberg's chart.

As you'll recall, the 6th house rules the liver and kidney area. Spielberg's rising sign is Gemini, and its ruler, Mercury, is placed in the 6th house conjunct with Ketu. Although this placement shows a latent 6th house health issue, it is one that probably wouldn't arise until his Mercury mahadasha began. Look at

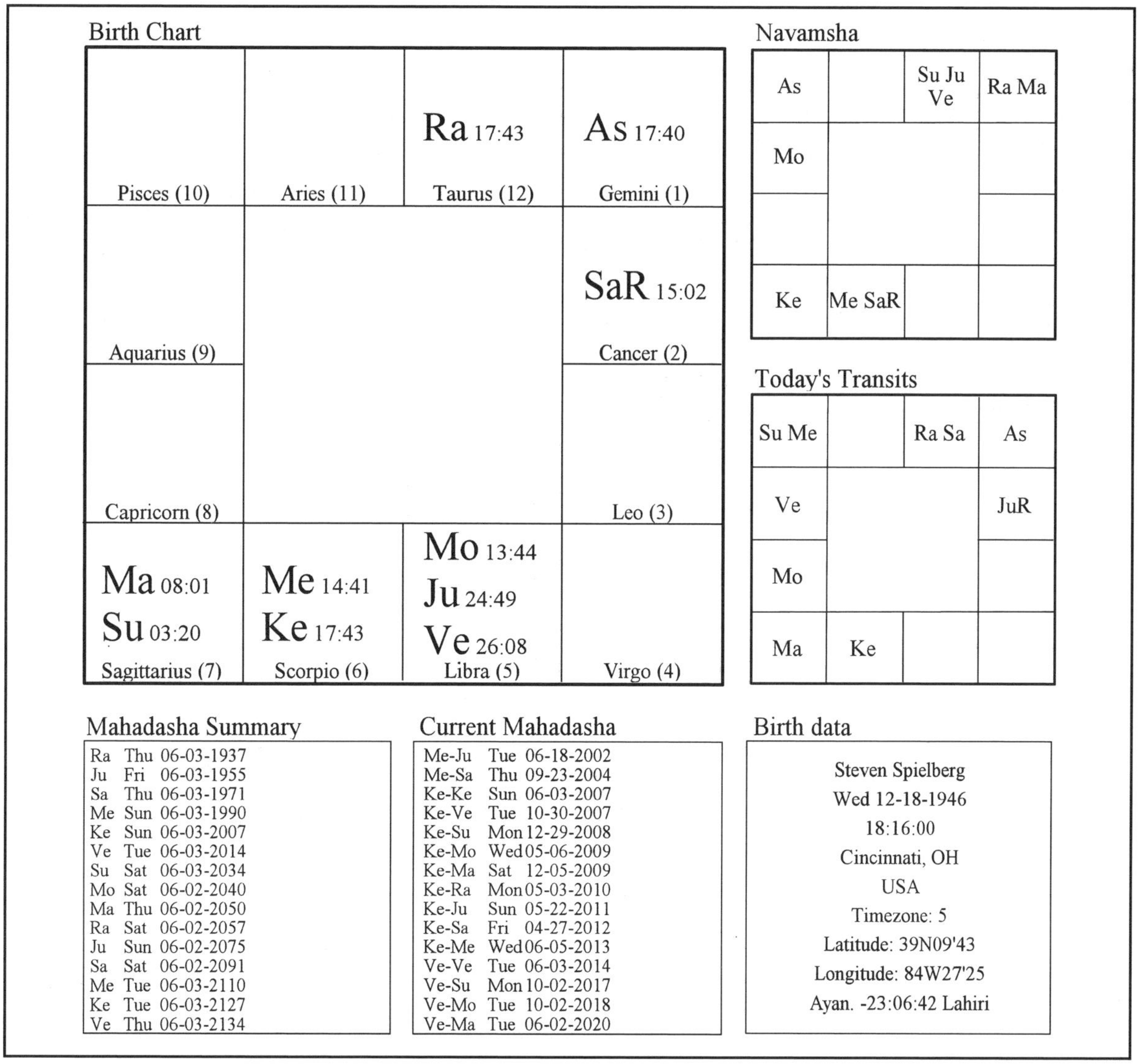

Birth Chart

Pisces (10)	Aries (11)	**Ra** 17:43 Taurus (12)	**As** 17:40 Gemini (1)
Aquarius (9)			**SaR** 15:02 Cancer (2)
Capricorn (8)			Leo (3)
Ma 08:01 **Su** 03:20 Sagittarius (7)	**Me** 14:41 **Ke** 17:43 Scorpio (6)	**Mo** 13:44 **Ju** 24:49 **Ve** 26:08 Libra (5)	Virgo (4)

Navamsha

As		Su Ju Ve	Ra Ma
Mo			
Ke	Me SaR		

Today's Transits

Su Me		Ra Sa	As
Ve			JuR
Mo			
Ma	Ke		

Mahadasha Summary

Ra	Thu	06-03-1937
Ju	Fri	06-03-1955
Sa	Thu	06-03-1971
Me	Sun	06-03-1990
Ke	Sun	06-03-2007
Ve	Tue	06-03-2014
Su	Sat	06-03-2034
Mo	Sat	06-02-2040
Ma	Thu	06-02-2050
Ra	Sat	06-02-2057
Ju	Sun	06-02-2075
Sa	Sat	06-02-2091
Me	Tue	06-03-2110
Ke	Tue	06-03-2127
Ve	Thu	06-03-2134

Current Mahadasha

Me-Ju	Tue	06-18-2002
Me-Sa	Thu	09-23-2004
Ke-Ke	Sun	06-03-2007
Ke-Ve	Tue	10-30-2007
Ke-Su	Mon	12-29-2008
Ke-Mo	Wed	05-06-2009
Ke-Ma	Sat	12-05-2009
Ke-Ra	Mon	05-03-2010
Ke-Ju	Sun	05-22-2011
Ke-Sa	Fri	04-27-2012
Ke-Me	Wed	06-05-2013
Ve-Ve	Tue	06-03-2014
Ve-Su	Mon	10-02-2017
Ve-Mo	Tue	10-02-2018
Ve-Ma	Tue	06-02-2020

Birth data

Steven Spielberg
Wed 12-18-1946
18:16:00
Cincinnati, OH
USA
Timezone: 5
Latitude: 39N09'43
Longitude: 84W27'25
Ayan. -23:06:42 Lahiri

Chart 44—Steven Spielberg

the Mahadasha Summary and you'll notice that he is in the Mercury cycle now. It began in 1990, and since longer mahadashas take more time to get up to speed, it wasn't until the first bhukti occurred in October of 1992 that he fully came under its influence.

When the malefic Rahu bhukti started, in the late fall of 1999, it probably enlivened the latent health issue in Spielberg's 6th house because Rahu opposes his Mercury within 3 degrees. On February 7th, 2000, it was announced that he'd had a kidney removed after an "irregularity" was discovered during a routine physical examination.

Looking at his other planets, the indications in Spielberg's chart that he was destined for greatness couldn't be more obvious. The 5th house, the house of destiny, is occupied by all three benefics——the Moon, Jupiter, and Venus. The Moon rules his 2nd house, the house of creative imagination and wealth. Jupiter rules both his 7th and 10th houses, the houses of professional collaboration and of career, and Venus rules his 5th house in artistic, driven Libra. With such powerful planets in the 5th house, it's no wonder he charged admission to his home movies while his sister sold popcorn when they were children.

Let's look at the chart of Billie Jean King, the great female tennis champion.

Birth Chart

		MaR 24:32	SaR 01:53
Pisces (3)	Aries (4)	Taurus (5)	Gemini (6)
Aquarius (2)			Ra 17:11 Cancer (7)
Ke 17:11 As 04:09 Capricorn (1)			Ju 03:16 Leo (8)
Sagittarius (12)	Su 06:31 Me 13:29 Scorpio (11)	Libra (10)	Mo 07:40 Ve 20:00 Virgo (9)

Navamsha

Mo	Ju		Ke
As			Ve
			MaR Su
Ra	Me	SaR	

Today's Transits

Su Me		Ra Sa	As
Ve			JuR
Mo			
Ma	Ke		

Mahadasha Summary

Su	Sat	12-10-1938
Mo	Sat	12-09-1944
Ma	Fri	12-10-1954
Ra	Sun	12-10-1961
Ju	Mon	12-10-1979
Sa	Sun	12-10-1995
Me	Tue	12-09-2014
Ke	Tue	12-09-2031
Ve	Thu	12-09-2038
Su	Sun	12-09-2058
Mo	Mon	12-08-2064
Ma	Sun	12-09-2074
Ra	Tue	12-09-2081
Ju	Wed	12-09-2099
Sa	Tue	12-10-2115

Current Mahadasha

Sa-Ve	Mon	09-30-2002
Sa-Su	Wed	11-30-2005
Sa-Mo	Sun	11-12-2006
Sa-Ma	Thu	06-12-2008
Sa-Ra	Wed	07-22-2009
Sa-Ju	Mon	05-28-2012
Me-Me	Tue	12-09-2014
Me-Ke	Sun	05-07-2017
Me-Ve	Fri	05-04-2018
Me-Su	Thu	03-04-2021
Me-Mo	Sat	01-08-2022
Me-Ma	Sat	06-10-2023
Me-Ra	Thu	06-06-2024
Me-Ju	Thu	12-24-2026
Me-Sa	Sat	03-31-2029

Birth data

Billie Jean King
Mon 11-22-1943
11:45:00
Long Beach, CA
USA
Timezone: 8
Latitude: 33N46'01
Longitude: 118W11'18
Ayan. -23:04:10 Lahiri

Chart 45—Billie Jean King

Billie Jean's rising sign is Capricorn, a strong earth sign, making her practical and a fighter for what she believes in. The ruler of Capricorn, Saturn, is placed retrograde in her 6th house, the house of enemies. Saturn is an influence that shows conventionality, a conservative nature, and is strongly masculine in energy. Indeed, at the time of King's athletic success, tennis was a man's sport, with male tennis champions making far more prize money and getting more exposure than women did. So the Saturn in Billie Jean's 6th house shows the male-dominated establishment she found herself up against.

Being of an earthy, persevering nature, with the ability to overcome such obstacles, King lobbied constantly and broke through the barriers to establish the first successful women's professional tennis tour. Since Saturn rules her rising sign, she expressed an energy and a will that appeared very male. So she gained credibility, and soon overcame the obstacles by essentially beating the men at their own game.

The skill with which she redefined women's tennis was no doubt affected by Ketu in her rising sign, an influence that brings clever maneuvering. Her ability to shake the tennis institution to its core would be due to her Saturn being retrograde, which enabled her to effect change at the deepest levels.

In 1972, quite fittingly, she was named *Sports Illustrated*'s "Sportsperson of the Year," the first woman so honored.

For another tennis example, let's look at the chart of John McEnroe (Chart 46).

John has Virgo rising, with Rahu in the rising sign a few degrees from the ascendant degree. This position brings McEnroe aggression, frustration, intensity, and anger. It also brings him a lot of worldly success. (Although it's unclear in what sign Rahu is exalted, most agree that Rahu is extremely well placed in Virgo.)

A great deal of McEnroe's frustration has come from his Virgo rising nature. This rising sign brought McEnroe a perfectionist tendency, so detail became all-important to him. When line judges or chair umpires called shots incorrectly, McEnroe would have his worst tirades. Whether or not he expressed it (and he usually did), he always felt their lack of perfection intensely.

The Rahu also made McEnroe an unconventional player. Many seasoned tennis commentators were sometimes amazed that he could even get shots back with his grip, stance, and positioning. Even during slow-motion films of his play, in which pros would analyze his serve and overall game, they had trouble understanding how he played tennis so well, so unconventional was his game.

Now look at his 6th house. The Sun, Mercury, and Venus are all placed there, showing that he faced enormous competition. McEnroe's 6th house indicates he was up against a slew of enemies and challenges, just as a warrior would be. Not only did McEnroe fight, he enjoyed the fight. You can tell because his 6th house ruler, Saturn, is placed in the 4th house, the house of happiness.

Not only did the Rahu give him the

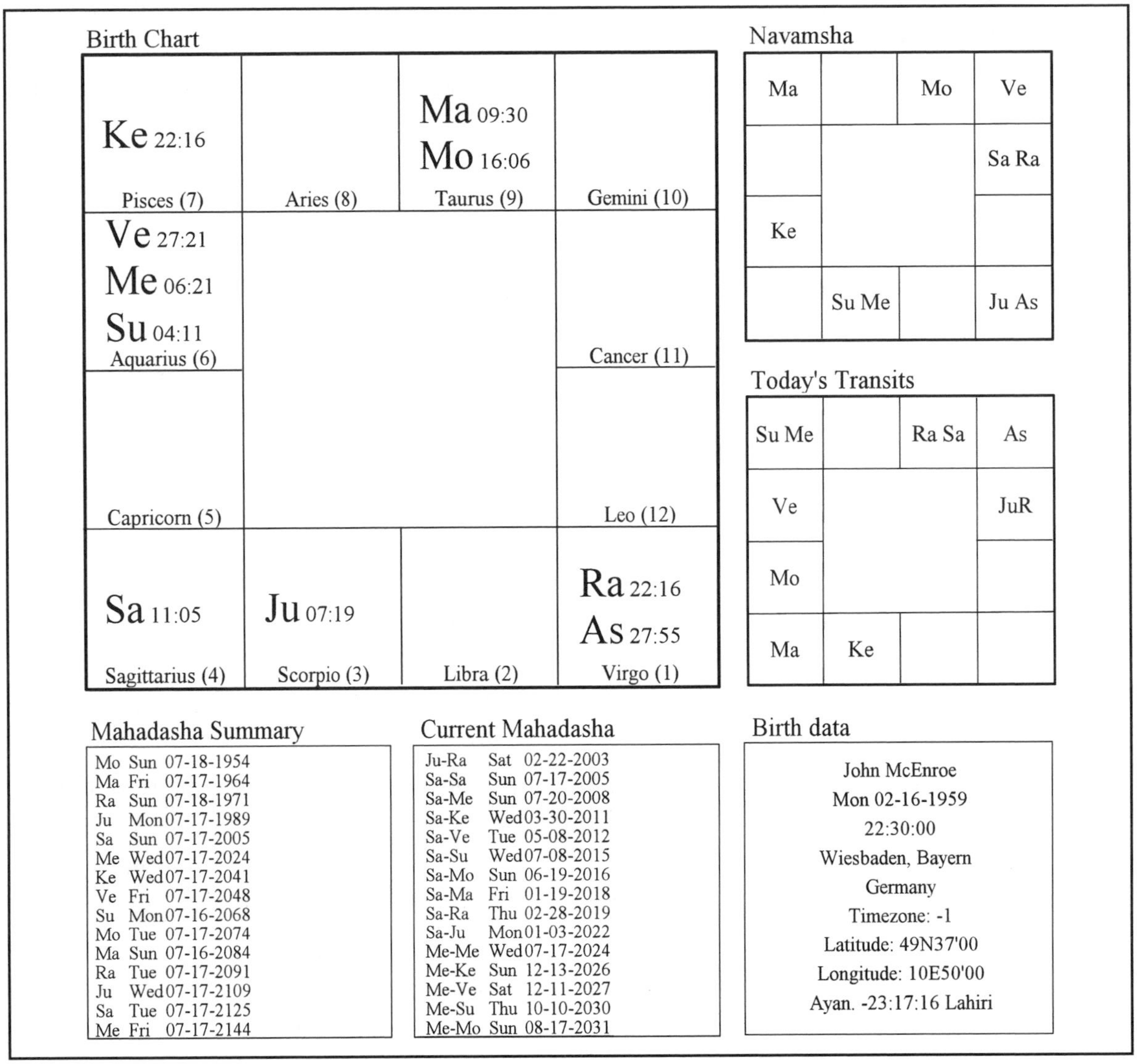

Birth Chart

Ke 22:16 Pisces (7)	Aries (8)	**Ma** 09:30 **Mo** 16:06 Taurus (9)	Gemini (10)
Ve 27:21 **Me** 06:21 **Su** 04:11 Aquarius (6)			Cancer (11)
Capricorn (5)			Leo (12)
Sa 11:05 Sagittarius (4)	**Ju** 07:19 Scorpio (3)	Libra (2)	**Ra** 22:16 **As** 27:55 Virgo (1)

Navamsha

Ma	Mo	Ve
		Sa Ra
Ke		
	Su Me	Ju As

Today's Transits

Su Me	Ra Sa	As
Ve		JuR
Mo		
Ma	Ke	

Mahadasha Summary

Mo	Sun	07-18-1954
Ma	Fri	07-17-1964
Ra	Sun	07-18-1971
Ju	Mon	07-17-1989
Sa	Sun	07-17-2005
Me	Wed	07-17-2024
Ke	Wed	07-17-2041
Ve	Fri	07-17-2048
Su	Mon	07-16-2068
Mo	Tue	07-17-2074
Ma	Sun	07-16-2084
Ra	Tue	07-17-2091
Ju	Wed	07-17-2109
Sa	Tue	07-17-2125
Me	Fri	07-17-2144

Current Mahadasha

Ju-Ra	Sat	02-22-2003
Sa-Sa	Sun	07-17-2005
Sa-Me	Sun	07-20-2008
Sa-Ke	Wed	03-30-2011
Sa-Ve	Tue	05-08-2012
Sa-Su	Wed	07-08-2015
Sa-Mo	Sun	06-19-2016
Sa-Ma	Fri	01-19-2018
Sa-Ra	Thu	02-28-2019
Sa-Ju	Mon	01-03-2022
Me-Me	Wed	07-17-2024
Me-Ke	Sun	12-13-2026
Me-Ve	Sat	12-11-2027
Me-Su	Thu	10-10-2030
Me-Mo	Sun	08-17-2031

Birth data

John McEnroe

Mon 02-16-1959

22:30:00

Wiesbaden, Bayern

Germany

Timezone: -1

Latitude: 49N37'00

Longitude: 10E50'00

Ayan. -23:17:16 Lahiri

Chart 46—John McEnroe

strength and ability to overcome his competition, but it was also during his Rahu mahadasha that he rose to the highest levels in his sport, winning Wimbledon three times and the U.S. Open four times.

REMEDIES

Again, it's important to mention that sometimes suffering can be the catalyst for people's rise to greatness. This is especially true for 6th house issues. Had Oprah not experienced disappointment in life to the degree that she did, perhaps she wouldn't have had such a positive impact on so many people. I would recommend that Oprah strengthen the Moon in her chart. She entered a ten-year Moon mahadasha in September of 2000, and her Moon could use some strengthening. This has already been amplified by Saturn's two-and-a-half-year transit opposing her Moon, which began in the summer of 2000 and lasted through 2002.

She would do well to adopt the Moon mantra, especially on Mondays, and to eat a little less food on that day. A large Indian or Sri Lankan moonstone would also help, as long as the stone was pure in color without blue tints (which would increase the energy of Saturn).

In McEnroe's case, I would recommend he appease the Jupiter in his chart. This can be accomplished by chanting Jupiter mantras on Thursdays, and eating a little less that day. He can also try wearing a yellow sapphire on the index finger of the right hand. This might increase the power in his 4th and 7th houses because Jupiter rules both, but because Jupiter is a malefic for Virgo rising he should experiment with it first. By strengthening his 7th house he would bring more joy to his intimate relationship and marriage house; by strengthening his 4th house, he would bring more happiness into his life. I once heard him doing the play-by-play for a grand-slam tennis match, and when the winner was crowned, McEnroe commented that he hoped the winner could enjoy the glory, since he had been unable to enjoy his times as champion.

Since Spielberg is now in his Mercury mahadasha, it's a time for him to be cautious about his health, particularly now that Saturn is making a two-year transit over his rising sign. Also, beginning in September of 2004, when the Saturn bhukti runs during his Mercury mahadasha, he may experience some added stress. The Ketu mahadasha (which begins in June of 2007) won't help matters, so he should have strong health-strengthening fire rituals performed for these situations. He would also do well to adopt the Mercury mantra and to chant it on Wednesdays, and eat less on that day. He should wear an emerald or green tourmaline on the 5th finger of his right hand.

STRENGTHENING YOUR 6th HOUSE

This is a difficult house for which to make general recommendations. Although malefic planets can express themselves well here, they can also bring health problems. By giving a malefic planet more strength, you may also be increasing the possibility of health problems. Since benefics are generally not well placed in the 6th house, even though you *can* bring them more strength, you always do so in the context of 6th house issues.

The safest remedy for the 6th house is to strengthen the ruler of the house itself (as long as it's well placed). By chanting to the ruler of the 6th house on the day associated with that house, and eating a little bit less on that day, you are helping the house considerably.

If the 6th house has brought you health problems, you can make dramatic inroads toward recovery by having powerful Vedic fire rituals performed for the complaint. Since the 6th house is an upachaya, or improving house, any powerful remedy has the ability to bring about significant results.

SUMMARY

Most people would agree that they learned, and grew more dramatically, from experiences of antagonism than those of comfort and ease. Remember that pressure creates diamonds. Your greatest adversary can actually be your greatest ally in disguise. When His Holiness the Dalai Lama is asked to comment on how he feels about the Chinese invading his country and killing millions of his people, he remarks that he sees the Chinese as his teachers, since they have taught him to cultivate patience. Everyone has a certain amount of antagonism in his or her life, and it's not so much what happens that matters, it's how you react to what happens.

Once you have succeeded at overcoming inner and outer conflicts to some degree, and learn to stand strong for what you believe in, you are ready to unite with another in a deep intimate relationship. That is why the 7th house, the house of marriage, follows the 6th house of enemies. It is here that you find a kindred soul with whom to share life's journey. Though marriage doesn't have to be taken literally, this is still the house that shows a spark of synergy, where a like-minded soul and you meet and realize you can help one another on the path.

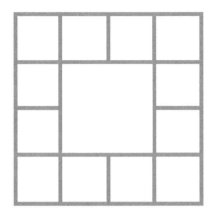

THE 7th HOUSE

Marriage

This house deals primarily with partnerships, and as such, it indicates the nature of your spouse and married life. It can also signify business partnerships, and can show foreign travel, usually connected with business. The 7th house is associated with the organs of the lower abdomen.

From a Vedic astrological perspective, intimate contact between two people creates effects that potentially play out for lifetimes. Imprints from past encounters, friendships, loves, and partnerships affect our psyche in direct proportion to the intensity of the event. Given the long-reaching effects we engender through our intimate relationships, it's important to realize the need to act consciously, carefully, and kindly toward others.

If we choose intimate or marriage partners casually, as if we were cruising through television channels, we do so somewhat unconsciously, and thus find we tend to attract the same types of people. Again and again, we will encounter problematic partners, people who rub us the wrong way in the same kinds of ways, regardless of how different they "appear" on the outside.

You can look to the 7th house to break that pattern. Do you want to know why you always attract needy types, strong types, bossy types, abusive types, nurturing types? Look to the indications displayed by the 7th house, and see what lies beneath your motivations, your impulses, your desires, and your behavior. Then, recognize that you can change the pattern just by being conscious of what drives you.

THE NATURE OF THE 7th HOUSE

Find the 7th house in your chart. If you are Libra rising, your 7th house is Aries. If you are Gemini rising, Sagittarius is your 7th house. Pay close attention to the zodiac sign of the 7th house because the nature of that sign will show you who would be the ideal person to be your life partner.

For instance, if Capricorn is your 7th

house, then you'll do best with grounded, businesslike personalities. If your 7th house is Scorpio, a deep, passionate type is a better choice.

Also, pay attention to the ruling planet of the other person's 7th house. This will inform you how the person best responds to stimuli. Houses ruled by Mercury, for instance, are interested in conversation. Houses ruled by Mars might get bored by lots of talking; they want to go on a hike.

HOW THE 7th HOUSE EXPRESSES ITSELF

Locate the planet that rules your 7th house (Table B), and find where it's placed in your chart. Then read the description below that pertains to this placement.

The 7th House Ruler placed in the 1st house indicates a marriage or business partnership that brings much benefit to your sense of self and purpose. These relationships enhance your self-esteem and help you find direction in life. Marriage or partnership is a wonderful support system for you and it provides you with a strong foundation.

The 7th House Ruler placed in the 2nd house indicates that your partner has good communication skills. Also, by virtue of your association with that person, whether a spouse or a business partner, you are able to make money. You may consider starting a business together.

The 7th House Ruler placed in the 3rd house indicates that your spouse or business partner is driven, courageous, and inspired. He or she may also be talented in the arts. As the 3rd house is associated with adventure, this is not the best placement for marriage, since your partner may always have an eye out for a person who seems more interesting.

The 7th House Ruler placed in the 4th house shows that you and your spouse create a warm, nurturing home environment. Marriage also brings you great happiness. A business partnership may involve real estate or home renovation.

The 7th House Ruler placed in the 5th house indicates that your marriage is based on deep love and affection, not convenience or ulterior motives. You probably feel as if you've known your spouse forever. This is a good position for children, and happy relationships with them.

The 7th House Ruler placed in the 6th house indicates that your spouse may be a healer or may be in the medical profession. He or she may also attract jealous competitors. This position can sometimes indicate that a spouse suffers from health problems, or the possibility of a difficult marriage.

The 7th House Ruler placed in the 7th house indicates a powerful spouse or business partner, and a strong positive relationship with him or her. This position also suggests you have a charisma that tends to attract lots of suitors, either for marriage or for partnership.

The 7th House Ruler placed in the 8th house indicates a spouse who is interested in mysticism or the occult. He or she may also accrue money through some unearned means, such as an inheritance or lottery. This position can indicate more than one marriage, ill health for a spouse, or loss from a business partnership.

The 7th House Ruler placed in the 9th house indicates that your spouse or partner may be deeply spiritual. Your association with this marriage or business partner increases your luck. Your spouse's father may also be involved in the venture, as in a family business.

The 7th House Ruler placed in the 10th house shows that your spouse or business partner is instrumental in enhancing your career. You may be in business with your spouse, or he or she may be strongly career driven.

The 7th House Ruler placed in the 11th house indicates that your association with your spouse or business partner gives you numerous opportunities for happiness or success. You are lucky in speculative ventures because of your partner's influence or insight. He or she may have a friend who facilitates such ventures, and who is a strong positive influence.

The 7th House Ruler placed in the 12th house is generally not favorable, showing the possibility of unhappiness in marriage, more than one marriage, and the ill health of a partner. It can also show a partner who is spiritually oriented or who is from a faraway place.

IF THERE ARE PLANETS IN THE 7th HOUSE

To help fine-tune the descriptions below, you'll want to assess whether the planet is welcome in the house in which it is placed (Table G). If the planet is in the house of a friend, the positive nature of the following description is enhanced. If the planet is in the house of an enemy, more of the negative possibilities need to be considered.

Sun (Su) in the 7th house shows a partner who is powerful yet who can remain aloof. He or she may also be somewhat irritable by nature.

Moon (Mo) in the 7th house indicates that marriage is beneficial, but if afflicted can show the inability to settle down with just one person.

Mars (Ma) in the 7th house shows strong kuja dosha, which can indicate more than one marriage. The partner could also be powerful or controlling.

Mercury (Me) in the 7th house, if unafflicted, brings an intelligent partner who appears younger than his or her years. Otherwise it could indicate a mentally unstable mate.

Jupiter (Ju) in the 7th house brings a prosperous, supportive, caring partner. If afflicted, your partner may not get recognition equal to the amount of work he or she performs, or may run into legal problems.

Venus (Ve) in the 7th house brings a beautiful partner who enjoys refinement and aesthetic sensibilities. Afflicted, it can make you promiscuous.

Saturn (Sa) in the 7th house indicates that you may marry an older person, or one who is more mature than you are, or you may delay marriage. Afflicted, Saturn can bring loneliness in marriage.

Rahu (Ra) in the 7th house is not a good position for the longevity of a marriage. It also shows an overpowering partner, or one from an indigenous culture.

Ketu (Ke) in the 7th house brings a mystical or spiritual partner. Afflicted, it can lead to more than one marriage, or a partner who comes from a foreign land.

OTHER CONSIDERATIONS

- Note the element associated with your 7th house. Remember that fire signs are driven; earth signs are patient; air signs are creative; and water signs are emotional.
- Also note the quality of your 7th house. Cardinal signs initiate; fixed signs stabilize; and mutable signs seek change.

Now check any aspects to the 7th house:

- Are any planets located in the same house as, or opposed to any planet in, the 7th house? If so, are those planets friendly, neutral, or enemies? (See Table F.) For instance, say your Mars is placed in the 7th house and opposed by its enemy Saturn. This planetary combination shows the possibility of violence in the partnership.
- Remember that Mars energizes the house it's in, as well as the 4th, 7th, and 8th houses from itself. This means if Mars is placed in the 12th, 1st, or 4th house of your chart, it throws an aspect onto your 7th house, making your partner proactive, passionate, and possibly promiscuous.
- Saturn restricts or brings discipline to the house it's in, as well as the 3rd, 7th, and 10th houses from itself. This means if Saturn is placed in the 10th, 1st, or 5th house of your chart, it throws an aspect onto your 7th house, bringing delays in meeting a spouse, or causing you to be attracted to older, more mature types.
- Jupiter expands or brings optimism to the house it's in, as well as the 5th, 7th, and 9th houses from itself. This means that if Jupiter is placed in the 11th, 1st, or 3rd house of your chart, it throws an aspect onto your 7th house, increasing the benefits of married life.
- If you want to find out when your chart's 7th house energies will be enlivened, look to the 7th house ruler, or any planet located in the 7th house. Examine the

Mahadasha Summary of your chart to see when that planet will come into power, and that will give you your answer. To find shorter periods when 7th house issues will be highlighted, look to the 7th house ruler or any planet located in the 7th house, and find the time its bhukti will run.

- Notice any influence transiting planets are having on your 7th house, or 7th house ruler. Jupiter passing over the 7th very often brings marriage. Saturn or Rahu transits put your partnership through a certain amount of stress that can either solidify or break up the relationship. You can chant to the planet that is favorably transiting your rising sign, on the appropriate day for that planet, to enhance its effects.

THE INSTITUTION OF MARRIAGE

Vedic astrology makes an important distinction between an intimate relationship and marriage. Although marriage may seem like a mere formality in our contemporary society, from a Vedic astrological standpoint, an indissoluble bond is created by joining in matrimony that does not exist in a courtship, even if the courtship has lasted a decade.

It's not uncommon for couples who have dated or even lived together for years to decide eventually to marry. However, if the planets in their charts do not support marriage, soon after the wedding the couple may feel like strangers. They sense that they made a big mistake. This happens because during courtship, antagonistic planets between two people slide over each other easily, as if Teflon coated. Points of contention or great differences don't strongly impede the way they get along. In fact, disagreements are often explained away as being unimportant or even viewed as the spice that keeps things interesting. Generally, the rough spots don't stay difficult for long.

But when a couple whose planets are antagonistic decides to marry, those planets lock together. Suddenly those points of stress that could once slip in and out of tension are locked, and a person may feel trapped, suffocated, or overwhelmed by the energy of the other. Or they can feel a sudden distance, as if their spouse was just a friend instead of a husband or a wife (same-sex marriage works the same way). The little things that used to be endearing idiosyncrasies during a courtship can become intensely annoying or off-putting in a marriage. Nonetheless, if you are committed to making a marriage work, and you are willing to concentrate on healing the negativity between yourself and your partner, you *can* make the marriage last. Your own will, passion, and compassion can bring about enormous results. But please, consult the planets first!

COMPATIBILITY

When seeking to determine compatibility between two people, the Kuta System is traditionally employed in Vedic astrology. It's a rather complex system of twelve factors based on the Moon's position in the charts. Because most Vedic astrological software can calculate this with a push of a button, and there is some doubt as to the efficacy of this system without studying the overall makeup of the charts, I have decided instead to compare charts in this chapter by visually laying them atop one another—a technique called synastry. This allows us to gauge the relationship between the rising signs and planetary positions between charts in the context of compatibility. Although this is not technically a Vedic astrological appraoch, most Vedic astrologers I know use it. And I feel certain you will find it most accurate and useful.

Since this chapter is already quite involved, I have not mentioned the navamsha chart much in the following examples. But don't pretend it's not there. The navamsha chart is known as the "marriage chart," and as such should be looked at as closely as the birth chart in compatibility issues. All you'll need to do is analyze the navamsha chart in exactly the way I analyze the birth chart. Ask yourself the same questions: Are the rising signs compatible? How about the Moons? And the other planets? I feel confident that if more people utilized the information you are about to gather in the following chapter, many more marriages would remain intact.

When analyzing two charts for compatibility in marriage, it's important that the Moons and Venuses be well placed. Good placements include conjunction (in the same house), sextile (the 3rd house from itself), trine (the 5th house from itself), and opposition (the 7th house from itself).

Harmony in relationships is challenged when planets are in square (the 4th house from itself), or in the 6th, 8th, or 2nd and 12th houses from each other.

The rising signs can be in square as long as you thrive on being with someone whose external expression of himself or herself is quite different from your own. Otherwise, the rising signs should be conjunct, in sextile, trine, or opposition positions.

When considering planetary compatibility, recognize that the house that planet occupies will inflect the characteristic of the planet with its own temperament. So even if the aspects are favorable, the way those planets interact may not be satisfactory.

For instance, say one person has Venus in Cancer, while the partner has Venus in Scorpio. Though their Venuses are in trine, and favorable, the Cancer Venus wants soft, nurturing expressions of love, while Scorpio Venus wants intense, energetic exchanges.

For compatibility in business, the rules change. In many cases business partners don't necessarily want their planets in compatible positions since one brings strength where the other has weakness, and vice versa. This opposition helps with the overall success of a company. You don't need a warm, fuzzy relationship in business. You need someone with an edge to motivate and challenge you. The only difficulty comes when your differences are so disharmonious that they impede the conduct of business.

Let's look at some compatibility in charts.

For an example of a nice courtship that became a marriage from hell, consider the charts of Sharon (Chart 47) and Ken (Chart 48).

Sharon was born with Pisces rising. Looking at her 7th house, which is Virgo, we see no planets. But Virgo's ruler, Mercury, is in her 8th house, the house of loss, which indi-

cates the potential failure of her first marriage. An astrologer could see this woman's chart on the day of her birth and know that she was likely to suffer at least one divorce because of this planetary configuration. Although we don't know Ken's time of birth, what's more important in this example are the planets he has in Virgo, since Virgo is Sharon's 7th house.

Birth Chart

As 09:28 Pisces (1)	 Aries (2)	**Ra** 18:47 Taurus (3)	 Gemini (4)
  Aquarius (12)			**SaR** 15:43 Cancer (5)
Mo 07:38 Capricorn (11)			 Leo (6)
  Sagittarius (10)	**Su** 12:50 **Ke** 18:47 **Ma** 22:56 Scorpio (9)	**Ju** 20:43 **VeR** 25:53 **MeR** 28:32 Libra (8)	 Virgo (7)

Navamsha

Mo	Ju	VeR	MeR Ra
Ma			
Ke	SaR	Su	As

Today's Transits

Su Me		Ra Sa	As
Ve			JuR
Mo			
Ma	Ke		

Mahadasha Summary

Su	Sun	12-21-1941
Mo	Mon	12-21-1947
Ma	Sat	12-21-1957
Ra	Sun	12-20-1964
Ju	Tue	12-21-1982
Sa	Mon	12-21-1998
Me	Wed	12-20-2017
Ke	Wed	12-20-2034
Ve	Fri	12-20-2041
Su	Tue	12-20-2061
Mo	Tue	12-20-2067
Ma	Mon	12-20-2077
Ra	Tue	12-19-2084
Ju	Thu	12-21-2102
Sa	Wed	12-21-2118

Current Mahadasha

Sa-Me	Sun	12-23-2001
Sa-Ke	Wed	09-01-2004
Sa-Ve	Tue	10-11-2005
Sa-Su	Thu	12-11-2008
Sa-Mo	Mon	11-23-2009
Sa-Ma	Fri	06-24-2011
Sa-Ra	Thu	08-02-2012
Sa-Ju	Tue	06-09-2015
Me-Me	Wed	12-20-2017
Me-Ke	Mon	05-18-2020
Me-Ve	Sat	05-15-2021
Me-Su	Fri	03-15-2024
Me-Mo	Sun	01-19-2025
Me-Ma	Sun	06-21-2026
Me-Ra	Fri	06-18-2027

Birth data

Sharon
Thu 11-28-1946
14:00:00
Miami, FL
USA
Timezone: 5
Latitude: 25N46'26
Longitude: 80W11'38
Ayan. -23:06:39 Lahiri

Chart 47—Sharon

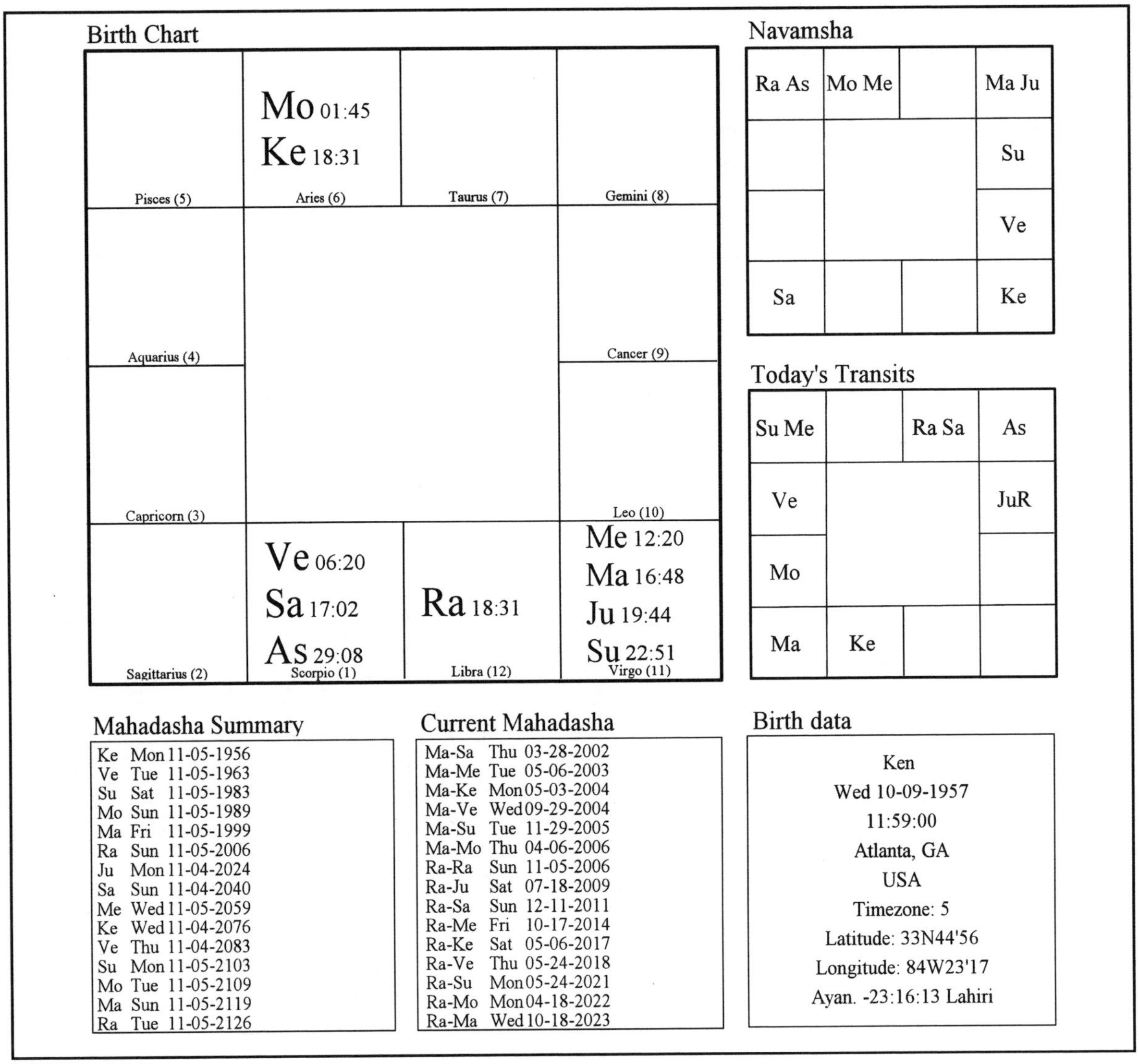

Birth Chart

Pisces (5)	Aries (6) Mo 01:45 Ke 18:31	Taurus (7)	Gemini (8)
Aquarius (4)			Cancer (9)
Capricorn (3)			Leo (10)
Sagittarius (2) Ve 06:20 Sa 17:02 As 29:08	Scorpio (1)	Libra (12) Ra 18:31	Virgo (11) Me 12:20 Ma 16:48 Ju 19:44 Su 22:51

Navamsha

Ra As	Mo Me		Ma Ju
			Su
			Ve
Sa			Ke

Today's Transits

Su Me		Ra Sa	As
Ve			JuR
Mo			
Ma	Ke		

Mahadasha Summary

Ke	Mon	11-05-1956
Ve	Tue	11-05-1963
Su	Sat	11-05-1983
Mo	Sun	11-05-1989
Ma	Fri	11-05-1999
Ra	Sun	11-05-2006
Ju	Mon	11-04-2024
Sa	Sun	11-04-2040
Me	Wed	11-05-2059
Ke	Wed	11-04-2076
Ve	Thu	11-04-2083
Su	Mon	11-05-2103
Mo	Tue	11-05-2109
Ma	Sun	11-05-2119
Ra	Tue	11-05-2126

Current Mahadasha

Ma-Sa	Thu	03-28-2002
Ma-Me	Tue	05-06-2003
Ma-Ke	Mon	05-03-2004
Ma-Ve	Wed	09-29-2004
Ma-Su	Tue	11-29-2005
Ma-Mo	Thu	04-06-2006
Ra-Ra	Sun	11-05-2006
Ra-Ju	Sat	07-18-2009
Ra-Sa	Sun	12-11-2011
Ra-Me	Fri	10-17-2014
Ra-Ke	Sat	05-06-2017
Ra-Ve	Thu	05-24-2018
Ra-Su	Mon	05-24-2021
Ra-Mo	Mon	04-18-2022
Ra-Ma	Wed	10-18-2023

Birth data

Ken
Wed 10-09-1957
11:59:00
Atlanta, GA
USA
Timezone: 5
Latitude: 33N44'56
Longitude: 84W23'17
Ayan. -23:16:13 Lahiri

Chart 48—Ken

Ken has Mercury (a neutral planet, taking on the power of the planet most powerfully influencing it—in this case, malefic Mars), Jupiter, and Sun all placed in Virgo. Although Ken's Jupiter would normally be beneficial for Sharon because it aspects her rising sign, his Jupiter falls unfortunately close to the Sun, creating a combustion. The beneficial effects of Jupiter are lessened greatly by the Sun.

With four intense planets occupying Sharon's 7th house, Ken's and her relationship was a whirlwind of intense sexuality, passion, obsession, and arguments. In Ken, Sharon had finally found the hot-blooded lover she wanted, and they decided to marry.

If only they had known about Vedic astrology!

When the Mars of one person occupies the 7th house of the person he or she marries, there is a tendency for that person to be promiscuous. The Mars in Virgo for Ken also aspects his Aries Moon, giving him an explosive temper. Sharon's Saturn hits its enemy Mars in Ken's chart almost to the exact degree from Cancer. Finally, Sharon's Mars and Sun sit directly on their enemy, Saturn, in Ken's chart, in the house of intensely emotional Scorpio.

This all makes for a highly inflammatory relationship. The passion Ken and Sharon felt turned to antagonism the moment they married. The catalyst planets, the Saturn and Mars in her chart, locked strongly with their enemies, Mars and Sun in his chart.

Even though neither Sharon nor Ken intentionally set out to hurt each other, the nature of their planets when locked in by marriage became extremely antagonistic. Because neither knew how to face the emotional work they needed to do, theirs became a marriage of emotional highs and lows. Within a short period of time he began cheating on her (his Mars in her 7th). Then he became physically abusive. Sharon finally decided to divorce him after he battered her and broke her ribs.

Just as the influences of difficult planets can be amplified, so too can the positive effects of planets. When well-placed planets are further enhanced by marriage, the results can be rewarding on every level. For instance,

I have a young client who married a woman and soon thereafter was worth more than $1 million. Why?

Her exalted Sun sits on his rising sign, enhancing his confidence. Her powerful Venus aspects his 2nd house, bringing support to his house of wealth. Her exalted Mars placed in his 10th house gave him the energy to succeed professionally. Finally, his Venus in the 4th house (material prosperity) is empowered by being conjunct her exalted Jupiter, opposed by her exalted Mars. With a woman like that, a man can go places. Her planets fortify not just his wealth houses but his entire chart.

KUJA DOSHA

Kuja dosha is a specific placement of Mars in the chart that can bring obstacles to the peaceful enjoyment of married life. It's a very common phenomenon (about 6 out of 10 charts have it). It occurs when Mars is in the 1st house (unless in Aries), in the 4th house (unless in Scorpio), in the 7th house (unless in Capricorn or Pisces), in the 8th house (unless in Cancer), or in the 12th house (unless in Sagittarius). If kuja dosha is strong in a chart, it can indicate the possibility of more than one marriage if the first marriage takes place before the person is thirty years of age.

The easiest way to neutralize kuja dosha is to marry someone else who has it. In fact, I have seen several charts of people who have been married most of their lives in relative happiness, both of whom have kuja dosha. Had one or the other been without kuja dosha, that same marriage might not have lasted a fraction of that time. Or, if the marriage had lasted, it would have been a very unhappy one. The challenge inherent in finding another person who also has kuja dosha is that other people who also have it may seem boring to you.

A common tendency in people with kuja dosha is to choose excitement over commitment. I've heard clients say, "I'd rather have a marriage that lasts six months with someone I feel passionate about than one that lasts a lifetime with someone boring." Sound familiar?

In addition to kuja dosha, Rahu (the north lunar node) and Ketu (the south lunar node) can also cause disturbances to marriage when either is placed in the 1st house. (Because the lunar nodes always travel in opposition, if one is in the 1st house, the other is automatically in the 7th.)

Rahu or Ketu in the 1st or 7th houses causes relationship upheavals in a slightly different fashion than kuja dosha, however.

Mars is the planet of energy. In kuja dosha, its energetic expression wants to be free and independent (1st house), extremely sexual (4th, 8th, and 12th houses), or promiscuous (7th house). Rahu in the 1st house, on the other hand, affects one's confidence. To compensate for a feeling of inadequacy, the person will generally act in an egocentric and overly confident manner.

That's a tough person to be married to, especially if he or she is not willing to deal with his or her sense of inadequacy and instead constantly tries to cover it up.

If a person marries someone with Rahu in the 7th, on the other hand, it's possible that marriage partner is from a foreign country, or has a different cultural/religious background. Even then, they may still be strong-willed and controlling (or both).

A good example can be seen in the charts of Melanie Griffith and Antonio Banderas.

Look at Griffith's chart (Chart 49), with Aries rising, Ketu in her 1st house, and Rahu in the 7th. Now look at Banderas's chart (Chart 50). He has Aquarius rising, with Ketu also in his 1st house and Rahu in the 7th. Since these positions don't favor happiness in marriage, it's no wonder both Melanie and Antonio were previously divorced.

With Rahu placed in the 7th house in both of their charts, it makes sense that each would marry a person from a different cultural background. Although Ketu in their 1st houses creates difficulty in marriage, when both charts have that same position, they balance each other. Because they have gone through similar life experiences, they feel as if they're on the same page, and have learned similar lessons.

Glancing at the rest of their planets, you'll notice that their Suns are both in Cancer, Venuses are both in Leo, Moons are in a harmonious sextile, and rising signs are also in sextile. However, since Rahu shows a powerful, sometimes controlling presence, and they both have Rahu placed in their marriage house, this indicates they have both married headstrong people.

Look at Antonio's Mars in Taurus, a stubborn, fixed sign. Now look at the retrograde

Saturn in Melanie's chart in Scorpio, a deeply intense, emotional sign. Mars and Saturn, strong enemies, oppose one another just a few degrees apart. Fireworks!

Let's also look at an example of kuja dosha, specifically when one person has it and the other doesn't. A good example would be John F. Kennedy and Jackie Onassis.

As we are only speaking in terms of intimacy and marriage, we will only address those aspects of the charts. JFK's chart (Chart 51) shows a man of tremendous sexual appetite. We can see this from (among other planetary combinations) his Mars and Mercury in the 8th house and his Moon in the 12th. Mars in the 8th house also indicates strong kuja dosha.

Birth Chart				Navamsha			
	Ke 21:43 As 26:47			Ju	Ra		Ma Mo
Pisces (12)	Aries (1)	Taurus (2)	Gemini (3)	Su			
			Su 23:58				
Aquarius (11)			Cancer (4)	As	SaR Ve	Me Ke	
			Ma 07:57 Me 21:07 Ve 24:52				
Mo 19:41				**Today's Transits**			
Capricorn (10)			Leo (5)	Su Me		Ra Sa	As
	SaR 14:24	Ra 21:43	Ju 07:17	Ve			JuR
				Mo			
Sagittarius (9)	Scorpio (8)	Libra (7)	Virgo (6)	Ma	Ke		

Mahadasha Summary		Current Mahadasha		Birth data
Mo Wed 05-03-1950		Sa-Sa Wed 05-02-2001		Melanie Griffith
Ma Mon 05-02-1960		Sa-Me Wed 05-05-2004		Fri 08-09-1957
Ra Wed 05-03-1967		Sa-Ke Sat 01-13-2007		23:49:00
Ju Thu 05-02-1985		Sa-Ve Fri 02-22-2008		New York, NY
Sa Wed 05-02-2001		Sa-Su Sun 04-24-2011		USA
Me Sat 05-02-2020		Sa-Mo Thu 04-05-2012		Timezone: 5
Ke Sat 05-02-2037		Sa-Ma Mon 11-04-2013		Latitude: 40N42'51
Ve Mon 05-02-2044		Sa-Ra Sun 12-14-2014		Longitude: 74W00'23
Su Fri 05-02-2064		Sa-Ju Fri 10-20-2017		Ayan. -23:16:08 Lahiri
Mo Fri 05-02-2070		Me-Me Sat 05-02-2020		
Ma Wed 05-01-2080		Me-Ke Thu 09-29-2022		
Ra Fri 05-02-2087		Me-Ve Tue 09-26-2023		
Ju Sat 05-02-2105		Me-Su Mon 07-27-2026		
Sa Fri 05-02-2121		Me-Mo Wed 06-02-2027		
Me Mon 05-02-2140		Me-Ma Tue 10-31-2028		

Chart 49—Melanie Griffith

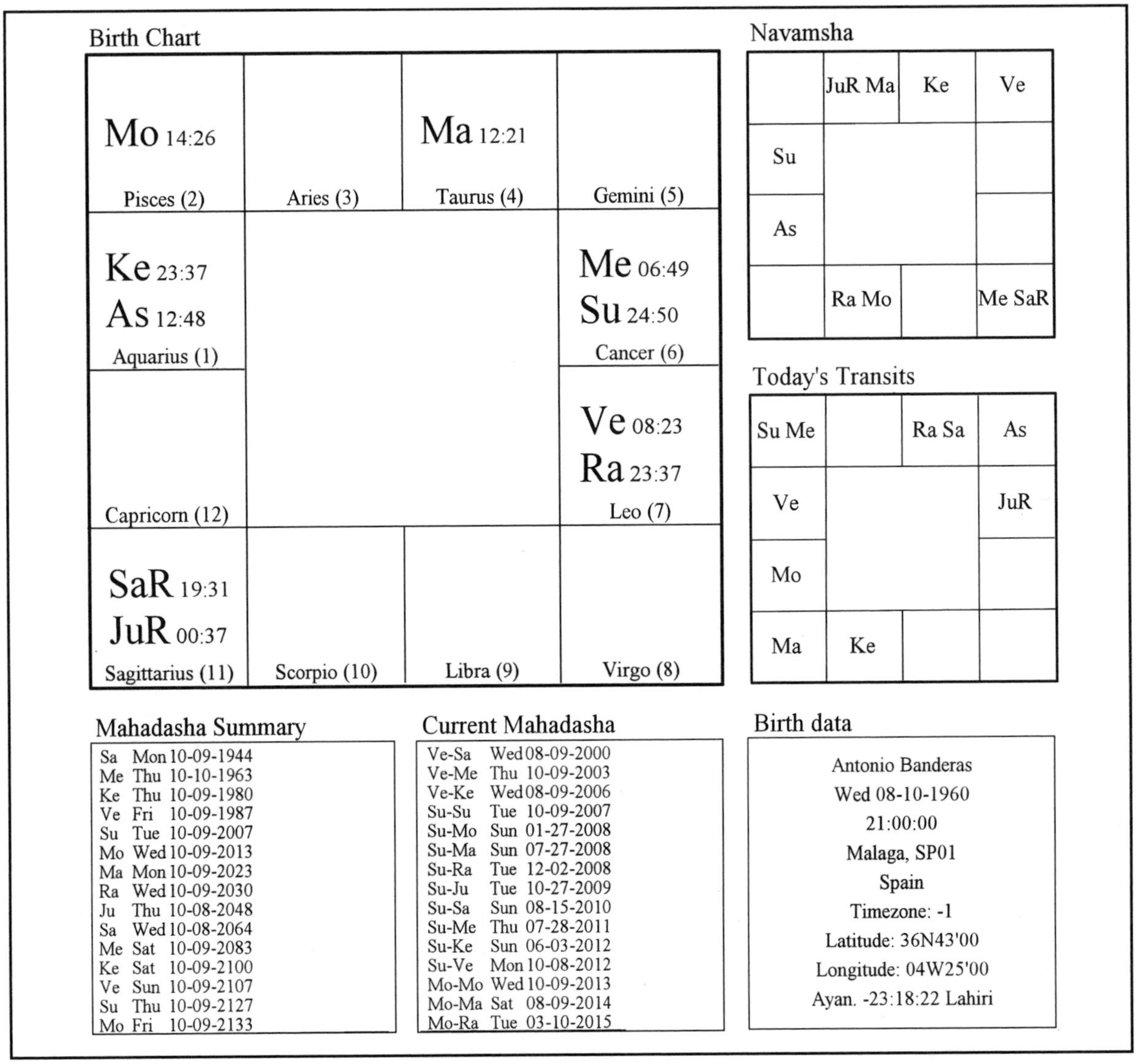

Birth Chart

Mo 14:26		**Ma** 12:21	
Pisces (2)	Aries (3)	Taurus (4)	Gemini (5)
Ke 23:37 **As** 12:48			**Me** 06:49 **Su** 24:50
Aquarius (1)			Cancer (6)
			Ve 08:23 **Ra** 23:37
Capricorn (12)			Leo (7)
SaR 19:31 **JuR** 00:37			
Sagittarius (11)	Scorpio (10)	Libra (9)	Virgo (8)

Navamsha

	JuR Ma	Ke	Ve
Su			
As			
	Ra Mo		Me SaR

Today's Transits

Su Me		Ra Sa	As
Ve			JuR
Mo			
Ma	Ke		

Mahadasha Summary

Sa	Mon	10-09-1944
Me	Thu	10-10-1963
Ke	Thu	10-09-1980
Ve	Fri	10-09-1987
Su	Tue	10-09-2007
Mo	Wed	10-09-2013
Ma	Mon	10-09-2023
Ra	Wed	10-09-2030
Ju	Thu	10-08-2048
Sa	Wed	10-08-2064
Me	Sat	10-09-2083
Ke	Sat	10-09-2100
Ve	Sun	10-09-2107
Su	Thu	10-09-2127
Mo	Fri	10-09-2133

Current Mahadasha

Ve-Sa	Wed	08-09-2000
Ve-Me	Thu	10-09-2003
Ve-Ke	Wed	08-09-2006
Su-Su	Tue	10-09-2007
Su-Mo	Sun	01-27-2008
Su-Ma	Sun	07-27-2008
Su-Ra	Tue	12-02-2008
Su-Ju	Tue	10-27-2009
Su-Sa	Sun	08-15-2010
Su-Me	Thu	07-28-2011
Su-Ke	Sun	06-03-2012
Su-Ve	Mon	10-08-2012
Mo-Mo	Wed	10-09-2013
Mo-Ma	Sat	08-09-2014
Mo-Ra	Tue	03-10-2015

Birth data

Antonio Banderas

Wed 08-10-1960

21:00:00

Malaga, SP01

Spain

Timezone: -1

Latitude: 36N43'00

Longitude: 04W25'00

Ayan. -23:18:22 Lahiri

Chart 50—Antonio Banderas

Although Jackie (Chart 52) does not have kuja dosha, Ketu in her rising sign and Rahu in the 7th show a fair amount of unhappiness in married life. Due to her Rahu in the 7th, the chart also indicates that at some point she would be attracted to a person of a different religious or cultural background (Ari Onassis).

JFK's strong Saturn, which strikes Jackie's Sun, Mercury, and Moon by aspect very directly in her 7th house, shows that she could not feel fulfillment in this relationship. In fact, she would feel restricted (his Saturn on her Sun), mentally agitated (his Saturn on her Mercury), and depressed as a result (his

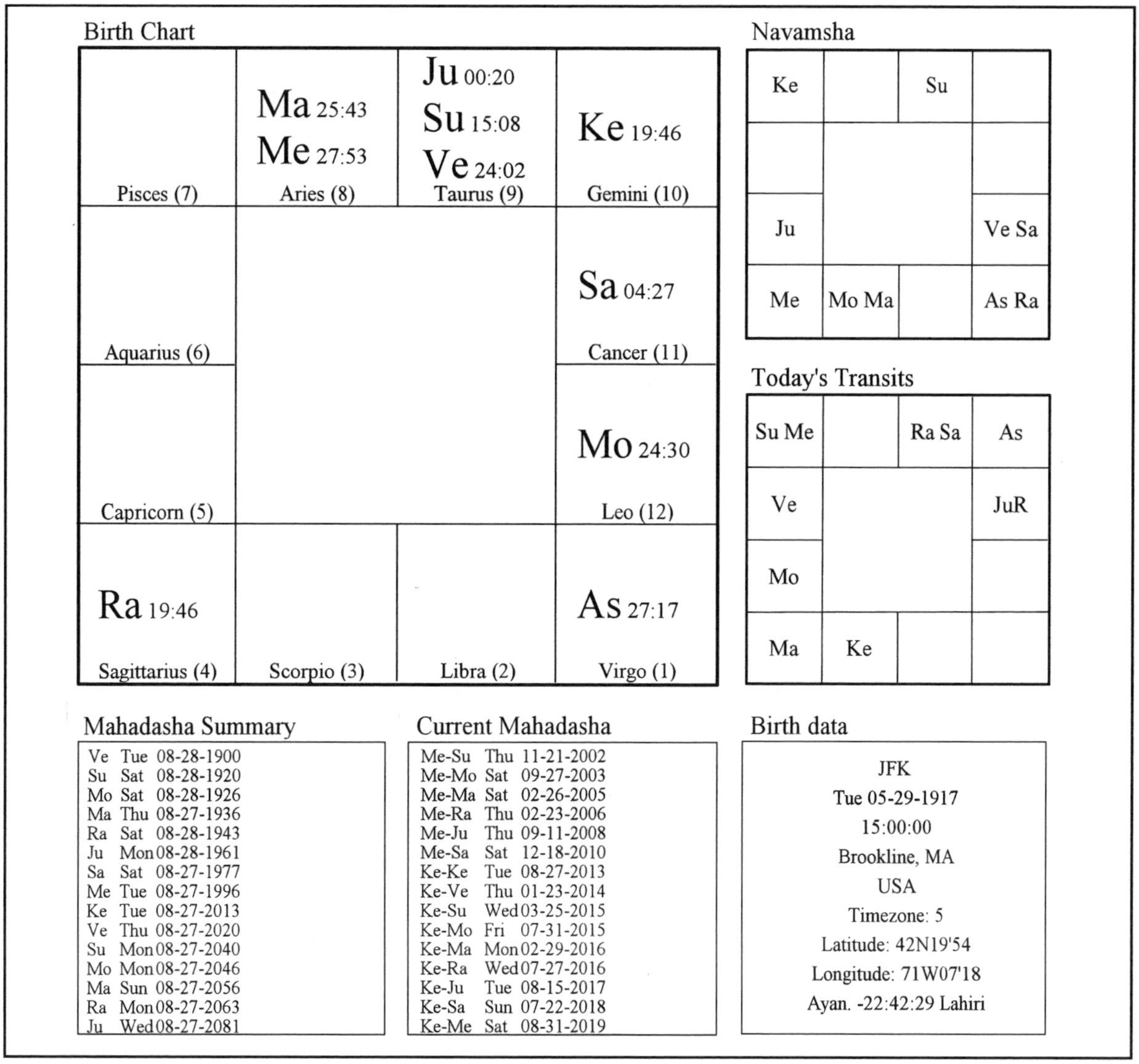

Birth Chart			
	Ma 25:43 Me 27:53	Ju 00:20 Su 15:08 Ve 24:02	Ke 19:46
Pisces (7)	Aries (8)	Taurus (9)	Gemini (10)
			Sa 04:27
Aquarius (6)			Cancer (11)
			Mo 24:30
Capricorn (5)			Leo (12)
Ra 19:46			As 27:17
Sagittarius (4)	Scorpio (3)	Libra (2)	Virgo (1)

Navamsha			
Ke		Su	
Ju			Ve Sa
Me	Mo Ma		As Ra

Today's Transits			
Su Me		Ra Sa	As
Ve			JuR
Mo			
Ma	Ke		

Mahadasha Summary

Ve	Tue	08-28-1900
Su	Sat	08-28-1920
Mo	Sat	08-28-1926
Ma	Thu	08-27-1936
Ra	Sat	08-28-1943
Ju	Mon	08-28-1961
Sa	Sat	08-27-1977
Me	Tue	08-27-1996
Ke	Tue	08-27-2013
Ve	Thu	08-27-2020
Su	Mon	08-27-2040
Mo	Mon	08-27-2046
Ma	Sun	08-27-2056
Ra	Mon	08-27-2063
Ju	Wed	08-27-2081

Current Mahadasha

Me-Su	Thu	11-21-2002
Me-Mo	Sat	09-27-2003
Me-Ma	Sat	02-26-2005
Me-Ra	Thu	02-23-2006
Me-Ju	Thu	09-11-2008
Me-Sa	Sat	12-18-2010
Ke-Ke	Tue	08-27-2013
Ke-Ve	Thu	01-23-2014
Ke-Su	Wed	03-25-2015
Ke-Mo	Fri	07-31-2015
Ke-Ma	Mon	02-29-2016
Ke-Ra	Wed	07-27-2016
Ke-Ju	Tue	08-15-2017
Ke-Sa	Sun	07-22-2018
Ke-Me	Sat	08-31-2019

Birth data

JFK

Tue 05-29-1917

15:00:00

Brookline, MA

USA

Timezone: 5

Latitude: 42N19'54

Longitude: 71W07'18

Ayan. -22:42:29 Lahiri

Chart 51—JFK

Saturn throwing an aspect onto her Moon).

In contrast, if we consider JFK and Marilyn Monroe's charts, though their intimate connection is only rumored, we see an entirely different picture. (See Chart 53 for Marilyn.)

Unlike JFK and Jackie's rising signs, which are in the 2nd and 12th houses from one another, JFK and Marilyn's are in sextile, a very friendly, favorable position.

Their Suns are conjunct, showing close physical rapport. Her Venus is conjunct with his Mars in his 8th house, a combination of planets that expresses intense sexual passion in the house considered strongly sensual in

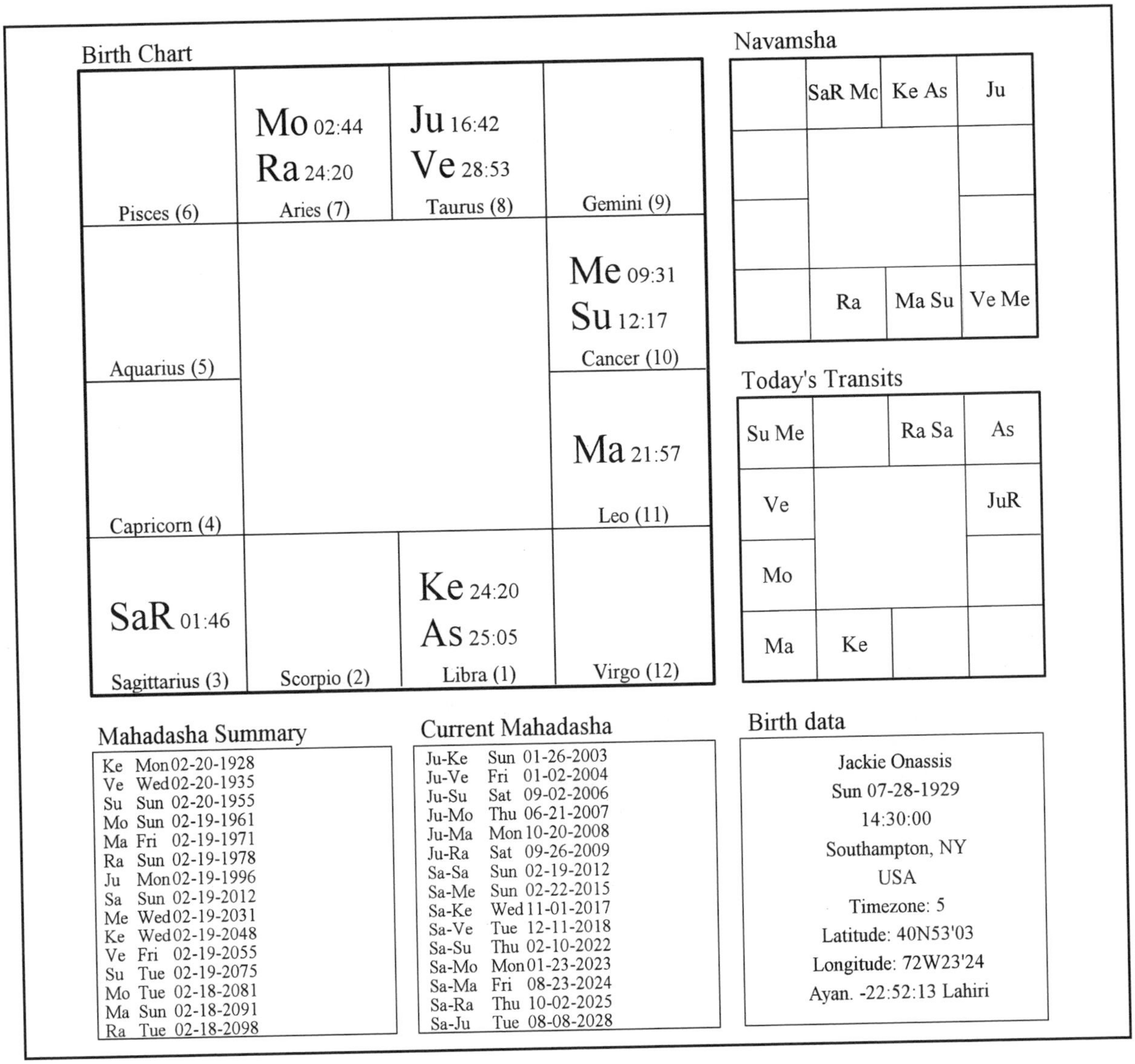

Birth Chart

	Mo 02:44 **Ra** 24:20	**Ju** 16:42 **Ve** 28:53	
Pisces (6)	Aries (7)	Taurus (8)	Gemini (9)
Aquarius (5)			**Me** 09:31 **Su** 12:17 Cancer (10)
Capricorn (4)			**Ma** 21:57 Leo (11)
SaR 01:46 Sagittarius (3)	Scorpio (2)	**Ke** 24:20 **As** 25:05 Libra (1)	Virgo (12)

Navamsha

	SaR Mc	Ke As	Ju
	Ra	Ma Su	Ve Me

Today's Transits

Su Me		Ra Sa	As
Ve			JuR
Mo			
Ma	Ke		

Mahadasha Summary

Ke	Mon	02-20-1928
Ve	Wed	02-20-1935
Su	Sun	02-20-1955
Mo	Sun	02-19-1961
Ma	Fri	02-19-1971
Ra	Sun	02-19-1978
Ju	Mon	02-19-1996
Sa	Sun	02-19-2012
Me	Wed	02-19-2031
Ke	Wed	02-19-2048
Ve	Fri	02-19-2055
Su	Tue	02-19-2075
Mo	Tue	02-18-2081
Ma	Sun	02-18-2091
Ra	Tue	02-18-2098

Current Mahadasha

Ju-Ke	Sun	01-26-2003
Ju-Ve	Fri	01-02-2004
Ju-Su	Sat	09-02-2006
Ju-Mo	Thu	06-21-2007
Ju-Ma	Mon	10-20-2008
Ju-Ra	Sat	09-26-2009
Sa-Sa	Sun	02-19-2012
Sa-Me	Sun	02-22-2015
Sa-Ke	Wed	11-01-2017
Sa-Ve	Tue	12-11-2018
Sa-Su	Thu	02-10-2022
Sa-Mo	Mon	01-23-2023
Sa-Ma	Fri	08-23-2024
Sa-Ra	Thu	10-02-2025
Sa-Ju	Tue	08-08-2028

Birth data

Jackie Onassis
Sun 07-28-1929
14:30:00
Southampton, NY
USA
Timezone: 5
Latitude: 40N53'03
Longitude: 72W23'24
Ayan. -22:52:13 Lahiri

Chart 52—Jackie Onassis

nature. The planets that express Marilyn's sexual magnetism (Mars and Jupiter) are in opposition to JFK's Moon in the 12th, another sensual house, indicating enjoyment of sensual pleasures.

Because JFK's Saturn is placed on Marilyn's rising sign, it shows he controlled the sit-uation. In addition, this Saturn placement also aspects her Venus quite strongly. For true love to occur, the Venus should be free from any aspect by Saturn. So this was not a relation-ship of love, or even deep affection. Rather, it was a relationship of passion.

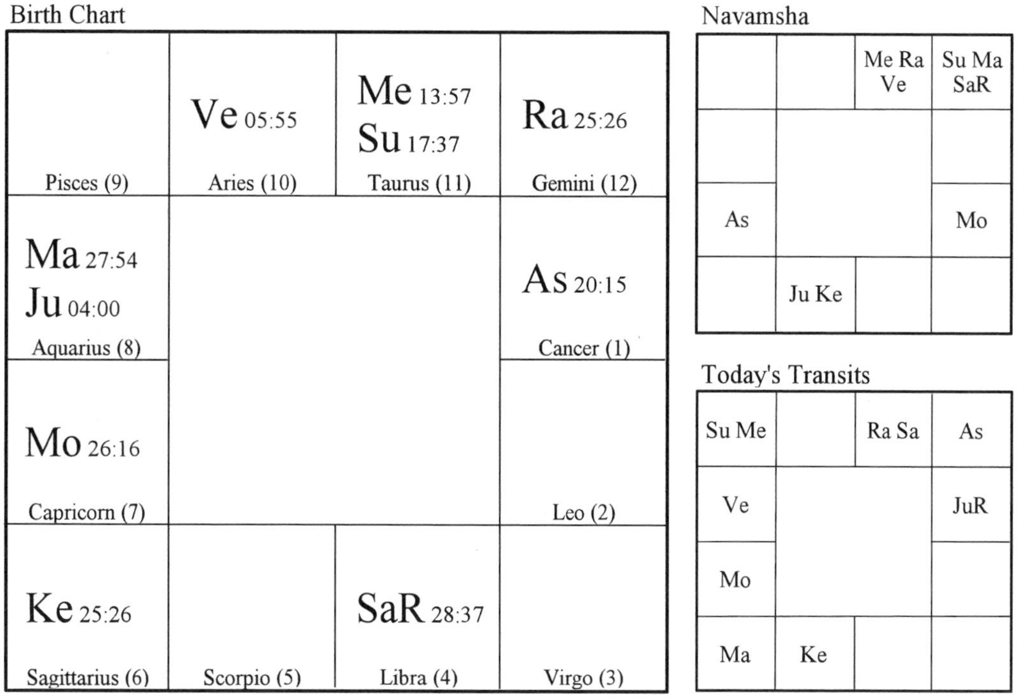

Birth Chart

	Ve 05:55	Me 13:57 Su 17:37	Ra 25:26
Pisces (9)	Aries (10)	Taurus (11)	Gemini (12)
Ma 27:54 Ju 04:00			As 20:15
Aquarius (8)			Cancer (1)
Mo 26:16			
Capricorn (7)			Leo (2)
Ke 25:26		SaR 28:37	
Sagittarius (6)	Scorpio (5)	Libra (4)	Virgo (3)

Navamsha

		Me Ra Ve	Su Ma SaR
As			Mo
	Ju Ke		

Today's Transits

Su Me		Ra Sa	As
Ve			JuR
Mo			
Ma	Ke		

Mahadasha Summary

Ma	Fri	11-14-1924
Ra	Sun	11-15-1931
Ju	Mon	11-14-1949
Sa	Sun	11-14-1965
Me	Wed	11-14-1984
Ke	Wed	11-14-2001
Ve	Thu	11-14-2008
Su	Mon	11-13-2028
Mo	Tue	11-14-2034
Ma	Sun	11-13-2044
Ra	Tue	11-14-2051
Ju	Wed	11-13-2069
Sa	Tue	11-13-2085
Me	Fri	11-14-2104
Ke	Fri	11-14-2121

Current Mahadasha

Ke-Su	Thu	06-12-2003
Ke-Mo	Sat	10-18-2003
Ke-Ma	Tue	05-18-2004
Ke-Ra	Thu	10-14-2004
Ke-Ju	Tue	11-01-2005
Ke-Sa	Sun	10-08-2006
Ke-Me	Sat	11-17-2007
Ve-Ve	Thu	11-13-2008
Ve-Su	Thu	03-15-2012
Ve-Mo	Fri	03-15-2013
Ve-Ma	Fri	11-14-2014
Ve-Ra	Thu	01-14-2016
Ve-Ju	Mon	01-14-2019
Ve-Sa	Tue	09-14-2021
Ve-Me	Wed	11-13-2024

Birth data

Marilyn Monroe
Tue 06-01-1926
09:30:00
Los Angeles, CA
USA
Timezone: 8
Latitude: 34N03'08
Longitude: 118W14'34
Ayan. -22:49:29 Lahiri

Chart 53—Marilyn Monroe

SATURN IN COMPATIBILITY

Sometimes what is lacking in a person's life can be completed by a marriage partner, even if the marriage is not considered ideal from a planetary point of view. In the case of Paul Newman and Joanne Woodward, for example, notice how her Saturn sits firmly on his ascendant, aspecting his rising sign planets, including Venus, as well as aspecting his Moon.

Ordinarily, this Saturn/Venus connection would cause a fair amount of stress in a relationship, as evidenced in JFK and Marilyn's charts, except in cases where one spouse

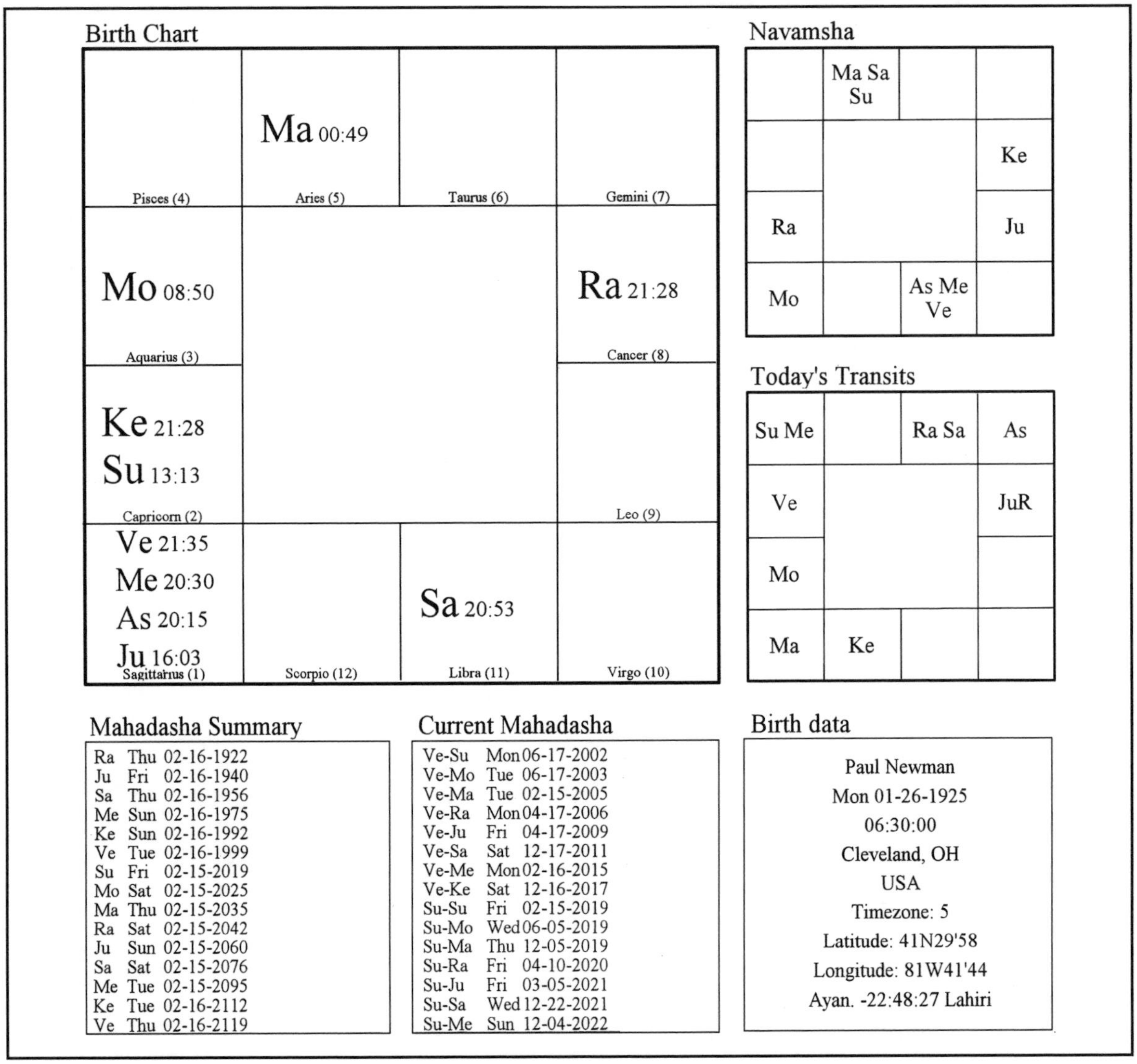

Birth Chart

Pisces (4)	Aries (5) Ma 00:49	Taurus (6)	Gemini (7)
Mo 08:50 Aquarius (3)			Ra 21:28 Cancer (8)
Ke 21:28 Su 13:13 Capricorn (2)			Leo (9)
Ve 21:35 Me 20:30 As 20:15 Ju 16:03 Sagittarius (1)	Scorpio (12)	Sa 20:53 Libra (11)	Virgo (10)

Navamsha

	Ma Sa Su		
			Ke
Ra			Ju
Mo	As Me Ve		

Today's Transits

Su Me		Ra Sa	As
Ve			JuR
Mo			
Ma	Ke		

Mahadasha Summary

Ra	Thu	02-16-1922
Ju	Fri	02-16-1940
Sa	Thu	02-16-1956
Me	Sun	02-16-1975
Ke	Sun	02-16-1992
Ve	Tue	02-16-1999
Su	Fri	02-15-2019
Mo	Sat	02-15-2025
Ma	Thu	02-15-2035
Ra	Sat	02-15-2042
Ju	Sun	02-15-2060
Sa	Sat	02-15-2076
Me	Tue	02-15-2095
Ke	Tue	02-16-2112
Ve	Thu	02-16-2119

Current Mahadasha

Ve-Su	Mon	06-17-2002
Ve-Mo	Tue	06-17-2003
Ve-Ma	Tue	02-15-2005
Ve-Ra	Mon	04-17-2006
Ve-Ju	Fri	04-17-2009
Ve-Sa	Sat	12-17-2011
Ve-Me	Mon	02-16-2015
Ve-Ke	Sat	12-16-2017
Su-Su	Fri	02-15-2019
Su-Mo	Wed	06-05-2019
Su-Ma	Thu	12-05-2019
Su-Ra	Fri	04-10-2020
Su-Ju	Fri	03-05-2021
Su-Sa	Wed	12-22-2021
Su-Me	Sun	12-04-2022

Birth data

Paul Newman
Mon 01-26-1925
06:30:00
Cleveland, OH
USA
Timezone: 5
Latitude: 41N29'58
Longitude: 81W41'44
Ayan. -22:48:27 Lahiri

Chart 54—Paul Newman

benefits by (or enjoys) being controlled and dominated by the other.

But in Paul and Joanne's case, it's different. Look at their conjunct Moons. This connection between Moons cannot be underestimated, since it brings a great sense of knowing the other person, as if you've always been together. From that connection comes deep trust.

Since Paul lost his father in his teens (a man who never thought Paul would succeed at acting, and died before his son "made it"), Joanne's Saturn brings a grounded discipline to Paul. Saturn represents a male energy that

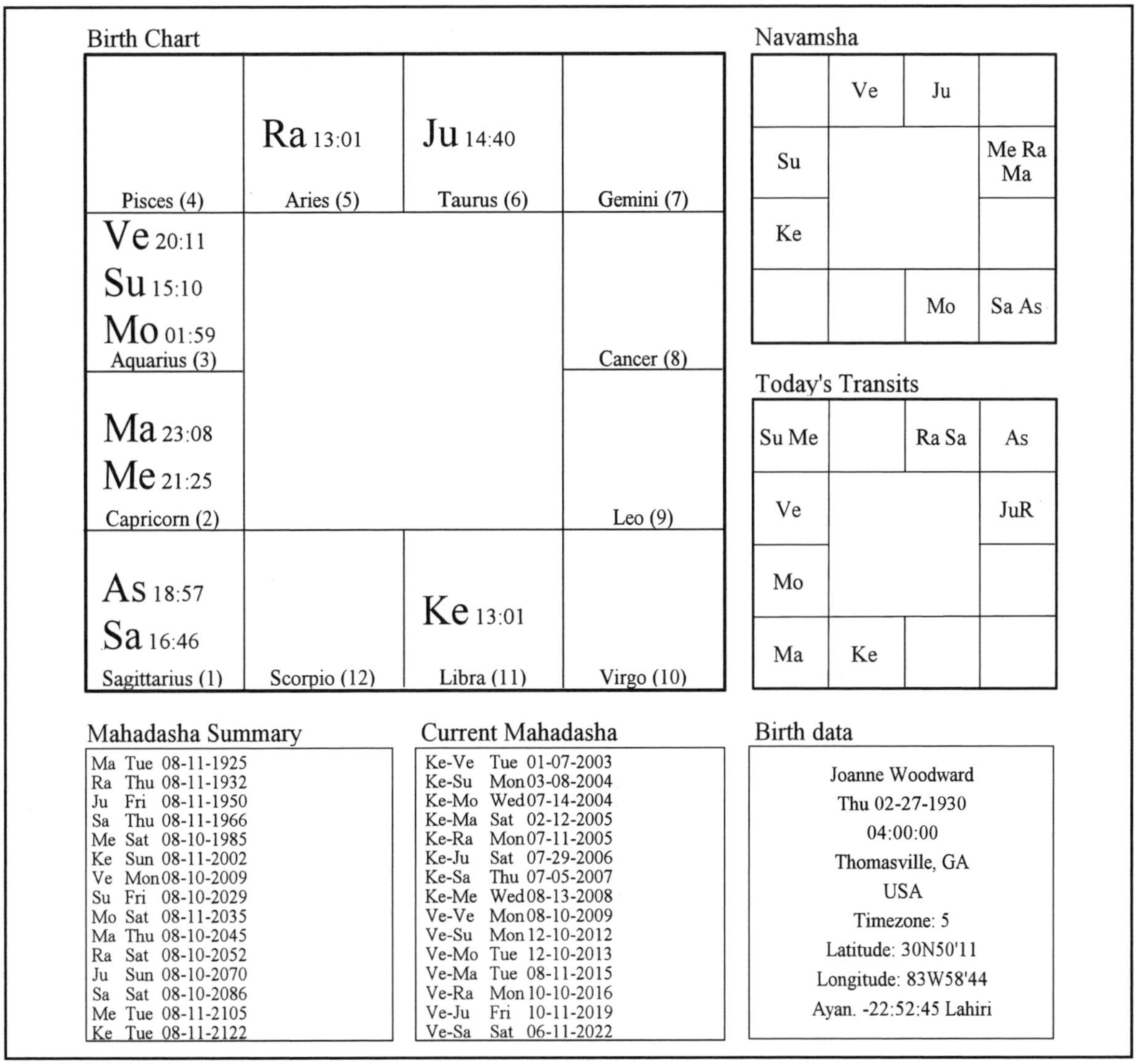

Birth Chart

	Ra 13:01	Ju 14:40	
Pisces (4)	Aries (5)	Taurus (6)	Gemini (7)
Ve 20:11 Su 15:10 Mo 01:59 Aquarius (3)			Cancer (8)
Ma 23:08 Me 21:25 Capricorn (2)			Leo (9)
As 18:57 Sa 16:46 Sagittarius (1)	Scorpio (12)	Ke 13:01 Libra (11)	Virgo (10)

Navamsha

	Ve	Ju	
Su			Me Ra Ma
Ke			
		Mo	Sa As

Today's Transits

Su Me		Ra Sa	As
Ve			JuR
Mo			
Ma	Ke		

Mahadasha Summary

Ma	Tue	08-11-1925
Ra	Thu	08-11-1932
Ju	Fri	08-11-1950
Sa	Thu	08-11-1966
Me	Sat	08-10-1985
Ke	Sun	08-11-2002
Ve	Mon	08-10-2009
Su	Fri	08-10-2029
Mo	Sat	08-11-2035
Ma	Thu	08-10-2045
Ra	Sat	08-10-2052
Ju	Sun	08-10-2070
Sa	Sat	08-10-2086
Me	Tue	08-11-2105
Ke	Tue	08-11-2122

Current Mahadasha

Ke-Ve	Tue	01-07-2003
Ke-Su	Mon	03-08-2004
Ke-Mo	Wed	07-14-2004
Ke-Ma	Sat	02-12-2005
Ke-Ra	Mon	07-11-2005
Ke-Ju	Sat	07-29-2006
Ke-Sa	Thu	07-05-2007
Ke-Me	Wed	08-13-2008
Ve-Ve	Mon	08-10-2009
Ve-Su	Mon	12-10-2012
Ve-Mo	Tue	12-10-2013
Ve-Ma	Tue	08-11-2015
Ve-Ra	Mon	10-10-2016
Ve-Ju	Fri	10-11-2019
Ve-Sa	Sat	06-11-2022

Birth data

Joanne Woodward

Thu 02-27-1930

04:00:00

Thomasville, GA

USA

Timezone: 5

Latitude: 30N50'11

Longitude: 83W58'44

Ayan. -22:52:45 Lahiri

Chart 55—Joanne Woodward

is mature in nature, a paternal influence. On some level, her presence must convey a feeling to Paul that he is deeply cared for. This feeling transcends the inability of his planets to be at their best in matters of love, and it exists because of the presence of her Saturn.

An example of a Saturn aspecting a spouse's planets detrimentally can be seen in the charts of Prince Charles and Lady Diana (Charts 56 and 57).

First of all, his controlling Mars sits at almost the exact degree of her ascendant. As the ruler of her rising sign, her own Mars is strongly placed in her 10th house, showing

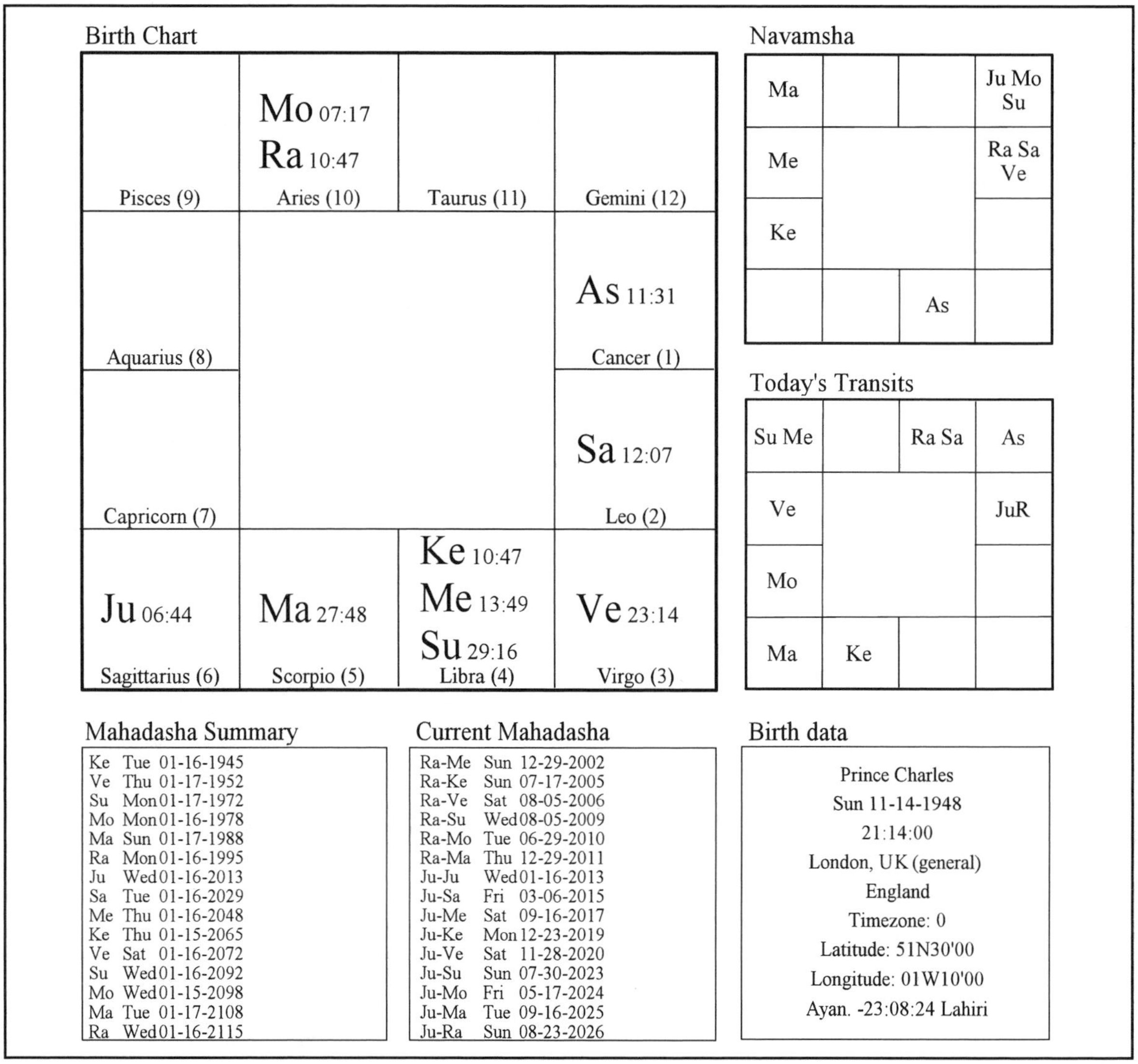

Birth Chart

Pisces (9)	Aries (10)	Taurus (11)	Gemini (12)
	Mo 07:17 Ra 10:47		
Aquarius (8)			Cancer (1)
			As 11:31
Capricorn (7)			Leo (2)
			Sa 12:07
Sagittarius (6)	Scorpio (5)	Libra (4)	Virgo (3)
Ju 06:44	Ma 27:48	Ke 10:47 Me 13:49 Su 29:16	Ve 23:14

Navamsha

Ma			Ju Mo Su
Me			Ra Sa Ve
Ke			
		As	

Today's Transits

Su Me		Ra Sa	As
Ve			JuR
Mo			
Ma	Ke		

Mahadasha Summary

Ke	Tue	01-16-1945
Ve	Thu	01-17-1952
Su	Mon	01-17-1972
Mo	Mon	01-16-1978
Ma	Sun	01-17-1988
Ra	Mon	01-16-1995
Ju	Wed	01-16-2013
Sa	Tue	01-16-2029
Me	Thu	01-16-2048
Ke	Thu	01-15-2065
Ve	Sat	01-16-2072
Su	Wed	01-16-2092
Mo	Wed	01-15-2098
Ma	Tue	01-17-2108
Ra	Wed	01-16-2115

Current Mahadasha

Ra-Me	Sun	12-29-2002
Ra-Ke	Sun	07-17-2005
Ra-Ve	Sat	08-05-2006
Ra-Su	Wed	08-05-2009
Ra-Mo	Tue	06-29-2010
Ra-Ma	Thu	12-29-2011
Ju-Ju	Wed	01-16-2013
Ju-Sa	Fri	03-06-2015
Ju-Me	Sat	09-16-2017
Ju-Ke	Mon	12-23-2019
Ju-Ve	Sat	11-28-2020
Ju-Su	Sun	07-30-2023
Ju-Mo	Fri	05-17-2024
Ju-Ma	Tue	09-16-2025
Ju-Ra	Sun	08-23-2026

Birth data

Prince Charles

Sun 11-14-1948

21:14:00

London, UK (general)

England

Timezone: 0

Latitude: 51N30'00

Longitude: 01W10'00

Ayan. -23:08:24 Lahiri

Chart 56—Prince Charles

ambition and drive. When a person has this much drive and yet is dominated by a spouse's planet, the result is stifling.

His Saturn is also conjunct with that very same Mars in her 10th house, restricting it further. On top of that, his Saturn opposes her Moon, causing her to suffer emotionally because of her restricted situation. So where Paul Newman thrives in the structure that Joanne Woodward's Saturn brings him, Lady Diana found the same situation (with Prince Charles) unbearable.

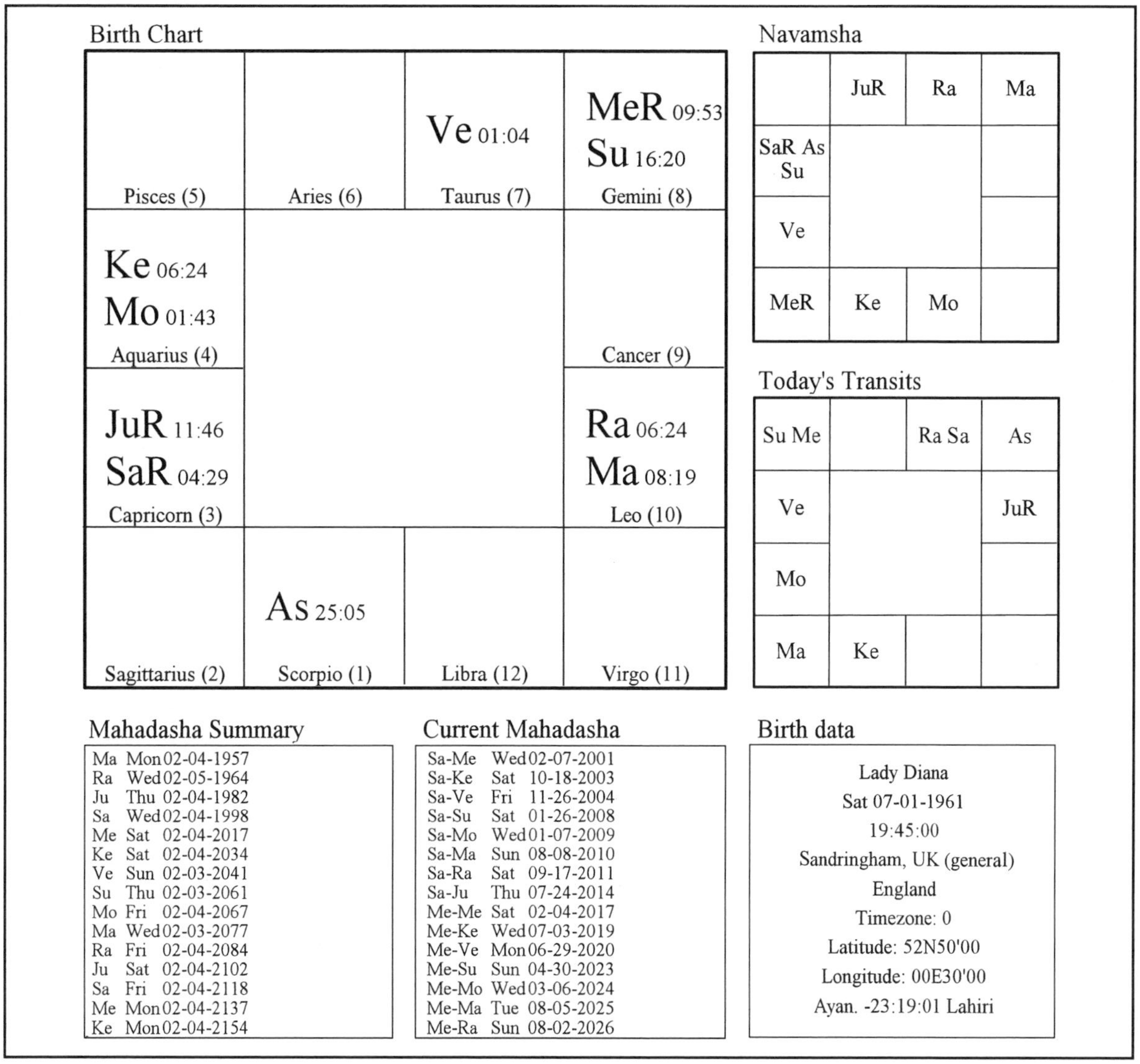

Birth Chart

		Ve 01:04	MeR 09:53 Su 16:20
Pisces (5)	Aries (6)	Taurus (7)	Gemini (8)
Ke 06:24 Mo 01:43 Aquarius (4)			Cancer (9)
JuR 11:46 SaR 04:29 Capricorn (3)			Ra 06:24 Ma 08:19 Leo (10)
Sagittarius (2)	As 25:05 Scorpio (1)	Libra (12)	Virgo (11)

Navamsha

	JuR	Ra	Ma
SaR As Su			
Ve			
MeR	Ke	Mo	

Today's Transits

Su Me		Ra Sa	As
Ve			JuR
Mo			
Ma	Ke		

Mahadasha Summary

Ma	Mon	02-04-1957
Ra	Wed	02-05-1964
Ju	Thu	02-04-1982
Sa	Wed	02-04-1998
Me	Sat	02-04-2017
Ke	Sat	02-04-2034
Ve	Sun	02-03-2041
Su	Thu	02-03-2061
Mo	Fri	02-04-2067
Ma	Wed	02-03-2077
Ra	Fri	02-04-2084
Ju	Sat	02-04-2102
Sa	Fri	02-04-2118
Me	Mon	02-04-2137
Ke	Mon	02-04-2154

Current Mahadasha

Sa-Me	Wed	02-07-2001
Sa-Ke	Sat	10-18-2003
Sa-Ve	Fri	11-26-2004
Sa-Su	Sat	01-26-2008
Sa-Mo	Wed	01-07-2009
Sa-Ma	Sun	08-08-2010
Sa-Ra	Sat	09-17-2011
Sa-Ju	Thu	07-24-2014
Me-Me	Sat	02-04-2017
Me-Ke	Wed	07-03-2019
Me-Ve	Mon	06-29-2020
Me-Su	Sun	04-30-2023
Me-Mo	Wed	03-06-2024
Me-Ma	Tue	08-05-2025
Me-Ra	Sun	08-02-2026

Birth data

Lady Diana
Sat 07-01-1961
19:45:00
Sandringham, UK (general)
England
Timezone: 0
Latitude: 52N50'00
Longitude: 00E30'00
Ayan. -23:19:01 Lahiri

Chart 57—Lady Diana

SUN AND MOON IN COMPATIBILITY

Compatibility, although strongly determined by 7th house indications, is affected by many other factors as well. As mentioned previously, the Moon has more significance in Vedic astrology than the Sun.

When looking at the Moons of two people, we look for a harmonious association. This tells us if there could be emotional, sexual, and psychological compatibility. In contrast, their Suns can be more dynamically placed, within reason, since some couples relish their differences more than their similarities.

It's easier to think in terms of feeling emotionally stable with the person you're with (harmonious Moons), and from that foundation expressing your disparate characteristics (less harmonious Suns). It's more difficult to work from a base of emotional instability (less harmonious Moons), and express your similar external characteristics (harmonious Suns). This is another example of why the Moon is more important than the Sun in Vedic astrology.

It's also important to assess the other planets in both charts when considering compatibility: Mars (energy), Saturn (discipline), Venus (love), Mercury (communication), and Jupiter (religious or spiritual orientation) all

Birth Chart

Pisces (8)	Aries (9)	Taurus (10)	Gemini (11)
	Ke 02:03 **Ma** 22:06		
Aquarius (7)			Cancer (12)
			Ve 07:15 **Su** 29:49
Capricorn (6)			Leo (1)
			MeR 12:22 **As** 14:58 **Mo** 18:15
Sagittarius (5)	Scorpio (4)	Libra (3)	Virgo (2)
	SaR 25:51	**Ra** 02:03 **Ju** 03:06	

Navamsha

Su	Ke		
SaR			MeR
			As
		Ra Ma Ju	Ve Mo

Today's Transits

Su Me		Ra Sa	As
Ve			JuR
Mo			
Ma	Ke		

Mahadasha Summary

Ve	Sun	03-25-1951
Su	Thu	03-25-1971
Mo	Thu	03-24-1977
Ma	Wed	03-25-1987
Ra	Thu	03-24-1994
Ju	Sat	03-24-2012
Sa	Fri	03-24-2028
Me	Sun	03-24-2047
Ke	Sun	03-23-2064
Ve	Tue	03-24-2071
Su	Sat	03-24-2091
Mo	Sat	03-23-2097
Ma	Fri	03-25-2107
Ra	Sat	03-24-2114
Ju	Mon	03-24-2132

Current Mahadasha

Ra-Me	Wed	03-06-2002
Ra-Ke	Wed	09-22-2004
Ra-Ve	Tue	10-11-2005
Ra-Su	Sat	10-11-2008
Ra-Mo	Fri	09-04-2009
Ra-Ma	Sun	03-06-2011
Ju-Ju	Sat	03-24-2012
Ju-Sa	Mon	05-12-2014
Ju-Me	Tue	11-22-2016
Ju-Ke	Thu	02-28-2019
Ju-Ve	Tue	02-04-2020
Ju-Su	Wed	10-05-2022
Ju-Mo	Mon	07-24-2023
Ju-Ma	Fri	11-22-2024
Ju-Ra	Wed	10-29-2025

Birth data

Madonna

Sat 08-16-1958

07:05:00

Bay City, MI

USA

Timezone: 5

Latitude: 43N35'40

Longitude: 83W53'20

Ayan. -23:16:54 Lahiri

Chart 58—Madonna

have great significance in relationship charts.

To show the power of these planets in action, let's look to several celebrity charts. Take for example the charts of Sean Penn and Madonna.

Of course, Madonna's Leo Moon makes her seek the limelight, in which she thrives. But the Sun, as ruler of her 1st house, is placed very late in her 12th house. Further, retrograde Saturn hits her rising sign directly. Both placements indicate a woman who lacks real confidence and so seeks the admiration of others. When she married Sean Penn, however, his planets brought her strength in that area due to his powerful Sun (ruler of Leo), Venus, and Rahu sitting atop her Mercury and Moon.

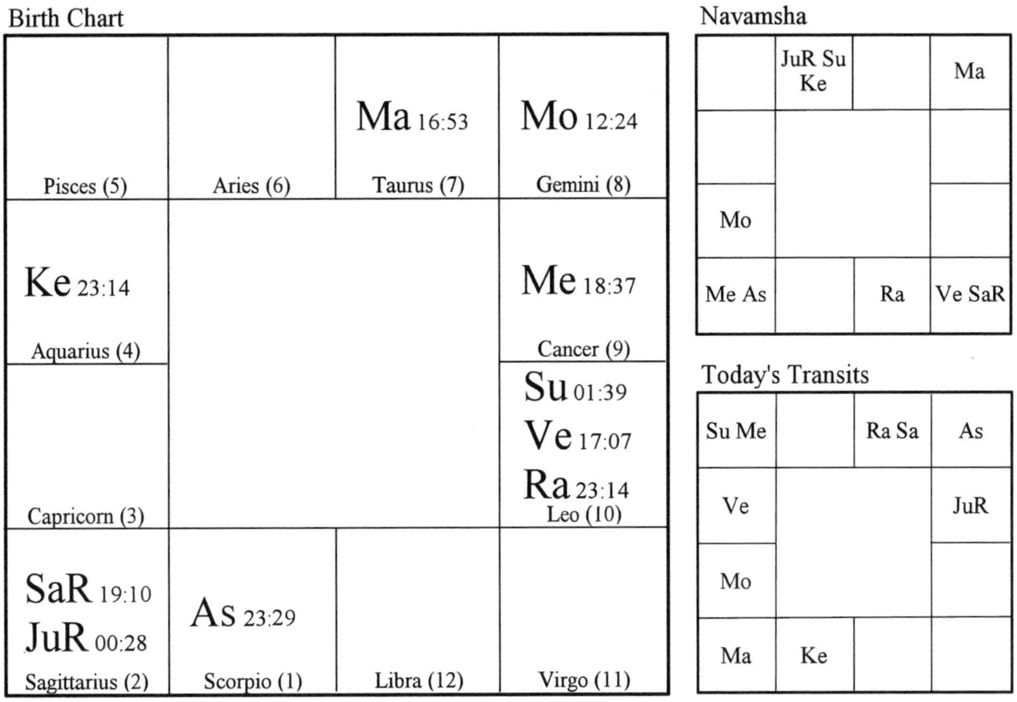

Birth Chart

		Ma 16:53	Mo 12:24
Pisces (5)	Aries (6)	Taurus (7)	Gemini (8)
Ke 23:14			Me 18:37
Aquarius (4)			Cancer (9)
			Su 01:39 / Ve 17:07 / Ra 23:14
Capricorn (3)			Leo (10)
SaR 19:10 / JuR 00:28	As 23:29		
Sagittarius (2)	Scorpio (1)	Libra (12)	Virgo (11)

Navamsha

	JuR Su Ke		Ma
Mo			
Me As		Ra	Ve SaR

Today's Transits

Su Me		Ra Sa	As
Ve			JuR
Mo			
Ma	Ke		

Mahadasha Summary

Ra	Sun	11-16-1952
Ju	Mon	11-16-1970
Sa	Sun	11-16-1986
Me	Wed	11-16-2005
Ke	Wed	11-16-2022
Ve	Fri	11-16-2029
Su	Mon	11-15-2049
Mo	Tue	11-16-2055
Ma	Sun	11-16-2065
Ra	Tue	11-15-2072
Ju	Wed	11-15-2090
Sa	Tue	11-16-2106
Me	Fri	11-16-2125
Ke	Fri	11-16-2142
Ve	Sun	11-16-2149

Current Mahadasha

Sa-Ra	Thu	06-29-2000
Sa-Ju	Tue	05-06-2003
Me-Me	Wed	11-16-2005
Me-Ke	Sun	04-13-2008
Me-Ve	Sat	04-11-2009
Me-Su	Thu	02-09-2012
Me-Mo	Sun	12-16-2012
Me-Ma	Sat	05-17-2014
Me-Ra	Fri	05-15-2015
Me-Ju	Fri	12-01-2017
Me-Sa	Sun	03-08-2020
Ke-Ke	Wed	11-16-2022
Ke-Ve	Fri	04-14-2023
Ke-Su	Thu	06-13-2024
Ke-Mo	Sat	10-19-2024

Birth data

Sean Penn

Wed 08-17-1960

15:17:00

Burbank, CA

USA

Timezone: 8

Latitude: 34N10'51

Longitude: 118W18'29

Ayan. -23:18:23 Lahiri

Chart 59—Sean Penn

Because Madonna's Scorpio Saturn aspects her rising sign, and Sean's Sun is also there, they must have had power struggles. To complicate matters, Madonna's Aries Mars aspects her Scorpio Saturn, which can amplify feelings of jealousy, revenge, and manipulation.

While they might have tried to work it out, it probably would have been too much of a challenge for either of them. Their Mercuries, in the 2nd and 12th houses from each other, indicate poor communication skills. More importantly, Sean processes information in a strongly emotional way (Cancer). His Mercury draws him inward, which makes him changeable, moody, and stubborn. He has trouble thinking objectively.

Madonna's Mercury operates almost antithetically (Leo). It makes her outwardly expressive, but of superficial emotions instead of feelings deeply felt. Her Mercury also gives her a strong tendency to exaggerate and not deal with the real issues at hand (especially when they are emotionally charged).

Along with their Saturn and Sun conflict, their Mars and Saturn (the planets of war) aspect each other strongly, not unlike the aspect between O. J. Simpson and Nicole Brown (although obviously that's an extreme case).

Madonna must have felt conflicted with Sean because she loved the security his planets brought to her rising sign, and yet there was resentment due to the power struggle between his Sun and her Saturn. Their Mars placements don't work well together either. She was explosive, impulsive, and pushed everything; he liked control, and didn't like being pushed. In fact, his Taurus Mars can be terribly stubborn. Looking to the other planets, their Venuses (located in the 2nd and 12th houses from each other) show that true love is very complicated. Madonna's own Saturn aspects her Venus in her rising sign, which is terrific for career, but difficult for love.

Let's take a look now at another famous celebrity couple.

Why did Brad Pitt (Chart 60) and Gwyneth Paltrow (Chart 61) split up? First, let's pretend that we don't know Gwyneth's time of birth. There will be instances when you won't have the birth time of a chart you want to analyze. Because the larger, slower moving planets do not move much during a twenty-four-hour period, they will still occupy the same houses regardless of the birth time. In a case like this, we use noon as a midpoint in the day to create a general chart to see where those slower moving planets are placed.

So, you can disregard Gwyneth's rising sign, since it's random. Instead, notice Gwyneth's Moon and Saturn conjoined in Taurus. The Moon, in its house of exaltation, brings her qualities of charisma, refinement, and emotional stability. But Saturn restricts the full expression of the Moon so that she might feel at times emotionally inhibited, perhaps shy or moody. Is this someone who's completely emotionally available? Not really. Rumor has it that Brad pursued Gwyneth and over the period of their courtship proposed marriage to her several times, and in each instance she put him off.

Birth Chart

Ju 16:29			Ra 18:43
Pisces (5)	Aries (6)	Taurus (7)	Gemini (8)
Aquarius (4)			Cancer (9)
Sa 25:47 Ve 00:07			Leo (10)
Capricorn (3)			
Mo 29:29 Me 22:45 Ke 18:43 Ma 16:40 Su 02:30	As 18:58		
Sagittarius (2)	Scorpio (1)	Libra (12)	Virgo (11)

Navamsha

Ra	Su		
Ve			Sa
As Mo	Ju	Me	Ma Ke

Today's Transits

Su Me		Ra Sa	As
Ve			JuR
Mo			
Ma	Ke		

Mahadasha Summary		Current Mahadasha		Birth data
Su	Sat 09-08-1962	Ra-Ma	Wed 08-21-2002	Brad Pitt
Mo	Sun 09-08-1968	Ju-Ju	Mon 09-08-2003	Wed 12-18-1963
Ma	Fri 09-08-1978	Ju-Sa	Wed 10-26-2005	06:33:00
Ra	Sun 09-08-1985	Ju-Me	Fri 05-09-2008	Shawnee, OK
Ju	Mon 09-08-2003	Ju-Ke	Sat 08-14-2010	USA
Sa	Sun 09-08-2019	Ju-Ve	Thu 07-21-2011	Timezone: 6
Me	Wed 09-08-2038	Ju-Su	Fri 03-21-2014	Latitude: 35N19'38
Ke	Wed 09-08-2055	Ju-Mo	Wed 01-07-2015	Longitude: 96W55'30
Ve	Thu 09-07-2062	Ju-Ma	Sun 05-08-2016	Ayan. -23:20:56 Lahiri
Su	Mon 09-07-2082	Ju-Ra	Fri 04-14-2017	
Mo	Tue 09-07-2088	Sa-Sa	Sun 09-08-2019	
Ma	Sun 09-07-2098	Sa-Me	Sun 09-11-2022	
Ra	Tue 09-08-2105	Sa-Ke	Wed 05-21-2025	
Ju	Wed 09-08-2123	Sa-Ve	Tue 06-30-2026	
Sa	Tue 09-08-2139	Sa-Su	Wed 08-29-2029	

Chart 60—Brad Pitt

Although Venus and Saturn are friends, that is not always the case in matters of love. Notice Brad's Saturn opposes Gwyneth's Venus very closely by degree. Again, Saturn is a restricting influence, and for Venus to operate at her best she needs to be free of such restrictions. Even thought their Venuses also oppose one another in the same houses, the aspect is quite wide (almost 28 degrees) and therefore weak in contrast to the Saturn/Venus connection.

Also, notice Gwyneth's cluster of planets in Virgo, and Brad's five planets in Sagittarius. Your eye naturally gravitates to places where

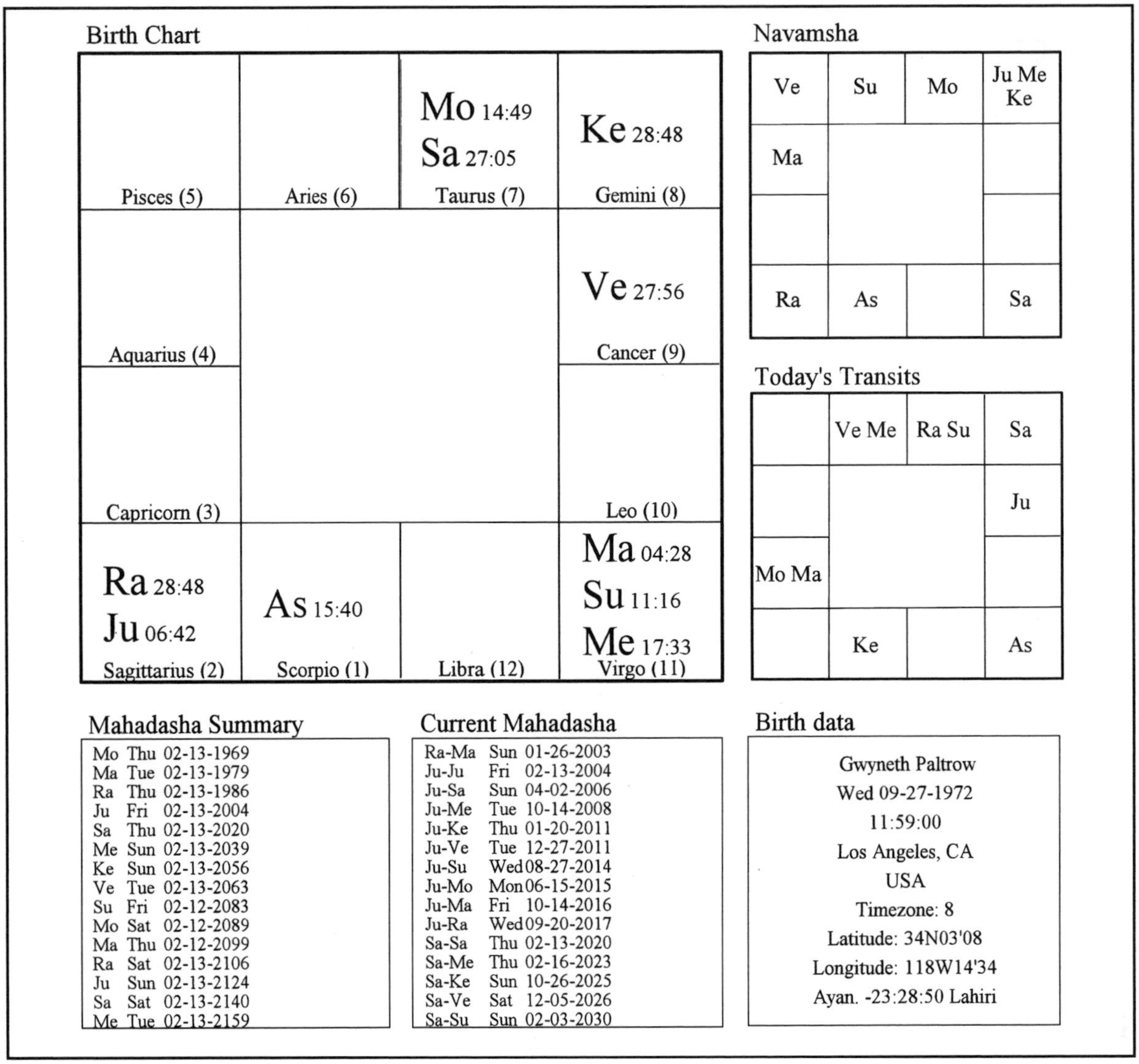

Birth Chart

Pisces (5)	Aries (6)	Mo 14:49 Sa 27:05 Taurus (7)	Ke 28:48 Gemini (8)
Aquarius (4)			Ve 27:56 Cancer (9)
Capricorn (3)			Leo (10)
Ra 28:48 Ju 06:42 Sagittarius (2)	As 15:40 Scorpio (1)	Libra (12)	Ma 04:28 Su 11:16 Me 17:33 Virgo (11)

Navamsha

Ve	Su	Mo	Ju Me Ke
Ma			
Ra	As		Sa

Today's Transits

	Ve Me	Ra Su	Sa
			Ju
Mo Ma			
	Ke		As

Mahadasha Summary

Mo	Thu	02-13-1969
Ma	Tue	02-13-1979
Ra	Thu	02-13-1986
Ju	Fri	02-13-2004
Sa	Thu	02-13-2020
Me	Sun	02-13-2039
Ke	Sun	02-13-2056
Ve	Tue	02-13-2063
Su	Fri	02-12-2083
Mo	Sat	02-12-2089
Ma	Thu	02-12-2099
Ra	Sat	02-13-2106
Ju	Sun	02-13-2124
Sa	Sat	02-13-2140
Me	Tue	02-13-2159

Current Mahadasha

Ra-Ma	Sun	01-26-2003
Ju-Ju	Fri	02-13-2004
Ju-Sa	Sun	04-02-2006
Ju-Me	Tue	10-14-2008
Ju-Ke	Thu	01-20-2011
Ju-Ve	Tue	12-27-2011
Ju-Su	Wed	08-27-2014
Ju-Mo	Mon	06-15-2015
Ju-Ma	Fri	10-14-2016
Ju-Ra	Wed	09-20-2017
Sa-Sa	Thu	02-13-2020
Sa-Me	Thu	02-16-2023
Sa-Ke	Sun	10-26-2025
Sa-Ve	Sat	12-05-2026
Sa-Su	Sun	02-03-2030

Birth data

Gwyneth Paltrow
Wed 09-27-1972
11:59:00
Los Angeles, CA
USA
Timezone: 8
Latitude: 34N03'08
Longitude: 118W14'34
Ayan. -23:28:50 Lahiri

Chart 61—Gwyneth Paltrow

planets are clustered because that is where a great deal of the chart's energy is expressed. Notice that Gwyneth's Mars, Sun, and Mercury sit four houses from (square) Brad's five Sagittarius planets. Squares are planetary formations that designate stress. In what way do these stresses, or incompatibilities, play out

in these two charts? In terms of the planets themselves: energy (Mars), personality (Sun), and communication (Mercury).

We see an even more extreme example in the charts of Bruce Willis (Chart 62) and Demi Moore (Chart 63). Theirs was a marriage that perhaps had more to do with business than love. They helped one another professionally. His Saturn sitting on her Venus at the exact degree makes it difficult to experience lasting feelings of deep love. But the Saturn/Venus connection brings great power to anyone involved in the arts.

In fact, their charts are quite poor indicators of compatibility. Their Suns are in the 6th and 8th houses from one another. His exalted Saturn sits on her debilitated Sun, Mercury, and Venus. Further, her debilitated Mars aspects his Saturn (creating conflict), and strikes his Venus almost directly (creating passion).

They both have strong oppositions between Mars and Saturn in their charts, showing inner turmoil that can manifest as external conflict. Those difficult planetary positions, when looking at the two charts

Birth Chart				Navamsha			
Su 05:06 Pisces (7)	Ma 21:34 Aries (8)	Taurus (9)	Ke 08:04 Ju 26:39 Gemini (10)	Mo		Ju	SaR Ra
Me 09:09 Aquarius (6)			Cancer (11)	As			Ve Su
Ve 24:05 Mo 09:16 Capricorn (5)			Leo (12)	Ke Me		Ma	
Ra 08:04 Sagittarius (4)	Scorpio (3)	SaR 27:39 Libra (2)	As 04:26 Virgo (1)				

Today's Transits			
Su Me		Ra Sa	As
Ve			JuR
Mo			
Ma	Ke		

Mahadasha Summary

Su	Sat	07-16-1949
Mo	Sat	07-16-1955
Ma	Fri	07-16-1965
Ra	Sun	07-16-1972
Ju	Mon	07-16-1990
Sa	Sun	07-16-2006
Me	Tue	07-15-2025
Ke	Wed	07-16-2042
Ve	Thu	07-15-2049
Su	Mon	07-15-2069
Mo	Tue	07-15-2075
Ma	Sun	07-15-2085
Ra	Tue	07-15-2092
Ju	Wed	07-16-2110
Sa	Tue	07-16-2126

Current Mahadasha

Ju-Ma	Sun	03-16-2003
Ju-Ra	Fri	02-20-2004
Sa-Sa	Sun	07-16-2006
Sa-Me	Sun	07-19-2009
Sa-Ke	Wed	03-28-2012
Sa-Ve	Mon	05-06-2013
Sa-Su	Wed	07-06-2016
Sa-Mo	Sun	06-18-2017
Sa-Ma	Thu	01-17-2019
Sa-Ra	Wed	02-26-2020
Sa-Ju	Mon	01-02-2023
Me-Me	Tue	07-15-2025
Me-Ke	Sun	12-12-2027
Me-Ve	Fri	12-08-2028
Me-Su	Thu	10-09-2031

Birth data

Bruce Willis
Sat 03-19-1955
18:32:00
Idar, GERMANY (general)
Germany
Timezone: -1
Latitude: 49N43'00
Longitude: 07E18'00
Ayan. -23:14:11 Lahiri

Chart 62—Bruce Willis

together, are in square position to each other (four houses apart). This amplifies the already difficult planetary placements.

Their Moons are also in square, showing a lack of real emotional, psychological, or sexual compatibility. Looking a little more deeply, the position of Demi's Moon shows us a woman who suffers from great loneliness, for no planet conjoins the Moon nor occupies a house on either side of the Moon. That means even in the midst of being surrounded by deeply loved ones, she can feel desperately lonely. Bruce's powerful Mars on that Moon must not have helped much, as this position stimulates antagonism and fighting.

Birth Chart

Pisces (2)	Mo 25:12 Aries (3)	Taurus (4)	Gemini (5)
As 29:03 Ju 09:47 Aquarius (1)			Ra 10:00 Ma 21:16 Cancer (6)
Sa 12:20 Ke 10:00 Capricorn (12)			Leo (7)
Sagittarius (11)	Scorpio (10)	Me 17:41 Su 25:40 VeR 27:12 Libra (9)	Virgo (8)

Navamsha

Me	Ke Sa	Su	VeR As
Ma			
Ju	Mo	Ra	

Today's Transits

Su Me		Ra Sa	As
Ve			JuR
Mo			
Ma	Ke		

Mahadasha Summary

Ve	Wed	01-17-1945
Su	Sun	01-17-1965
Mo	Sun	01-17-1971
Ma	Sat	01-17-1981
Ra	Sun	01-17-1988
Ju	Tue	01-17-2006
Sa	Mon	01-17-2022
Me	Wed	01-16-2041
Ke	Wed	01-16-2058
Ve	Fri	01-16-2065
Su	Tue	01-16-2085
Mo	Tue	01-16-2091
Ma	Mon	01-17-2101
Ra	Wed	01-18-2108
Ju	Thu	01-17-2126

Current Mahadasha

Ra-Su	Tue	08-06-2002
Ra-Mo	Mon	06-30-2003
Ra-Ma	Wed	12-29-2004
Ju-Ju	Tue	01-17-2006
Ju-Sa	Thu	03-06-2008
Ju-Me	Fri	09-17-2010
Ju-Ke	Sun	12-23-2012
Ju-Ve	Fri	11-29-2013
Ju-Su	Sat	07-30-2016
Ju-Mo	Thu	05-18-2017
Ju-Ma	Mon	09-17-2018
Ju-Ra	Sat	08-24-2019
Sa-Sa	Mon	01-17-2022
Sa-Me	Sun	01-19-2025
Sa-Ke	Thu	09-30-2027

Birth data

Demi Moore
Sun 11-11-1962
14:16:00
Roswell, NM
USA
Timezone: 7
Latitude: 33N23'39
Longitude: 104W31'21
Ayan. -23:20:02 Lahiri

Chart 63—Demi Moore

ANTAGONISTIC COMPATIBILITY— TONYA HARDING AND NANCY KERRIGAN

As mentioned earlier, sometimes people become connected because of antagonistic karmas carried over from past lives. Many of these situations seem unavoidable. This is why we see generations of warring families, cultures, and religions in various parts of the world. Remember, by reacting unconsciously or impulsively you keep karma and retribution in motion.

On January 6th, 1994, figure skater Nancy Kerrigan was struck with a metal baton above the knee. Tonya Harding was

Birth Chart

	Mo 25:14 SaR 25:34		As 24:23
Pisces (10)	Aries (11)	Taurus (12)	Gemini (1)
Ra 05:05			
Aquarius (9)			Cancer (2)
			Ke 05:05
Capricorn (8)			Leo (3)
	Me 06:44	VeR 22:23 Ju 23:52 Su 26:55	Ma 21:36
Sagittarius (7)	Scorpio (6)	Libra (5)	Virgo (4)

Navamsha

	VeR	Ju As Ke	Su
			Ma
		Ra Mo SaR	Me

Today's Transits

Su Me		Ra Sa	As
Ve			JuR
Mo			
Ma	Ke		

Mahadasha Summary

Ve	Sat	01-03-1953
Su	Wed	01-03-1973
Mo	Wed	01-03-1979
Ma	Tue	01-03-1989
Ra	Wed	01-03-1996
Ju	Fri	01-03-2014
Sa	Wed	01-02-2030
Me	Sat	01-02-2049
Ke	Sat	01-02-2066
Ve	Mon	01-02-2073
Su	Fri	01-02-2093
Mo	Fri	01-02-2099
Ma	Thu	01-03-2109
Ra	Fri	01-03-2116
Ju	Sun	01-03-2134

Current Mahadasha

Ra-Sa	Thu	02-08-2001
Ra-Me	Tue	12-16-2003
Ra-Ke	Tue	07-04-2006
Ra-Ve	Mon	07-23-2007
Ra-Su	Fri	07-23-2010
Ra-Mo	Thu	06-16-2011
Ra-Ma	Sat	12-15-2012
Ju-Ju	Fri	01-03-2014
Ju-Sa	Sun	02-21-2016
Ju-Me	Mon	09-03-2018
Ju-Ke	Wed	12-09-2020
Ju-Ve	Mon	11-15-2021
Ju-Su	Tue	07-16-2024
Ju-Mo	Sun	05-04-2025
Ju-Ma	Thu	09-03-2026

Birth data

Tonya Harding

Thu 11-12-1970

20:22:00

Portland, OR

USA

Timezone: 8

Latitude: 45N31'25

Longitude: 122W40'30

Ayan. -23:27:08 Lahiri

Chart 64—Tonya Harding

later implicated in the plot to destroy her competitor's chances at winning in the upcoming Winter Olympic games in Lillehammer.

Look at their two charts. Their rising signs are in square positions to one another, showing innate antagonism.

When you go to analyze the nature of any relationship, you'll want to look closely at the 7th houses of both charts. Tonya's Mars, the planet of war, sits in Nancy's 7th house; Nancy's Mars sits in Tonya's 7th house. This tells us everything.

Other signs of incompatibility are also evident in these charts. For instance, their Suns are in the 2nd and 12th houses from each other; their Jupiters are in the 2nd and 12th

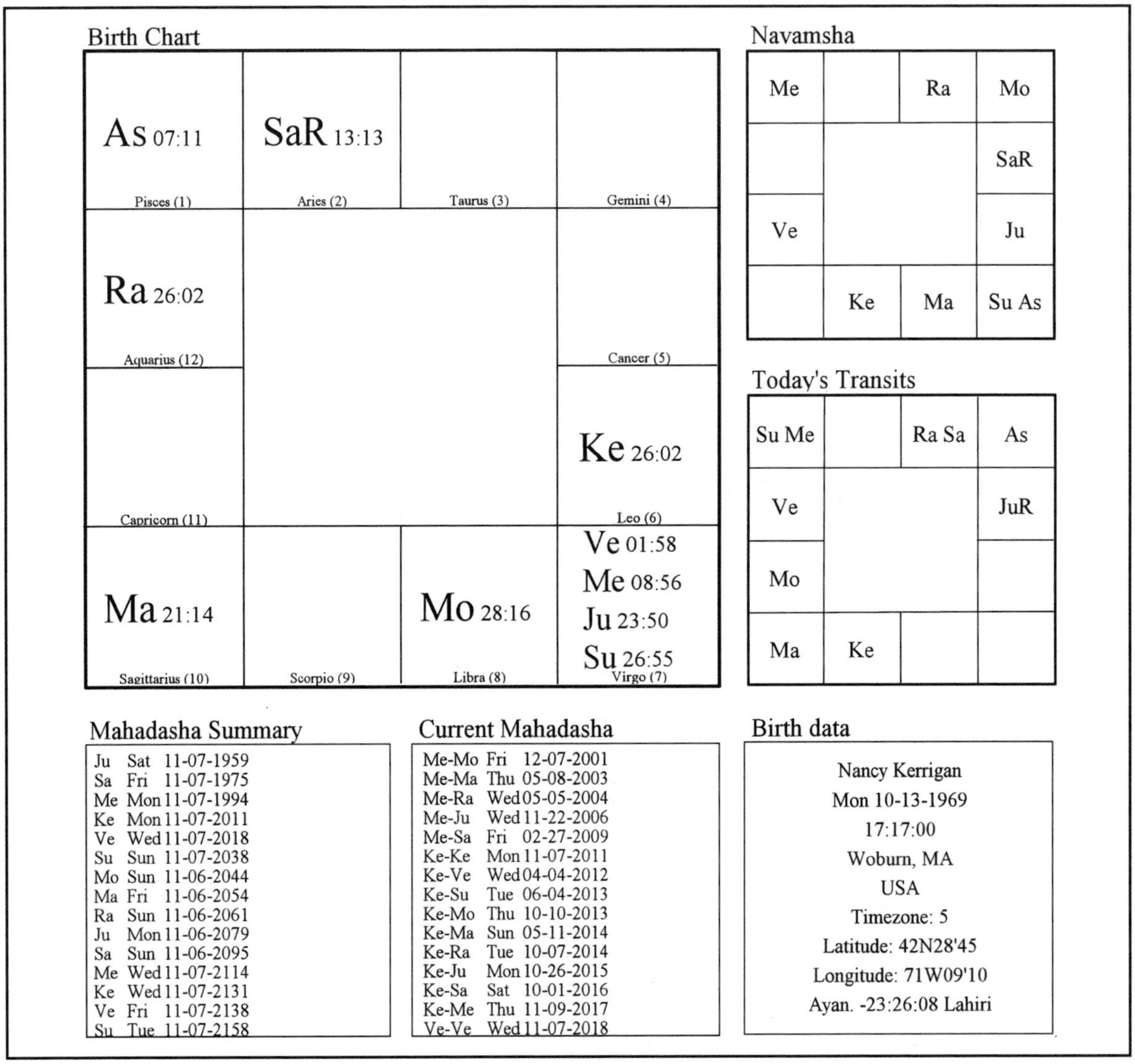

Birth Chart

As 07:11	**SaR** 13:13		
Pisces (1)	Aries (2)	Taurus (3)	Gemini (4)
Ra 26:02			
Aquarius (12)			Cancer (5)
			Ke 26:02
Capricorn (11)			Leo (6)
Ma 21:14	**Mo** 28:16		**Ve** 01:58 **Me** 08:56 **Ju** 23:50 **Su** 26:55
Sagittarius (10)	Scorpio (9)	Libra (8)	Virgo (7)

Navamsha

Me		Ra	Mo
			SaR
Ve			Ju
		Ke	Ma	Su As

Today's Transits

Su Me		Ra Sa	As
Ve			JuR
Mo			
Ma		Ke	

Mahadasha Summary

Ju	Sat	11-07-1959
Sa	Fri	11-07-1975
Me	Mon	11-07-1994
Ke	Mon	11-07-2011
Ve	Wed	11-07-2018
Su	Sun	11-07-2038
Mo	Sun	11-06-2044
Ma	Fri	11-06-2054
Ra	Sun	11-06-2061
Ju	Mon	11-06-2079
Sa	Sun	11-06-2095
Me	Wed	11-07-2114
Ke	Wed	11-07-2131
Ve	Fri	11-07-2138
Su	Tue	11-07-2158

Current Mahadasha

Me-Mo	Fri	12-07-2001
Me-Ma	Thu	05-08-2003
Me-Ra	Wed	05-05-2004
Me-Ju	Wed	11-22-2006
Me-Sa	Fri	02-27-2009
Ke-Ke	Mon	11-07-2011
Ke-Ve	Wed	04-04-2012
Ke-Su	Tue	06-04-2013
Ke-Mo	Thu	10-10-2013
Ke-Ma	Sun	05-11-2014
Ke-Ra	Tue	10-07-2014
Ke-Ju	Mon	10-26-2015
Ke-Sa	Sat	10-01-2016
Ke-Me	Thu	11-09-2017
Ve-Ve	Wed	11-07-2018

Birth data

Nancy Kerrigan
Mon 10-13-1969
17:17:00
Woburn, MA
USA
Timezone: 5
Latitude: 42N28'45
Longitude: 71W09'10
Ayan. -23:26:08 Lahiri

Chart 65—Nancy Kerrigan

houses; they have both a Sun/Saturn and Moon/Saturn opposition; and Nancy's retrograde and debilitated Saturn aspects Tonya's rising sign.

But this was more than a case of incompatibility. Tonya's Mars sits on Nancy's Venus, Mercury, Sun, and Jupiter. That her Mars sits so close to Nancy's Sun, her planet

of physical health, shows one of the problems. The other problem is that Tonya's Mars and Nancy's Mars are in square, in *full* antagonism, almost to the exact degree! And they converge on Nancy's 10th house, her house of career, the house that indicates her success as a skater.

At the time of the attack, Taurus was rising.

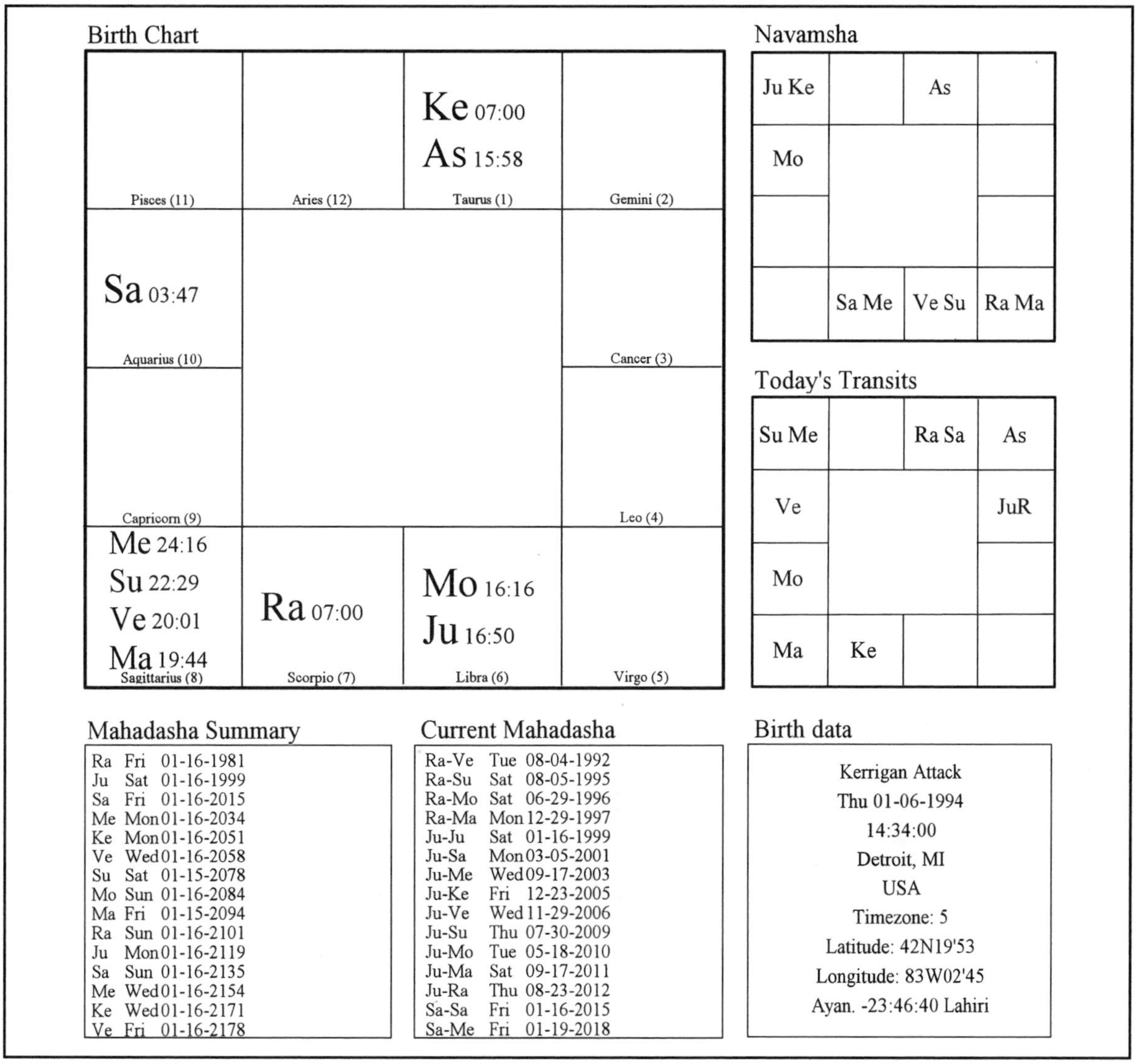

Birth Chart

Pisces (11)	Aries (12)	Taurus (1) Ke 07:00 As 15:58	Gemini (2)
Aquarius (10) Sa 03:47			Cancer (3)
Capricorn (9)			Leo (4)
Sagittarius (8) Me 24:16 Su 22:29 Ve 20:01 Ma 19:44	Scorpio (7) Ra 07:00	Libra (6) Mo 16:16 Ju 16:50	Virgo (5)

Navamsha

Ju Ke		As	
Mo			
	Sa Me	Ve Su	Ra Ma

Today's Transits

Su Me		Ra Sa	As
Ve			JuR
Mo			
Ma	Ke		

Mahadasha Summary

Ra	Fri	01-16-1981
Ju	Sat	01-16-1999
Sa	Fri	01-16-2015
Me	Mon	01-16-2034
Ke	Mon	01-16-2051
Ve	Wed	01-16-2058
Su	Sat	01-15-2078
Mo	Sun	01-16-2084
Ma	Fri	01-15-2094
Ra	Sun	01-16-2101
Ju	Mon	01-16-2119
Sa	Sun	01-16-2135
Me	Wed	01-16-2154
Ke	Wed	01-16-2171
Ve	Fri	01-16-2178

Current Mahadasha

Ra-Ve	Tue	08-04-1992
Ra-Su	Sat	08-05-1995
Ra-Mo	Sat	06-29-1996
Ra-Ma	Mon	12-29-1997
Ju-Ju	Sat	01-16-1999
Ju-Sa	Mon	03-05-2001
Ju-Me	Wed	09-17-2003
Ju-Ke	Fri	12-23-2005
Ju-Ve	Wed	11-29-2006
Ju-Su	Thu	07-30-2009
Ju-Mo	Tue	05-18-2010
Ju-Ma	Sat	09-17-2011
Ju-Ra	Thu	08-23-2012
Sa-Sa	Fri	01-16-2015
Sa-Me	Fri	01-19-2018

Birth data

Kerrigan Attack
Thu 01-06-1994
14:34:00
Detroit, MI
USA
Timezone: 5
Latitude: 42N19'53
Longitude: 83W02'45
Ayan. -23:46:40 Lahiri

Chart 66—Attack Chart

The ruler of Taurus, Venus, was in the fateful 8th house, the house of loss. Malefic Mars turns a difficult situation into a volatile one when it hits that Venus to within a degree. Malefic Sun compounds the situation and turns Mercury malefic, too. So these four planets sit in Sagittarius on top of Nancy's Mars at the time of the incident. And what house is Sagittarius for Nancy? Her career house. And what part of the body is indicated by the 10th house? The knees.

Now look at Tonya's 6th house Mercury, the house of enemies, at the time of the assault. Transiting Saturn in Aquarius aspects her 6th house Scorpio, affecting judgment due to its influence on the Mercury located there. Scorpio, being the house of secretive and perverse dealings, was further aggravated by the Rahu, which was also transiting that house. Now look how close the aspects were between Tonya's natal Mercury and the malefic Rahu and aspecting Saturn. All planets are within 3 degrees of one another, having a highly malefic impact upon Tonya's house of enemies. Also, at the time of the attack, the four Sagittarius planets that indicate Kerrigan's injury occupy Tonya's 7th house.

MANIFESTATION

Many people feel that if they work hard in several areas of their lives, the rest of their lives will naturally fall into place. This is why there are so many forty-something men and women who wonder why their soul mates have not shown up yet. They assumed it would just happen if they created financial security and work stability and kept their eyes open.

Manifesting love requires more than just hoping. If you're not intentional and clear about who you want in your life and why, you are living in dreams. Those dreams have as little likelihood of manifesting as a wish to win the lottery without buying a ticket. If you don't become intentional in what you desire, you get whatever happens to come along. And you'll find yourself spending all your time compromising because the person who showed up is so far from what you really wanted.

Once you become intentional about bringing a person into your life, how do you attract that person?

REMEDIES FOR YOUR 7th HOUSE

Locate your 7th house. Recognize that the qualities inherent in that house are generally ones you'd appreciate in a mate. For Aries rising people, Libra qualities are attractive. Gemini people are attracted by Sagittarians. Leos are attracted by Aquarians, and so on. You may want to refer back to Table A to review the signs. What you find out may be a surprise. You may discover you've been after the wrong type of person all along.

You can empower the 7th house and its ruler by chanting the appropriate mantras on the designated days associated with the ruler, and eating less on those days. You can also chant the Venus mantra on Fridays, since that planet is associated with love. Venus is also strengthened by offering a small amount of sugar to the base of a tree on Fridays. This is an old Indian custom that proves to be very effective. Wearing a stone for Venus also enhances the energy, as would a Vedic fire ritual for attracting love.

As you analyze your mahadasha and bhukti cycles, you'll be able to anticipate the times when love is coming your way. The Venus mahadasha is generally very good for love, as is the Venus bhukti. The planet that rules your 7th house or any planet that occupies the 7th can also be positive during their mahadasha and bhukti cycles. Also, pay attention to the planets that transit your chart.

Whenever the transit of a beneficent planet like Jupiter or Venus connects with the planet that rules your 7th house, be aware that love is nearby. Also, when Jupiter or Venus transit your 1st or 7th houses, or throw an aspect onto those houses, you can have luck in love. In fact, when Jupiter transits your 1st or 7th house, it's almost inevitable you'll meet someone to fall in love with.

SUMMARY

The 7th house shows the culmination of a major cycle of life: First you are born into the world, then you recognize your talents and abilities, and then you learn how to apply them. Then, after working to meet your basic needs of food and home, and overcoming the obstacles to finding your place in the world, you are finally able to attract a significant other. But there's more to life than that.

Some people are automatically drawn to the deeper significance of life from early on. Others go through a type of midlife crisis after they have accumulated everything they thought would bring them happiness, but still find themselves feeling discontented. The 8th house is the next place to go. It is a hidden, secret house, showing subconscious motivations, deep creative wellsprings, and the lower power centers of your body where anger, lust, and rage reside. The energy contained in the 8th house has the power to be transmuted through the alchemy of exploration, but most people want to avoid such a journey. People's primal passions and energies are scary enough when on occasion they raise their heads. To consciously dive into their abode often seems ill advised.

However, remember that the beautiful lotus flower has its roots buried in the mud of a pond. It is from this slime that the flower gets its nourishment. There are tremendous nutrients contained in the 8th house, and making the conscious decision to explore its depths will bring great luster to your life.

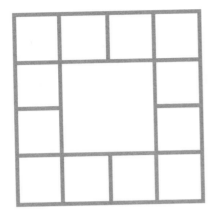

THE 8th HOUSE

Transformation

The 8th house is one of three dusthana (malefic) houses in the Vedic system, along with the 6th (also technically upachaya) and 12th houses. It is a house that indicates longevity, as well as the opportunity to accrue unearned money, whether through lottery, inheritance, insurance settlements, or alimony.

People with strong 8th houses may also have an interest in metaphysics or mysticism. The 8th house favors research, working behind the scenes, and hidden pursuits. Eighth house–focused people may also have an innate sensuality, a sexual charisma that draws people to them. Sometimes they are unaware of this sensuality and don't realize they are putting that energy out there.

The 8th house, on the other hand, can indicate chronic difficulties, problems that may not easily be overcome. Whether challenges of money, health, or love, they may plague a person for a very long time and may not be easily remedied.

THE NATURE OF THE 8th HOUSE

Find the 8th house in your chart. If you are Aquarius rising, your 8th house is Virgo. If you are Aries rising, Scorpio is your 8th house. Pay close attention to the zodiac sign of the 8th house because the nature of that sign will show you the way that 8th house issues function.

For instance, if Libra is your 8th house, you work behind the scenes artistically, like a set designer or ghost writer. If your 8th house is Aries, you may need to learn how to express emotions that you keep bottled up.

HOW THE 8th HOUSE EXPRESSES ITSELF

Locate the planet that rules your 8th house (see Table B), and find where it's placed in your chart. Then read the description below that pertains to this placement.

The 8th House Ruler placed in the 1st house is a difficult position about which to make a blanket statement. If the ruler is well placed and strong, the indications are that you are curious about the underlying mysteries of life, you will have a long life, and luck with unearned money. Yet, if the ruler is poorly placed and weak, the exact opposite can be true.

The 8th House Ruler placed in the 2nd house favors your ability to generate unearned income because the 2nd house relates to money. However, this position adversely affects your happiness while growing up, and can negatively affect your mouth, teeth, or speaking ability. It may also indicate the possibility for addictions.

The 8th House Ruler placed in the 3rd house indicates that metaphysics and mysticism may permeate your creative endeavors. You may have difficulty with siblings, or they may have health problems. This position usually shows a lack of adventurousness.

The 8th House Ruler placed in the 4th house is a position in which happiness is usually challenged, and the problem may be associated with the mother. However, by cultivating a spiritual practice, and contemplating the transitory nature of life, you can develop an inner contentment that is independent of material attainment.

The 8th House Ruler placed in the 5th house is generally not a favorable placement for children. It indicates few children, and difficulty with them. It also creates obstacles for pregnancy. However, this position is strong for making money through speculation and entrepreneurial pursuits.

The 8th House Ruler placed in the 6th house indicates the possibility of chronic ill health, particularly in the lower digestive and reproductive areas. You may encounter jealous people who will be unable to succeed at bringing you down. You may also have innate healing ability.

The 8th House Ruler placed in the 7th house is generally not a good position for marriage. The spouse may either suffer from chronic illness or be mystically oriented. The spouse may also be involved with behind-the-scenes activities, such as research or ghostwriting books.

The 8th House Ruler placed in the 8th house usually favors the most uplifting 8th house indications, bringing a long life, deep interest in esoteric knowledge, money through inheritance or chance, and a sensual, charismatic personality.

The 8th House Ruler placed in the 9th house is not favorable for the father, or your relationship with him, although it does show the possibility of gaining inheritance from him. Generally luck is spoiled in this position, but your luck can be enhanced with the help of an older mentor.

The 8th House Ruler placed in the 10th house is a good position for a psychoanalyst or dream interpreter. There may be delays in finding your life's work. You excel at research, and delving beneath the surface of things can bring great satisfaction in a career path. You might do well as a private investigator, for instance.

The 8th House Ruler placed in the 11th house favors the gift of the unexpected. Speculative ventures can suddenly prove successful through the efforts of a friend or a new opportunity. Generally this is not a good placement for siblings, and you might experience falling out with friends.

The 8th House Ruler placed in the 12th house indicates long-distance travel, but also ill health or accidents that occur away from home or abroad. However, in certain cases, this placement can strongly enhance profound spiritual growth.

IF THERE ARE PLANETS IN THE 8th HOUSE

To help fine-tune the descriptions below, you'll want to assess whether the planet is welcome in the house in which it is placed (Table G). If the planet is in the house of a friend, the positive nature of the following description is enhanced. If the planet is in the house of an enemy, more of the negative possibilities need to be considered.

Sun (Su) in the 8th house can indicate skill and knowledge of metaphysics, but brings weakness to the body. Not a good position for the father or your relationship with him.

Moon (Mo) in the 8th house shows inner charisma, sensuality, and enthusiasm. Not a good position for the mother, or your relationship with her.

Mars (Ma) in the 8th house brings intense sensuality to the chart, and promiscuity is possible. This position shows the possibility of accidents.

Mercury (Me) in the 8th house, if unafflicted, brings enthusiasm, insight into things metaphysical, and a keen memory. Afflicted, it can bring nervous disorders and speech impediments.

Jupiter (Ju) in the 8th house brings luck with inheritance or other forms of unearned money, like winning the lottery. If not well placed, you can have health problems in the liver/kidney area.

Venus (Ve) in the 8th house brings sensuality to the chart as well as luck with unearned money. A poorly aspected Venus can bring disappointment in love or health issues that are sexual in nature.

Saturn (Sa) in the 8th house is well placed, indicating a long life. However, unearned money is not likely to come your way, as you work diligently for everything you get.

Rahu (Ra) in the 8th house can bring tremendous luck in speculative ventures, but can also indicate you'll lose everything you make. Insatiable desires can bring aggravation and jealousy.

Ketu (Ke) in the 8th house is a deeply mystical position. You may immerse yourself in metaphysical studies. This placement can also bring mysterious health complaints to the reproductive system, which are not easy to diagnose or treat.

OTHER CONSIDERATIONS

- Note the element associated with your 8th house. Remember that fire signs are driven; earth signs are patient; air signs are creative; and water signs are emotional.
- Also note the quality of your 8th house. Cardinal signs initiate; fixed signs stabilize; and mutable signs seek change.

Now check any aspects to the 8th house:

- Are any planets located in the same house as, or opposing any planet in, the 8th house? If so, are those planets friendly, neutral, or enemies? (See Table F.) For instance, say your Sun is placed in the 8th house and opposed by its enemy Saturn. This planetary combination can indicate a dispute around inheritance.

- Remember that Mars energizes the house it's in, as well as the 4th, 7th, and 8th houses from itself. This means if Mars is placed in the 1st, 2nd, or 5th houses of your chart, it throws an aspect onto your 8th house, bringing luck with unearned money, or making you susceptible to accidents if you don't stay alert.
- Saturn restricts or brings discipline to the house it's in, as well as the 3rd, 7th, and 10th houses from itself. This means if Saturn is placed in the 11th, 2nd, or 6th houses of your chart, it throws an aspect onto your 8th house, limiting your luck with unearned money, and making you work for everything you get.
- Jupiter expands or brings optimism to the house it's in, as well as to the 5th, 7th, and 9th houses from itself. This means if Jupiter is placed in the 12th, 2nd, or 4th houses of your chart, it throws an aspect onto your 8th house, increasing your luck with unearned money. This aspect also supports research, especially as it relates to legal issues or spiritual wisdom.
- If you want to find out when your chart's 8th house energies will be enlivened, look to the 8th house ruler, or any planet located in the 8th house. Examine the Mahadasha Summary of your chart to see when that planet will come into power, and that will give you your answer. To find shorter periods when 8th house issues will be highlighted, look to the 8th house ruler or any planet located in the 8th house, and find the time its bhukti will run.

• Notice any influence transiting planets are having on your 8th house, or 8th house ruler. Jupiter passing over the 8th can bring deep spiritual aspirations or unexpected windfalls. Mars over the 8th is not a time to take risks, especially if injury is possible. You can chant to the planet that is favorably transiting your rising sign on the appropriate day for that planet to enhance its effects.

CHART EXAMPLES

A challenging 8th house situation can be seen in the chart of River Phoenix.

Notice that his rising sign is Libra, and the

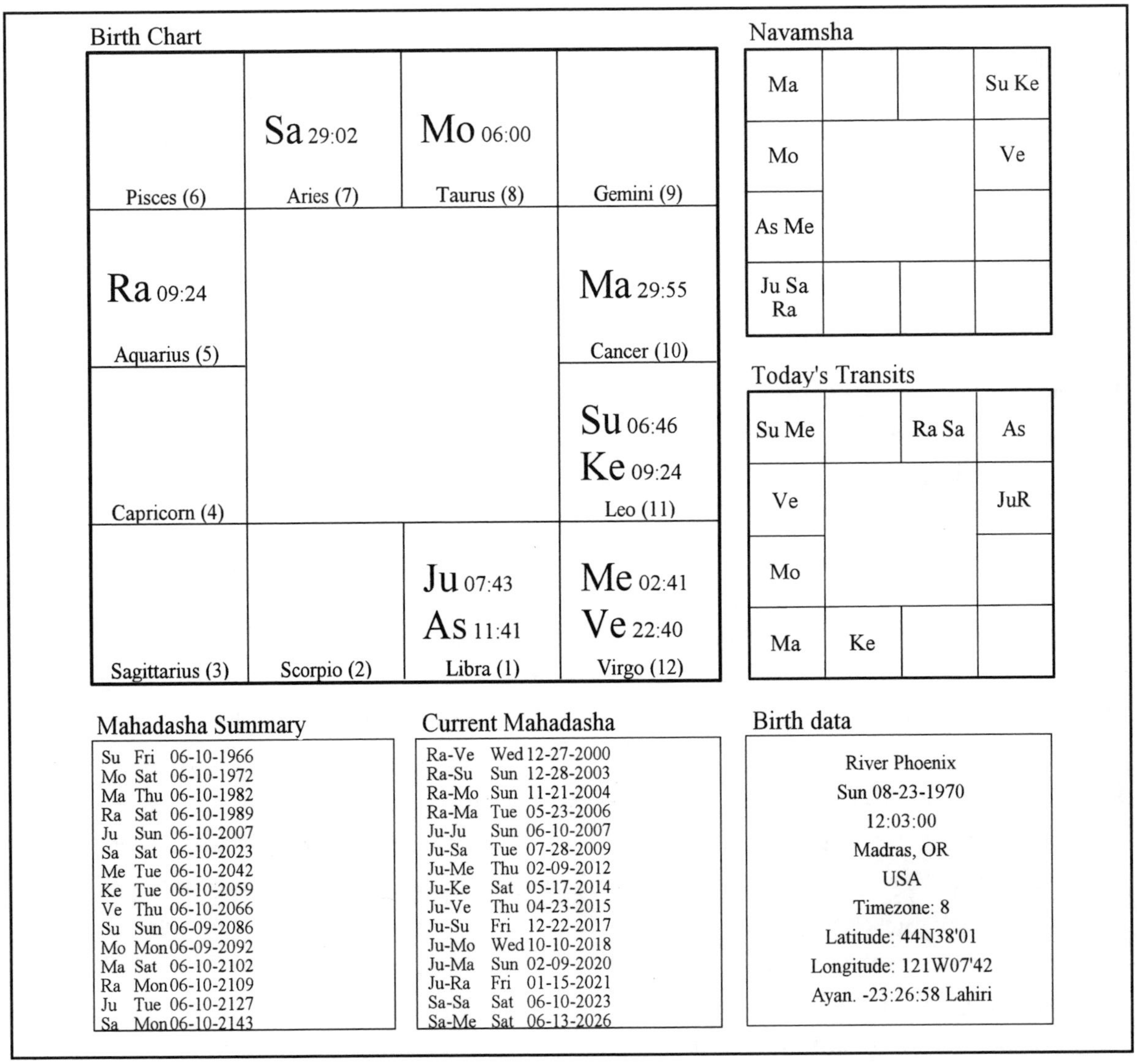

Birth Chart

	Sa 29:02	Mo 06:00	
Pisces (6)	Aries (7)	Taurus (8)	Gemini (9)
Ra 09:24			Ma 29:55
Aquarius (5)			Cancer (10)
			Su 06:46 Ke 09:24
Capricorn (4)			Leo (11)
		Ju 07:43 As 11:41	Me 02:41 Ve 22:40
Sagittarius (3)	Scorpio (2)	Libra (1)	Virgo (12)

Navamsha

Ma			Su Ke
Mo			Ve
As Me			
Ju Sa Ra			

Today's Transits

Su Me		Ra Sa	As
Ve			JuR
Mo			
Ma	Ke		

Mahadasha Summary

Su	Fri	06-10-1966
Mo	Sat	06-10-1972
Ma	Thu	06-10-1982
Ra	Sat	06-10-1989
Ju	Sun	06-10-2007
Sa	Sat	06-10-2023
Me	Tue	06-10-2042
Ke	Tue	06-10-2059
Ve	Thu	06-10-2066
Su	Sun	06-09-2086
Mo	Mon	06-09-2092
Ma	Sat	06-10-2102
Ra	Mon	06-10-2109
Ju	Tue	06-10-2127
Sa	Mon	06-10-2143

Current Mahadasha

Ra-Ve	Wed	12-27-2000
Ra-Su	Sun	12-28-2003
Ra-Mo	Sun	11-21-2004
Ra-Ma	Tue	05-23-2006
Ju-Ju	Sun	06-10-2007
Ju-Sa	Tue	07-28-2009
Ju-Me	Thu	02-09-2012
Ju-Ke	Sat	05-17-2014
Ju-Ve	Thu	04-23-2015
Ju-Su	Fri	12-22-2017
Ju-Mo	Wed	10-10-2018
Ju-Ma	Sun	02-09-2020
Ju-Ra	Fri	01-15-2021
Sa-Sa	Sat	06-10-2023
Sa-Me	Sat	06-13-2026

Birth data

River Phoenix
Sun 08-23-1970
12:03:00
Madras, OR
USA
Timezone: 8
Latitude: 44N38'01
Longitude: 121W07'42
Ayan. -23:26:58 Lahiri

Chart 67—River Phoenix

ruler of his rising sign, Venus, is placed in the 12th house and in debilitation (though in the same house as his exalted Mercury, which strengthens it a bit). Let's check the navamsha to see if the natal planets get any help. His navamsha rising sign is Capricorn, ruled by Saturn, which is also in the 12th house. This placement confirms the gravity of River's situation, for when the ruler of the rising sign is placed in the 12th house, a person's confidence is harmed and they become highly susceptible to outside influences, such as peer groups.

River's 8th house is Taurus, which is ruled by Venus. Venus is placed in his 12th house. The 8th house ruler in the 12th house doesn't favor longevity. However, his exalted Moon is placed in the 8th house, which does indicate longevity. That's why it's important to study the houses from different angles.

One of the concerns in this chart is the Saturn aspecting the rising sign from its place of debilitation in Aries, and in sandhi (the fateful last degrees of that sign). Mars also hits the rising sign with a 4th house aspect, and is also in debilitation and in sandhi.

Now look at the actual position of the Saturn and Mars. They are within one degree of each other, and as you'll remember, these two planets are strong enemies. When two enemies converge on a person's rising sign, that person's physical well-being must be questioned.

Two indications in the chart support the popular belief that River began using drugs during the filming of the movie *My Own Private Idaho*. Apparently he went deep into the psyche of the character he was playing—a narcoleptic street hustler—and, as already mentioned, River was very impressionable. One's 2nd house indicates addictions, and in River's case, the 2nd house is dark and secretive Scorpio, ruled by Mars, and that Mars is placed in his 10th house (the house of career) in sandhi and debilitation.

So according to the chart, it was exactly because of some influence in his career that River would start to use drugs. Now look at the 10th house, which is ruled by Cancer in River's chart. What planet rules Cancer? The Moon does. And the Moon is placed in River's fateful 8th house, another indication that his career would bring his demise.

Now look at the chart for the day of his death.

Amazingly, the debilitated Sun and Mars in the fateful last degrees and Jupiter are all in Libra, his rising sign. Located between malefic Sun and Mars is Mercury, a neutral planet until influenced by surrounding planets. Hemmed in by malefics, it too becomes a malefic. Now check the strength of Libra in this chart. Venus, the ruler of Libra, is placed in the fateful 12th house, the house of loss.

More importantly, these planets all sit on River's rising sign, which is also Libra. Now look at the Saturn in Capricorn. Notice that it is in sandhi (the fateful last degrees) and remember that Saturn influences the house it's in and the 3rd, 7th, and 10th houses from itself. Look at the 10th house aspect. It strikes Libra too, and hits its enemy Mars to almost the exact degree and minute.

So, not only do we have an exact conver-

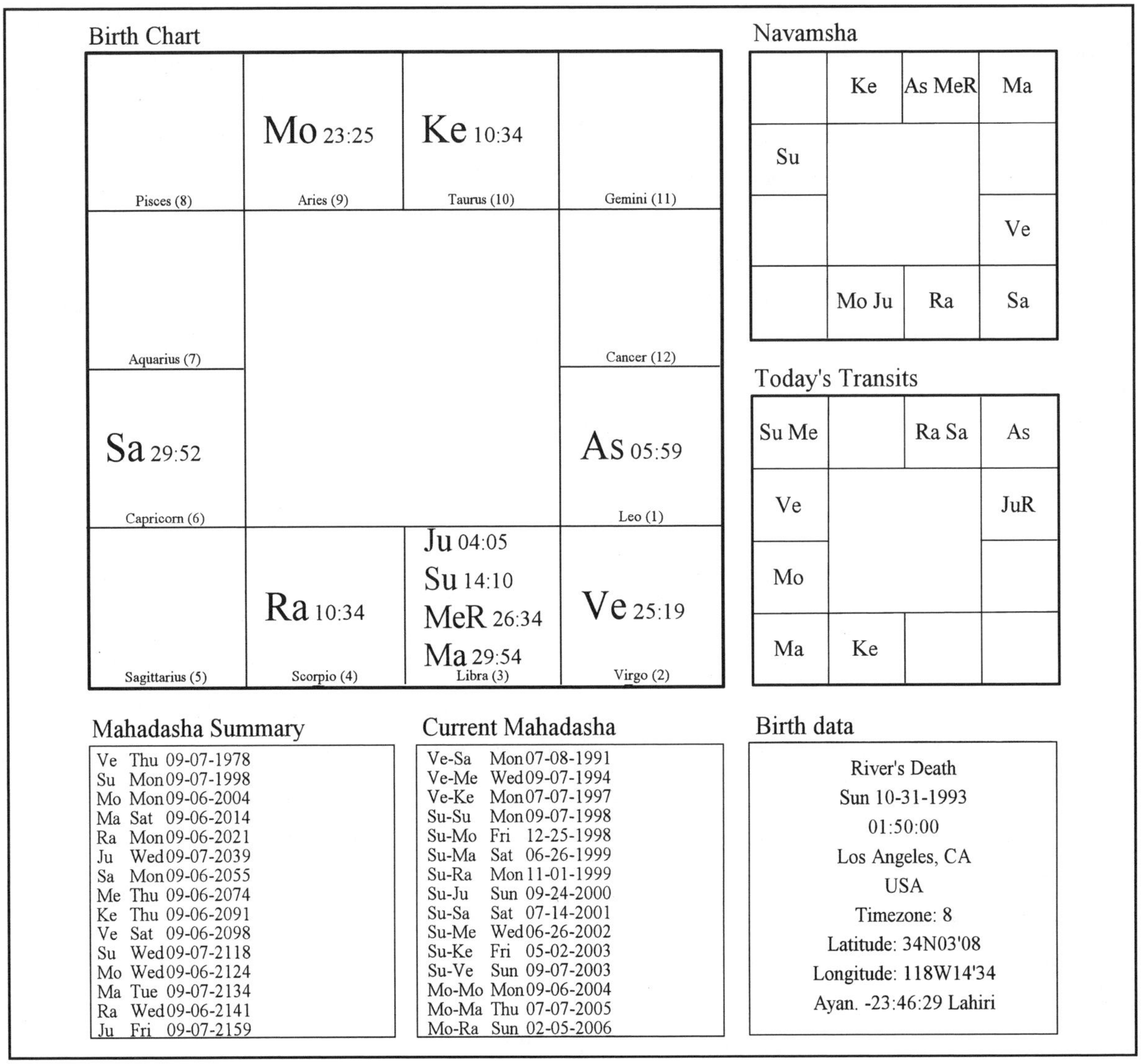

Birth Chart

Pisces (8)	Aries (9)	Taurus (10)	Gemini (11)
	Mo 23:25	Ke 10:34	

Aquarius (7)			Cancer (12)

Capricorn (6)			Leo (1)
Sa 29:52			As 05:59

Sagittarius (5)	Scorpio (4)	Libra (3)	Virgo (2)
Ra 10:34		Ju 04:05 / Su 14:10 / MeR 26:34 / Ma 29:54	Ve 25:19

Navamsha

	Ke	As MeR	Ma
Su			
			Ve
	Mo Ju	Ra	Sa

Today's Transits

Su Me		Ra Sa	As
Ve			JuR
Mo			
Ma	Ke		

Mahadasha Summary

Ve	Thu	09-07-1978
Su	Mon	09-07-1998
Mo	Mon	09-06-2004
Ma	Sat	09-06-2014
Ra	Mon	09-06-2021
Ju	Wed	09-07-2039
Sa	Mon	09-06-2055
Me	Thu	09-06-2074
Ke	Thu	09-06-2091
Ve	Sat	09-06-2098
Su	Wed	09-07-2118
Mo	Wed	09-06-2124
Ma	Tue	09-07-2134
Ra	Wed	09-06-2141
Ju	Fri	09-07-2159

Current Mahadasha

Ve-Sa	Mon	07-08-1991
Ve-Me	Wed	09-07-1994
Ve-Ke	Mon	07-07-1997
Su-Su	Mon	09-07-1998
Su-Mo	Fri	12-25-1998
Su-Ma	Sat	06-26-1999
Su-Ra	Mon	11-01-1999
Su-Ju	Sun	09-24-2000
Su-Sa	Sat	07-14-2001
Su-Me	Wed	06-26-2002
Su-Ke	Fri	05-02-2003
Su-Ve	Sun	09-07-2003
Mo-Mo	Mon	09-06-2004
Mo-Ma	Thu	07-07-2005
Mo-Ra	Sun	02-05-2006

Birth data

River's Death
Sun 10-31-1993
01:50:00
Los Angeles, CA
USA
Timezone: 8
Latitude: 34N03'08
Longitude: 118W14'34
Ayan. -23:46:29 Lahiri

Chart 68—River's Death

gence of enemies Saturn and Mars on River's rising sign in his natal chart, but at the time of his death, those transiting planets hit each other again to the exact degree.

Now let's look at a positive 8th house indication. This, again, is the chart of Shirley MacLaine.

First look at her rising sign, Virgo, and the Jupiter placed there. This brings her an eye for detail and perfectionism, ideal traits for a performer, and the Jupiter imbues the chart with grace. Now look at her 6th house Aquarius. Saturn and Venus are conjoined in the 6th house, and Table F tells us that these planets are great friends. So her 6th house, the house of competitors, is strong. She was destined to break into the entertainment business by overcoming competition.

The way she did that was a bit unusual, but nonetheless it gave her the opportunity she wanted. She was the understudy for the Broadway performer Carol Haney in the 1954 production of *The Pajama Game*, when Carol broke her ankle (a 6th house event). Jumping into the part, she was spotted and offered a movie contract. This shows the strength of her 6th house planets.

Shirley's great charisma is indicated in her 8th house, Aries, which Mars rules. Mars is placed in its own sign in her chart, conjunct with exalted Sun. This is a powerful combination of planets. They give her impulsive

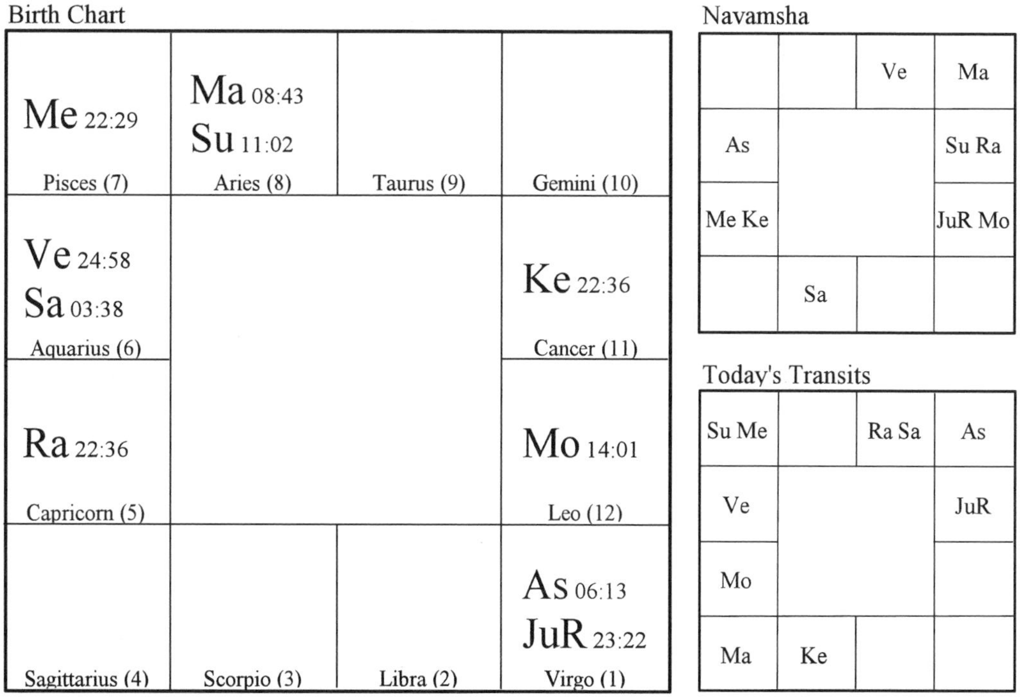

Birth Chart

Me 22:29	Ma 08:43 Su 11:02	Taurus (9)	Gemini (10)
Pisces (7)	Aries (8)		
Ve 24:58 Sa 03:38			Ke 22:36
Aquarius (6)			Cancer (11)
Ra 22:36			Mo 14:01
Capricorn (5)			Leo (12)
			As 06:13 JuR 23:22
Sagittarius (4)	Scorpio (3)	Libra (2)	Virgo (1)

Navamsha

		Ve	Ma
As			Su Ra
Me Ke			JuR Mo
	Sa		

Today's Transits

Su Me		Ra Sa	As
Ve			JuR
Mo			
Ma	Ke		

Mahadasha Summary

Ve	Fri	04-07-1933
Su	Tue	04-07-1953
Mo	Tue	04-07-1959
Ma	Sun	04-06-1969
Ra	Tue	04-06-1976
Ju	Wed	04-06-1994
Sa	Tue	04-06-2010
Me	Fri	04-06-2029
Ke	Fri	04-06-2046
Ve	Sun	04-06-2053
Su	Thu	04-06-2073
Mo	Thu	04-06-2079
Ma	Tue	04-05-2089
Ra	Thu	04-05-2096
Ju	Sat	04-07-2114

Current Mahadasha

Ju-Ve	Sun	02-17-2002
Ju-Su	Mon	10-18-2004
Ju-Mo	Sat	08-06-2005
Ju-Ma	Wed	12-06-2006
Ju-Ra	Mon	11-12-2007
Sa-Sa	Tue	04-06-2010
Sa-Me	Tue	04-09-2013
Sa-Ke	Fri	12-18-2015
Sa-Ve	Thu	01-26-2017
Sa-Su	Sat	03-28-2020
Sa-Mo	Wed	03-10-2021
Sa-Ma	Sun	10-09-2022
Sa-Ra	Sat	11-18-2023
Sa-Ju	Thu	09-24-2026
Me-Me	Fri	04-06-2029

Birth data

Shirley MacLaine
Tue 04-24-1934
15:57:00
Richmond, VA
USA
Timezone: 5
Latitude: 37N33'13
Longitude: 77W27'38
Ayan. -22:56:33 Lahiri

Chart 69—Shirley MacLaine

creativity, keep her young at heart, and provide her with tremendous energy and an athlete's body and stamina.

The 8th house planets are hidden, glow from within, and exude playfulness and sensuality. They also indicate that she practices and hones her skills in secret, since the 8th is the house of hidden pursuits. This would also account for her considerable interest in spiritual studies and pursuits.

Another chart with strong 8th house planets is Marilyn Monroe's.

Her planets work in much the same way that Shirley's do. Marilyn's 8th house is Aquarius, and her Jupiter and Mars are conjunct there. While Shirley's exalted Sun and

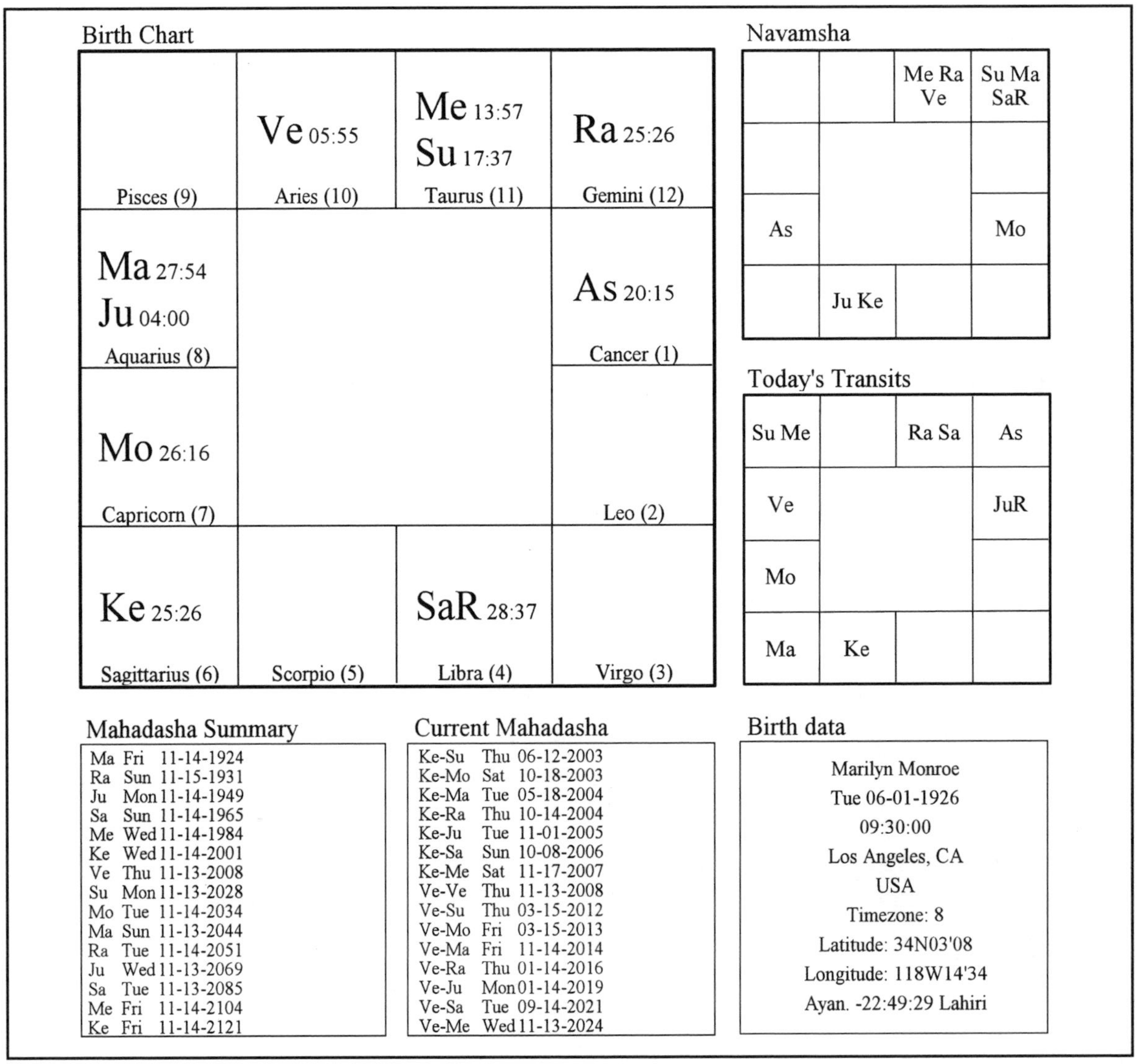

Birth Chart

	Ve 05:55	Me 13:57 Su 17:37	Ra 25:26
Pisces (9)	Aries (10)	Taurus (11)	Gemini (12)
Ma 27:54 Ju 04:00			As 20:15
Aquarius (8)			Cancer (1)
Mo 26:16			
Capricorn (7)			Leo (2)
Ke 25:26	SaR 28:37		
Sagittarius (6)	Scorpio (5)	Libra (4)	Virgo (3)

Navamsha

		Me Ra Ve	Su Ma SaR
As			Mo
	Ju Ke		

Today's Transits

Su Me		Ra Sa	As
Ve			JuR
Mo			
Ma	Ke		

Mahadasha Summary

Ma	Fri	11-14-1924
Ra	Sun	11-15-1931
Ju	Mon	11-14-1949
Sa	Sun	11-14-1965
Me	Wed	11-14-1984
Ke	Wed	11-14-2001
Ve	Thu	11-13-2008
Su	Mon	11-13-2028
Mo	Tue	11-14-2034
Ma	Sun	11-13-2044
Ra	Tue	11-14-2051
Ju	Wed	11-13-2069
Sa	Tue	11-13-2085
Me	Fri	11-14-2104
Ke	Fri	11-14-2121

Current Mahadasha

Ke-Su	Thu	06-12-2003
Ke-Mo	Sat	10-18-2003
Ke-Ma	Tue	05-18-2004
Ke-Ra	Thu	10-14-2004
Ke-Ju	Tue	11-01-2005
Ke-Sa	Sun	10-08-2006
Ke-Me	Sat	11-17-2007
Ve-Ve	Thu	11-13-2008
Ve-Su	Thu	03-15-2012
Ve-Mo	Fri	03-15-2013
Ve-Ma	Fri	11-14-2014
Ve-Ra	Thu	01-14-2016
Ve-Ju	Mon	01-14-2019
Ve-Sa	Tue	09-14-2021
Ve-Me	Wed	11-13-2024

Birth data

Marilyn Monroe
Tue 06-01-1926
09:30:00
Los Angeles, CA
USA
Timezone: 8
Latitude: 34N03'08
Longitude: 118W14'34
Ayan. -22:49:29 Lahiri

Chart 70—Marilyn Monroe

Mars are powerful planets placed in a fiery, cardinal house (Aries), Marilyn's are strongly sensual planets in an airy sign, particularly when Jupiter, not normally considered a sensual planet, conjoins and adds excess to the energy of Mars. So, as much as Shirley exudes a dynamic charisma, Marilyn exuded deep sensuality.

Another way 8th house issues present themselves can be seen in the chart of Ken Starr, the presiding attorney on the Whitewater investigation committee.

Starr's rising sign is Sagittarius, not an uncommon 1st house for someone involved in the legal profession. The ruler of his rising sign is Jupiter, and that Jupiter is placed in the 10th house, indicating a strong career pull and the likelihood of great success in that

Birth Chart				Navamsha			
	Mo 08:09	Ra 25:40					Mo
Pisces (4)	Aries (5)	Taurus (6)	Gemini (7)	Ke			
			Sa 05:24 Su 05:30 MeR 23:02	MeR			Sa Su Ra Ju Ve
Aquarius (3)			Cancer (8)		Ma	As	
			Ve 16:20 Ma 25:28				
Capricorn (2)			Leo (9)				

Today's Transits

Su Me		Ra Sa	As
Ve			JuR
Mo			
Ma	Ke		

As 20:20	Ke 25:40		Ju 26:19
Sagittarius (1)	Scorpio (12)	Libra (11)	Virgo (10)

Mahadasha Summary

Ke	Fri	04-10-1942
Ve	Sun	04-10-1949
Su	Wed	04-09-1969
Mo	Thu	04-10-1975
Ma	Tue	04-09-1985
Ra	Thu	04-09-1992
Ju	Fri	04-09-2010
Sa	Thu	04-09-2026
Me	Sun	04-09-2045
Ke	Sun	04-09-2062
Ve	Tue	04-09-2069
Su	Fri	04-08-2089
Mo	Sat	04-09-2095
Ma	Thu	04-09-2105
Ra	Sat	04-09-2112

Current Mahadasha

Ra-Ke	Wed	10-09-2002
Ra-Ve	Tue	10-28-2003
Ra-Su	Fri	10-27-2006
Ra-Mo	Fri	09-21-2007
Ra-Ma	Sun	03-22-2009
Ju-Ju	Fri	04-09-2010
Ju-Sa	Mon	05-28-2012
Ju-Me	Tue	12-09-2014
Ju-Ke	Thu	03-16-2017
Ju-Ve	Tue	02-20-2018
Ju-Su	Wed	10-21-2020
Ju-Mo	Mon	08-09-2021
Ju-Ma	Fri	12-09-2022
Ju-Ra	Wed	11-15-2023
Sa-Sa	Thu	04-09-2026

Birth data

Ken Starr
Sun 07-21-1946
18:45:00
Vernon, TX
USA
Timezone: 6
Latitude: 34N09'16
Longitude: 99W15'53
Ayan. -23:06:22 Lahiri

Chart 71—Kenneth Starr

career. That his 10th house is Virgo brings the qualities of that sign to his profession.

Virgo qualities include groundedness, precision, and good communication skills, with a very good memory for facts and figures. There may also be an interest in history.

Now look at Starr's 8th house, Cancer. Cancer is ruled by the Moon, which is placed in the 5th house, and aspected strongly by Saturn in the 8th house (throwing a 10th house aspect). The 5th house, as we now know, is strongly related to destiny. So by digging into 8th house issues that by their very nature are hidden and behind the scenes, he is playing out his destiny.

But he must necessarily become a controversial figure, since two powerful enemies afflict his 8th house—the Sun and Saturn. The Mercury, a neutral planet until influenced by an aspecting planet, also becomes malefic and is placed in the 8th house.

As Saturn rules his 2nd and 3rd houses (Capricorn and Aquarius), this indicates that some of the conflict in his life comes from his speaking (2nd house) about efforts he has made (3rd house) to uphold his duty as independent counsel (Saturn). Saturn's conflict comes from its connection with the Sun, which rules Starr's 9th house, Leo, the seat of power and indicative of the person in a leadership position.

Because the 8th house signifies research and hidden information, his chart shows his involvement in such matters perfectly.

Now look at another chart with the same rising sign, but with different results.

Troy Aikman, recently a quarterback for the Dallas Cowboys football team, has earned three Super Bowl rings and a Super Bowl Most Valuable Player Award. His chart shows his rising sign is Sagittarius, and the ruler of his rising sign, Jupiter, is placed in his 8th house, Cancer, where it is exalted and retrograde. Unlike the conflict-ridden 8th house of Ken Starr's, Troy's 8th house is expansive and extremely strong. First, because Jupiter is the largest planet, it brings a certain mass wherever it is placed. The 8th house often shows a person's downfall, but Jupiter in the 8th house is difficult to knock over. Its mass is just too great. So Troy can stay on his feet, even during intense pressure from the other team to knock him down.

Also, retrograde Jupiter is buoyant, so it gives him a lightness on his feet, and the smarts (Jupiter is the planet of wisdom and knowledge) to get out of trouble and execute the best plays. That his 8th house is watery Cancer gives him the ability to intuit appropriate reactions by "feeling" his way through difficult situations. Jupiter's retrograde nature brings him an economy of movement and cleverness.

It's interesting to note that we have often spoken of Mars and Saturn as planets that antagonize one another in dynamic, sometimes volatile ways. Notice that Troy has a Mars and Saturn opposition to almost the exact degree. His Moon is also aspected by these planets, as it sits very close to their degree of effect.

Because football can be violent, these planets work well for him. Do you see how important it is to see everything in its proper context? Whereas Mars and Saturn in opposition generally bring some form of violence, these planets give him added strength.

Does that mean Troy is entirely beyond their challenging effects? No. During his Saturn mahadasha he ran into some trouble, when the Mars bhukti was running. The Mars bhukti of his Saturn mahadasha ran between December 6, 1989, and January 15, 1991, during which Troy was injured. These planets impacted his 3rd house; you'll remember that the arms are the part of the body indicated by the 3rd house. On December 28, 1990, Troy went on the injured reserve list with a shoulder injury and subsequently missed the entire season.

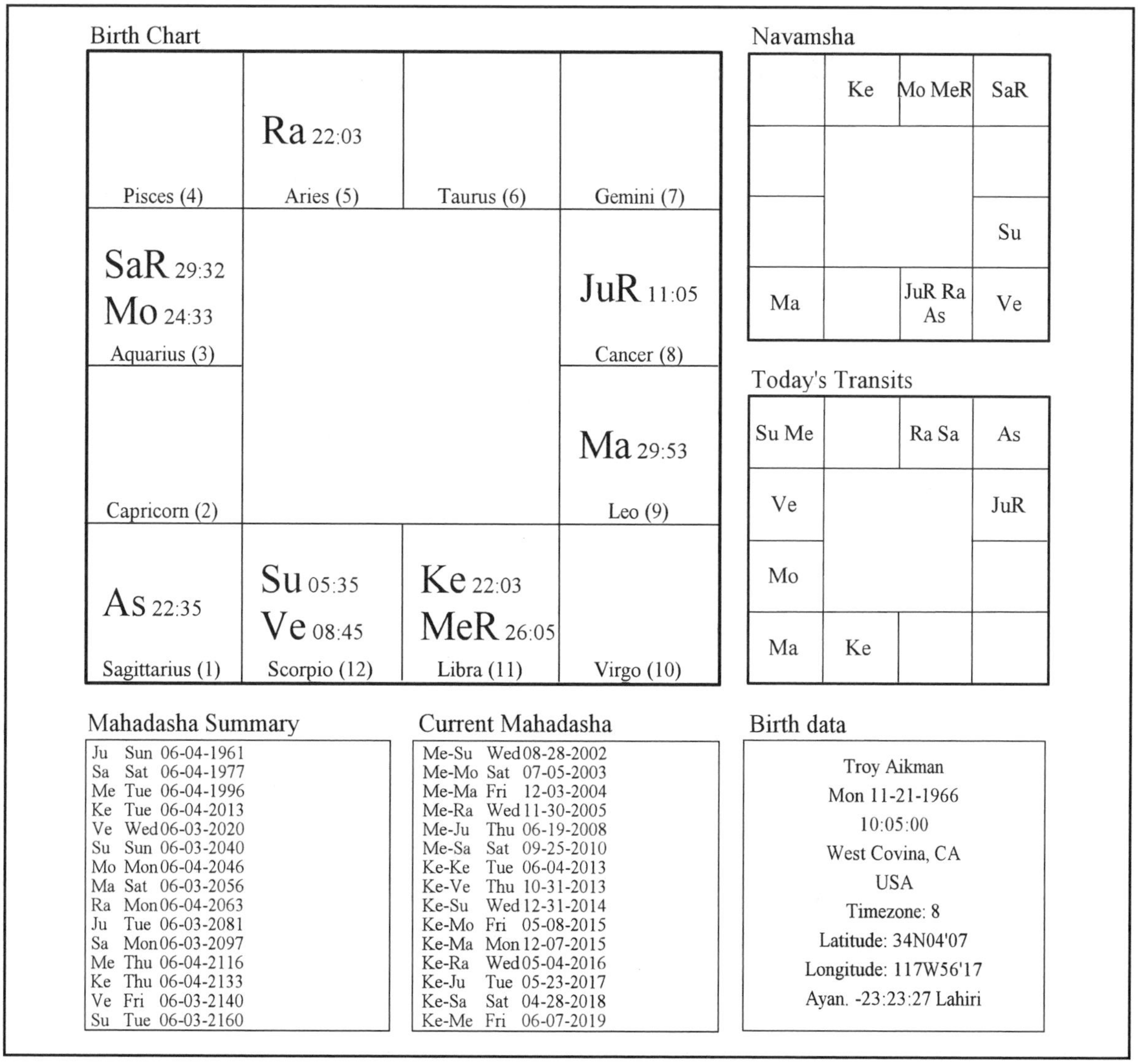

Birth Chart

Pisces (4)	Ra 22:03 Aries (5)	Taurus (6)	Gemini (7)
SaR 29:32 Mo 24:33 Aquarius (3)			JuR 11:05 Cancer (8)
Capricorn (2)			Ma 29:53 Leo (9)
As 22:35 Sagittarius (1)	Su 05:35 Ve 08:45 Scorpio (12)	Ke 22:03 MeR 26:05 Libra (11)	Virgo (10)

Navamsha

	Ke	Mo MeR	SaR
			Su
Ma		JuR Ra As	Ve

Today's Transits

Su Me		Ra Sa	As
Ve			JuR
Mo			
Ma	Ke		

Mahadasha Summary

Ju	Sun	06-04-1961
Sa	Sat	06-04-1977
Me	Tue	06-04-1996
Ke	Tue	06-04-2013
Ve	Wed	06-03-2020
Su	Sun	06-03-2040
Mo	Mon	06-04-2046
Ma	Sat	06-03-2056
Ra	Mon	06-04-2063
Ju	Tue	06-03-2081
Sa	Mon	06-03-2097
Me	Thu	06-04-2116
Ke	Thu	06-04-2133
Ve	Fri	06-03-2140
Su	Tue	06-03-2160

Current Mahadasha

Me-Su	Wed	08-28-2002
Me-Mo	Sat	07-05-2003
Me-Ma	Fri	12-03-2004
Me-Ra	Wed	11-30-2005
Me-Ju	Thu	06-19-2008
Me-Sa	Sat	09-25-2010
Ke-Ke	Tue	06-04-2013
Ke-Ve	Thu	10-31-2013
Ke-Su	Wed	12-31-2014
Ke-Mo	Fri	05-08-2015
Ke-Ma	Mon	12-07-2015
Ke-Ra	Wed	05-04-2016
Ke-Ju	Tue	05-23-2017
Ke-Sa	Sat	04-28-2018
Ke-Me	Fri	06-07-2019

Birth data

Troy Aikman
Mon 11-21-1966
10:05:00
West Covina, CA
USA
Timezone: 8
Latitude: 34N04'07
Longitude: 117W56'17
Ayan. -23:23:27 Lahiri

Chart 72—Troy Aikman

While you might think his Moon would be adversely affected by Saturn's being so close to it and being opposed by Mars, in fact, the Saturn brings Troy's Moon the necessary discipline and emotional steadiness to think clearly under fire. Again, what would ordinarily indicate a negative situation for a person ends up serving him very well because he uses combative energy on a regular basis.

However, notice the late degree his Mars and Saturn occupy in their respective positions—both are in sandhi (the fateful last degrees). Also, you'll recall that when the 1st house ruler is located in the 8th house there is the possibility of a head injury. After suffering at least ten concussions in twelve years of play, Aikman was finally let go in the spring of 2001.

This decision came soon after his Mercury mahadasha came into power. Notice that his Mercury is retrograde in his chart and conjunct with malefic Ketu and opposing Rahu by a close degree. Since mahadashas bring about the latent energy of planets, it wasn't until his Mercury became enlivened that people realized how dangerous his situation was. Why did it take so long? Because both his Mercury and Jupiter are retrograde in his chart, indicating that some of his tendencies can be hidden and revealed at a later time.

Now with Troy's Mercury cycle in power, no longer did people focus on his powerful, persevering nature (his Saturn mahadasha qualities). Instead they worried that he might not get up again if he took another hit to the head (a Mercury mahadasha concern—

remember, Mercury rules the mind, intellect, and brain).

How do we know these concussions posed a real threat to Troy? Look to his navamsha chart. His rising sign is Libra, and Jupiter is placed there (an enemy for Libra rising—Table G) along with malefic Rahu. The ruler of the sign, Venus, is located in the 12th house of loss. You bet he has a problem.

REMEDIES

Had River Phoenix's parents been able understand how susceptible their child was to outside influences, they surely would have monitored the professional choices he was making more carefully. When one has an understanding of Vedic astrology, it becomes quite easy to determine, from an afflicted 2nd house, for instance, that a child might have a propensity for addictions.

In River's case, his rising sign weakness could have been strongly improved by appeasing his Jupiter, since that planet is such a prominent feature in the chart. Although Jupiter does not give as much benefit in Libra rising as it would in another sign (it's in an enemy's house), it can still have a powerful positive influence on the chart.

Since Mars and Saturn hit his rising sign to the exact degree in malefic aspect, it would have helped to have strong death-averting Vedic fire rituals performed for this chart (mrtunjaya yagyas). Though a death-averting ritual does not necessarily change a person's destiny if he or she is destined to die young, it does remove any residual obstacles to a person's well-being.

In addition, strengthening Jupiter with mantra repetition on Thursdays and eating less that day might have helped. Also, wearing a yellow sapphire on the index finger of the right hand would have brought great benefit. The Venus could have been strengthened in the same way. By bringing strength to the powerful benefics in this chart, you can offset the negative influences from other planets, without needing to deal directly with them. Rather than wrestle with darkness, it's easier to just turn on the light.

What about Ken Starr? His chart is somewhat geared for controversy, due to the exact conjunction between Saturn and Sun in his 8th house. Though it is unlikely that Ken Starr would consult a Vedic astrologer, chant mantras, or arrange for a fire ritual, by taking such measures he could ease the potential for conflict in his chart by strengthening his Jupiter, which rules both his rising sign and the 10th house of career.

Chanting for Jupiter on Thursdays and eating less that day would help. When he enters an especially difficult period of conflict, he could soften the intensity by having fire rituals performed just before the anticipated event. In addition, he would do well to strengthen his Sun, the ruler of his 9th house of grace, which is strongly afflicted by Saturn. Chanting the Sun mantra on Sundays and eating less that day, along with wearing a ruby or red spinel, would help considerably.

As we discussed earlier, Troy Aikman entered his seventeen-year Mercury cycle in 1996, which means that interesting opportunities are also available to him for remedying some of his placements. Because his Ketu sits close to his retrograde Mercury, and Rahu opposes it, he would do well to chant the Mercury mantra on Wednesdays and eat less that day. An emerald or green tourmaline worn on the fifth finger of the right hand would also help. Without strengthening the Mercury during this time, there can be some confusion or misunderstanding that can play out in the houses that Mercury rules: the 7th house of marriage, and the 10th house of career.

Since retiring, Troy has taken a job as a football commentator. This is an ideal professional choice because Mercury has everything to do with teaching, instructing, and informing. However, there are rumors that he plans a comeback. As I just mentioned, there can be confusion during his Mercury major cycle in the houses Mercury rules, one of which is career. To return would be a poor, and potentially lethal, choice.

REMEDIES FOR YOUR 8th HOUSE

The 8th house is like the 6th house, except it doesn't have the benefit of being an upachaya, or improving house. For this reason, chronic habits or health complaints that aren't easily remedied will sometimes be reflected here. This is compounded by the fact, as was explained in the section on the 6th house, that strengthening the 8th house planets may aggravate the problem instead of alleviating it.

Each chart is unique and it's impossible to make a blanket statement about improving the 8th house without seeing the specific chart. The reason this is an issue with the 6th, 8th, and 12th houses is because they are malefic houses (dusthanas), and they deserve extra care.

However, you can always strengthen the 8th house ruler by chanting mantras to it on the day associated with that planet. You can also eat less that day. Chronic health or psychological 8th house issues are best dealt with by employing Vedic fire rituals. These can be performed either for the specific problem itself, or for the planet causing the mischief.

SUMMARY

The experiences of the 8th house are not always easy to transcend. Life can be difficult enough with the lights on; entering the 8th house is like making that same journey in the dark. It's not easy to find logical reasons or explanations for 8th house issues, and at times this house can be humbling. Faith is your greatest guide as you explore these depths. Ultimately, the universe is evolutionary in nature and will lead you in an uplifting direction if you allow it.

Once you plumb the depths of the 8th house, you are able to come into contact with the divine nature of your being. The 8th house is the house of transition from the more mundane levels of life to the exalted. Leaving the 8th house, you head toward the mid-heaven, where you express yourself as a complete and whole human being. The natural progression, then, is to the 9th house, which represents the deepest spiritual truths and the connection to spiritual mentors. Using our earlier analogy, if the 8th house is the mud from which the lotus blossoms, the 9th house takes us to the petals of the lotus itself.

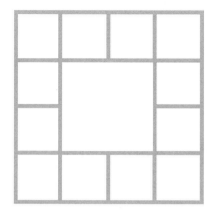

THE 9th HOUSE

The Father

An extremely favorable house, the 9th house indicates the father or fatherlike figures, such as mentors, teachers, or spiritual advisors.

The 9th house also includes overall luck, long-distance travel (though not necessarily the longest trips possible—for example, for those in North America, a trip to Europe as opposed to a trip to Asia), and spiritual growth in theory and practice. It is considered one of the most auspicious signs if well fortified. One's spiritual path, particularly one's faith and devotion, can be seen in the 9th house, especially by noting what planets occupy the sign and the position of its ruler.

For instance, Venus in the 9th house shows a person who may resonate to the feminine principle of divinity (e.g., Mary in Christianity, Tara in Tibetan Buddhism, Saraswati in Hinduism) or who has a woman as a spiritual teacher. This person also has a devotion and faith that exist quite naturally.

Saturn, on the other hand, can give you a more conventional, traditional, and disciplined approach to religion. Rahu in the 9th gives an unconventional approach to religion, an eclectic orientation to spirituality, and difficulty with organized religion.

The 9th house also has anatomical significance in the area between the lower hip and thighs.

THE NATURE OF THE 9th HOUSE

Find the 9th house in your chart. If you are Leo rising, your 9th house is Aries. If you are Libra rising, Gemini is your 9th house. Pay close attention to the zodiac sign of the 9th house because the nature of that sign will show you the way 9th house issues function.

For instance, if your 9th house is Sagittarius, your father may be philosophically oriented (or a lawyer). If your 9th house is Virgo, your father may be hypercritical.

HOW THE 9th HOUSE EXPRESSES ITSELF

Locate the planet that rules your 9th house (see Table B), and find where it's placed in your chart. Then read the description below that pertains to this placement.

The 9th House Ruler placed in the 1st house shows that you have natural luck. People may be amazed at how readily things happen for you. Your father is a positive influence in your life, and you have a certain refinement and charisma, even an air of royalty.

The 9th House Ruler placed in the 2nd house indicates that you speak convincingly and with wisdom about spiritual or philosophical matters. Your father may be instrumental in helping you generate income. Overall, money comes to you easily, but be conscious of how you spend it, and aim to spend wisely.

The 9th House Ruler placed in the 3rd house enhances all 3rd house indications. Relationships with siblings (usually younger ones) flourish, and your brothers and sisters may be philosophical and live lives of grace. Creative endeavors and courageous pursuits are all positively indicated. Efforts may involve spiritual matters.

The 9th House Ruler placed in the 4th house enhances all 4th house matters, so your mother benefits or your association with her is good. By focusing on your spiritual life, all worldly benefit and happiness come to you.

The 9th House Ruler placed in the 5th house indicates that much luck comes to you in speculative ventures. You have a strong spiritual connectedness, and your father or mentor is a powerful, wise presence. Children benefit you and they experience luck in their lives.

The 9th House Ruler placed in the 6th house shows the likelihood that your father is a healer. Otherwise, this position does not generally favor the health of the father, and he could be sickly and weak. Or the father could seem as if he is your enemy. You have luck in overcoming disputes and antagonists.

The 9th House Ruler placed in the 7th house enhances luck through marriage or partnership. Your spouse may be spiritually oriented and there may be a fair amount of foreign travel with him or her. Your father plays a positive role in this union or is supportive of it.

The 9th House Ruler placed in the 8th house is one of the few placements in which the 9th house ruler is not particularly well placed. Although it can show the pursuit of deep spiritual knowledge or philosophical concerns studied in private, it more likely indicates not much luck and difficulty for the father.

The 9th House Ruler placed in the 9th house is an extremely favorable position and lets all of the 9th house indications flourish. There may be long-distance travel associated with your gaining deep spiritual insight or philosophical understanding. Luck is also enhanced, as are the indications for the father.

The 9th House Ruler placed in the 10th house indicates that your father is strongly career oriented and powerful in his profession, and can help bolster your career. Likewise, you have luck in your career, and bring a certain refinement and righteousness there. This position can sometimes favor great leadership abilities in career.

The 9th House Ruler placed in the 11th house allows you to benefit greatly from friends or siblings (usually older). Luck in speculative ventures is also strongly enhanced. Opportunities abound, so that doors seem to open for you when you least expect them to, including while abroad.

The 9th House Ruler placed in the 12th house, as with the 8th house position, does not generally enhance 9th house results. Unless you are strongly spiritually oriented, and involved in long-distance pilgrimages or retreats for spiritual purposes, this position usually ruins your luck and indicates poor health or other difficulties for your father.

IF THERE ARE PLANETS IN THE 9th HOUSE

To help fine-tune the descriptions below, you'll want to assess whether the planet is welcome in the house in which it is placed (Table G). If the planet is in the house of a friend, the positive nature of the following description is enhanced. If the planet is in the house of an enemy, more of the negative possibilities need to be considered.

Sun (Su) in the 9th house indicates a father who is prominent, or the possibility that you will connect with a helpful mentor in life. Afflicted, your father's health or your relationship with your father may suffer.

Moon (Mo) in the 9th house brings luck and good fortune, as well as supportive parents. A poorly placed Moon indicates problems with parents, and mental unhappiness as a result.

Mars (Ma) in the 9th house brings strength to spiritual endeavors and overall drive. Afflicted, this position can indicate accidents or ill health for the father.

Mercury (Me) in the 9th house, if unafflicted, brings keen insight into spiritual truths, and overall luck. Afflicted, this position can show delusion in the mind about spiritual knowledge.

Jupiter (Ju) in the 9th house brings great luck and good fortune. This position shows a life filled with grace. Afflicted, the father is weakened and you have to create your own opportunities—they won't just fall in your lap.

Venus (Ve) in the 9th house indicates that women bring luck to you in your life. You have refinement and heightened aesthetic sensibilities. Otherwise, luck is spoiled and your father creates obstacles for you.

Saturn (Sa) in the 9th house indicates your father may be severe and conservative, yet long-lived. Opportunities do not come easily to you, and wisdom comes only after many years and much life experience. You may adopt a foreign religion.

Rahu (Ra) in the 9th house shows that you don't do well in organized religions, but instead may have a more eclectic approach to spirituality. This placement also shows conflict with the father or a father who suffers from ill health.

Ketu (Ke) in the 9th house brings a deep connection to spiritual matters, but if afflicted may indicate that you can be led astray by charismatic religious leaders who are deceptive false gurus.

OTHER CONSIDERATIONS

- Note the element associated with your 9th house. Remember that fire signs are driven; earth signs are patient; air signs are creative; and water signs are emotional.
- Also note the quality of your 9th house. Cardinal signs initiate; fixed signs stabilize; and mutable signs seek change.

Now check any aspects to the 9th house:

- Are any planets located in the same house as, or opposing any planet in, the 9th house? If so, are those planets friendly, neutral, or enemies? (See Table F.) For

instance, say your Rahu is placed in the 9th house and opposed by its enemy Sun. This planetary combination shows the possibility that your father will have allergies.

- Remember that Mars energizes the house it's in, as well as the 4th, 7th, and 8th houses from itself. This means if Mars is placed in the 2nd, 3rd, or 6th houses of your chart, it throws an aspect onto your 9th house. This brings the possibility of trouble when traveling long distances, or conflicts with the father (or he may experience conflict, illness, or accidents in his life). On the positive side, it also brings you a passion for spiritual truths and a tendency to align with a powerful spiritual teacher or life mentor.

- Saturn restricts or brings discipline to the house it's in, as well as the 3rd, 7th, and 10th houses from itself. This means if Saturn is placed in the 12th, 3rd, or 7th houses of your chart, it throws an aspect onto your 9th house, making your father conservative by nature, or something of a strict influence in your life.

- Jupiter expands or brings optimism to the house it's in, as well as the 5th, 7th, and 9th houses from itself. This means if Jupiter is placed in the 1st, 3rd, or 5th houses of your chart, it throws an aspect onto your 9th house, increasing luck, spiritual knowledge, and benefit from a father, mentor, or spiritual teacher.

- If you want to find out when your chart's 9th house energies will be enlivened, look to the 9th house ruler, or any planet located in the 9th house. Examine the Mahadasha Summary of your chart to see when that planet will come into power, and that will give you your answer. To find shorter periods when 9th house issues will be highlighted, look to the 9th house ruler or any planet located in the 9th house, and find the time its bhukti will run.

• Notice any influence transiting planets are having on your 9th house. Jupiter passing over the 9th can bring a spiritual teacher into your life. A Saturn transit can bring some restriction to your father. You can chant to the planet that is favorably transiting your rising sign, on the appropriate day for that planet, to enhance its effects.

EXAMPLE CHARTS

When we consider that George Lucas created an antagonistic character like Darth Vader based on his father (it is said he used the name Vader as a thin guise for the German word for father, *vater*), you have to wonder about the 9th house in his chart.

At first glance, Lucas's 9th house does not look that challenging. His rising sign is Aries, so his 9th house is Sagittarius. His 9th house ruler (Jupiter) is placed in the 4th house (Cancer), its house of exaltation. At face value, this looks exceptionally strong.

However, remember that Mars rules Aries, and look where George's Mars is placed in his chart. It is in the same house as his Jupiter, the indicator of his father. But Cancer is where the Mars is debilitated, so it is at its most weak.

Why is that a problem? Because Mars is the planet of power, and when it's the ruler of your rising sign and in debilitation, it indicates you have little sense of power, more so in George's case because his Mars is conjunct with malefic Rahu. And why doesn't he have power? Because a powerful, big planet in exaltation is keeping him from his own power. That planet is Jupiter, the indicator of his father (in this case).

To get a second opinion of the chart, let's look at the navamsha chart. The rising sign there is Scorpio, and the ruler of Scorpio is Mars, and that Mars is located in Cancer again, its place of debilitation. When the same planet is located in the same position in both the natal and navamsha charts, it is called vargottama, and indicates a powerful affirmation of that planet. In this case the affirmation is that in both the natal and navamsha charts, the ruler of the rising sign is Mars, and in both charts that Mars is in its house of debilitation.

This indicates a struggle to find one's self-worth in the midst of restriction. What about the indication for the father in the navamsha chart? The 9th house is Cancer, which is ruled by the Moon, and that Moon is in the fateful 8th house. So the indications are quite poor for the father in the navamsha chart as well.

When, due to painful external circumstances, a creatively talented person like George Lucas is forced to seek solace within his own imagination, humanity tends to benefit, provided the artist is successful in completing

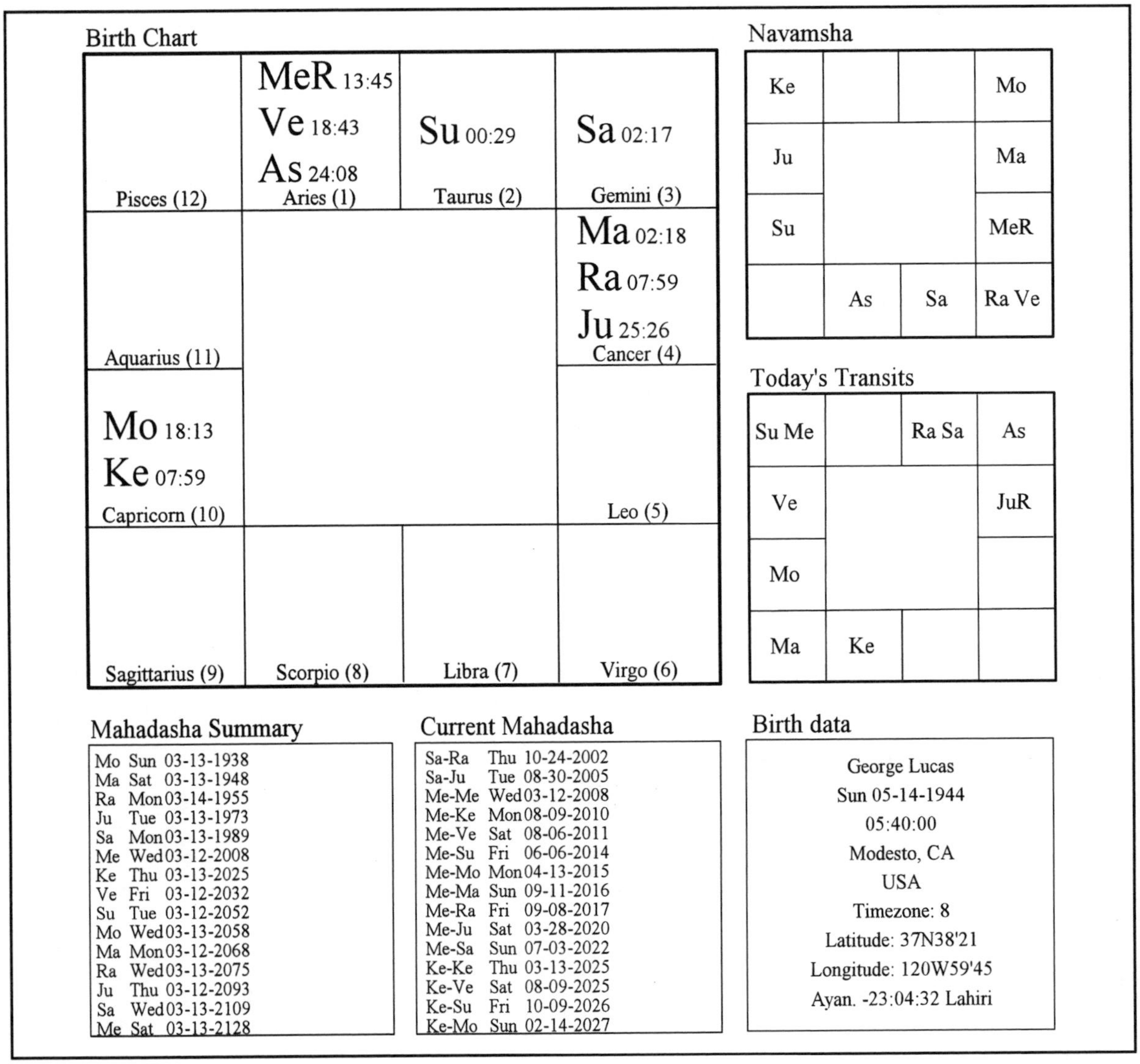

Birth Chart

Pisces (12)	MeR 13:45 Ve 18:43 As 24:08 Aries (1)	Su 00:29 Taurus (2)	Sa 02:17 Gemini (3)
Aquarius (11)			Ma 02:18 Ra 07:59 Ju 25:26 Cancer (4)
Mo 18:13 Ke 07:59 Capricorn (10)			Leo (5)
Sagittarius (9)	Scorpio (8)	Libra (7)	Virgo (6)

Navamsha

Ke			Mo
Ju			Ma
Su			MeR
	As	Sa	Ra Ve

Today's Transits

Su Me		Ra Sa	As
Ve			JuR
Mo			
Ma	Ke		

Mahadasha Summary

Mo	Sun	03-13-1938
Ma	Sat	03-13-1948
Ra	Mon	03-14-1955
Ju	Tue	03-13-1973
Sa	Mon	03-13-1989
Me	Wed	03-12-2008
Ke	Thu	03-13-2025
Ve	Fri	03-12-2032
Su	Tue	03-12-2052
Mo	Wed	03-13-2058
Ma	Mon	03-12-2068
Ra	Wed	03-13-2075
Ju	Thu	03-12-2093
Sa	Wed	03-13-2109
Me	Sat	03-13-2128

Current Mahadasha

Sa-Ra	Thu	10-24-2002
Sa-Ju	Tue	08-30-2005
Me-Me	Wed	03-12-2008
Me-Ke	Mon	08-09-2010
Me-Ve	Sat	08-06-2011
Me-Su	Fri	06-06-2014
Me-Mo	Mon	04-13-2015
Me-Ma	Sun	09-11-2016
Me-Ra	Fri	09-08-2017
Me-Ju	Sat	03-28-2020
Me-Sa	Sun	07-03-2022
Ke-Ke	Thu	03-13-2025
Ke-Ve	Sat	08-09-2025
Ke-Su	Fri	10-09-2026
Ke-Mo	Sun	02-14-2027

Birth data

George Lucas
Sun 05-14-1944
05:40:00
Modesto, CA
USA
Timezone: 8
Latitude: 37N38'21
Longitude: 120W59'45
Ayan. -23:04:32 Lahiri

Chart 73—George Lucas

the journey and translating it in ways others can share.

Richard's chart (Chart 74) is another one that shows an unusual issue around a father.

This chart shows Richard with Aries rising. His 9th house, then, is Sagittarius, which is ruled by Jupiter. Notice that Jupiter is retrograde and located in the 10th house, Capricorn. As you learned in Table E, Capricorn is the house where Jupiter is in its place of debilitation. Since the 9th house ruler placed in the 10th house indicates a father who brings career benefit to that person, you would expect that in Richard's case. His

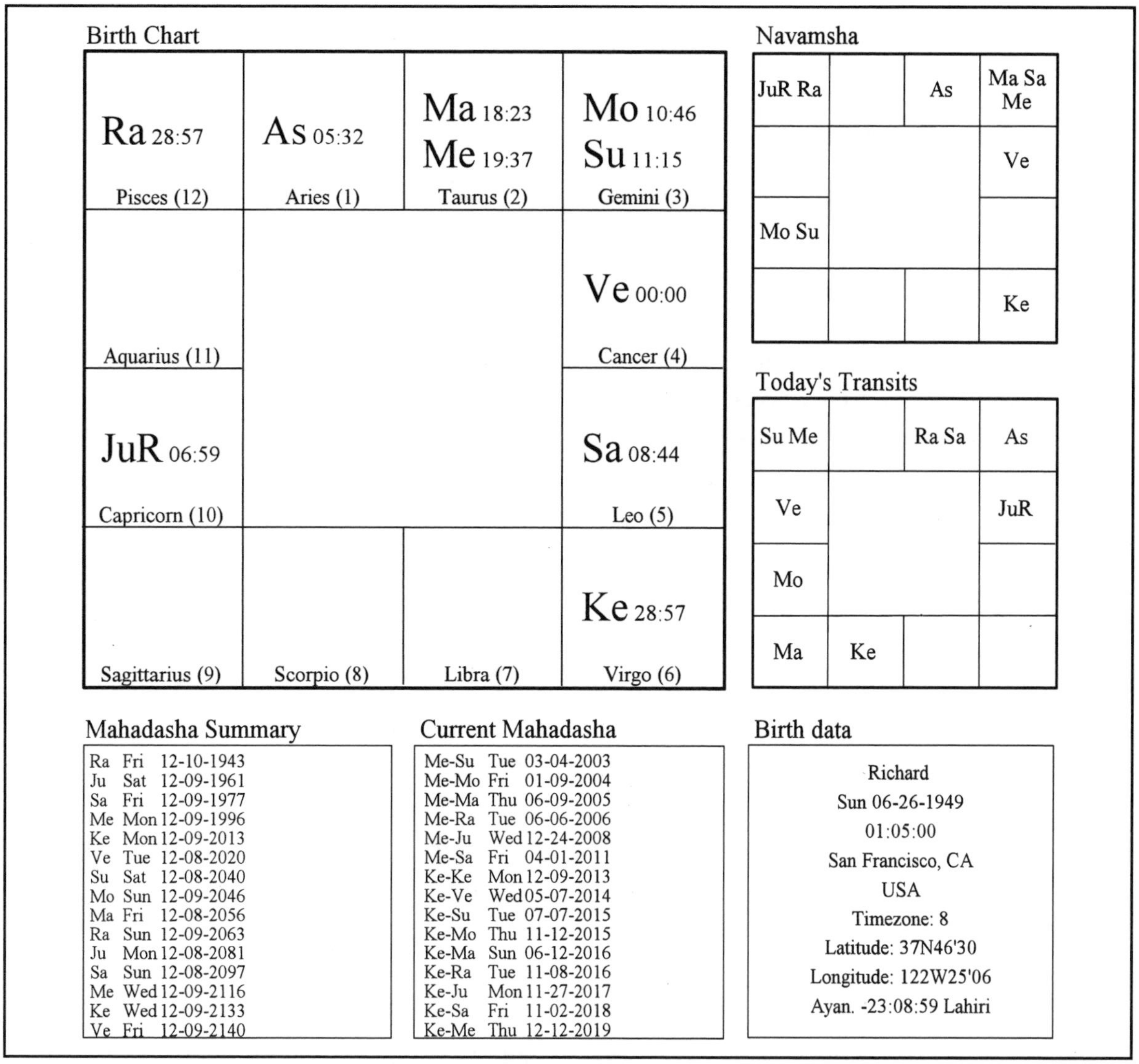

Birth Chart

Ra 28:57 Pisces (12)	As 05:32 Aries (1)	Ma 18:23 Me 19:37 Taurus (2)	Mo 10:46 Su 11:15 Gemini (3)
  Aquarius (11)			Ve 00:00 Cancer (4)
JuR 06:59 Capricorn (10)			Sa 08:44 Leo (5)
  Sagittarius (9)	Scorpio (8)	Libra (7)	Ke 28:57 Virgo (6)

Navamsha

JuR Ra		As	Ma Sa Me
			Ve
Mo Su			
			Ke

Today's Transits

Su Me		Ra Sa	As
Ve			JuR
Mo			
Ma	Ke		

Mahadasha Summary

Ra	Fri	12-10-1943
Ju	Sat	12-09-1961
Sa	Fri	12-09-1977
Me	Mon	12-09-1996
Ke	Mon	12-09-2013
Ve	Tue	12-08-2020
Su	Sat	12-08-2040
Mo	Sun	12-09-2046
Ma	Fri	12-08-2056
Ra	Sun	12-09-2063
Ju	Mon	12-08-2081
Sa	Sun	12-08-2097
Me	Wed	12-09-2116
Ke	Wed	12-09-2133
Ve	Fri	12-09-2140

Current Mahadasha

Me-Su	Tue	03-04-2003
Me-Mo	Fri	01-09-2004
Me-Ma	Thu	06-09-2005
Me-Ra	Tue	06-06-2006
Me-Ju	Wed	12-24-2008
Me-Sa	Fri	04-01-2011
Ke-Ke	Mon	12-09-2013
Ke-Ve	Wed	05-07-2014
Ke-Su	Tue	07-07-2015
Ke-Mo	Thu	11-12-2015
Ke-Ma	Sun	06-12-2016
Ke-Ra	Tue	11-08-2016
Ke-Ju	Mon	11-27-2017
Ke-Sa	Fri	11-02-2018
Ke-Me	Thu	12-12-2019

Birth data

Richard

Sun 06-26-1949

01:05:00

San Francisco, CA

USA

Timezone: 8

Latitude: 37N46'30

Longitude: 122W25'06

Ayan. -23:08:59 Lahiri

Chart 74—Richard

father owned car dealerships, and from the time he was young, Richard spent all of his time on the lots. He began working for his father as a young man, and in a few short years understood everything about the business. Although this was an invaluable education, the part that especially served Richard well was how to bargain (a retrograde Jupiter function) and get what he wanted in life.

The retrograde motion of Jupiter, however, and its location in its house of debilitation indicate a certain difficulty for the father. When Jupiter is in retrograde, it can indicate a person who obsesses about what it means to be successful in life, and the luxuries that he or she would be able to afford. However, since Jupiter is weak in Capricorn, the chances are slim that the person would ever realize such success. Jupiter in Capricorn shows a person who works very hard but never gets recognition or remuneration equal to the amount of effort put forth. This situation was aggravated by the fact that many of Richard's father's friends experienced great material success in life.

According to Richard, as the years went on, though his father's obsession intensified, he was never able to achieve the level of material wealth he had set as a goal for himself. Eventually the frustration of "failing" began to eat away at him, his health spiraled downward, and he died soon thereafter. Though this was difficult for Richard to watch, it enabled him to make the necessary adjustments in his own life so that his expectations equaled his ability to meet them.

Demi Moore is another who learned to succeed in spite of challenging family circumstances. Let's look again at her chart.

Though we'll eventually look at Demi's 9th house, let's first explore her chart using what we've learned so far about the other houses. Her rising sign is Aquarius, and the planet that rules Aquarius is Saturn. Saturn is in her 12th house, conjunct with Ketu and opposed by Mars in its sign of debilitation. Not only does this indicate a woman with poor self-esteem; it indicates a life filled with considerable conflict, as well, because Mars and Saturn are enemies. As a girl Demi was surrounded by alcoholism and abuse. Her parents divorced twice and she was forced to move more than forty times. The position of her rising sign is also in the fateful last degree of the sign, indicating weakness.

You'll also remember that when the 1st house ruler is in the 12th house, there is a possibility of a problem in the head region. Demi suffered from having crossed eyes when she was young, and needed two operations to correct the situation. This is indicated by Ketu aspecting the ruler of her rising sign, Saturn, in her 12th house. Ketu brings a mysterious, unusual element in malefic aspect, thus the crossed eyes.

However, Jupiter sits well placed in the rising sign, showing that despite the challenges inherent in this chart, she has grace behind her. The 2nd house ruler placed in the 1st house indicates that she is a self-made woman. Notice that Jupiter also rules her 11th house, which indicates opportunities and friendships. Demi got her break when she lived next to Natassja Kinski, who rehearsed scripts with Demi. Through this beneficial friendship she fueled her career.

Her 3rd house Moon brings her creative ability, along with a fiery temperament (Aries is a fire sign). Her skill at portraying deep emotional scenes (in *St. Elmo's Fire* and *About Last Night*) is due to this lunar position. It enables her to portray the emotional side of a character by pulling from her own painful emotional experiences.

Her 3rd house ruler, Mars, placed in the house of its debilitation, Cancer, the 6th house, shows strong determination, particularly with her acting ability. Her skills didn't

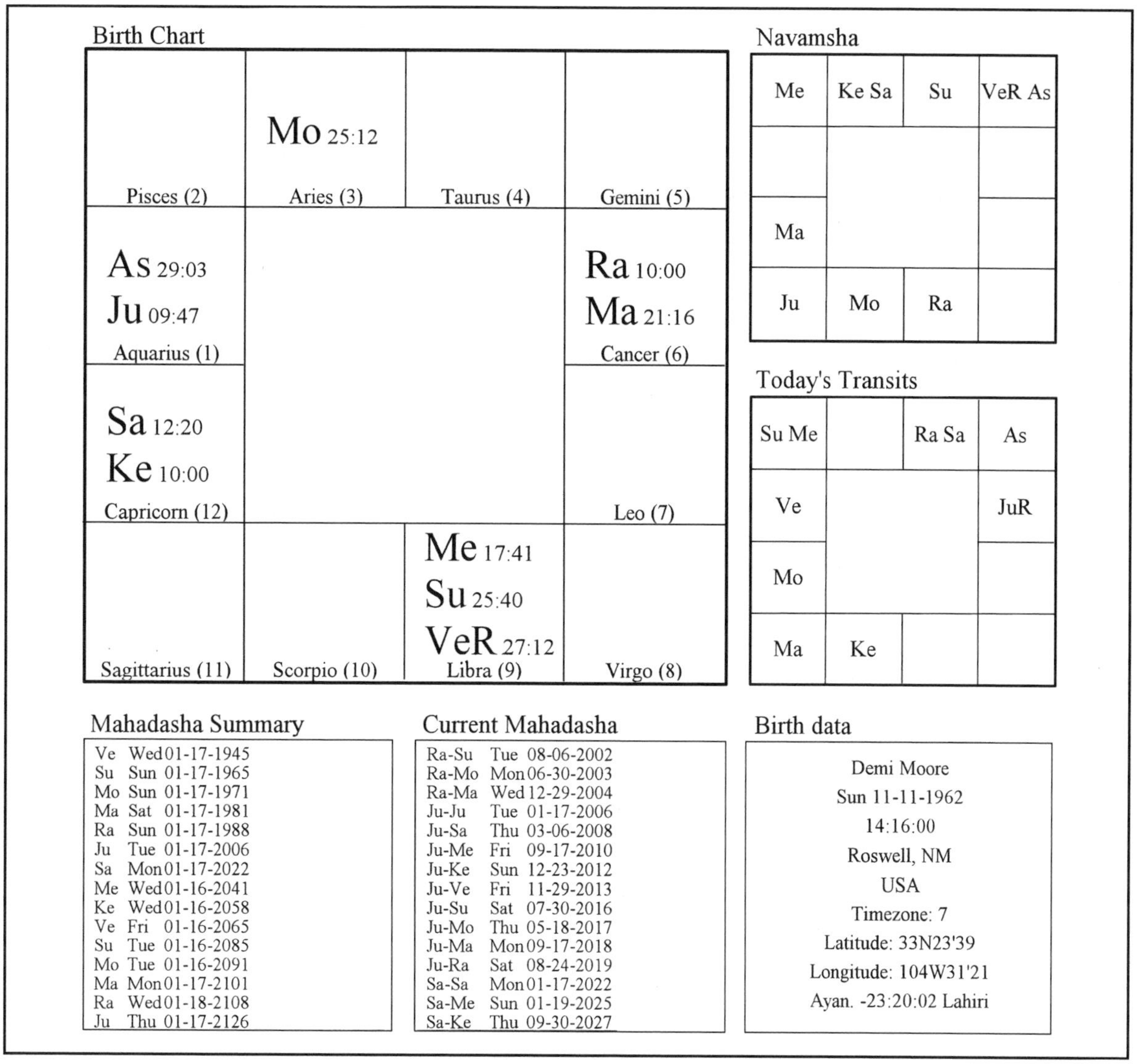

Birth Chart			
Pisces (2)	**Mo** 25:12 Aries (3)	Taurus (4)	Gemini (5)
As 29:03 **Ju** 09:47 Aquarius (1)			**Ra** 10:00 **Ma** 21:16 Cancer (6)
Sa 12:20 **Ke** 10:00 Capricorn (12)			Leo (7)
Sagittarius (11)	Scorpio (10)	**Me** 17:41 **Su** 25:40 **VeR** 27:12 Libra (9)	Virgo (8)

Navamsha			
Me	Ke Sa	Su	VeR As
Ma			
Ju	Mo	Ra	

Today's Transits			
Su Me		Ra Sa	As
Ve			JuR
Mo			
Ma	Ke		

Mahadasha Summary

Ve	Wed 01-17-1945
Su	Sun 01-17-1965
Mo	Sun 01-17-1971
Ma	Sat 01-17-1981
Ra	Sun 01-17-1988
Ju	Tue 01-17-2006
Sa	Mon 01-17-2022
Me	Wed 01-16-2041
Ke	Wed 01-16-2058
Ve	Fri 01-16-2065
Su	Tue 01-16-2085
Mo	Tue 01-16-2091
Ma	Mon 01-17-2101
Ra	Wed 01-18-2108
Ju	Thu 01-17-2126

Current Mahadasha

Ra-Su	Tue 08-06-2002
Ra-Mo	Mon 06-30-2003
Ra-Ma	Wed 12-29-2004
Ju-Ju	Tue 01-17-2006
Ju-Sa	Thu 03-06-2008
Ju-Me	Fri 09-17-2010
Ju-Ke	Sun 12-23-2012
Ju-Ve	Fri 11-29-2013
Ju-Su	Sat 07-30-2016
Ju-Mo	Thu 05-18-2017
Ju-Ma	Mon 09-17-2018
Ju-Ra	Sat 08-24-2019
Sa-Sa	Mon 01-17-2022
Sa-Me	Sun 01-19-2025
Sa-Ke	Thu 09-30-2027

Birth data

Demi Moore
Sun 11-11-1962
14:16:00
Roswell, NM
USA
Timezone: 7
Latitude: 33N23'39
Longitude: 104W31'21
Ayan. -23:20:02 Lahiri

Chart 75—Demi Moore

come completely naturally, but only through work and practice.

Mars also rules her 10th house, the house of career. So when the 10th house ruler is placed in the 6th house, it shows that one fights one's way through any career obstacles in order to achieve success. It didn't come eas-

ily. She had to beat out thousands of actresses for a role in the soap opera *General Hospital*.

Her 7th house ruler, the Sun, is placed in its house of debilitation, Libra, and is aspected by Saturn (throwing a 10th house aspect). It doesn't surprise us, then, that she has been married more than once.

Now look at her 9th house, Libra. Mercury, Sun, and retrograde Venus are in her 9th house. The Sun is in its place of debilitation, and the entire house is aspected by Mars (4th house aspect) and Saturn (10th house aspect). Mercury, a neutral planet taking on the influence of planets around it, becomes malefic due to the aspects of the Mars, Sun, and Saturn. The Jupiter in her rising sign also aspects the 9th house. So the 9th house appears to be filled with struggle and drama.

Look at the navamsha. Venus is placed in her rising sign, Gemini, in the navamsha. The ruler of Gemini—Mercury—is placed in the 10th house of career, showing that as a strong focus. Aquarius is her 9th house, ruled by Saturn, and that Saturn is placed in debilitation in Aries in her 11th house. So what can be seen from this is that her father was of no help. Indeed, he was unemployable and gambled away whatever money he had, and he and Demi's mother were married and divorced from each other several times.

More amazingly, when he committed suicide just before Demi's sixteenth birthday, she found out he wasn't even her biological father. Demi's real father left before Demi was born.

As the 9th house also indicates luck, Demi's chart indicates that hers is spoiled (as you can imagine). However, because Venus is placed in the house it rules, and her rising sign Jupiter aspects the sign, Demi has been able to make her own luck. Even though she ran up against many hardships, her planets supported her lifting of herself out of what might otherwise have been a tragic life.

Now, let's look at the chart of a successful healer.

Karen's chart (Chart 76) has Taurus rising. Touching on a few aspects of the chart before getting to the 9th house, notice that retrograde Jupiter is in Karen's 2nd house, which is Gemini, indicating great wealth. The retrograde aspect of Jupiter enables Karen to hold onto the wealth she makes. How do you think she makes her money? Look at where the 2nd house ruler is placed. Mercury rules Gemini, and Karen's Mercury is placed in the 6th house of her chart, the house of health and healing. So she makes a great deal of money from a healing practice. To confirm this indication, look at the 10th house (house of career) and notice that it is Aquarius, which is ruled by Saturn. Along with the fact that Aquarius is a humanitarian house and tends to make a person altruistically motivated, its ruler Saturn is placed in exaltation in Karen's 6th house, also the position for healing.

When might you expect that Karen would make her money? Look at the Mahadasha Summary and notice that Jupiter began its cycle in late October, 1992. By late 1993, she was making money hand over fist.

Now look at Karen's 9th house, Capricorn, which is also ruled by Saturn. The Moon and Rahu are placed in the 9th house. Since the Moon is associated with the mother, its traits are those traditionally attributed to her: nurturing, caring, protecting, feeding, and embracing. When the Moon is well placed in the 9th house, it shows a father who expresses those qualities. How might the father make his living? The ruler of Karen's 9th house, Saturn, is placed in her 6th house. So the father is a healer, too.

Although Capricorn is a down-to-earth sign, providing a practical and traditional nature, Rahu (which conjoins the Moon in Karen's 9th house) indicates that her father would embrace alternative types of healing.

As I've mentioned several times, Rahu tends to make people alternative minded. So, Karen's father began by practicing traditional medicine, but then began incorporating alternative methods of healing.

Paul's chart (Chart 77) reflects another interesting patriarchal family dynamic.

Paul's rising sign is Capricorn, ruled by

Birth Chart				Navamsha			
Pisces (11)	Aries (12)	**As** 19:51 Taurus (1)	**JuR** 03:15 Gemini (2)		Me		As
				Ve Ra			
Aquarius (10)			**Ke** 05:36 Cancer (3)	Mo			Ke
Ra 05:36 **Mo** 01:01 Capricorn (9)			**Ma** 26:28 Leo (4)		Sa Ma	JuR	Su
Sagittarius (8)	Scorpio (7)	**Sa** 05:59 **Me** 22:14 Libra (6)	**Ve** 03:35 **Su** 29:10 Virgo (5)				

Today's Transits			
Su Me		Ra Sa	As
Ve			JuR
Mo			
Ma	Ke		

Mahadasha Summary		Current Mahadasha		Birth data
Su Mon 10-29-1951		Ju-Ve Sat 09-09-2000		Karen
Mo Tue 10-29-1957		Ju-Su Sun 05-11-2003		Thu 10-15-1953
Ma Sun 10-29-1967		Ju-Mo Fri 02-27-2004		20:20:00
Ra Tue 10-29-1974		Ju-Ma Tue 06-28-2005		Charleston, WV
Ju Wed 10-28-1992		Ju-Ra Sun 06-04-2006		USA
Sa Tue 10-28-2008		Sa-Sa Tue 10-28-2008		Timezone: 5
Me Fri 10-29-2027		Sa-Me Tue 11-01-2011		Latitude: 38N20'59
Ke Fri 10-28-2044		Sa-Ke Fri 07-11-2014		Longitude: 81W37'58
Ve Sat 10-28-2051		Sa-Ve Thu 08-20-2015		Ayan. -23:12:56 Lahiri
Su Wed 10-28-2071		Sa-Su Fri 10-19-2018		
Mo Thu 10-28-2077		Sa-Mo Tue 10-01-2019		
Ma Tue 10-28-2087		Sa-Ma Sun 05-02-2021		
Ra Thu 10-28-2094		Sa-Ra Fri 06-10-2022		
Ju Fri 10-28-2112		Sa-Ju Wed 04-16-2025		
Sa Thu 10-28-2128		Me-Me Fri 10-29-2027		

Chart 76—Karen

Saturn, which is placed in his 9th house of Virgo. Venus is also in Virgo, its sign of debilitation. Venus is the planet of love, but when it sits in debilitation it is unable to give the results one might expect. The love that Paul would expect to receive from his father was rarely met, and this is compounded by the fact that Saturn sits so close to the Venus. Although Saturn and Venus work well together in many ways—for instance, in bringing forth skills in design, work with colors and textures, photography, and graphic arts—it's not easy for these planets to express love.

Look at the ruler of Paul's 9th house, Mercury, which is placed in the 8th house. As you may recall, this placement is poor for the

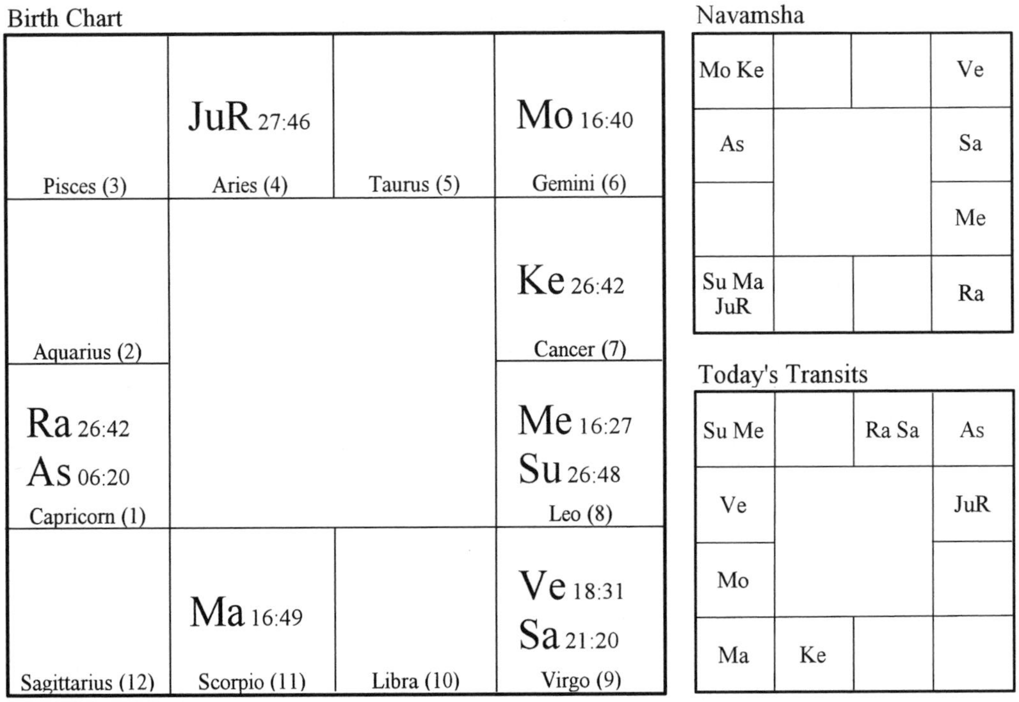

Birth Chart

	JuR 27:46		Mo 16:40
Pisces (3)	Aries (4)	Taurus (5)	Gemini (6)
Aquarius (2)			Ke 26:42
			Cancer (7)
Ra 26:42 As 06:20			Me 16:27 Su 26:48
Capricorn (1)			Leo (8)
	Ma 16:49		Ve 18:31 Sa 21:20
Sagittarius (12)	Scorpio (11)	Libra (10)	Virgo (9)

Navamsha

Mo Ke			Ve
As			Sa
			Me
Su Ma JuR			Ra

Today's Transits

Su Me		Ra Sa	As
Ve			JuR
Mo			
Ma	Ke		

Mahadasha Summary

Ra	Thu	03-09-1939
Ju	Fri	03-08-1957
Sa	Thu	03-08-1973
Me	Sun	03-08-1992
Ke	Sun	03-08-2009
Ve	Tue	03-08-2016
Su	Fri	03-07-2036
Mo	Sat	03-08-2042
Ma	Thu	03-07-2052
Ra	Sat	03-08-2059
Ju	Sun	03-07-2077
Sa	Sat	03-07-2093
Me	Tue	03-08-2112
Ke	Tue	03-08-2129
Ve	Thu	03-08-2136

Current Mahadasha

Me-Ra	Tue	09-04-2001
Me-Ju	Tue	03-23-2004
Me-Sa	Thu	06-29-2006
Ke-Ke	Sun	03-08-2009
Ke-Ve	Tue	08-04-2009
Ke-Su	Mon	10-04-2010
Ke-Mo	Wed	02-09-2011
Ke-Ma	Sat	09-10-2011
Ke-Ra	Mon	02-06-2012
Ke-Ju	Sun	02-24-2013
Ke-Sa	Fri	01-31-2014
Ke-Me	Wed	03-11-2015
Ve-Ve	Tue	03-08-2016
Ve-Su	Mon	07-08-2019
Ve-Mo	Tue	07-07-2020

Birth data

Paul

Fri 09-12-1952

17:00:00

Harrisburg, PA

USA

Timezone: 5

Latitude: 40N16'25

Longitude: 76W53'05

Ayan. -23:11:58 Lahiri

Chart 77—Paul

father, and even though Paul's father didn't suffer from ill health or experience a short life, he was psychologically very weak. In fact, from a very young age Paul became the man of the family. His mother and siblings would always come to him—not the father—with their problems.

We know that the 9th house ruler placed in the 8th house brings problems to the father, but it's important to be able to fine-tune our understanding of the nature of the problem and its severity. How would we know, for instance, that Paul's father was just a weak man and didn't really suffer more than just psychologically? Look at Jupiter placed in Paul's 4th house, Aries, and recall that Jupiter throws an aspect on the 5th house from itself. This planet hits the ruler of Paul's 9th house strongly, bringing protection and support, which are qualities of Jupiter.

If you need to fine-tune the prediction even more, remember that you can use the house you want to analyze as if it's the rising sign, and analyze the chart accordingly. Paul's 9th house is Virgo, so if we want to explore the father we will use Virgo as the rising sign, with Saturn and debilitated Venus conjoined there. Already this tells us a lot about Paul's father.

Saturn in the rising sign shows restriction and shyness. More importantly, debilitated Venus rules the father's 9th house, which is Taurus. This shows us that the father received no love from his father, and probably never knew how to give to his son what he himself never received.

Now let's look at the 9th house in terms of its spiritual indications by examining the chart of Pope John Paul II (Chart 78).

Though his birth information is somewhat debatable, it seems that the Pope's rising sign is Leo, and the ruler of the rising sign, Sun, is placed in the 10th house, the house of career. Generally, with Leo rising—a dramatic sign that attracts the limelight—and with its ruler placed in the 10th house, tremendous career success would be anticipated. But Saturn sits in his rising sign, bringing humility and understatement, though not lessening the impact he can have on the masses. Saturn also brings the inherent need to be of service to others.

This is the ideal chart for a religious leader, because it combines charisma with a tempered ego. His Moon in its exalted house of Taurus brings the charisma, and Saturn aspecting it results in humility (10th house aspect by Saturn).

His 9th house is Aries, ruled by Mars, which is placed in the 2nd house. This enables him to speak convincingly and with wisdom about spiritual and philosophical matters. The retrograde nature of that Mars enables him to pull from an inward source, to tap inspiration from within.

Additionally, look at his 9th house planets. Venus, Ketu, and Mercury are in the 9th house, aspected by Mars, and opposed by Rahu. The Ketu hemmed in by the Venus and Mercury keeps the focus of 9th house issues introspective and spiritual by nature.

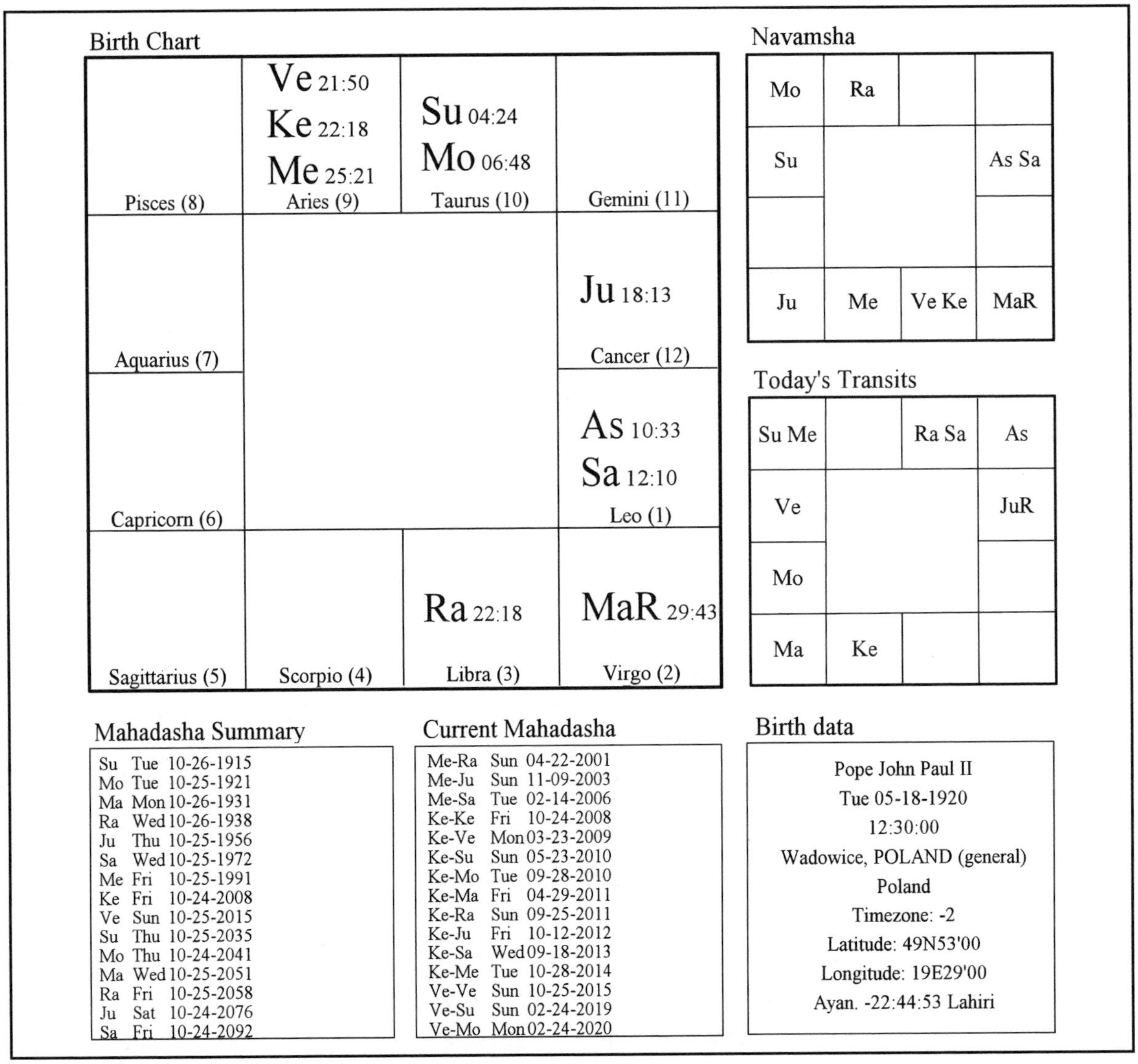

Birth Chart

Pisces (8)	Ve 21:50 Ke 22:18 Me 25:21 Aries (9)	Su 04:24 Mo 06:48 Taurus (10)	Gemini (11)
Aquarius (7)			Ju 18:13 Cancer (12)
Capricorn (6)			As 10:33 Sa 12:10 Leo (1)
Sagittarius (5)	Scorpio (4)	Ra 22:18 Libra (3)	MaR 29:43 Virgo (2)

Navamsha

Mo	Ra		
Su			As Sa
Ju	Me	Ve Ke	MaR

Today's Transits

Su Me		Ra Sa	As
Ve			JuR
Mo			
Ma	Ke		

Mahadasha Summary

Su	Tue	10-26-1915
Mo	Tue	10-25-1921
Ma	Mon	10-26-1931
Ra	Wed	10-26-1938
Ju	Thu	10-25-1956
Sa	Wed	10-25-1972
Me	Fri	10-25-1991
Ke	Fri	10-24-2008
Ve	Sun	10-25-2015
Su	Thu	10-25-2035
Mo	Thu	10-24-2041
Ma	Wed	10-25-2051
Ra	Fri	10-25-2058
Ju	Sat	10-24-2076
Sa	Fri	10-24-2092

Current Mahadasha

Me-Ra	Sun	04-22-2001
Me-Ju	Sun	11-09-2003
Me-Sa	Tue	02-14-2006
Ke-Ke	Fri	10-24-2008
Ke-Ve	Mon	03-23-2009
Ke-Su	Sun	05-23-2010
Ke-Mo	Tue	09-28-2010
Ke-Ma	Fri	04-29-2011
Ke-Ra	Sun	09-25-2011
Ke-Ju	Fri	10-12-2012
Ke-Sa	Wed	09-18-2013
Ke-Me	Tue	10-28-2014
Ve-Ve	Sun	10-25-2015
Ve-Su	Sun	02-24-2019
Ve-Mo	Mon	02-24-2020

Birth data

Pope John Paul II

Tue 05-18-1920

12:30:00

Wadowice, POLAND (general)

Poland

Timezone: -2

Latitude: 49N53'00

Longitude: 19E29'00

Ayan. -22:44:53 Lahiri

Chart 78—Pope John Paul II

REMEDIES

It is sometimes the case with deeply creative people that the pain they experience in life catalyzes their greatest works of art. I'm not suggesting that you have to live a life of agony in order to create magnificently, and we've mentioned several people in this book who have proven that to be true (e.g., Steven Spielberg and Michael Crichton). Yet the question remains: Had George Lucas been able to soothe the conflict with his father through planetary remedial measures, would he have still created the *Star Wars* trilogy?

Regardless, the ruler of his rising sign is weak and needs strengthening. Mars sits in debilitation in Cancer, and can be empowered by Mars mantras on Tuesdays and eating less food on that day. A large red coral worn as a ring or pendant would also help greatly.

In addition, Lucas could strengthen the Venus in his chart, which sits in his rising sign and rules his 2nd house. The Sun in the 2nd house must have been another paternal influence that limited his ability to speak his mind. Bringing power to the Venus would simultaneously strengthen his rising sign and empower his house of verbal communication. George would do well to chant Venus mantras on Fridays, and to eat less food on that day as well.

Richard, our young car salesman, would do well to strengthen the Jupiter in his chart, which sits in debilitation and in retrograde. Although the retrograde motion of Jupiter enables Richard to bargain hunt and help the downtrodden, it is still the weakest planet in the chart. Chanting the Jupiter mantra on Thursdays and eating less that day would help considerably, as would wearing a yellow sapphire. Not only would the effects bring more consistent luck in his life, but they would empower his 4th house Venus, which is associated with material and spiritual prosperity.

Demi would also do well to strengthen her Jupiter. Sitting in the rising sign, it has the ability to smooth out many of her emotional rough edges. Her Moon could also use some help. Notice that her Moon sits all by itself. No planet shares the house with the Moon, nor is a planet located in the houses on either side of the Moon. This creates for a person a deep inner loneliness that cannot be quenched by friends or lovers. A large moonstone pendant would help matters, as would chanting the Moon mantras on Mondays and eating less food that day.

STRENGTHENING YOUR 9th HOUSE

Because the 9th house is deeply spiritual in nature, one of the benefits of strengthening it is that many other elements of your life naturally fall into place. Often, those intensely sought-after goals or strong unfulfilled desires simply drop away.

You can empower any benefic in the 9th house by chanting its mantra on the appropriate day, and eating less on that day. Although it's best not to chant to any malefic 9th house planet, you can strengthen the ruler of the 9th house, and any planet that favorably aspects the 9th, by chanting their mantras on the appropriate days. Since both the Sun and Jupiter are indicators (karakas) for the 9th house, you can also empower the 9th house with Sun or Jupiter mantras chanted on Sunday or Thursday, respectively.

SUMMARY

The 9th house provides you the opportunity to tap into your spiritual nature. What you find there might be surprising. To illustrate this point, there is an oft-told story in India about a lion cub that somehow became separated from its mother and was adopted by a family of donkeys. As the years passed, the lion was raised as a donkey and acted like one in every respect. One day, a spiritual master heard the lion braying, and he approached him and explained to the lion that he was confused. The lion had forgotten that he was the king of the jungle, and instead thought himself to be a beast of burden.

Once you come to recognize your true nature in the 9th house, you are ready to come out into the world through the 10th house. The 10th house is where you shine, and as such represents vocational pursuits, indicating that you are ready to fully express yourself professionally, ideally in a way that is a pure extension of your being. That's why the 9th house precedes the 10th, so you can first come to know your true inner pulse before you express it outwardly.

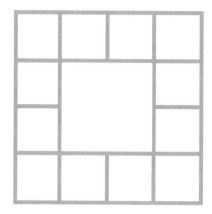

THE 10th HOUSE

Career

The main focus of this house is your career, your job, and as an extension of that, fame, leadership, or authority (or lack thereof). Anatomically, the 10th house is associated with the knees.

The 10th house, like the 3rd, 6th, and 11th houses, is an upachaya house. This means that it is a house that improves over time with effort, even if it is afflicted.

THE NATURE OF THE 10th HOUSE

Find the 10th house in your chart. If you are Aries rising, your 10th house is Capricorn. If you are Gemini rising, Pisces is your 10th house. Pay close attention to the zodiac sign of the 10th house because the nature of that sign will show you the way 10th house issues function.

For instance, if Gemini is your 10th house, you could make your living as a teacher or writer. If your 10th house is Capricorn, you may be drawn to business.

HOW THE 10th HOUSE EXPRESSES ITSELF

Locate the planet that rules your 10th house (see Table B), and find where it's placed in your chart. Then read the description below that pertains to this placement.

The 10th House Ruler placed in the 1st house indicates that you are a career-minded person whose profession is dependent on your physical traits and skills. You may be entrepreneurial by nature, and will rarely stop before getting what you want. This position usually indicates a self-made person.

The 10th House Ruler placed in the 2nd house indicates that your career plays out through 2nd house issues. Overall, this is a good placement for earning ability, and your profession can involve speaking, lecturing, teaching, and even dealing with money.

The 10th House Ruler placed in the 3rd house indicates that your creative abilities are not just hobbies; they designate your career path. Your skills in acting, writing, dance, or literature should be cultivated because they show how you will likely make your living. This position favors courage, and the possibility that a sibling (probably younger) will enhance your career in some way.

The 10th House Ruler placed in the 4th house shows that your career enhances your ability to own property and homes, and therefore indicates a successful vocational path. Your career also brings you a great deal of happiness, and benefits your mother, too.

The 10th House Ruler placed in the 5th house favors an early drive toward your career goals because the 5th house is the house of destiny. The path to realizing these goals will be well defined and obstacles will naturally drop away. This is also a position that can indicate a career in speculation.

The 10th House Ruler placed in the 6th house indicates that you have to overcome people who try to hold you back or discredit you. There may be obstacles to finding your career path, or you may (initially) work hard without being fairly compensated. Your career may also involve the healing arts or medicine.

The 10th House Ruler placed in the 7th house indicates that your career is enhanced by being associated with a partner or a spouse. You work well in collaboration with others. This is a powerful position for the career, indicating success.

The 10th House Ruler placed in the 8th house indicates that your career could involve the mystical or metaphysical. It may be difficult to find your career path. Either you work many different types of jobs, or you lose jobs you like. You can also be involved in hidden activities like research or ghostwriting.

The 10th House Ruler placed in the 9th house is very favorable for the overall luck and success of your career. Your vocational pursuits may involve philosophy or spiritual activities, or a certain amount of long-distance travel. Your career path may also be influenced by your father, or may benefit him.

The 10th House Ruler placed in the 10th house is perhaps the most powerful placement for the career house, showing a person with great leadership ability who either stands at the helm, or operates in a strong, responsibility-bearing manner.

The 10th House Ruler placed in the 11th house indicates that a sibling (usually older) may be involved in your career, or enhance your vocational pursuits somehow. Your career could involve speculation, or friends may help to further it. Professionally you connect with powerful and influential people.

The 10th House Ruler placed in the 12th house doesn't generally favor happiness in your career. You can have trouble finding your career path or be disappointed in the one you've chosen. On the positive side, it can also indicate working in a spiritual environment or being involved with foreign ventures.

IF THERE ARE PLANETS IN THE 10th HOUSE

To help fine-tune the descriptions below, you'll want to assess whether the planet is welcome in the house in which it is placed (Table G). If the planet is in the house of a friend, the positive nature of the following description is enhanced. If the planet is in the house of an enemy, more of the negative possibilities need to be considered.

Sun (Su) in the 10th house indicates success in your chosen career, particularly as an administrator or at the helm of a company. If afflicted, this position indicates the frustration of feeling capable, but not getting the chance to prove yourself.

Moon (Mo) in the 10th house shows popularity in your chosen profession. You may be involved in providing nurturing energy in your career (as a counselor or therapist), and may cater specifically to women. If afflicted, this position shows subservience in the career and many vocational changes.

Mars (Ma) in the 10th house brings great power to the career house. You may be a professional athlete or in the military. If not well placed, this position shows difficulty in settling down to just one career, due to impatience.

Mercury (Me) in the 10th house, if unafflicted, indicates a career as a teacher, speaker, or writer. Otherwise, you tend to go unnoticed at work and are seen as weak-minded.

Jupiter (Ju) in the 10th house shows early success in your chosen profession, and a sense early in life of how you will make your living. It could show a career as a counselor/advisor, teacher, banker, or broker. Otherwise, you will not be compensated in an amount equal to the work you do.

Venus (Ve) in the 10th house shows you could work in women's fashion, design, interior decorating, or any of the fine arts. If afflicted, women will create obstacles to your career path.

Saturn (Sa) in the 10th house, if well placed, brings great strength to your career over time. It might show someone in a responsible leadership position, or indicate a career in agriculture. If afflicted, you may end up working only menial jobs.

Rahu (Ra) in the 10th house indicates the possibility that you will have an impact upon large masses of people through your chosen career. Otherwise, you may run into career conflicts and power struggles, especially while dealing with foreigners.

Ketu (Ke) in the 10th house enables you to incorporate mysticism into your chosen career. Otherwise, you might experience losses in your career due to deception.

OTHER CONSIDERATIONS

- Note the element associated with your 10th house. Remember that fire signs are driven; earth signs are patient; air signs are creative; and water signs are emotional.
- Also note the quality of your 10th house. Cardinal signs initiate; fixed signs stabilize; and mutable signs seek change.

Now check the aspects to the 10th house:

- Are any planets located in the same house as, or opposing any planet in, the 10th house? If so, are those planets friendly, neutral, or enemies? (See Table F.) For instance, say your Venus is placed in the 10th house and opposed by its friend Saturn. This planetary combination shows interest in colors, textures, and graphic design.
- Remember that Mars energizes the house it's in, as well as the 4th, 7th, and 8th houses from itself. This means if Mars is placed in the 3rd, 4th, or 7th house of your chart, it throws an aspect onto your 10th house, keeping you one step ahead of the competition, and making you willing to take professional risks in order to succeed.
- Saturn restricts or brings discipline to the house it's in, as well as the 3rd, 7th, and 10th houses from itself. This means if Saturn is placed in the 1st, 4th, or 8th house of your chart, it throws an aspect onto your 10th house, bringing perseverance and discipline to your work habits.

- Jupiter expands or brings optimism to the house it's in, as well as the 5th, 7th, and 9th houses from itself. This means if Jupiter is placed in the 2nd, 4th, or 6th house of your chart, it throws an aspect onto your 10th house, increasing career expansion and opportunity.
- If you want to find out when your chart's 10th house energies will be enlivened, look to the 10th house ruler, or any planet located in the 10th house. Examine the Mahadasha Summary of your chart to see when that planet will come into power, and that will give you your answer. To find shorter periods when 10th house issues will be highlighted, look to the 10th house ruler or any planet located in the 10th house, and find the time its bhukti will run.
- Notice any influence transiting planets are having on your 10th house. Saturn passing over can cause a change of careers. Jupiter can indicate a job promotion. Ketu may bring deception into the workplace. You can chant to the planet that is favorably transiting your rising sign, on the appropriate day for that planet, to enhance its effects.

EXAMPLE CHARTS

Remember my aunt, the Olympic athlete, mentioned in the section on the 4th house?

Barbara excelled in international meets (her specialty was high jump) but injured her back twice prior to the 1956 Olympics. She

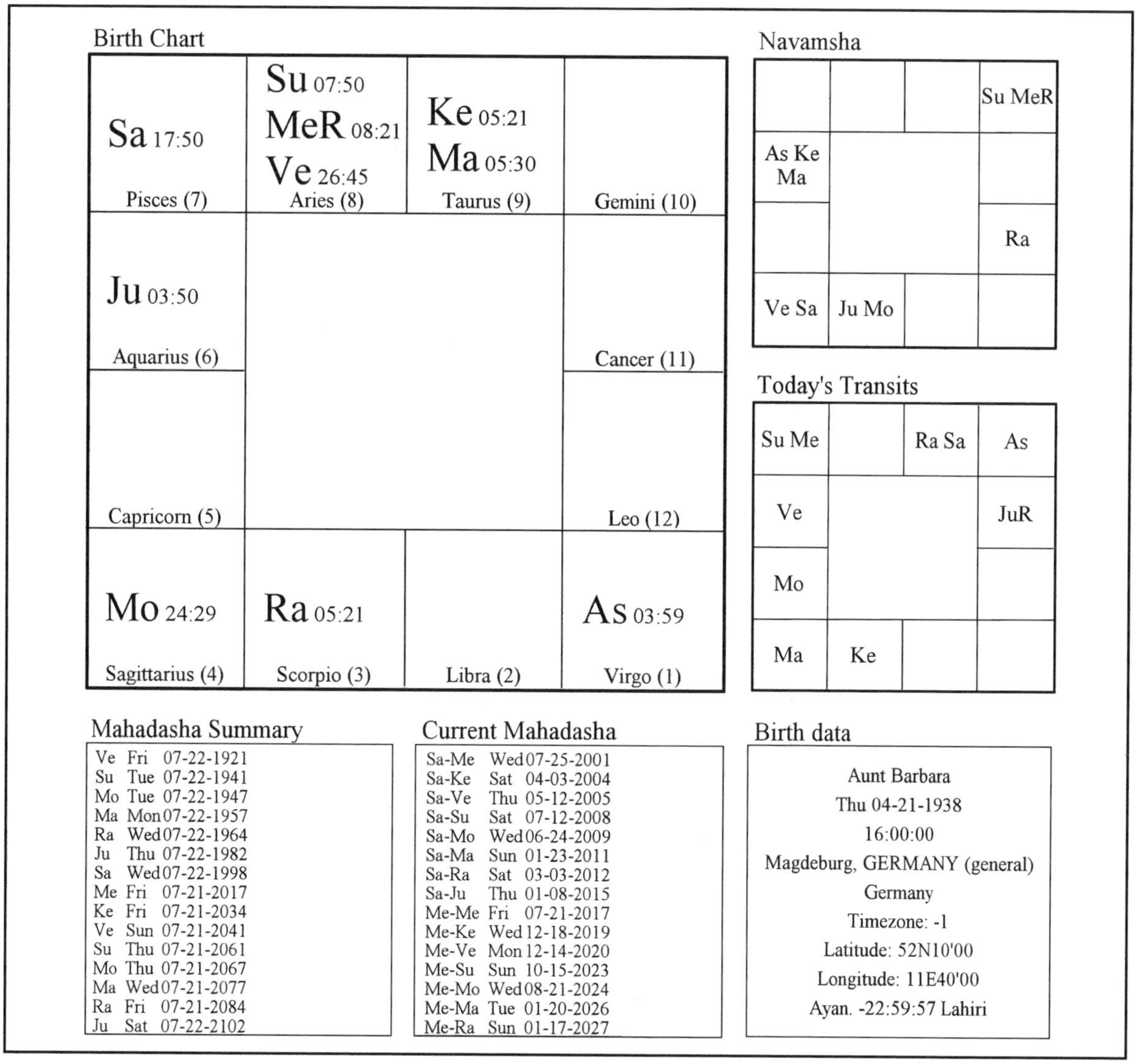

Birth Chart

Sa 17:50 Pisces (7)	**Su** 07:50 **MeR** 08:21 **Ve** 26:45 Aries (8)	**Ke** 05:21 **Ma** 05:30 Taurus (9)	Gemini (10)
Ju 03:50 Aquarius (6)			Cancer (11)
Capricorn (5)			Leo (12)
Mo 24:29 Sagittarius (4)	**Ra** 05:21 Scorpio (3)	Libra (2)	**As** 03:59 Virgo (1)

Navamsha

			Su MeR
As Ke Ma			
			Ra
Ve Sa	Ju Mo		

Today's Transits

Su Me		Ra Sa	As
Ve			JuR
Mo			
Ma	Ke		

Mahadasha Summary

Ve	Fri	07-22-1921
Su	Tue	07-22-1941
Mo	Tue	07-22-1947
Ma	Mon	07-22-1957
Ra	Wed	07-22-1964
Ju	Thu	07-22-1982
Sa	Wed	07-22-1998
Me	Fri	07-21-2017
Ke	Fri	07-21-2034
Ve	Sun	07-21-2041
Su	Thu	07-21-2061
Mo	Thu	07-21-2067
Ma	Wed	07-21-2077
Ra	Fri	07-21-2084
Ju	Sat	07-22-2102

Current Mahadasha

Sa-Me	Wed	07-25-2001
Sa-Ke	Sat	04-03-2004
Sa-Ve	Thu	05-12-2005
Sa-Su	Sat	07-12-2008
Sa-Mo	Wed	06-24-2009
Sa-Ma	Sun	01-23-2011
Sa-Ra	Sat	03-03-2012
Sa-Ju	Thu	01-08-2015
Me-Me	Fri	07-21-2017
Me-Ke	Wed	12-18-2019
Me-Ve	Mon	12-14-2020
Me-Su	Sun	10-15-2023
Me-Mo	Wed	08-21-2024
Me-Ma	Tue	01-20-2026
Me-Ra	Sun	01-17-2027

Birth data

Aunt Barbara

Thu 04-21-1938

16:00:00

Magdeburg, GERMANY (general)

Germany

Timezone: -1

Latitude: 52N10'00

Longitude: 11E40'00

Ayan. -22:59:57 Lahiri

Chart 79—Barbara

broke her lower back once, and strained it another time by falling incorrectly in the pit, yet she was still forced to compete in the Olympics. The back injury is due to her 10th house ruler being combust in the 8th house, and two malefics conjunct *to the exact degree* in her 9th house, aspected by Saturn. Perhaps it was because of her conditioning (strong 8th house planets) that she did not suffer more from this challenging planetary setup. Her success, however, is more obvious from her navamsha than it is from the 10th house indication in her natal chart.

Notice that Mars and Ketu are placed in

the rising sign of the navamsha in Aquarius. Mars in the rising sign indicates an athlete. But Mars sits in the house of an enemy (Aquarius), is conjunct Ketu (deception), and is aspected by enemy Saturn. Her 10th house is Scorpio, and Scorpio's ruler, Mars, is in the rising sign. Because the 1st house ruler is the body, when the 10th house ruler is placed in the rising sign, it shows using the body in some way professionally.

Both powerful Jupiter and the Moon placed in her 10th house (which is ruled by Mars) indicate her career success. But because the Moon is debilitated in Scorpio, this speaks again to her unhappiness. Since the Moon is in her 10th house, her emotional upset is connected with her forced career as an athlete. Though she won many international medals, she left them behind when her Mars mahadasha came into power in 1957. That very year she hired a guide to get her across the border and through mine fields away from her country once and for all. Isn't it amazing how accurate the mahadasha system can be for predicting major life changes (and how ironic that her talents as an athlete gave her the speed and agility to literally run from her country)?

Let's look at a chart that shows a completely different career path—that of the renowned newscaster Walter Cronkite (Chart 80).

Though there is some question as to Cronkite's time of birth, notice that his rising sign is Libra, which shows great diplomacy and balance. Librans are also charming and tactful, and have the ability to be persuasive, which is a particularly good quality for a newscaster who needs to gain the trust of his viewers. Notice too that Mercury is placed in his rising sign, which indicates intelligence and skill with words. It also shows a keen intellect and a talkative nature.

The Sun is also placed in his rising sign, in the last degrees of the sign of its debilitation. This position makes him a perfect conduit for reading the news, as it shows his personality will not get in the way. Since a debilitated Sun shows a certain lack of ego, Cronkite was successful at being unbiased in his presentation.

The ruler of Libra, Venus, is placed in his 12th house, indicating a person who sacrifices his own concerns for that of the many. The 12th house Venus also enhances his inner charisma and innate attractiveness.

Cronkite's 10th house is Cancer, which is ruled by the Moon. The Moon is placed in his 9th house, showing career success, including the possibility of travel associated with the career. This placement applies very well to Cronkite, who often acted as a foreign correspondent.

Ketu and retrograde Saturn both occupy his 10th house. As can be seen in Table G, Saturn is a benefic planet for Libra rising, and does very well in the 10th house. This is because Saturn brings a traditional, structured, conventional approach to work that follows slow logical steps, which is important especially in the midst of a late-breaking story when it's sometimes up to the newscaster to piece the puzzle together.

This leads us to the influence of Ketu in

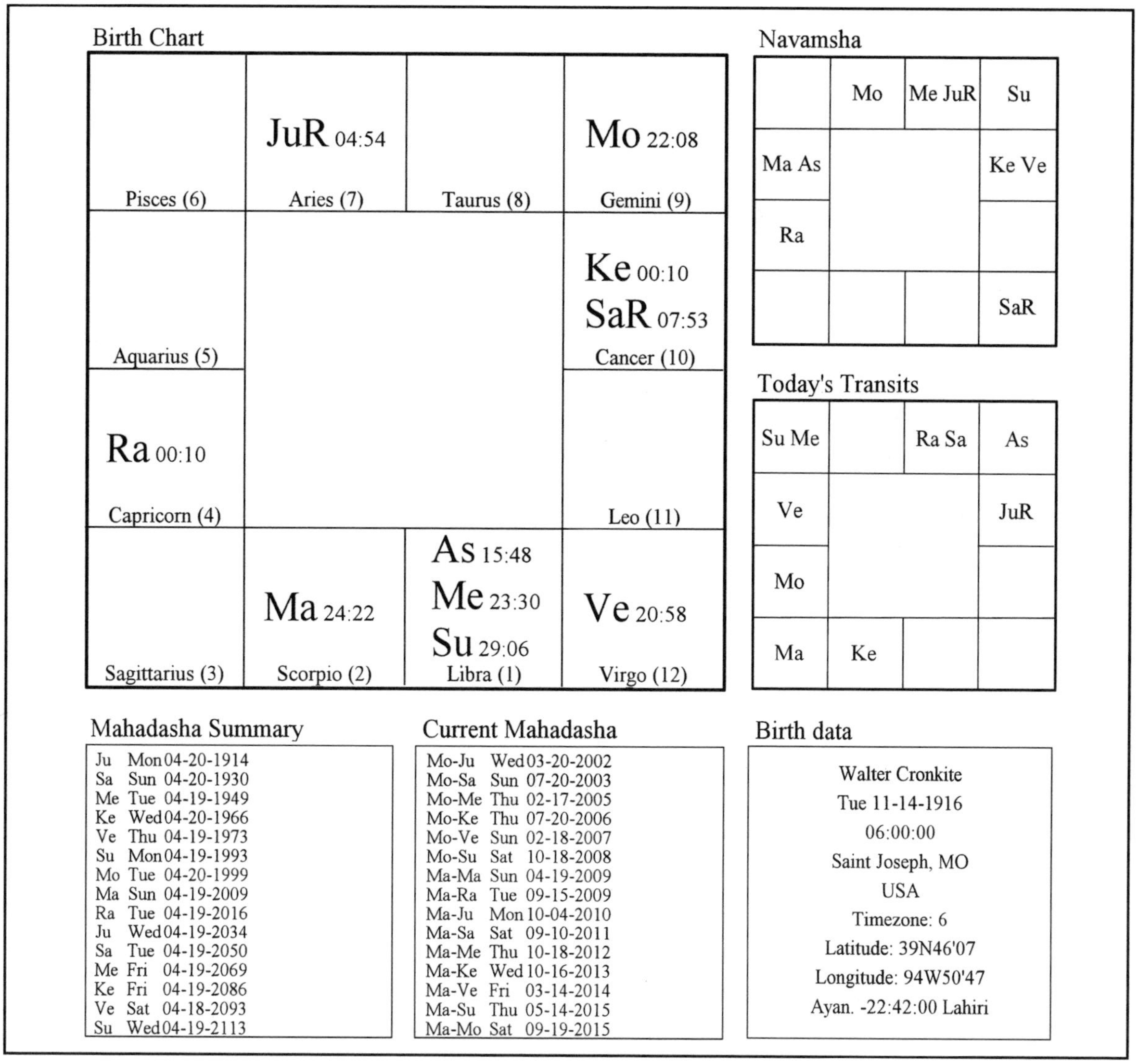

Birth Chart

	JuR 04:54	Mo 22:08	
Pisces (6)	Aries (7)	Taurus (8)	Gemini (9)
Aquarius (5)		Ke 00:10 / SaR 07:53 — Cancer (10)	
Ra 00:10 — Capricorn (4)		Leo (11)	
Ma 24:22 — Sagittarius (3)	Scorpio (2)	As 15:48 / Me 23:30 / Su 29:06 — Libra (1)	Ve 20:58 — Virgo (12)

Navamsha

	Mo	Me JuR	Su
Ma As			Ke Ve
Ra			
			SaR

Today's Transits

Su Me		Ra Sa	As
Ve			JuR
Mo			
Ma	Ke		

Mahadasha Summary

Ju	Mon	04-20-1914
Sa	Sun	04-20-1930
Me	Tue	04-19-1949
Ke	Wed	04-20-1966
Ve	Thu	04-19-1973
Su	Mon	04-19-1993
Mo	Tue	04-20-1999
Ma	Sun	04-19-2009
Ra	Tue	04-19-2016
Ju	Wed	04-19-2034
Sa	Tue	04-19-2050
Me	Fri	04-19-2069
Ke	Fri	04-19-2086
Ve	Sat	04-18-2093
Su	Wed	04-19-2113

Current Mahadasha

Mo-Ju	Wed	03-20-2002
Mo-Sa	Sun	07-20-2003
Mo-Me	Thu	02-17-2005
Mo-Ke	Thu	07-20-2006
Mo-Ve	Sun	02-18-2007
Mo-Su	Sat	10-18-2008
Ma-Ma	Sun	04-19-2009
Ma-Ra	Tue	09-15-2009
Ma-Ju	Mon	10-04-2010
Ma-Sa	Sat	09-10-2011
Ma-Me	Thu	10-18-2012
Ma-Ke	Wed	10-16-2013
Ma-Ve	Fri	03-14-2014
Ma-Su	Thu	05-14-2015
Ma-Mo	Sat	09-19-2015

Birth data

Walter Cronkite
Tue 11-14-1916
06:00:00
Saint Joseph, MO
USA
Timezone: 6
Latitude: 39N46'07
Longitude: 94W50'47
Ayan. -22:42:00 Lahiri

Chart 80—Walter Cronkite

the 10th house. This position shows the possibility of unexpected, uncontrollable situations affecting a career, and as we all know, what will show up in tomorrow's news is anyone's guess. The fast-moving Mercury (with the quickest orbit) placed in his Libra, which is a cardinal sign showing tremendous drive,

enabled Cronkite to make quick adjustments and excel in his field.

Now, see if you can determine what this next person does for a living before I reveal it.

David's rising sign is Leo (Chart 81), ruled by the Sun. At first glance we know he likes being in the limelight, which many Leos do.

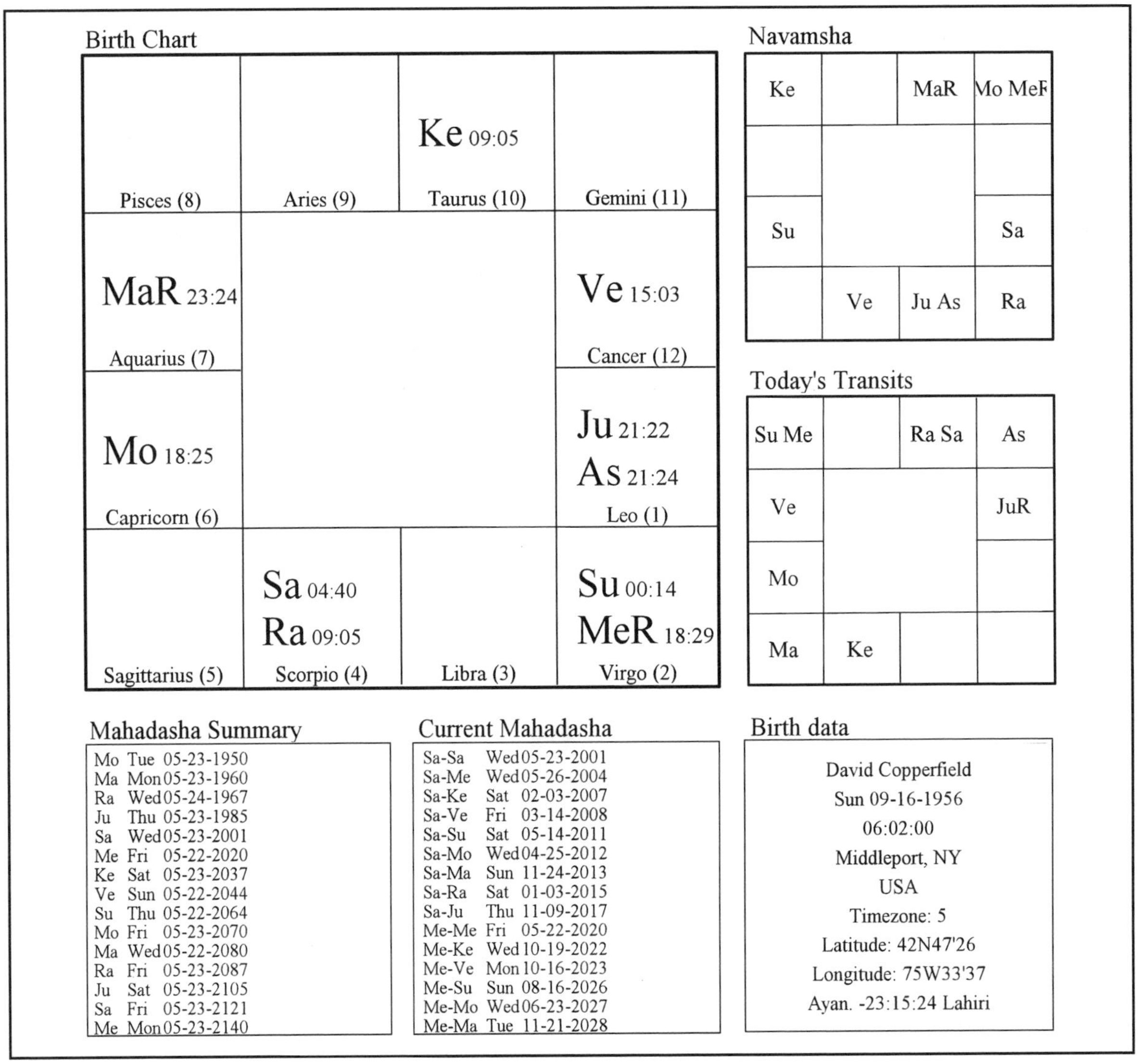

Birth Chart

Pisces (8)	Aries (9)	Taurus (10) Ke 09:05	Gemini (11)
MaR 23:24 Aquarius (7)			Ve 15:03 Cancer (12)
Mo 18:25 Capricorn (6)			Ju 21:22 As 21:24 Leo (1)
Sagittarius (5)	Sa 04:40 Ra 09:05 Scorpio (4)	Libra (3)	Su 00:14 MeR 18:29 Virgo (2)

Navamsha

Ke		MaR	Mo MeR
Su			Sa
	Ve	Ju As	Ra

Today's Transits

Su Me		Ra Sa	As
Ve			JuR
Mo			
Ma	Ke		

Mahadasha Summary

Mo	Tue	05-23-1950
Ma	Mon	05-23-1960
Ra	Wed	05-24-1967
Ju	Thu	05-23-1985
Sa	Wed	05-23-2001
Me	Fri	05-22-2020
Ke	Sat	05-23-2037
Ve	Sun	05-22-2044
Su	Thu	05-22-2064
Mo	Fri	05-23-2070
Ma	Wed	05-22-2080
Ra	Fri	05-23-2087
Ju	Sat	05-23-2105
Sa	Fri	05-23-2121
Me	Mon	05-23-2140

Current Mahadasha

Sa-Sa	Wed	05-23-2001
Sa-Me	Wed	05-26-2004
Sa-Ke	Sat	02-03-2007
Sa-Ve	Fri	03-14-2008
Sa-Su	Sat	05-14-2011
Sa-Mo	Wed	04-25-2012
Sa-Ma	Sun	11-24-2013
Sa-Ra	Sat	01-03-2015
Sa-Ju	Thu	11-09-2017
Me-Me	Fri	05-22-2020
Me-Ke	Wed	10-19-2022
Me-Ve	Mon	10-16-2023
Me-Su	Sun	08-16-2026
Me-Mo	Wed	06-23-2027
Me-Ma	Tue	11-21-2028

Birth data

David Copperfield
Sun 09-16-1956
06:02:00
Middleport, NY
USA
Timezone: 5
Latitude: 42N47'26
Longitude: 75W33'37
Ayan. -23:15:24 Lahiri

Chart 81—David

Jupiter is placed in the rising sign close to the ascendant degree, showing a strong influence of enthusiasm and optimism—what might be called a contagious personality. This is enhanced by the Venus/Moon opposition in the 6th and 12th houses.

Looking at his 10th house, we see that it is Taurus, which is ruled by Venus. Venus is placed in the 12th house, showing the possibility of career failure. Do you think this is the case here? Look again at the rising sign and notice that Mars and Saturn throw powerful aspects onto the Jupiter. Also, glance at the navamsha and see powerful Jupiter sitting in the rising sign. The 10th house ruler, the Moon, sits in the 9th house of luck conjunct with retrograde Mercury in its own house. No, this is not a chart indicating career failure.

Look at the 2nd house to determine David's earning ability. We see that the ruler of the rising sign, Sun, is placed there, along with the ruler of the 2nd house itself, Mercury (retrograde). Both indications show good wealth potential, so it's not likely that the person's career has faltered. As we'll learn later, the 12th house is a deeply secretive house, so it's possible this person makes their living by being involved with things hidden.

Look again at the 2nd house. The Sun and Mercury conjoined there show us that David is extremely capable with words, and can persuade people easily with them. But Mercury in retrograde gives the impression that what is being spoken is not the whole truth. There is the possibility of deception, since retrogration keeps things hidden.

If we look at the 10th house, we see that Ketu is placed there. In Table D, Ketu is associated with mysticism or things mysterious, and in fact its influence is apt in this particular chart. If we put all the evidence together, we have a charismatic person in the limelight with good earning ability who can convince you of things through a certain amount of deception. The 10th house ruler is in the secret 12th house, and mysterious Ketu occupies the 10th house itself.

This is the chart of David Copperfield, the magician.

Now let's look at Harrison Ford's chart.

After some minor success in his acting career, Ford became frustrated at not being able to break through as a major actor. He took up carpentry when he was in his early thirties. Due to his rising sign in Virgo, his eye for detail and perfectionism made him a successful woodworker, and he soon attracted prominent clients for custom projects. But look at his career house. The ruler of his rising sign, Mercury, is powerfully placed in his 10th house of career. There, it is conjoined with Jupiter, Sun, and Moon. With the strength of these planets it seems unlikely that he would have remained a carpenter for long, no matter how skilled he became.

His luck in the arts is also indicated by his 5th house of destiny—Capricorn—which is ruled by Saturn. That particular Saturn is conjunct with Venus in his 9th house, and Saturn and Venus are friendly planets, especially in Taurus. To remind you of the indications of the 5th house ruler placed in the 9th house, it is: "one of the finest placements of planetary rulers. You get tremendous grace from past life merit."

Further, Ford's 10th house Gemini is a mutable sign, meaning that he can easily get into character and convince you that he is, in fact, the person he is portraying. Rarely do you think you're watching Harrison Ford act. Instead, you see Indiana Jones or the President in *Air Force One*.

Also, notice that Ford's 2nd house ruler is placed in the 9th house, one of the best places for luck with money. His base compensation per movie is $20 million.

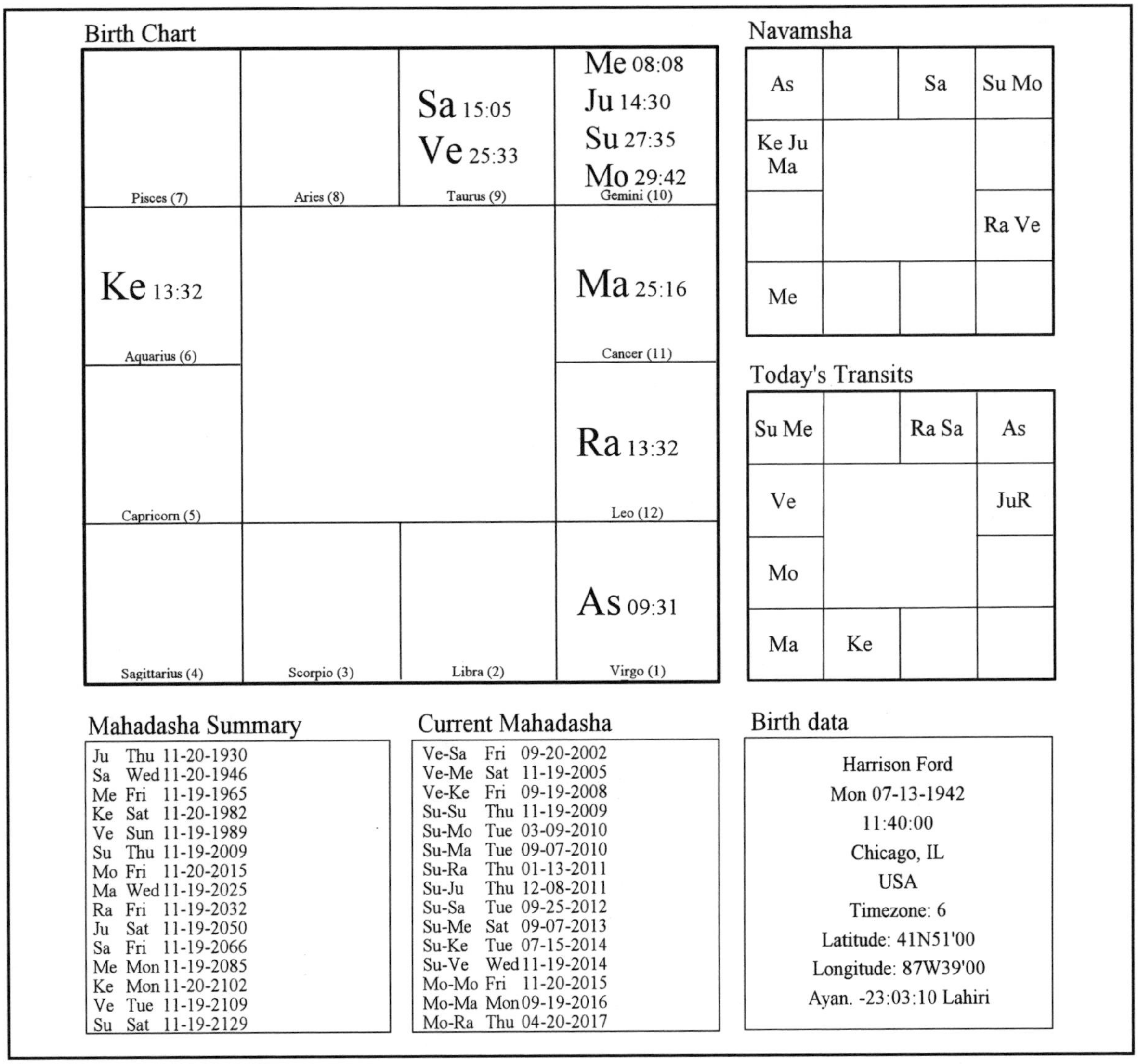

Birth Chart

Pisces (7)	Aries (8)	Taurus (9)	Gemini (10)
		Sa 15:05 Ve 25:33	Me 08:08 Ju 14:30 Su 27:35 Mo 29:42

Aquarius (6)			Cancer (11)
Ke 13:32			Ma 25:16

Capricorn (5)			Leo (12)
			Ra 13:32

Sagittarius (4)	Scorpio (3)	Libra (2)	Virgo (1)
			As 09:31

Navamsha

As		Sa	Su Mo
Ke Ju Ma			
			Ra Ve
Me			

Today's Transits

Su Me		Ra Sa	As
Ve			JuR
Mo			
Ma	Ke		

Mahadasha Summary

Ju	Thu	11-20-1930
Sa	Wed	11-20-1946
Me	Fri	11-19-1965
Ke	Sat	11-20-1982
Ve	Sun	11-19-1989
Su	Thu	11-19-2009
Mo	Fri	11-20-2015
Ma	Wed	11-19-2025
Ra	Fri	11-19-2032
Ju	Sat	11-19-2050
Sa	Fri	11-19-2066
Me	Mon	11-19-2085
Ke	Mon	11-20-2102
Ve	Tue	11-19-2109
Su	Sat	11-19-2129

Current Mahadasha

Ve-Sa	Fri	09-20-2002
Ve-Me	Sat	11-19-2005
Ve-Ke	Fri	09-19-2008
Su-Su	Thu	11-19-2009
Su-Mo	Tue	03-09-2010
Su-Ma	Tue	09-07-2010
Su-Ra	Thu	01-13-2011
Su-Ju	Thu	12-08-2011
Su-Sa	Tue	09-25-2012
Su-Me	Sat	09-07-2013
Su-Ke	Tue	07-15-2014
Su-Ve	Wed	11-19-2014
Mo-Mo	Fri	11-20-2015
Mo-Ma	Mon	09-19-2016
Mo-Ra	Thu	04-20-2017

Birth data

Harrison Ford

Mon 07-13-1942

11:40:00

Chicago, IL

USA

Timezone: 6

Latitude: 41N51'00

Longitude: 87W39'00

Ayan. -23:03:10 Lahiri

Chart 82—Harrison Ford

His 3rd house is Scorpio, and the ruler of Scorpio is Mars. Mars in his chart is in debilitation. Because the 3rd house represents courage, Ford does not give the overt sense that he is courageous. That's why he so convincingly plays Everyman, the self-deprecating person who reluctantly rises to do battle. In fact, Ford used to be a loner in school, who was constantly bullied by a group of troublemakers, until one day he decided to beat up the head bully. (Be careful of messing with people who have Cancer Mars! They may seem powerless but sometimes when they're pushed far enough they explode.)

This next example shows what happens when more than one planet converges on the 10th house. Let's look again at Michael Crichton's chart.

A great deal of Crichton's professional excellence is due both to his powerful Mercury in Virgo (showing his skills as a writer), and to the ruler of the 6th house being placed in his 1st house (which shows his interest in medicine). His converging 10th house planets, though they are notable, don't necessarily represent the specific professional skills he has. Rather, they enforce the multitalented nature of his 10th house. You'll see that he has four planets focused there: Moon in the actual house, and Mars, Venus, and Sun by opposition.

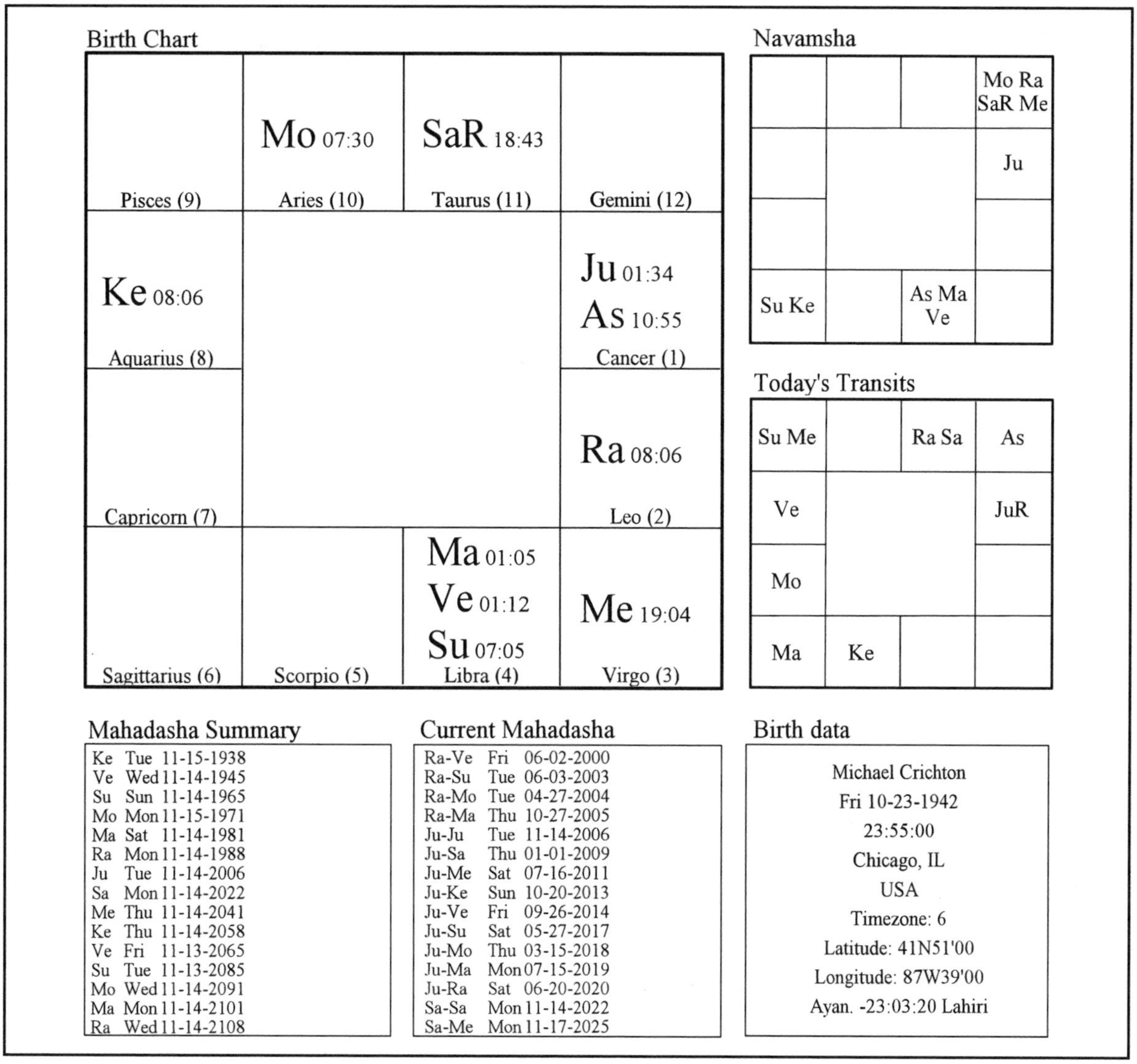

Birth Chart			
Pisces (9)	Mo 07:30 Aries (10)	SaR 18:43 Taurus (11)	Gemini (12)
Ke 08:06 Aquarius (8)			Ju 01:34 As 10:55 Cancer (1)
Capricorn (7)			Ra 08:06 Leo (2)
Sagittarius (6)	Scorpio (5)	Ma 01:05 Ve 01:12 Su 07:05 Libra (4)	Me 19:04 Virgo (3)

Navamsha			
			Mo Ra SaR Me
			Ju
Su Ke		As Ma Ve	

Today's Transits			
Su Me		Ra Sa	As
Ve			JuR
Mo			
Ma	Ke		

Mahadasha Summary

Ke	Tue	11-15-1938
Ve	Wed	11-14-1945
Su	Sun	11-14-1965
Mo	Mon	11-15-1971
Ma	Sat	11-14-1981
Ra	Mon	11-14-1988
Ju	Tue	11-14-2006
Sa	Mon	11-14-2022
Me	Thu	11-14-2041
Ke	Thu	11-14-2058
Ve	Fri	11-13-2065
Su	Tue	11-13-2085
Mo	Wed	11-14-2091
Ma	Mon	11-14-2101
Ra	Wed	11-14-2108

Current Mahadasha

Ra-Ve	Fri	06-02-2000
Ra-Su	Tue	06-03-2003
Ra-Mo	Tue	04-27-2004
Ra-Ma	Thu	10-27-2005
Ju-Ju	Tue	11-14-2006
Ju-Sa	Thu	01-01-2009
Ju-Me	Sat	07-16-2011
Ju-Ke	Sun	10-20-2013
Ju-Ve	Fri	09-26-2014
Ju-Su	Sat	05-27-2017
Ju-Mo	Thu	03-15-2018
Ju-Ma	Mon	07-15-2019
Ju-Ra	Sat	06-20-2020
Sa-Sa	Mon	11-14-2022
Sa-Me	Mon	11-17-2025

Birth data

Michael Crichton

Fri 10-23-1942

23:55:00

Chicago, IL

USA

Timezone: 6

Latitude: 41N51'00

Longitude: 87W39'00

Ayan. -23:03:20 Lahiri

Chart 83—Michael Crichton

His professional skills number four as well. As a physician, he graduated summa cum laude from Harvard undergrad, and received a medical degree at Harvard Medical School. As a teacher, he lectured in anthropology at prestigious Cambridge University. As a writer, he has written six novels, including *The Andromeda Strain*, and *The Terminal Man*, as well as the screenplays *Rising Sun*, *Jurassic Park*, *Twister*, and *Sphere*. As a director and producer he created *Westworld*, *Twister*, *Sphere*, and TV's *E.R.*

How might his debilitated Sun in Libra express itself? It may have weakened his threshold for physical trauma. When asked why he gave up medicine, he answered that

Birth Chart

	Me 01:34 Ju 09:38 Ve 14:42 Su 26:51		
Pisces (9)	Aries (10)	Taurus (11)	Gemini (12)
Ra 03:20			As 27:00
Aquarius (8)			Cancer (1)
			Ke 03:20
Capricorn (7)			Leo (2)
	Mo 09:33	MaR 13:52	SaR 15:46
Sagittarius (6)	Scorpio (5)	Libra (4)	Virgo (3)

Navamsha

As	Me	Ke SaR	Ju
MaR			
			Ve
Su	Ra		Mo

Today's Transits

Su Me		Ra Sa	As
Ve			JuR
Mo			
Ma	Ke		

Mahadasha Summary

Sa	Mon	06-28-1943
Me	Wed	06-27-1962
Ke	Thu	06-28-1979
Ve	Fri	06-27-1986
Su	Tue	06-27-2006
Mo	Wed	06-27-2012
Ma	Mon	06-27-2022
Ra	Wed	06-27-2029
Ju	Thu	06-27-2047
Sa	Wed	06-27-2063
Me	Sat	06-27-2082
Ke	Sat	06-27-2099
Ve	Sun	06-27-2106
Su	Thu	06-27-2126
Mo	Fri	06-27-2132

Current Mahadasha

Ve-Me	Thu 06-27-2002
Ve-Ke	Wed 04-27-2005
Su-Su	Tue 06-27-2006
Su-Mo	Sun 10-15-2006
Su-Ma	Sun 04-15-2007
Su-Ra	Tue 08-21-2007
Su-Ju	Tue 07-15-2008
Su-Sa	Sun 05-03-2009
Su-Me	Thu 04-15-2010
Su-Ke	Sun 02-20-2011
Su-Ve	Mon 06-27-2011
Mo-Mo	Wed 06-27-2012
Mo-Ma	Sat 04-27-2013
Mo-Ra	Tue 11-26-2013
Mo-Ju	Thu 05-28-2015

Birth data

Greg

Sat 05-10-1952

12:30:00

Fresno, CA

USA

Timezone: 8

Latitude: 36N44'52

Longitude: 119W46'17

Ayan. -23:11:38 Lahiri

Chart 84—Greg

when he saw accident victims in the emergency ward, or when he was performing surgery, or while he was drawing blood, he tended to faint!

Looking at two more powerful professional charts, imagine the level of success our drug smuggler might have reached had he been involved in a legitimate career.

To illustrate this point, look at Greg's chart next to actor Jack Nicholson's. Notice that the smuggler has four well-placed planets in his 10th house, and that they are opposed by powerful Mars. Mr. Nicholson, in contrast, has three planets in his 10th house that are not nearly as strong.

So, technically speaking, the indications in

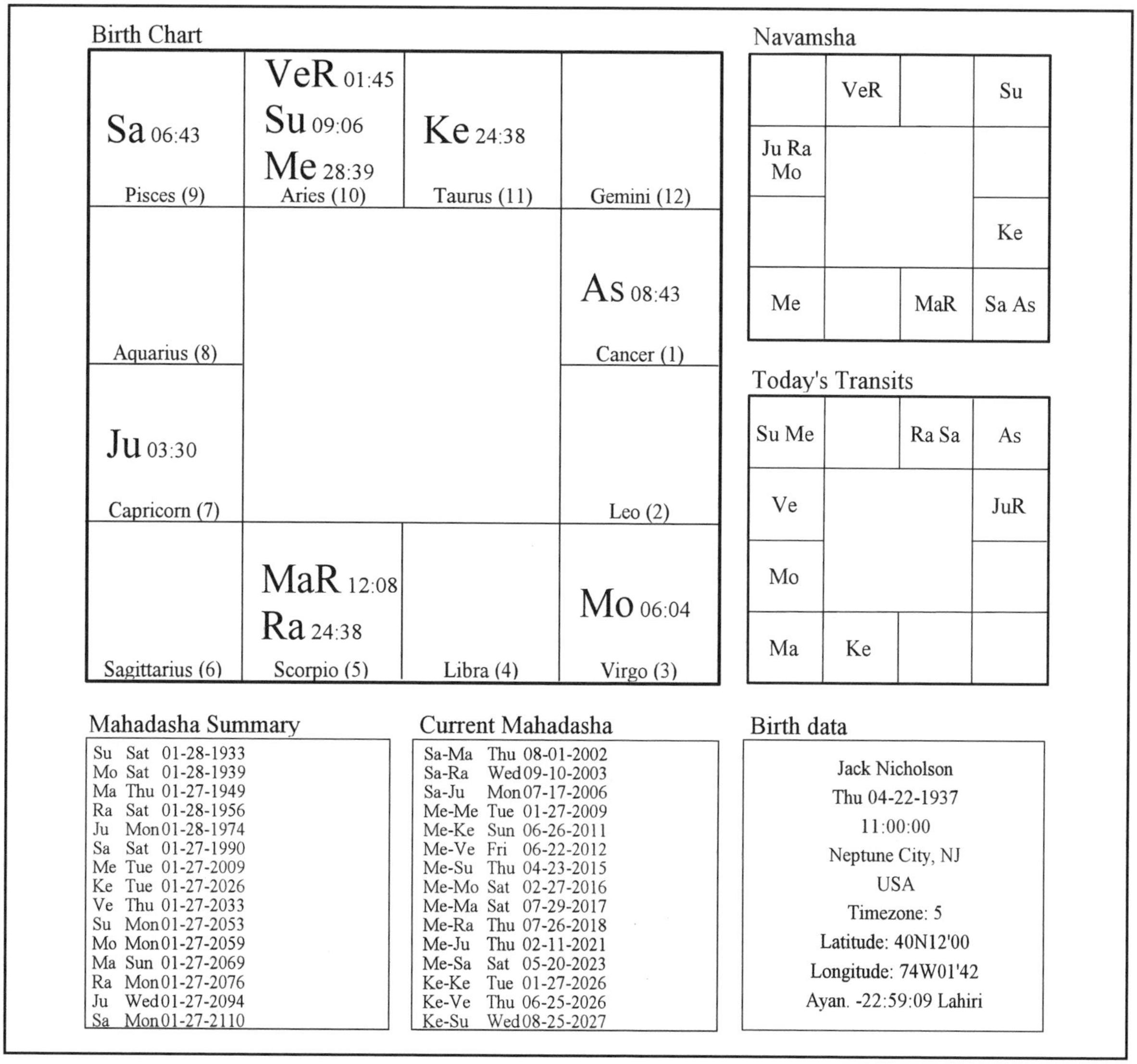

Birth Chart

Sa 06:43 Pisces (9)	VeR 01:45 Su 09:06 Me 28:39 Aries (10)	Ke 24:38 Taurus (11)	Gemini (12)
Aquarius (8)			As 08:43 Cancer (1)
Ju 03:30 Capricorn (7)			Leo (2)
Sagittarius (6)	MaR 12:08 Ra 24:38 Scorpio (5)	Libra (4)	Mo 06:04 Virgo (3)

Navamsha

	VeR		Su
Ju Ra Mo			Ke
Me		MaR	Sa As

Today's Transits

Su Me		Ra Sa	As
Ve			JuR
Mo			
Ma	Ke		

Mahadasha Summary

Su	Sat	01-28-1933
Mo	Sat	01-28-1939
Ma	Thu	01-27-1949
Ra	Sat	01-28-1956
Ju	Mon	01-28-1974
Sa	Sat	01-27-1990
Me	Tue	01-27-2009
Ke	Tue	01-27-2026
Ve	Thu	01-27-2033
Su	Mon	01-27-2053
Mo	Mon	01-27-2059
Ma	Sun	01-27-2069
Ra	Mon	01-27-2076
Ju	Wed	01-27-2094
Sa	Mon	01-27-2110

Current Mahadasha

Sa-Ma	Thu	08-01-2002
Sa-Ra	Wed	09-10-2003
Sa-Ju	Mon	07-17-2006
Me-Me	Tue	01-27-2009
Me-Ke	Sun	06-26-2011
Me-Ve	Fri	06-22-2012
Me-Su	Thu	04-23-2015
Me-Mo	Sat	02-27-2016
Me-Ma	Sat	07-29-2017
Me-Ra	Thu	07-26-2018
Me-Ju	Thu	02-11-2021
Me-Sa	Sat	05-20-2023
Ke-Ke	Tue	01-27-2026
Ke-Ve	Thu	06-25-2026
Ke-Su	Wed	08-25-2027

Birth data

Jack Nicholson
Thu 04-22-1937
11:00:00
Neptune City, NJ
USA
Timezone: 5
Latitude: 40N12'00
Longitude: 74W01'42
Ayan. -22:59:09 Lahiri

Chart 85—Jack Nicholson

Greg's chart for professional success are stronger than those of Jack Nicholson. In their navamshas, both have Sun in the 10th house, and the 10th house ruler placed in the 4th house, showing luck with property due to career success. The difference is that Jack expresses himself creatively due to his 3rd house Moon in Virgo, and Greg's energies are deeply secretive and hidden, due to his debilitated Moon in Scorpio.

Let's look at another interesting professional chart.

Fran is a professional stripper. Her rising sign is Taurus, and the ruler of Taurus is Venus, placed in its house of debilitation in Virgo. So she has a natural interest in the arts,

Birth Chart

	Mo 03:46 Ma 09:11 Pisces (11)	As 07:48 Aries (12)	Sa 08:16 Ke 11:33 Taurus (1)
			Sa 08:16 Ke 11:33 Gemini (2)
Aquarius (10)			Me 18:14 Cancer (3)
JuR 11:16 Capricorn (9)			Su 02:33 Leo (4)
Ra 11:33 Sagittarius (8)	Scorpio (7)	Libra (6)	Ve 06:40 Virgo (5)

Navamsha

Ve As	JuR Su	Mo	Ma
			Ra
Ke			
Me Sa			

Today's Transits

Su Me		Ra Sa	As
Ve			JuR
Mo			
Ma	Ke		

Mahadasha Summary

Ke	Wed	08-25-1971
Ve	Thu	08-24-1978
Su	Mon	08-24-1998
Mo	Tue	08-24-2004
Ma	Sun	08-24-2014
Ra	Tue	08-24-2021
Ju	Wed	08-24-2039
Sa	Tue	08-24-2055
Me	Fri	08-24-2074
Ke	Fri	08-24-2091
Ve	Sat	08-23-2098
Su	Wed	08-24-2118
Mo	Thu	08-24-2124
Ma	Tue	08-24-2134
Ra	Thu	08-24-2141

Current Mahadasha

Su-Me	Wed	06-12-2002
Su-Ke	Sat	04-19-2003
Su-Ve	Sun	08-24-2003
Mo-Mo	Tue	08-24-2004
Mo-Ma	Fri	06-24-2005
Mo-Ra	Mon	01-23-2006
Mo-Ju	Wed	07-25-2007
Mo-Sa	Sun	11-23-2008
Mo-Me	Thu	06-24-2010
Mo-Ke	Thu	11-24-2011
Mo-Ve	Sun	06-24-2012
Mo-Su	Sat	02-22-2014
Ma-Ma	Sun	08-24-2014
Ma-Ra	Tue	01-20-2015
Ma-Ju	Mon	02-08-2016

Birth data

Fran
Sun 08-19-1973
00:24:00
Toledo, OH
USA
Timezone: 5
Latitude: 41N39'50
Longitude: 83W33'19
Ayan. -23:29:37 Lahiri

Chart 86—Fran

but the debilitated Venus brings it out through sensuality and sexual expression.

Fran explained to me that the movement and sensuality of her art are very satisfying to her, but energetically she feels very vulnerable and doesn't like the projections of the men who watch her. However, the Sun in Leo indicates that she does like being the center of attention, and being in the limelight.

An interesting destiny chart is Sylvester Stallone's, which we discussed earlier.

Stallone's rising sign is Sagittarius, and the ruler of Sagittarius is Jupiter. That Jupiter is placed in his 10th house, the house of career.

Now look at Stallone's 10th house—Virgo. The ruler of Virgo is Mercury, and that

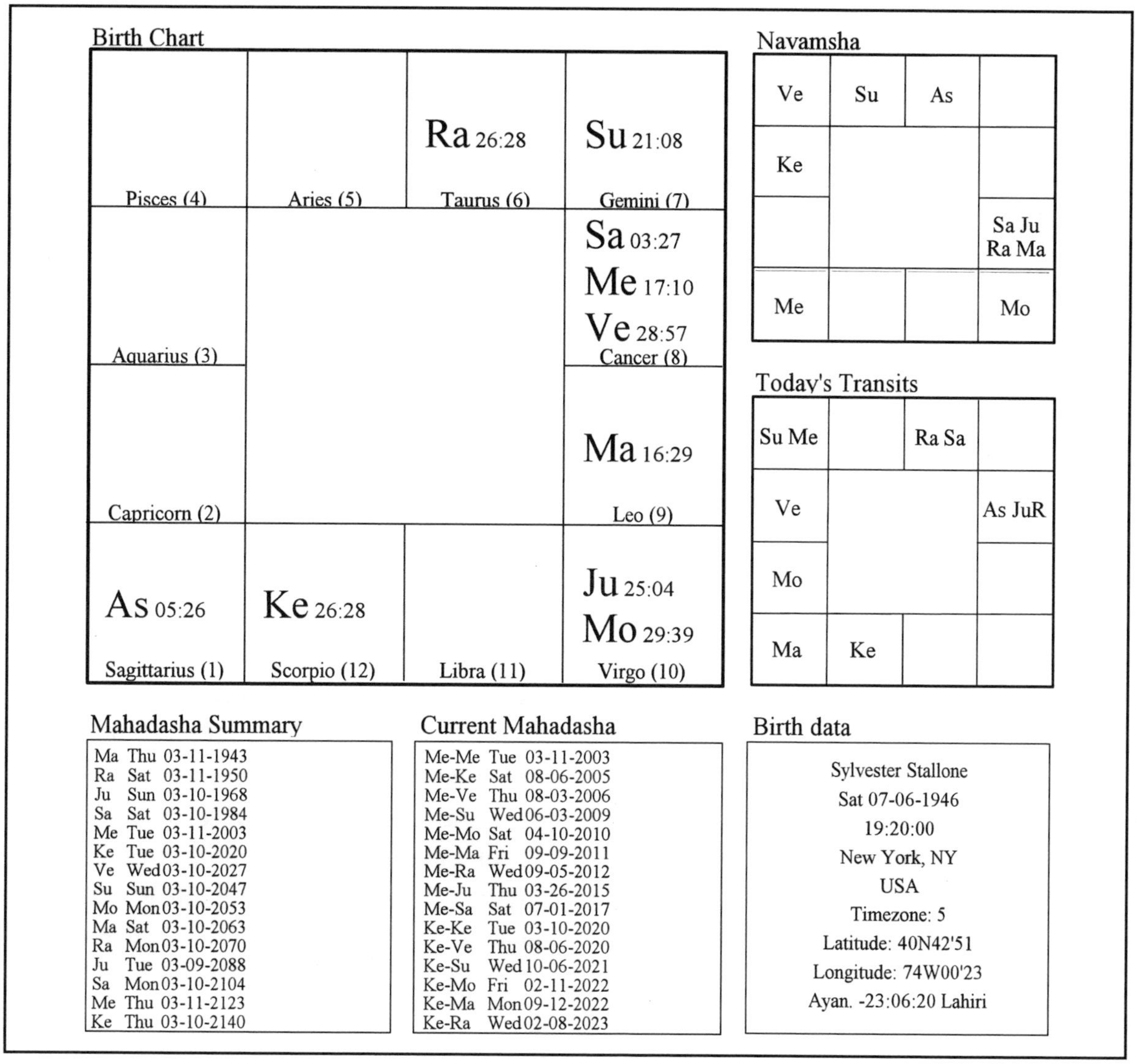

Birth Chart

		Ra 26:28	Su 21:08
Pisces (4)	Aries (5)	Taurus (6)	Gemini (7)
Aquarius (3)			Sa 03:27 Me 17:10 Ve 28:57 Cancer (8)
Capricorn (2)			Ma 16:29 Leo (9)
As 05:26 Sagittarius (1)	Ke 26:28 Scorpio (12)	Libra (11)	Ju 25:04 Mo 29:39 Virgo (10)

Navamsha

Ve	Su	As	
Ke			Sa Ju Ra Ma
Me			Mo

Today's Transits

Su Me		Ra Sa	
Ve			As JuR
Mo			
Ma	Ke		

Mahadasha Summary

Ma	Thu	03-11-1943
Ra	Sat	03-11-1950
Ju	Sun	03-10-1968
Sa	Sat	03-10-1984
Me	Tue	03-11-2003
Ke	Tue	03-10-2020
Ve	Wed	03-10-2027
Su	Sun	03-10-2047
Mo	Mon	03-10-2053
Ma	Sat	03-10-2063
Ra	Mon	03-10-2070
Ju	Tue	03-09-2088
Sa	Mon	03-10-2104
Me	Thu	03-11-2123
Ke	Thu	03-10-2140

Current Mahadasha

Me-Me	Tue	03-11-2003
Me-Ke	Sat	08-06-2005
Me-Ve	Thu	08-03-2006
Me-Su	Wed	06-03-2009
Me-Mo	Sat	04-10-2010
Me-Ma	Fri	09-09-2011
Me-Ra	Wed	09-05-2012
Me-Ju	Thu	03-26-2015
Me-Sa	Sat	07-01-2017
Ke-Ke	Tue	03-10-2020
Ke-Ve	Thu	08-06-2020
Ke-Su	Wed	10-06-2021
Ke-Mo	Fri	02-11-2022
Ke-Ma	Mon	09-12-2022
Ke-Ra	Wed	02-08-2023

Birth data

Sylvester Stallone
Sat 07-06-1946
19:20:00
New York, NY
USA
Timezone: 5
Latitude: 40N42'51
Longitude: 74W00'23
Ayan. -23:06:20 Lahiri

Chart 87—Sylvester Stallone

Mercury is in the 8th house. As described earlier, this combination brings many changes in one's career, or difficulty in finding one's career path. What makes this particularly frustrating for Stallone is that his Jupiter and Moon are in his 10th house. These are powerful planets, pushing him for greatness, and they bring him great aggravation when there are obstructions to his career path.

When might we estimate that Stallone would start to see some career results? Look at his Mahadasha Summary. His Jupiter came into power in 1968, and remember that it usually isn't until a person's first bhukti begins that the results of that mahadasha will be seen. This occurred in the summer of 1970.

It was in 1971 that he landed his role in Woody Allen's *Bananas*. By 1974 he had written and costarred in *The Lords of Flatbush*, and soon thereafter began working on the script for *Rocky*. If he had received a Vedic astrological reading when he was young, he would have been told that in the mid-'70s his career would flourish. This would have been a nice solace during some of his tough Rahu mahadasha years, 1950 to 1968.

As the 6th house is related to health, and Rahu is a malefic influence here, you might guess that he had some health issues early on. As it turns out, besides the forceps injury he sustained during birth (which we discussed earlier), Stallone was a sickly child who even suffered from rickets.

And because the 6th house also indicates enemies, you might imagine he would have some run-ins. By his early teens he had already changed schools twelve times, and had been expelled from many of them. Eventually, he was enrolled in a school for emotionally disturbed children.

However, so great was his feeling of career destiny that when he wrote *Rocky* as a struggling actor trying to break in, he had a pregnant wife and only a few hundred dollars left in the bank. The script was well written and he started to receive offers for it. But even when he was in such dire straits, he wouldn't sell the *Rocky* script if he couldn't star in it.

All of the actors of the time wanted to star in this picture, but Stallone wouldn't let go of the script without an acting lead. Finally, he got a small company to pick it up that let him carry the lead. The rest is history. *Rocky* became one of the biggest movie hits of all time, and earned Stallone an Academy Award for best picture.

REMEDIES

Cronkite could benefit by strengthening his Venus, which sits in debilitation in Virgo. By chanting the Venus mantras on Friday and eating less that day, he would feel more overall optimism in his life. He could also wear a diamond or white sapphire on the middle finger of his right hand to produce the same results. He might also experiment with Sun mantras or the wearing of a ruby or red spinel for his weak Sun. Otherwise, he would do well to consider writing, because the Sun/Mercury combination in his rising sign shows that he could excel in that field.

David would also do well to bring strength to his Sun, which is a bit weak in the natal chart, and is also in the house of an enemy in the navamsha. Also, since he began his nineteen-year Saturn mahadasha in the Spring of 2001, I would recommend he have fire rituals performed to ease that transition.

Looking more deeply into his chart, I would say that his life will probably become more difficult during his Saturn cycle, since that planet sits conjunct with malefic Rahu in his 4th house, and is in an enemy's house in both the natal and navamsha charts. This can affect the mother, vehicular traffic, and overall happiness. David should start Saturn mantras and eating less on Saturdays even before the Saturn period actually begins. Wearing a stone for Saturn can be tricky because on occasion it amplifies the negativity of that planet. David should experiment with such a stone before buying it. (He should get the stone on approval and keep it close for a few days. Soon thereafter, by either actual events, psychological shifts, or dreams, he will be able to determine whether the stone is helping or harming.)

Also, since Rahu indicates foreign cultures, David could transmute the energy of these planets to his advantage by going international with his magic show. This would satisfy the Saturn/Rahu conjunction, and those planets would then work in his favor.

Harrison Ford could benefit by bringing strength to his Venus and Mars. Even though they serve him well professionally, these planets actually cause him to be a bit shy in real life. Venus mantras on Fridays and Mars mantras on Tuesdays would help, as would eating less on those days. A diamond or white sapphire would also bring him benefit, but since Mars is an enemy for Virgo rising, instead of wearing a stone for Mars he would do better to have yagyas performed for that planet.

Ford was recently interviewed regarding the lifetime achievement award he received in 2000 from the American Film Institute. He explained that such an honor was a mixed blessing. It was wonderful to be held in such high esteem, but it was awful because he had to give an acceptance speech, and he is terrified of speaking in front of people.

Fran would benefit by chanting Venus mantras on Fridays and eating less that day. Also, Mercury and Jupiter are planets that could use strengthening. Since her 2nd house shows she can be prone to addictions, it's safer to strengthen the planet that rules her 2nd house, Mercury, than to deal with the two malefic planets occupying the house. This can be done by chanting Mercury mantras on Wednesdays and eating less that day, or by wearing an emerald or green tourmaline. The Jupiter can be empowered by chanting Jupiter mantras on Thursdays, and eating less on that day.

STRENGTHENING YOUR 10th HOUSE

Many planets do well in the 10th house. Malefic Mars, Rahu, even Saturn in many instances, as well as powerful benefics like Jupiter and Venus can thrive there. The challenge with 10th house planets occurs when multiple planets converge in the 10th and don't get along so well, or the ruler is poorly placed, or as a by-product of malefic planets located there, the 4th house and its indications suffer (the house that opposes the 10th).

If planets are favorably placed in the 10th, you can empower them with mantras, as long as you're aware of the repercussions they will have on the 4th house. Bringing strength to Mars in the 10th house is very good for anyone in a position of leadership or for an athlete, but can hurt the 4th house in such a way that vehicular accidents are more likely, and happiness may be sacrificed.

The safest way to strengthen the 10th house is to empower its ruler by chanting to that planet on the appropriate day, and eating less food on the day associated with that planet. Benefic planets can be strengthened, since benefic aspects onto the 4th house are seen as favorable.

If you are starting a business, or want to ask for a raise, or want to pursue a new career, you can have a Vedic astrologer determine the best time for such actions (muhurtha). You can also receive the best possible date to incorporate or establish a business. I have seen numerous occasions where struggling businesspeople have dissolved a company that was begun at an inauspicious time, and re-established their business with a Vedic astrologer's help on a much better date, with good results. In fact, the results can be remarkable.

Because a company chart is viewed just like an individual person's, imagine if you had control of the planets in such a way that a company could be brought into inception at the height of its Venus mahadasha, just when Venus was well placed in the company's 2nd house. This company would generate a lot of money right away. And let's say the Sun mahadasha that follows the Venus brings great prominence to the company, because the Sun is placed in the 10th house of the company, and so on. This is how an auspicious date for incorporation can work. It's the same as conceiving a child at the best possible time, when the planets are at their strongest.

SUMMARY

The beauty of the 10th house is that it's an upachaya house, meaning that whatever indications are there can be changed whenever you decide you're really ready to make a shift. Because the 10th house has this quality of malleability, take this opportunity to explore your chart and discover whether your strengths are truly being expressed through your vocational path.

Making career changes does not need to be dramatic. Small, incremental changes can also have significant effects. For instance, I have a client who was always so exhausted after work each day that he never had the energy to even consider changing his career path. The man has the chart of a caregiver, even though he does not work in that field. At my suggestion, he decided to donate an hour a week to a mentoring program for children. Within a few weeks, he became so energized by donating his time that he signed up for more hours. For the first time in years, there is a glow on his face and a sparkle in his eye.

So, it's not about finding more time in your day, it's about redirecting your energies in more efficient ways that speak more accurately to how your planets want to express themselves.

Once you have succeeded, you will have a large reservoir to pull from. This is a reservoir of opportunity, latent possibilities, or accrued merit. We have now moved from the 10th house of career to the 11th house of opportunity. This is a house of desires, like the 3rd, but from a place of deeper life experience. Your wishes and dreams in this house have matured, ripened, are less selfishly oriented, and become more humanitarian. This is where all the hard work pays off, and where friends rally to your side.

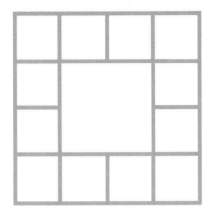

THE 11th HOUSE

Opportunity

The 11th house is the house of gains, and like the 3rd, 6th, and 10th houses, it is an upachaya house that improves with effort.

This house indicates siblings (usually older), entrepreneurial pursuits, friendships, unearned money, windfalls, and desires and wishes.

The 11th house also indicates the legs below the knees, including the shins and ankles. It also signifies your father's brothers.

THE NATURE OF THE 11th HOUSE

Find the 11th house in your chart. If you are Virgo rising, your 11th house is Cancer. If you are Pisces rising, Capricorn is your 11th house. Pay close attention to the zodiac sign of the 11th house because the nature of that sign will show you the way 11th house issues function.

For instance, if Gemini is your 11th house, then you have multitalented friends. If your 11th house is Aries, you'll want to curb your impulsive nature while speculating (e.g. making emotional decisions while trading stocks).

HOW THE 11th HOUSE EXPRESSES ITSELF

Locate the planet that rules your 11th house (see Table B), and find where it's placed in your chart. Then read the description below that pertains to this placement.

The 11th House Ruler placed in the 1st house indicates that your siblings (usually elder) bring you opportunities, as do your friends. Opportunities in general come easily to you; doors open where for most they close. You may take part in entrepreneurial pursuits that involve your personality and physical body.

The 11th House Ruler placed in the 2nd house indicates that money comes to you through speculative pursuits or unearned means. Friends or siblings can help you in generating income. You can be inspiring and motivate others through your speaking, imagination, or poetic abilities.

The 11th House Ruler placed in the 3rd house indicates that opportunities abound through creative efforts. Talents in art, literature, music, or dance are strongly enhanced by practice. If doors do not open for you, you will make them open. Siblings (usually younger ones) and friends can help make opportunities available.

The 11th House Ruler placed in the 4th house indicates that your mother creates opportunities for you and inspires you. You gain through real estate and other large fixed assets. Your friends and siblings (usually elder) bring you happiness.

The 11th House Ruler placed in the 5th house indicates that your children bring you benefits and opportunities. You may be strongly entrepreneurial, as either a stock trader, gambler, or speculator. Your friends or siblings may help you in speculative ventures.

The 11th House Ruler placed in the 6th house indicates that your opportunities are connected with the healing arts, or by overcoming enemies, legal disputes, or competitors. Opportunities do not automatically occur; you have to work to make them happen. A friend or sibling may suffer from ill health.

The 11th House Ruler placed in the 7th house indicates that your opportunities are enhanced through marriage or business partnership. A friend or elder sibling may introduce you to your marriage or business partner. This is generally a favorable position for marriage.

The 11th House Ruler placed in the 8th house favors unearned money or opportunities, especially through inheritance or lottery, but this is not generally a good position for a friend's or an elder sibling's health. Opportunities are difficult to come by with this position.

The 11th House Ruler placed in the 9th house indicates that your father or a mentor bring you benefits, especially in making opportunities available. You may have spiritual friends or an elder sibling who influence your spiritual orientation.

The 11th House Ruler placed in the 10th house is very favorable for career success. Friends or an elder sibling may help to enhance your career. Career opportunities occur naturally for you, and you may meet powerful and influential friends in professional settings.

The 11th House Ruler placed in the 11th house favors all house affairs. Opportunities, friendships, elder siblings, and speculative ventures are all enhanced.

The 11th House Ruler placed in the 12th house indicates that opportunities are not strong unless you seek them abroad, or through spiritual pursuits. Otherwise, this position can indicate difficulty for a close friend or elder sibling.

IF THERE ARE PLANETS IN THE 11th HOUSE

To help fine-tune the descriptions below, you'll want to assess whether the planet is welcome in the house in which it is placed (Table G). If the planet is in the house of a friend, the positive nature of the following description is enhanced. If the planet is in the house of an enemy, more of the negative possibilities need to be considered.

Sun (Su) in the 11th house brings a powerful male ally into your life and also shows a prominent older brother. Otherwise, you work hard for everything you get, and you may have a falling out with male friends.

Moon (Mo) in the 11th house shows that women friends bring you much benefit, and that your chart is well positioned for wealth. A poorly placed Moon shows strong ambition frustrated by circumstances not unfolding to meet those expectations.

Mars (Ma) in the 11th house indicates that you can accumulate great wealth through entrepreneurial pursuits, but it isn't a great position for the health and well-being of an older sibling.

Mercury (Me) in the 11th house, if unafflicted, shows you will surround yourself with learned and knowledgeable friends, particularly ones who are younger. Otherwise, it indicates an older sibling can be mentally imbalanced.

Jupiter (Ju) in the 11th house indicates great wealth. It also shows you will have deeply wise or spiritual friends. Otherwise, you may find it hard to find any real friends, and if you're a woman, you will be overparticular about the intimate partner you choose to be with.

Venus (Ve) in the 11th house shows you benefit from female friends. This is also a position indicating wealth. Otherwise, you have difficulty with women, and are frustrated with your inability to surround yourself with things of beauty and comfort.

Saturn (Sa) in the 11th house is a good position for tact and diplomacy. It brings you maturity and wisdom. Otherwise, you get few opportunities in life and have very little natural luck.

Rahu (Ra) in the 11th house can bring you tremendous wealth. However, you may find it difficult to hold on to that wealth. This position does not often favor an elder sibling, who may have a difficult life.

Ketu (Ke) in the 11th house brings a strong intuitive approach to investing and speculation. Your friends tend to be mystical in nature or from foreign lands. Otherwise, you can experience deception in friendships.

OTHER CONSIDERATIONS

- Note the element associated with your 11th house. Remember that fire signs are driven; earth signs are patient; air signs are creative; and water signs are emotional.
- Also note the quality of your 11th house. Cardinal signs initiate; fixed signs stabilize; and mutable signs seek change.

Now check any aspects to the 11th house:

- Are any planets located in the same house as, or opposing any planet in, the 11th house? If so, are those planets friendly, neutral, or enemies? (See Table F.) For instance, say your Sun is placed in the 11th house along with the Moon. This planetary combination shows that your elder sibling strives for independence in life.
- Remember that Mars energizes the house it's in, as well as the 4th, 7th, and 8th houses from itself. This means if Mars is placed in the 4th, 5th, or 8th houses of your chart, it throws an aspect onto your 11th house, bringing an interest in short-term investments with fast turnarounds, and the tendency to burn through friendships rather quickly.
- Saturn restricts or brings discipline to the house it's in, as well as to the 3rd, 7th, and 10th houses from itself. This means if Saturn is placed in the 2nd, 5th, or 9th house of your chart, it throws an aspect onto your 11th house, bringing mature friends, and restriction on the level of success possible through speculative endeavors.
- Jupiter expands or brings optimism to the house it's in, as well as the 5th, 7th, and 9th houses from itself. This means if Jupiter is placed in the 3rd, 5th, or 7th house of your chart, it throws an aspect onto your 11th house, increasing your luck in speculative ventures.
- If you want to find out when your chart's 11th house energies will be enlivened, look to the 11th house ruler, or any planet located in the 11th house. Examine the Mahadasha Summary of your chart to see when that planet will come into power, and that will give you your answer. To find shorter periods when 11th house issues will be highlighted, look to the 11th house ruler or any planet located in the 11th house, and find the time its bhukti will run.
- Notice any influence transiting planets are having on your 11th house. When Saturn transits the 11th house, you'll want to stay away from any type of risky or speculative endeavor. When Jupiter crosses this house, just the opposite is true. When Mars transits the 11th house, be careful how you deal with friends if you want to keep their friendship. You can chant to the planet that is favorably transiting your rising sign, on the appropriate day for that planet, to enhance its effects.

CHART EXAMPLES

Let's look at an example of an afflicted 11th house that affects a sibling.

Sally has Aquarius rising. Her 11th house, then, is Sagittarius, which is ruled by Jupiter. Notice that the 11th house ruler, Jupiter, is retrograde, and placed in the 12th house con-junct with retrograde Saturn. Whenever Jupiter and Saturn conjoin in a poorly placed house, there exists the possibility of a severe legal issue.

In this case, Sally's older brother was imprisoned, though he was not guilty of the crime. This occurred during her Jupiter mahadasha, which is the planet that rules her

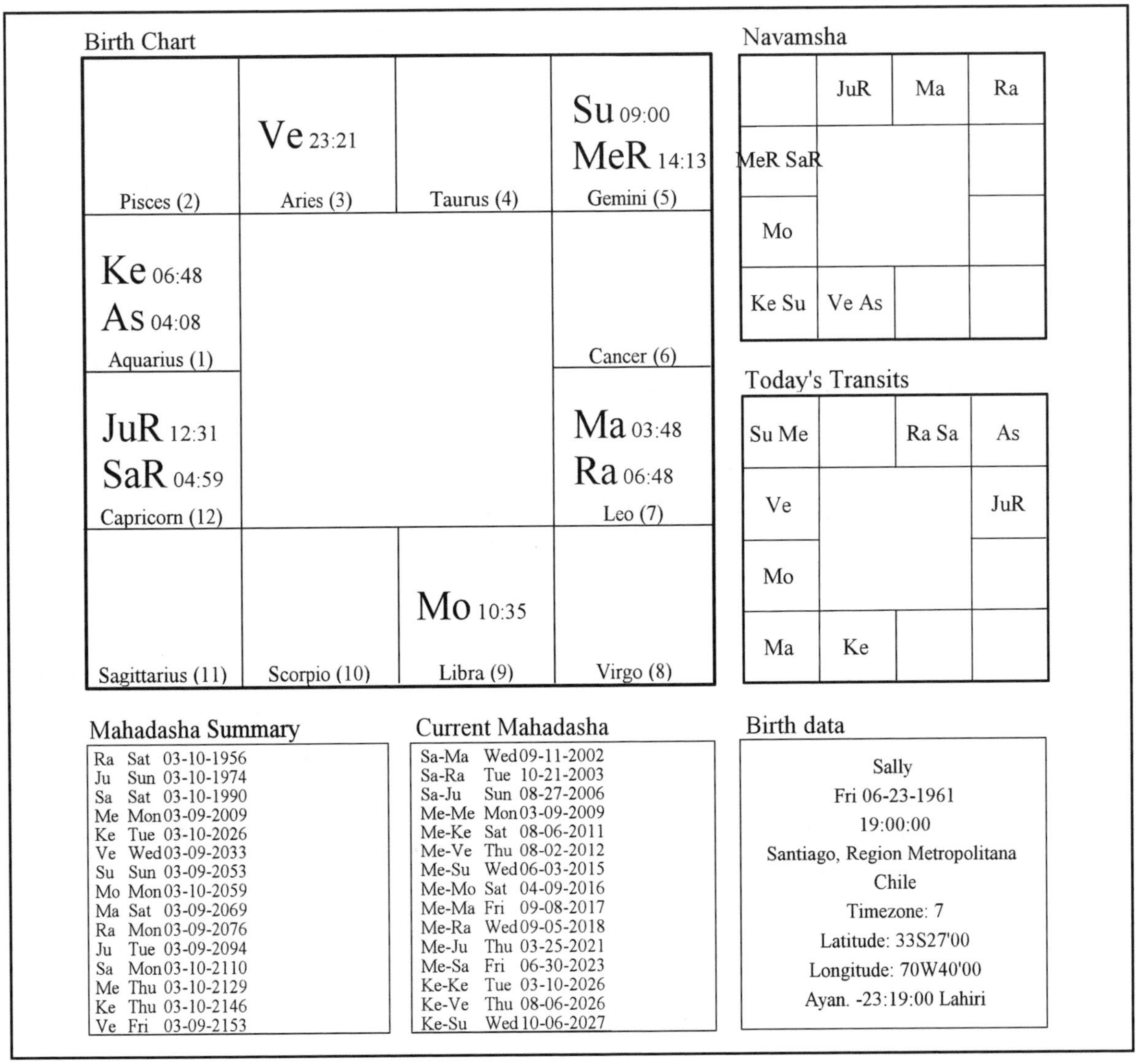

Birth Chart

Pisces (2)	**Ve** 23:21 Aries (3)	Taurus (4)	**Su** 09:00 **MeR** 14:13 Gemini (5)
Ke 06:48 **As** 04:08 Aquarius (1)			Cancer (6)
JuR 12:31 **SaR** 04:59 Capricorn (12)			**Ma** 03:48 **Ra** 06:48 Leo (7)
Sagittarius (11)	Scorpio (10)	**Mo** 10:35 Libra (9)	Virgo (8)

Navamsha

	JuR	Ma	Ra
MeR SaR			
Mo			
Ke Su	Ve As		

Today's Transits

Su Me		Ra Sa	As
Ve			JuR
Mo			
Ma	Ke		

Mahadasha Summary

Ra	Sat	03-10-1956
Ju	Sun	03-10-1974
Sa	Sat	03-10-1990
Me	Mon	03-09-2009
Ke	Tue	03-10-2026
Ve	Wed	03-09-2033
Su	Sun	03-09-2053
Mo	Mon	03-10-2059
Ma	Sat	03-09-2069
Ra	Mon	03-09-2076
Ju	Tue	03-09-2094
Sa	Mon	03-10-2110
Me	Thu	03-10-2129
Ke	Thu	03-10-2146
Ve	Fri	03-09-2153

Current Mahadasha

Sa-Ma	Wed	09-11-2002
Sa-Ra	Tue	10-21-2003
Sa-Ju	Sun	08-27-2006
Me-Me	Mon	03-09-2009
Me-Ke	Sat	08-06-2011
Me-Ve	Thu	08-02-2012
Me-Su	Wed	06-03-2015
Me-Mo	Sat	04-09-2016
Me-Ma	Fri	09-08-2017
Me-Ra	Wed	09-05-2018
Me-Ju	Thu	03-25-2021
Me-Sa	Fri	06-30-2023
Ke-Ke	Tue	03-10-2026
Ke-Ve	Thu	08-06-2026
Ke-Su	Wed	10-06-2027

Birth data

Sally
Fri 06-23-1961
19:00:00
Santiago, Region Metropolitana
Chile
Timezone: 7
Latitude: 33S27'00
Longitude: 70W40'00
Ayan. -23:19:00 Lahiri

Chart 88—Sally

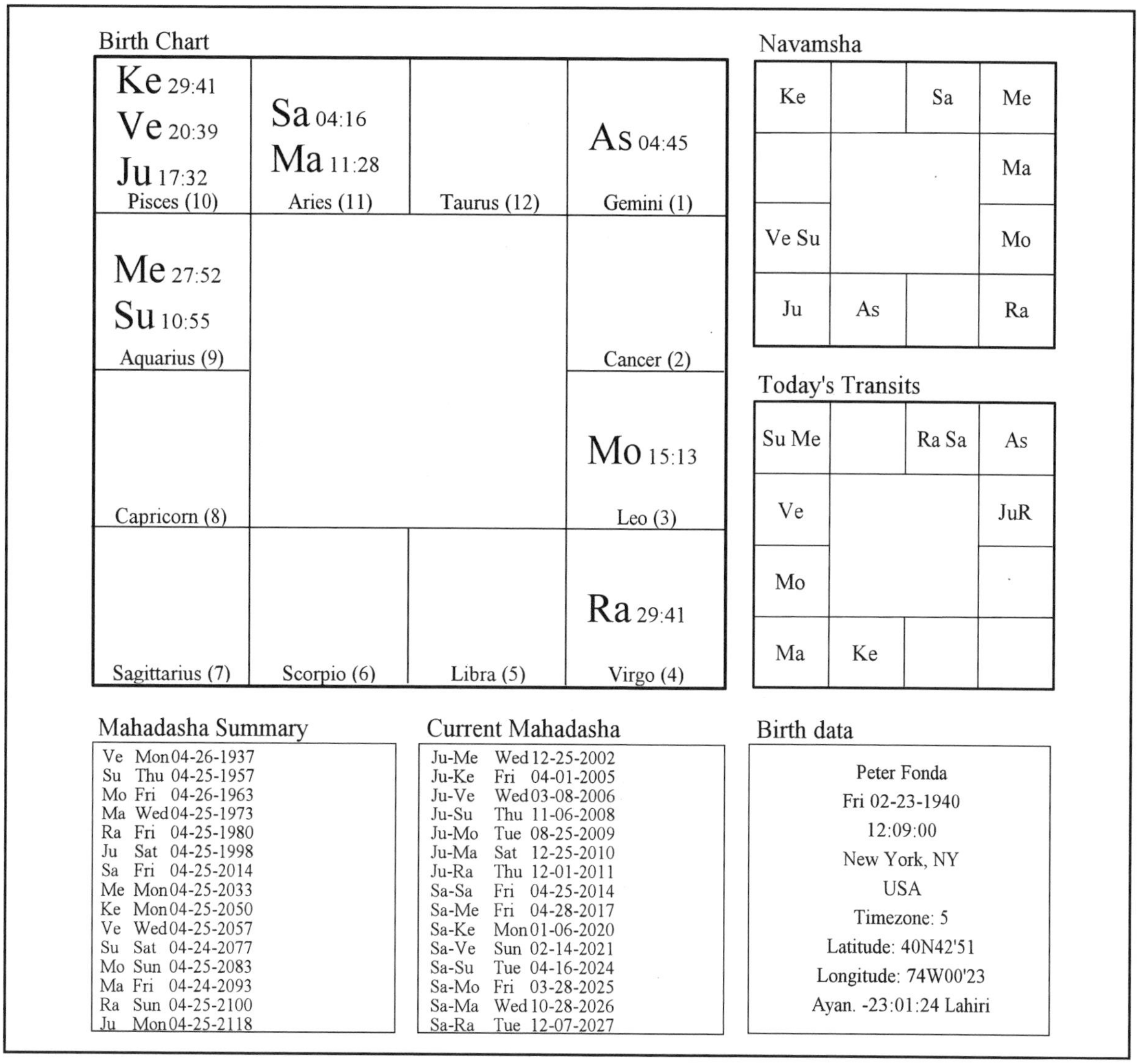

Birth Chart

Ke 29:41 Ve 20:39 Ju 17:32 Pisces (10)	Sa 04:16 Ma 11:28 Aries (11)	Taurus (12)	As 04:45 Gemini (1)
Me 27:52 Su 10:55 Aquarius (9)			Cancer (2)
Capricorn (8)			Mo 15:13 Leo (3)
Sagittarius (7)	Scorpio (6)	Libra (5)	Ra 29:41 Virgo (4)

Navamsha

Ke		Sa	Me
			Ma
Ve Su			Mo
Ju	As		Ra

Today's Transits

Su Me		Ra Sa	As
Ve			JuR
Mo			
Ma	Ke		

Mahadasha Summary

Ve	Mon 04-26-1937
Su	Thu 04-25-1957
Mo	Fri 04-26-1963
Ma	Wed 04-25-1973
Ra	Fri 04-25-1980
Ju	Sat 04-25-1998
Sa	Fri 04-25-2014
Me	Mon 04-25-2033
Ke	Mon 04-25-2050
Ve	Wed 04-25-2057
Su	Sat 04-24-2077
Mo	Sun 04-25-2083
Ma	Fri 04-24-2093
Ra	Sun 04-25-2100
Ju	Mon 04-25-2118

Current Mahadasha

Ju-Me	Wed 12-25-2002
Ju-Ke	Fri 04-01-2005
Ju-Ve	Wed 03-08-2006
Ju-Su	Thu 11-06-2008
Ju-Mo	Tue 08-25-2009
Ju-Ma	Sat 12-25-2010
Ju-Ra	Thu 12-01-2011
Sa-Sa	Fri 04-25-2014
Sa-Me	Fri 04-28-2017
Sa-Ke	Mon 01-06-2020
Sa-Ve	Sun 02-14-2021
Sa-Su	Tue 04-16-2024
Sa-Mo	Fri 03-28-2025
Sa-Ma	Wed 10-28-2026
Sa-Ra	Tue 12-07-2027

Birth data

Peter Fonda
Fri 02-23-1940
12:09:00
New York, NY
USA
Timezone: 5
Latitude: 40N42'51
Longitude: 74W00'23
Ayan. -23:01:24 Lahiri

Chart 89—Peter Fonda

house of older siblings. You can see by taking Sally's 11th house as the rising sign that well-placed Venus sits in Aries and is favorably opposed by the Moon. In a short amount of time, the truth of her brother's case was revealed and he was exonerated.

To see an example of a falling out among friends, let's look at Peter Fonda's chart.

Peter's rising sign is Gemini, and his 11th house is Aries, where Mars is located conjunct its enemy Saturn. This indicates that he would have a falling out with friends at some point, and that people he felt were friends would turn out to be antagonists.

Certainly the most publicly known example of this is his conflict with Terry Southern, the man who helped conceptualize and write the screenplay for the wildly successful 1969 film *Easy Rider*. Though there are many differing versions of the story, it seems Terry was cut out on the profits of the film and was unable to convince Peter Fonda (and Dennis Hopper) to help him out. This conflict came to a head during Peter's Mars mahadasha, which ran between 1973 and 1980.

Besides friendships, the 11th house also indicates older siblings. Aries, with Mars and Saturn placed there, indicates a person who is headstrong, ruthless, and outspoken, all of which seem to describe Peter's sister Jane well, from what we've read in the press. Want to find out about Jane's marriage chart? Use Peter's 11th house as the rising sign and look to the 7th house from it: Libra, ruled by Venus. That Venus is located in the 12th house of loss. So we would expect she would go through at least one marriage, which she has. How about her religious convictions? We look to the 9th house for that, which is Sagittarius, ruled by Jupiter. And that Jupiter is also placed in the 12th house. Those 12th house planets are joined by Ketu, indicating a certain unreliability or changeability, sometimes driven by mysterious causes or peer influence. That Jane could go from a free-thinking, independent, driven women to a shadow as a corporate wife, to a born-again Christian is an example of this.

How about Peter's daughter Bridget? Look to the 5th house of children. In this case it's Libra, ruled by Venus, the planet of the arts. That Venus is powerfully exalted in Pisces, conjunct Jupiter and Ketu, indicating a powerful artistic destiny. But looking at her marriage prospects, the 7th from the 5th, you'll see that nasty Saturn/Mars conjunction again in Aries. She'll need to be careful with her marriage choices.

Another problem with friends can be seen in Carrie Fisher's chart (Chart 90).

Carrie's rising sign is Sagittarius, which is ruled by Jupiter. That Jupiter is placed in her 9th house and opposed by Mars. The Jupiter/Mars connection brings with it the possibility of overindulgence, because Jupiter can bring excess and Mars fuels it. The debilitated Sun in her 11th house of friendship made her susceptibile to the influence of friends, primarily because a weak Sun doesn't give a person a strong sense of self. They rely on their friends to bring meaning into their lives. When might you think she would experience such difficulties? Probably when her Sun mahadasha ran. However, she was born during the Sun cycle and was only four years old when it ended. So we would look to the next challenging cycle for her. Notice that Saturn is placed in her 12th house (intense Scorpio) conjunct another malefic influence (Rahu) to the exact degree. Certainly when one of those planets runs its cycle she is bound to encounter difficulties.

Look at the Mahadasha Summary and notice that the Rahu came into power in 1977.

Soon thereafter, in November of 1978,

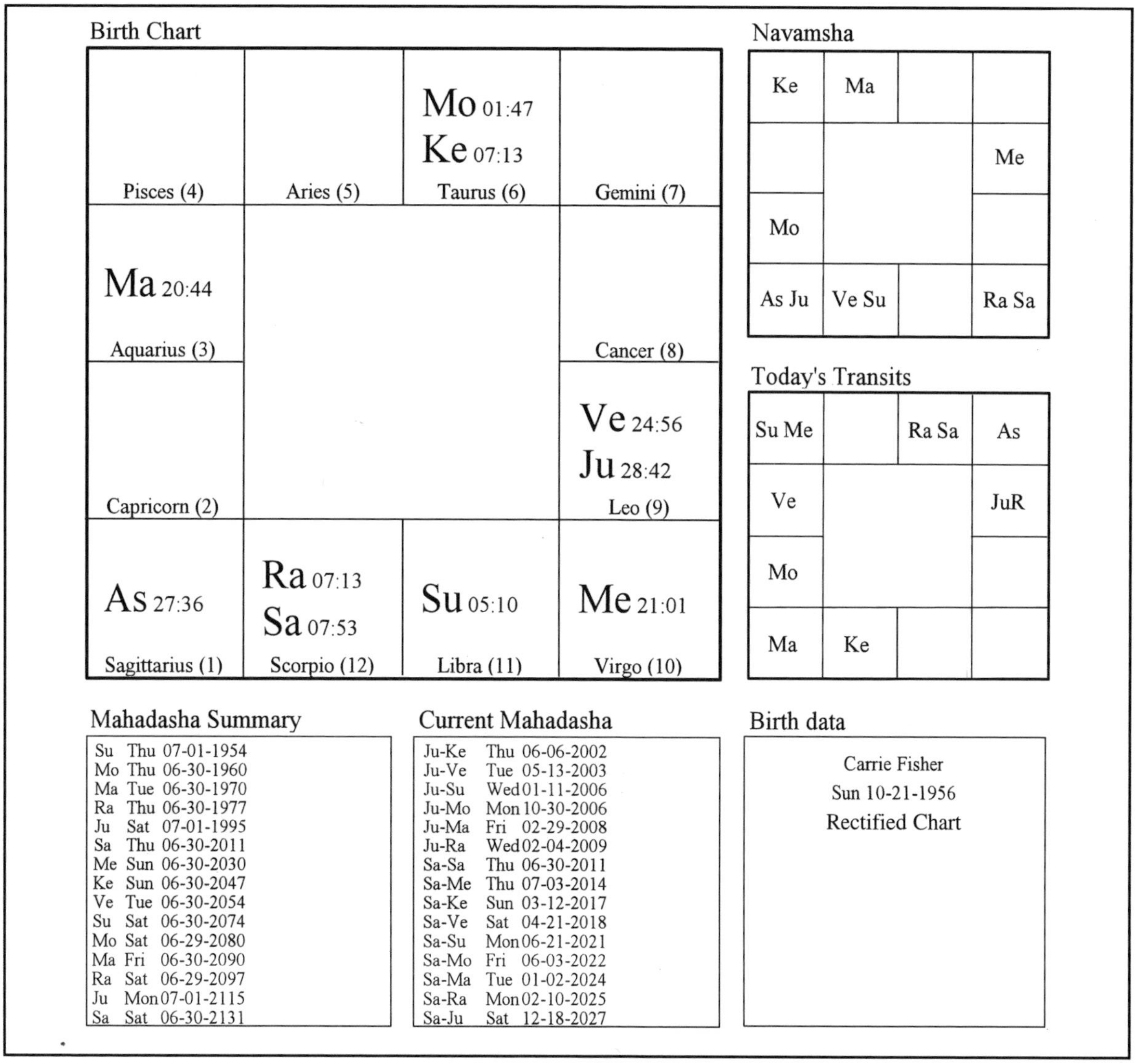

Birth Chart			
Pisces (4)	Aries (5)	**Mo** 01:47 **Ke** 07:13 Taurus (6)	Gemini (7)
Ma 20:44 Aquarius (3)			Cancer (8)
Capricorn (2)			**Ve** 24:56 **Ju** 28:42 Leo (9)
As 27:36 Sagittarius (1)	**Ra** 07:13 **Sa** 07:53 Scorpio (12)	**Su** 05:10 Libra (11)	**Me** 21:01 Virgo (10)

Navamsha			
Ke	Ma		
			Me
Mo			
As Ju	Ve Su		Ra Sa

Today's Transits			
Su Me		Ra Sa	As
Ve			JuR
Mo			
Ma	Ke		

Mahadasha Summary

Su	Thu	07-01-1954
Mo	Thu	06-30-1960
Ma	Tue	06-30-1970
Ra	Thu	06-30-1977
Ju	Sat	07-01-1995
Sa	Thu	06-30-2011
Me	Sun	06-30-2030
Ke	Sun	06-30-2047
Ve	Tue	06-30-2054
Su	Sat	06-30-2074
Mo	Sat	06-29-2080
Ma	Fri	06-30-2090
Ra	Sat	06-29-2097
Ju	Mon	07-01-2115
Sa	Sat	06-30-2131

Current Mahadasha

Ju-Ke	Thu	06-06-2002
Ju-Ve	Tue	05-13-2003
Ju-Su	Wed	01-11-2006
Ju-Mo	Mon	10-30-2006
Ju-Ma	Fri	02-29-2008
Ju-Ra	Wed	02-04-2009
Sa-Sa	Thu	06-30-2011
Sa-Me	Thu	07-03-2014
Sa-Ke	Sun	03-12-2017
Sa-Ve	Sat	04-21-2018
Sa-Su	Mon	06-21-2021
Sa-Mo	Fri	06-03-2022
Sa-Ma	Tue	01-02-2024
Sa-Ra	Mon	02-10-2025
Sa-Ju	Sat	12-18-2027

Birth data

Carrie Fisher
Sun 10-21-1956
Rectified Chart

Chart 90—Carrie Fisher

Carrie hosted *Saturday Night Live* and during that time befriended John Belushi, who led her into a life of deep and intense drug use. Due to her intensely addictive nature (2nd house ruler in the 12th and conjunct malefic Rahu), and fueled by this friendship (debilitated Sun in the 11th), Carrie was in and out of rehab clinics for more than a decade.

Now look at Warren Beatty's 11th house for the indication of his older sister.

Warren's rising sign is Virgo, so his 11th house is Cancer, which is ruled by the Moon. The Moon in his chart is in his 3rd house, Scorpio, conjoined by Mars and Rahu.

Because the 11th house also indicates older siblings, this Moon (remember the Moon is feminine in nature) indicates a sister.

Warren's sister is Shirley MacLaine. What can we see about her in his chart? As you now know, the 3rd house relates to creativity, and when you see several planets occupying a house of creativity, it can indicate more than one creative skill. Shirley acts, dances, sings, and writes books. Mars placed in the house it rules (Scorpio) gives added energy, bringing his sister an almost tireless amount of energy and enthusiasm.

What can we tell from Shirley's 11th house (specifically about the nature of her friendships) just by looking at it through her brother's chart? Because Shirley is indicated by Scorpio in Warren's chart, her 11th house is Virgo (eleven houses from Scorpio). Remember that Virgo is ruled by Mercury, and Mercury is located in Pisces along with the Saturn and Sun. Saturn and Sun when they're in the same house act as sparring brothers, each trying to assert his prowess and skill over the other. Of course, MacLaine was the only woman included in the Rat Pack, and those planets reflect the playful one-upmanship between Frank Sinatra, Dean Martin, Sammy Davis, Jr., and Peter Lawford, among others. The Mercury joining them in that house indicates that witty chatter, jokes, and song would be the medium through which they would play.

Kelly's chart (Chart 92) shows an afflicted 11th house and difficulty for an elder sibling.

Kelly was born with Gemini rising, and so her 11th house is ruled by Aries. If you'll recall, when we looked at the nature of each rising sign on pages 43–47, we said that Gemini is symbolized by the twins.

Appropriately enough, Kelly is a twin. Her brother was born just ahead of her, and so is considered older. So we can look to her 11th house for indications about him. Unfortunately, Saturn is placed in sandhi (the fateful last degrees) in retrograde in her 11th house, in the house of its enemy (Aries, ruled by Mars). Her brother didn't survive the birth. She, however, thrived.

Mindy's 11th house issue is her tendency to be intimidated by friends (Chart 93).

Mindy's rising sign is very late Libra. It's essential when you analyze charts to use the correct rising sign, because indications change so dramatically from sign to sign. On occasion you find a chart where the rising sign is on the cusp between two signs. When this happens, the person takes on qualities of both signs, with a little more emphasis on the sign the ascendant degree actually occupies, even if at zero degrees. Mindy's chart shows her rising sign to be within one degree of Scorpio, but still in Libra. She's a custom clothes designer, which certainly makes sense for a Libra rising person, since Libra is ruled by artistic Venus. But she also has a weight problem, which is indicated by the indulgent nature of Scorpio, and the expansive Jupiter placed in that house. In this way, Mindy actually takes on qualities of both signs.

Looking further, we see that her 11th house

Birth Chart

Ma 25:13 Pisces (10)	**SaR** 29:53 Aries (11)	**JuR** 22:21 Taurus (12)	**As** 24:59 Gemini (1)
Ke 24:38 Aquarius (9)			Cancer (2)
Ve 15:25 Capricorn (8)			**Ra** 24:38 Leo (3)
Su 00:34 Sagittarius (7)	**Me** 27:11 Scorpio (6)	**Mo** 25:41 Libra (5)	Virgo (4)

Navamsha

Me	Su	Ke As Ve Mo	
Ma			JuR
SaR	Ra		

Today's Transits

Su Me		Ra Sa	As
Ve			JuR
Mo			
Ma	Ke		

Mahadasha Summary

Ju	Tue 02-19-1935
Sa	Mon 02-19-1951
Me	Thu 02-19-1970
Ke	Thu 02-19-1987
Ve	Sat 02-19-1994
Su	Tue 02-18-2014
Mo	Wed 02-19-2020
Ma	Mon 02-18-2030
Ra	Wed 02-18-2037
Ju	Thu 02-18-2055
Sa	Wed 02-18-2071
Me	Sat 02-18-2090
Ke	Sat 02-19-2107
Ve	Mon 02-19-2114
Su	Thu 02-18-2134

Current Mahadasha

Ve-Ra	Fri 04-20-2001
Ve-Ju	Tue 04-20-2004
Ve-Sa	Wed 12-20-2006
Ve-Me	Thu 02-18-2010
Ve-Ke	Wed 12-19-2012
Su-Su	Tue 02-18-2014
Su-Mo	Sun 06-08-2014
Su-Ma	Mon 12-08-2014
Su-Ra	Tue 04-14-2015
Su-Ju	Tue 03-08-2016
Su-Sa	Sun 12-25-2016
Su-Me	Thu 12-07-2017
Su-Ke	Sun 10-14-2018
Su-Ve	Tue 02-19-2019
Mo-Mo	Wed 02-19-2020

Birth data

Kelly
Mon 12-15-1941
18:15:00
New York, NY
USA
Timezone: 5
Latitude: 40N42'51
Longitude: 74W00'23
Ayan. -23:02:43 Lahiri

Chart 92—Kelly

is Leo, ruled by the Sun. The Sun is placed in Leo, along with a slightly combust Mercury and retrograde Venus. Many of Mindy's friends are prominent in the community, indicated by the 11th house ruler placed in the 11th house. However, they often intimidate her, which is shown by delicate Mercury being a bit too close to the Sun, affecting her confidence and sense of self-worth (this is due also to her late-degree rising sign, which doesn't have much strength). Retrograde Venus (ironically) brings her an inner charisma that attracts the very people whom she feels stifled by, but makes her somewhat clumsy in social situations.

Does she make money? Jupiter in the 2nd house is one of the best placements for money, so yes. But the ruler of 2nd house Scorpio, Mars, is located in the 12th house of loss. So, although she earns well, she also runs into expenditures or can't seem to hold on to her money. Mars also rules her 7th house of marriage. When the 7th house ruler is placed in the 12th it indicates strong kuja dosha, an obstruction to the peaceful enjoyment of married life. More dramatically, her Mars is conjunct with malefic Rahu to the exact degree, and both planets (Rahu's not really a planet, but an influence) are hit by their enemy Saturn's 10th house aspect from Sagittarius. Needless to say, Mindy's love life leaves much to be desired.

Birth Chart

Ke 11:16 Pisces (6)	Aries (7)	Taurus (8)	Gemini (9)
Mo 02:15 Capricorn (4)		Aquarius (5)	Cancer (10) **VeR** 08:34 **Me** 21:12 **Su** 25:53 Leo (11)
Sa 07:12 Sagittarius (3)	**Ju** 02:58 Scorpio (2)	**As** 29:24 Libra (1)	**Ma** 11:04 **Ra** 11:16 Virgo (12)

Navamsha

	Ma Ra		Sa VeR As
			Ju
Mo			
	Su	Me Ke	

Today's Transits

Su Me		Ra Sa	As
Ve			JuR
Mo			
Ma	Ke		

Mahadasha Summary

Su	Thu	03-07-1957
Mo	Thu	03-07-1963
Ma	Wed	03-07-1973
Ra	Thu	03-06-1980
Ju	Sat	03-07-1998
Sa	Fri	03-07-2014
Me	Sun	03-06-2033
Ke	Sun	03-06-2050
Ve	Tue	03-06-2057
Su	Sat	03-06-2077
Mo	Sat	03-06-2083
Ma	Fri	03-06-2093
Ra	Sat	03-06-2100
Ju	Mon	03-07-2118
Sa	Sun	03-07-2134

Current Mahadasha

Ju-Me	Tue	11-05-2002
Ju-Ke	Thu	02-10-2005
Ju-Ve	Tue	01-17-2006
Ju-Su	Wed	09-17-2008
Ju-Mo	Mon	07-06-2009
Ju-Ma	Fri	11-05-2010
Ju-Ra	Wed	10-12-2011
Sa-Sa	Fri	03-07-2014
Sa-Me	Thu	03-09-2017
Sa-Ke	Mon	11-18-2019
Sa-Ve	Sat	12-26-2020
Sa-Su	Mon	02-26-2024
Sa-Mo	Fri	02-07-2025
Sa-Ma	Tue	09-08-2026
Sa-Ra	Mon	10-18-2027

Birth data

Mindy
Sat 09-12-1959
11:59:00
Northbrook, IL
USA
Timezone: 6
Latitude: 42N07'39
Longitude: 87W49'44
Ayan. -23:17:41 Lahiri

Chart 93—Mindy

In our next example, Oliver has difficulty with friends, too, but only when they're male.

Oliver's rising sign is Capricorn, with Saturn, the ruler of his rising sign, placed in his 11th house, which is ruled by Scorpio. In fact, four planets occupy the 11th house: Saturn, Sun, Mercury, and Rahu. We can see several things here. The emotional nature of the planets located in Scorpio become accentuated, due to Scorpio's water element, and there is also the indication that things can be obsessed about, due to Scorpio's fixed nature.

When you do find more than two planets in a house, as in this case, it can sometimes seem difficult to understand how they interact. It's best to look at each planet individually

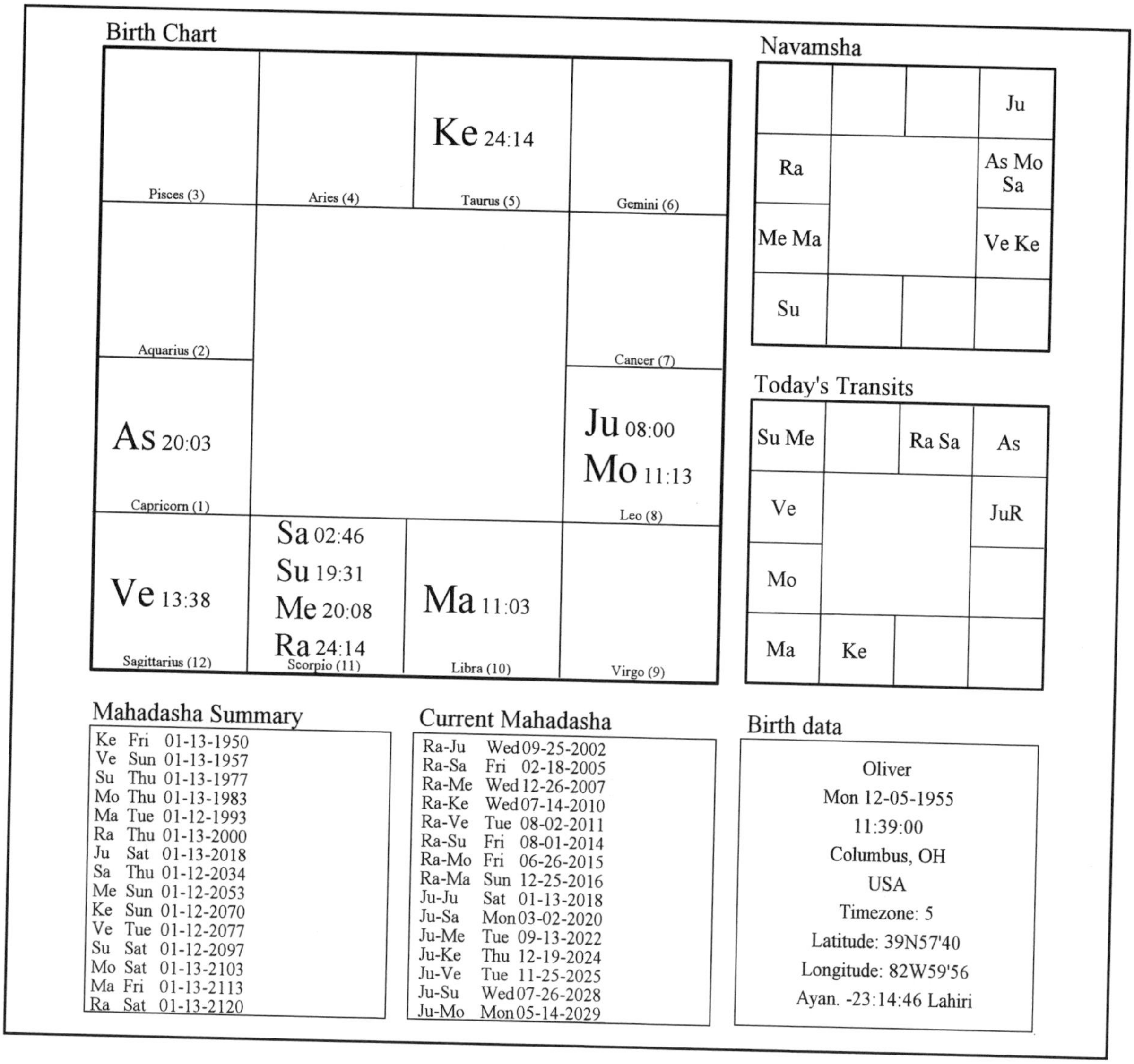

Birth Chart

		Ke 24:14	
Pisces (3)	Aries (4)	Taurus (5)	Gemini (6)
Aquarius (2)			Cancer (7)
As 20:03			Ju 08:00 / Mo 11:13
Capricorn (1)			Leo (8)
Ve 13:38	Sa 02:46 / Su 19:31 / Me 20:08 / Ra 24:14	Ma 11:03	
Sagittarius (12)	Scorpio (11)	Libra (10)	Virgo (9)

Navamsha

			Ju
Ra			As Mo Sa
Me Ma			Ve Ke
Su			

Today's Transits

Su Me		Ra Sa	As
Ve			JuR
Mo			
Ma	Ke		

Mahadasha Summary

Ke	Fri	01-13-1950
Ve	Sun	01-13-1957
Su	Thu	01-13-1977
Mo	Thu	01-13-1983
Ma	Tue	01-12-1993
Ra	Thu	01-13-2000
Ju	Sat	01-13-2018
Sa	Thu	01-12-2034
Me	Sun	01-12-2053
Ke	Sun	01-12-2070
Ve	Tue	01-12-2077
Su	Sat	01-12-2097
Mo	Sat	01-13-2103
Ma	Fri	01-13-2113
Ra	Sat	01-13-2120

Current Mahadasha

Ra-Ju	Wed 09-25-2002
Ra-Sa	Fri 02-18-2005
Ra-Me	Wed 12-26-2007
Ra-Ke	Wed 07-14-2010
Ra-Ve	Tue 08-02-2011
Ra-Su	Fri 08-01-2014
Ra-Mo	Fri 06-26-2015
Ra-Ma	Sun 12-25-2016
Ju-Ju	Sat 01-13-2018
Ju-Sa	Mon 03-02-2020
Ju-Me	Tue 09-13-2022
Ju-Ke	Thu 12-19-2024
Ju-Ve	Tue 11-25-2025
Ju-Su	Wed 07-26-2028
Ju-Mo	Mon 05-14-2029

Birth data

Oliver
Mon 12-05-1955
11:39:00
Columbus, OH
USA
Timezone: 5
Latitude: 39N57'40
Longitude: 82W59'56
Ayan. -23:14:46 Lahiri

Chart 94—Oliver

and determine first how they relate to the house they're in, and then how they relate to their surrounding planets.

Starting with Saturn, we see from Table G that it is placed in an enemy's house in Scorpio, and that it is conjunct with its enemy Sun (Table F). The Sun is comfortable in Scorpio but conjunct with its enemy Saturn. Mercury is neutral in Scorpio but hemmed in by two malefics, the Sun and Rahu. Further, Mercury is positioned within 1 degree of the Sun, making it combust. Lastly, Rahu, like Saturn, is not happy to be in Scorpio, and conjoins enemy Sun.

How do these relationships play out? Because Saturn rules Oliver's rising sign and conjoins its enemy in the 11th house, he tends to experience power struggles and conflicts with male friends in his life. He also has a natural resistance to authority and doesn't like feeling controlled or dominated by anyone. When the Sun is conjunct with its enemy Saturn, there is sometimes evidence of problems with the father that fuels this reaction to other men in a person's life.

Given that his planets are positioned in this way, do you see how it's possible that even if a male friend doesn't intend to create a dispute, Oliver can misread the messages he's receiving from that man and project on him his own patterning? This is a good example of the likelihood that we view the world, and react to it, through the inflected lens of our planets, rather than being able to comprehend what is truly before us.

Oliver's Mercury is strongly afflicted, bringing him nervousness, lack of confidence, poor eyesight, and breaks in education. In fact, he never finished college. The Rahu drives him to constantly prove that he is indeed competent, because his Mercury gives him the sense he's not. In order to compensate for his sense of unworthiness, powerful Rahu goes overboard in trying to prove otherwise, which also causes friction with friends.

Because the 11th house rules the ankles, it's also interesting to note that Oliver underwent several Achilles heel surgeries to repair torn tendons.

Now let's explore more deeply Richard's chart, which we looked at in our discussion of the 9th house.

Though we will eventually address his 11th house, let's first study Richard's chart using everything we've learned so far about the houses. His rising sign is Aries, ruled by Mars. As you can imagine, this rising sign makes Richard dynamic, headstrong, driven, and active. The militant nature of Mars is strongly expressed through him; he became an accomplished martial artist and had upper-level clearance in the military.

The ruler of his rising sign is placed in the 2nd house, the house of money. This is a good position for being able to accumulate money and for being generous with it. But notice that the Saturn hits his 2nd house, bringing some restriction to that house. However, also notice that Jupiter hits his 2nd house by aspect (5th house aspect), bringing expansion. As you can imagine, his fortunes have risen and fallen. He has several times gone from being a million-

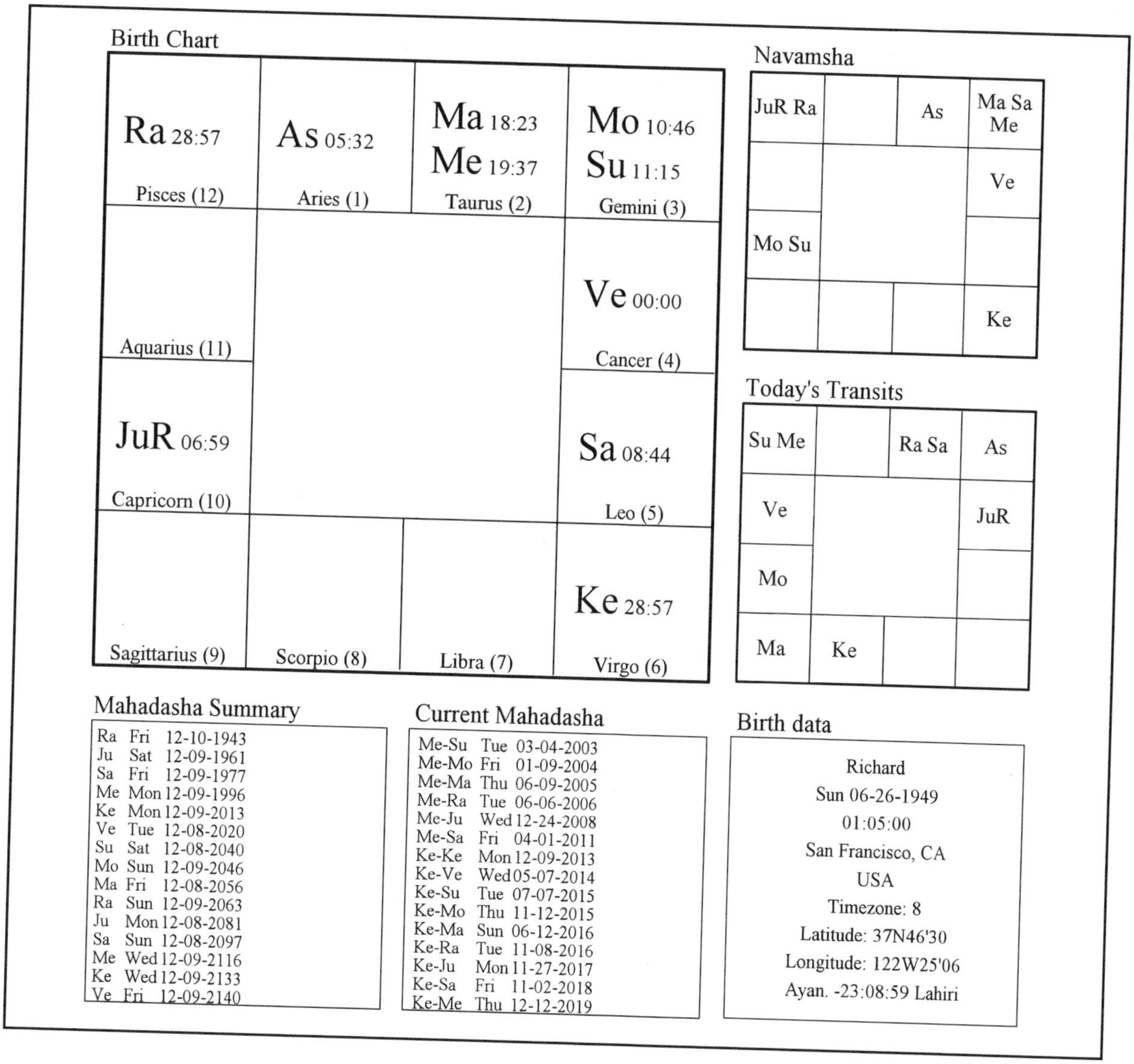

Birth Chart

Ra 28:57 Pisces (12)	As 05:32 Aries (1)	Ma 18:23 Me 19:37 Taurus (2)	Mo 10:46 Su 11:15 Gemini (3)
 Aquarius (11)			Ve 00:00 Cancer (4)
JuR 06:59 Capricorn (10)			Sa 08:44 Leo (5)
 Sagittarius (9)	Scorpio (8)	Libra (7)	Ke 28:57 Virgo (6)

Navamsha

JuR Ra		As	Ma Sa Me
			Ve
Mo Su			
			Ke

Today's Transits

Su Me		Ra Sa	As
Ve			JuR
Mo			
Ma	Ke		

Mahadasha Summary

Ra	Fri	12-10-1943
Ju	Sat	12-09-1961
Sa	Fri	12-09-1977
Me	Mon	12-09-1996
Ke	Mon	12-09-2013
Ve	Tue	12-08-2020
Su	Sat	12-08-2040
Mo	Sun	12-09-2046
Ma	Fri	12-08-2056
Ra	Sun	12-09-2063
Ju	Mon	12-08-2081
Sa	Sun	12-08-2097
Me	Wed	12-09-2116
Ke	Wed	12-09-2133
Ve	Fri	12-09-2140

Current Mahadasha

Me-Su	Tue	03-04-2003
Me-Mo	Fri	01-09-2004
Me-Ma	Thu	06-09-2005
Me-Ra	Tue	06-06-2006
Me-Ju	Wed	12-24-2008
Me-Sa	Fri	04-01-2011
Ke-Ke	Mon	12-09-2013
Ke-Ve	Wed	05-07-2014
Ke-Su	Tue	07-07-2015
Ke-Mo	Thu	11-12-2015
Ke-Ma	Sun	06-12-2016
Ke-Ra	Tue	11-08-2016
Ke-Ju	Mon	11-27-2017
Ke-Sa	Fri	11-02-2018
Ke-Me	Thu	12-12-2019

Birth data

Richard
Sun 06-26-1949
01:05:00
San Francisco, CA
USA
Timezone: 8
Latitude: 37N46'30
Longitude: 122W25'06
Ayan. -23:08:59 Lahiri

Chart 95—Richard

aire to being broke, but his generosity hasn't waned.

The 2nd house also indicates one's childhood, and remember that Saturn and Mars are enemies. Because they meet in his 2nd house, Richard's childhood suffered the results. His birth father was a powerful, overbearing man, and his stepfather abused him and his mother.

The 2nd house also relates to the mouth and eating. The way in which Richard's stepfather abused him was to slap him whenever he tried to eat. In order to eat food without getting hurt, he would wolf down as much food as he could before his stepfather noticed that he was eating. This gave him a lot of mental anguish and led to a weight problem, which is consistent with his delicate Mercury being aspected by two strong malefics, Mars and Saturn.

Richard's 3rd house, Gemini, is occupied by the Moon and Sun. These planets bring tremendous versatility and skill in the arts, particularly music. Richard plays several musical instruments, has overseen music production in a studio, and has organized large musical concerts in major cities worldwide. He has even performed stand-up comedy in Las Vegas.

His 4th house is Cancer, ruled by the Moon. That Moon is placed in the 3rd house. Since the 4th house deals with the home environment and "motherly energies," he constantly makes efforts (3rd house) to make sure people are nurtured in his home and fed well. Perhaps because he suffered so much in his home environment, he wants others to feel nurtured.

Venus is placed in his 4th house, showing that he benefits by women in his life, and has luck with homes and automobiles. Over the last twenty years, Richard has owned a number of remarkable homes, and has purchased almost every exotic car available. The power of his 4th house is enhanced by retrograde Jupiter throwing a beneficent aspect onto his 4th house from its house of debilitation. (Remember that debilitated planets in retrograde give *positive* results.)

The Saturn in his 5th house shows that he would not have many children (he has one), and since the 5th house rules the stomach area, that he would have some difficulty in that region. He was born with his stomach outside his body, and was one of few children to survive the type of operation needed to repair it. In fact, when he was born, the doctors were so sure he wouldn't survive that they set him aside to die a natural death. But he kept breathing!

In the navamsha, the severity of Richard's stomach situation is clearly seen. With Taurus rising, the 5th house is Virgo, ruled by Mercury. That Mercury is placed in the 2nd house conjunct with malefic Mars and Saturn. Also, the Ketu in the 5th house indicates a mysterious or highly unusual situation in the stomach area, which this most certainly was.

His 6th house is Virgo, a house associated with health and healing. That 6th house ruler (Mercury) is placed in his 2nd house, indicating that he can make money through healing. Richard has always had healing abilities, but was punished by his parents for using them when he was young. In his early twenties, however, he tapped back into his abilities and began healing many people.

At times the healings were dramatic. At one session a man came in by wheelchair, and was able to walk away on his own. You might imagine this could only occur through grace. Notice that grace-bestowing Jupiter throws a 9th house aspect onto his 6th house from Capricorn.

The 6th house also deals with enemies, and since the 6th house ruler is placed in the 2nd house, this chart shows that Richard could also make money through fighting. Although his martial art skills are formidable, and many people have wanted to study under him, his teacher made him promise never to teach, and he has lived by that promise.

His 7th house is Libra, ruled by Venus. Richard has been married several times, which is not that obvious in his natal chart, except that the 7th house ruler is in its weakest degree. However, look at the navamsha chart. With Taurus rising, his 7th house is Scorpio, ruled by Mars. That Mars is conjoined by Saturn and Mercury, which has turned malefic because of the influence of the other two malefic planets near it.

His 8th house Scorpio is ruled by Mars. That Mars is placed in his 2nd house. This is a good placement for inheritance, and in fact Richard did receive an inheritance that enabled him to buy several homes.

His 9th house, Sagittarius, is ruled by Jupiter, and that Jupiter is placed in its house of debilitation in retrograde. Generally when a planet is both retrograde and in its house of debilitation, the retrograde motion enables the planet to give exalted results. Richard has benefited by many mentors and spiritual advisors and teachers from many different religious traditions. In many cases, he is given a great deal of personal attention from these people.

His 10th house ruler is placed in the 5th house, indicating strongly destined career choices. But because the Sun is in an enemy's house and aspected by its enemy Mars, he has never really held down a conventional job. However, he has succeeded in many careers, mostly entrepreneurial in nature.

Richard's 11th house ruler is Saturn, as Aquarius is his 11th house. That Saturn is placed in his 5th house, showing one of the best possible positions for entrepreneurial luck. It is while being involved in speculative ventures that he has made his millions. But the Saturn also limits the number of his older siblings and close friends. He has no older siblings, and though people love being around him, he has very few close friends.

REMEDIES

Sally brother's situation could not be easily remedied through her chart. We would have to see his planets to determine what planets need strengthening in his chart. However, if that is not possible, a fire ritual could be performed for overall protection of the brother and be quite effective. The main issue to remedy in her chart is her 7th house of marriage, because Mars in the 7th house brings her kuja dosha, especially when compounded by malefic Rahu.

Rather than deal directly with those malefics, it would be better to strengthen the house itself, by empowering the Sun with mantras on Sundays and eating less on that day. Wearing a ruby or red spinel would also help. Sally would also benefit by chanting Moon mantras on Mondays, and eating less on that day, too. That would bring her more emotional fulfillment and happiness. She might experiment with Saturn chants, too, but very sparingly until she could see what effect they have. If she gains confidence and feelings of self-worth from the Saturn remedy she should continue, but if the opposite occurs, she should stop.

Mindy would do well to bring power to her Mercury by chanting Mercury mantras on Wednesdays and eating less on that day. She could also wear an emerald or green tourmaline on the fifth finger of her right hand. She might also try strengthening the Mars with mantras chanted on Tuesdays or wearing red coral.

Oliver should first strengthen his Mercury by drinking vata tea, an ayurvedic tea (found in most health food stores) that would soothe his nervous system. Since his Mercury is so afflicted, he tends to be reactive and never allows his system to calm down. He should be aware that as his nerves come into balance, there will still be the tendency to seek out drama or conflict, even when there is none. This is what happens when a person gets into habitual mind states.

Then he should begin chanting Mercury mantras particularly on Wednesdays, but in his case as often as possible. A Mercury stone would also help, as would a fire ritual to bolster the repair process to his nervous system. He can also strengthen Venus with mantras chanted on Fridays in order to improve his overall happiness.

Most importantly, Oliver should recognize that he should change his attitude toward work. His whole life he has worked as a menial laborer, yet his Mars sits strongly in his 10th house, one of the best possible placements for career leadership. I believe one reason he lashes out at everyone else is because his planets are not being utilized properly. All of his intensity could easily be supported and channeled through a powerful career in the arts, in the athletic arena, or in business.

STRENGTHENING YOUR 11th HOUSE

As with the other houses, the best way to strengthen the 11th house is to locate the planet that rules the 11th and appease it with chants on the appropriate day. However, if there is a planet placed in the 11th, you'll have to decide whether the nature of the planet is truly what you want to attract.

For instance, if Saturn occupies your 11th house and you bring it more strength, you may bring more discipline to your entrepreneurial efforts and attract mature and older friends, but you also may be limiting the amount of luck and opportunity that comes your way. Also, your entrepreneurial skills may come purely from intuition, due to the influence of the Moon or Ketu, for instance. If you strengthen a planet that's more of a mental planet, like Mercury, you may find that you intellectualize everything and lose your flow.

In addition, by bringing strength to a planet in the 11th house, you are necessarily affecting the 5th house, the house it opposes. So be careful if you choose to bring strength to a malefic planet in the 11th, as this can detrimentally impact your house of children.

SUMMARY

We spoke earlier about the four basic goals, or stages, of human existence: kama, artha, dharma, and moksha, meaning desire, wealth, purpose, and liberation. In traditional India, these four stages take place at specific times of a person's life, and are referred to as the *ashramas*. They include the time for learning (*bramacharya*), usually the first twenty-five years of life, followed by becoming a house-holder (*grhastha*) until around fifty, and then elder and advisor (*vanaprastha*), until finally becoming a full renunciate (*sannyasa*). The beauty of this system, among other things, is that the elder members of society are held in highest esteem.

Each house we have explored until now has addressed one of these stages except the last—moksha, or liberation. The last house of the zodiac, the 12th, speaks to this last stage. Does this mean that you have to be a very old person before you can experience the 12th house? Not at all. However, it's usually the case that a person is so preoccupied with the other eleven houses that only once those needs and desires have been fulfilled does a person find the opportunity to find the real meaning of life.

The irony of life, as reflected in the 12th house, is that despite all the activity represented by the other eleven houses you already had everything you needed all along. This is the most significant meaning of the 12th house: to become self-actualized, and see that you always were where you wanted to be. What you were searching for is actually inside. Thus, we have the symbolism of the circle that the 12th house brings to a close. In a sense, you return to where you began.

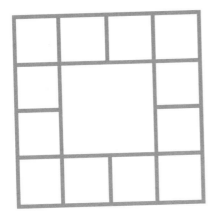

THE 12th HOUSE

Actualization

This house is one of three dusthana (malefic) houses in the Vedic system, including the 6th and 8th houses. In contrast to the 6th house, an upachaya house that can be improved through focus and hard work, the 8th and 12th houses tend to be more rigid and unchangeable.

The 12th house signifies long-distance travel or living abroad, sexual pleasure, loss, spiritual liberation, and transformation. Its association with confinement can express itself in a number of different ways. It can be voluntary confinement like a spiritual retreat or living in an ashram, or it can be involuntary like being hospitalized or imprisoned. Anatomically, the 12th house also rules the feet and the left eye.

THE NATURE OF THE 12th HOUSE

Find the 12th house in your chart. If you are Sagittarius rising, your 12th house is Scorpio. If you are Libra rising, Virgo is your 12th house.

Pay close attention to the zodiac sign of the 12th house because the nature of that sign will show you the way 12th house issues function.

For instance, if Scorpio is your 12th house, then you hide deep passionate feelings. If your 12th house is Pisces, you may be a deeply spiritual person.

HOW THE 12th HOUSE EXPRESSES ITSELF

Locate the planet that rules your 12th house (see Table B), and find where it's placed in your chart. Then read the description below that pertains to this placement.

The 12th House Ruler placed in the 1st house may bring you sensual pleasures, but it doesn't bring you much lasting happiness and can eventually sap your strength. You may be strongly spiritually oriented or a renunciate, or may suffer from lack of confidence and poor health.

The 12th House Ruler placed in the 2nd house can create misunderstanding or cause financial losses due to things you say or commitments you make. You may also be shy about speaking. This position can show loss of money, or accumulating money through either spiritual (positive) or deceptive (negative) methods. There may also be addictive tendencies.

The 12th House Ruler placed in the 3rd house indicates either that a deep spiritual connection infuses your creativity with energy, or that you lack creative ability altogether. Your sense of adventure may be spiritually oriented or inspired, or you may suffer on account of misdirected enthusiasm. Your sibling (usually younger) may be deeply spiritual, or suffers from health complaints, usually chronic.

The 12th House Ruler placed in the 4th house doesn't favor the mother or your relationship with her, nor does it indicate much luck with homes or automobiles, but it does indicate a strong spiritual nature. By delving into your spiritual side, your material comforts will naturally take care of themselves.

The 12th House Ruler placed in the 5th house indicates a reconnection with spirituality, because the 5th house is connected with your destiny, and spirituality is something you have cultivated in the past. This placement doesn't indicate many children, and there may be difficulties with them.

The 12th House Ruler placed in the 6th house indicates that assistants may steal from you or cause you losses. Health is generally not favored in this position; however, you can be involved in healing as long as it's spiritual in nature. Although this placement may bring enemies into your life, you can eventually defeat them.

The 12th House Ruler placed in the 7th house indicates that your spouse or business partner may be strongly spiritually oriented. Otherwise, this position can indicate the loss of a partner, or more than one partner. Your partner, whether in business or marriage, may also have chronic health problems.

The 12th House Ruler placed in the 8th house indicates that you can benefit unexpectedly from another person's death, usually through some type of inheritance. In some cases, this position can indicate a strong spiritual nature and great progress in spiritual practices. There can be health complaints, usually in the 8th house areas of reproductive organs.

The 12th House Ruler placed in the 9th house is a powerful spiritual placement, although it also indicates chronic health complaints for your father, or a father who does not live long. It can also indicate a falling out with teachers or mentors, or signify health problems for them. This position favors traveling abroad for the purpose of spiritual growth, like pilgrimage, but it can bring you difficulty in the thigh/hip area.

The 12th House Ruler placed in the 10th house indicates that your career either may be connected with spiritual pursuits or that there may be unhappiness around your career. You may also work abroad, or be involved in a career dealing with sensuality. This position can bring problems with the knees or lower back.

The 12th House Ruler placed in the 11th house does not favor speculation, unless it is conducted abroad or involves some type of spiritual venture. It can also indicate a sibling (usually older) who is either deeply spiritual, or has chronic health complaints or a short life. Opportunities come if they are deeply spiritual in nature, and you can have difficulty with your shins or ankles.

The 12th House Ruler placed in the 12th house indicates success abroad, and is a wonderful position for someone focused on attaining enlightenment. This placement favors any type of transformative work.

IF THERE ARE PLANETS IN THE 12th HOUSE

To help fine-tune the descriptions below, you'll want to assess whether the planet is welcome in the house in which it is placed (Table G). If the planet is in the house of a friend, the positive nature of the following description is enhanced. If the planet is in the house of an enemy, more of the negative possibilities need to be considered.

Sun (Su) in the 12th house brings power to the chart if the person is involved in deep personal growth and transformation. Otherwise, it shows weakness in the body and difficulty for the father.

Moon (Mo) in the 12th house shows inner charisma and a spiritual nature. If not well aspected, this position shows a person who can become obsessed with sex and whose mother suffers.

Mars (Ma) in the 12th house indicates great success in foreign countries. However, this position brings difficulty in marriage, and if afflicted can bring intense and constant sexual desires.

Mercury (Me) in the 12th house, if unafflicted, shows knowledge of the mysteries of life in such a way that they can be communicated. If not well aspected, this position shows the possibility of a speech defect or mental confusion.

Jupiter (Ju) in the 12th house may indicate that you are a spiritual teacher or advisor. Otherwise, this is not a favorable position for children and can bring a sensual nature that is not easily satisfied.

Venus (Ve) in the 12th house is a deeply spiritual placement. It also shows you like to work behind the scenes providing beauty and elegance for others. If not well aspected, there can be sexual problems, both psychologically and physically.

Saturn (Sa) in the 12th house brings tremendous discipline to your spiritual life. You are willing to undergo many hardships and delays to reach the highest state. If not well placed, this planet brings confinement and difficulty in obtaining wealth.

Rahu (Ra) in the 12th house can bring spiritual attainments through eclectic sources. Otherwise, this is not a good placement for overseas travel, where you may lose money or be robbed.

Ketu (Ke) in the 12th house indicates an unusually profound spiritual aspirant. This is a good placement for actualization. Otherwise, the possibility exists that you will be deceived on the spiritual path by pseudo gurus.

OTHER CONSIDERATIONS

- Note the element associated with your 12th house. Remember that fire signs are driven; earth signs are patient; air signs are creative; and water signs are emotional.
- Also note the quality of your 12th house. Cardinal signs initiate; fixed signs stabilize; and mutable signs seek change.

Now check any aspects to the 12th house:

- Are any planets located in the same house as, or opposing any planet in, the 12th house? If so, are those planets friendly, neutral, or enemies? (See Table F.) For instance, say your Ketu is placed in the 12th house along with its friend Mercury. This planetary combination shows not only the ability to understand profound spiritual truths, but to explain them to others.
- Remember that Mars energizes the house it's in, as well as the 4th, 7th, and 8th houses from itself. This means if Mars is placed in the 5th, 6th, or 9th house of your chart, it throws an aspect onto your 12th house, possibly increasing feelings of lust.
- Saturn restricts or brings discipline to the house it's in, as well as the 3rd, 7th, and 10th houses from itself. This means if Saturn is placed in the 3rd, 6th, or 10th house of your chart, it throws an aspect onto your 12th house, bringing perseverance on the spiritual path.
- Jupiter expands or brings optimism to the house it's in, as well as the 5th, 7th, and 9th houses from itself. This means if Jupiter is placed in the 4th, 6th, or 8th house of your chart, it throws an aspect onto your 12th house, enlivening your spiritual nature.
- If you want to find out when your chart's 12th house energies will be enlivened, look to the 12th house ruler, or any planet located in the 12th house. Examine the Mahadasha Summary of your chart to see when that planet will come into power, and that will give you your answer. To find shorter periods when 12th house issues will be highlighted, look to the 12th house ruler or any planet located in the

12th house, and find the time its bhukti will run.

- Notice any influence transiting planets are having on your 12th house. You can chant to the planet that is favorably transiting your rising sign, on the appropriate day for that planet, to enhance its effects.

CHART EXAMPLES

For an example of someone on the spiritual path, look again at Kelly's chart.

Her 12th house is Taurus, ruled by Venus. That Venus is placed in her 8th house. This indication is very positive for spiritually oriented people, which she is. This is further indicated by the Jupiter placed in retrograde

Birth Chart

Ma 25:13	SaR 29:53	JuR 22:21	As 24:59
Pisces (10)	Aries (11)	Taurus (12)	Gemini (1)
Ke 24:38			
Aquarius (9)			Cancer (2)
Ve 15:25			Ra 24:38
Capricorn (8)			Leo (3)
Su 00:34	Me 27:11	Mo 25:41	
Sagittarius (7)	Scorpio (6)	Libra (5)	Virgo (4)

Navamsha

Me	Su	Ke As Ve Mo	
Ma			JuR
SaR	Ra		

Today's Transits

Su Me		Ra Sa	As
Ve			JuR
Mo			
Ma	Ke		

Mahadasha Summary

Ju	Tue 02-19-1935
Sa	Mon 02-19-1951
Me	Thu 02-19-1970
Ke	Thu 02-19-1987
Ve	Sat 02-19-1994
Su	Tue 02-18-2014
Mo	Wed 02-19-2020
Ma	Mon 02-18-2030
Ra	Wed 02-18-2037
Ju	Thu 02-18-2055
Sa	Wed 02-18-2071
Me	Sat 02-18-2090
Ke	Sat 02-19-2107
Ve	Mon 02-19-2114
Su	Thu 02-18-2134

Current Mahadasha

Ve-Ra	Fri 04-20-2001
Ve-Ju	Tue 04-20-2004
Ve-Sa	Wed 12-20-2006
Ve-Me	Thu 02-18-2010
Ve-Ke	Wed 12-19-2012
Su-Su	Tue 02-18-2014
Su-Mo	Sun 06-08-2014
Su-Ma	Mon 12-08-2014
Su-Ra	Tue 04-14-2015
Su-Ju	Tue 03-08-2016
Su-Sa	Sun 12-25-2016
Su-Me	Thu 12-07-2017
Su-Ke	Sun 10-14-2018
Su-Ve	Tue 02-19-2019
Mo-Mo	Wed 02-19-2020

Birth data

Kelly

Mon 12-15-1941

18:15:00

New York, NY

USA

Timezone: 5

Latitude: 40N42'51

Longitude: 74W00'23

Ayan. -23:02:43 Lahiri

Chart 96—Kelly

in her 12th house. Kelly became involved with a spiritual teacher when her Venus mahadasha began in 1994 (interesting that the teacher is a woman, as Venus would indicate). Since then, she has committed herself fully to the practices, never letting up since she first began.

Ketu in her 9th house is a deeply spiritual influence, as is her Sun in Sagittarius. Kelly's money is very comfortable, since the 12th house ruler placed in the 8th house can bring inheritance, which she received.

Let's look at another interesting chart with regard to spirituality.

Mary has always been interested in spirituality, as evidenced by Ketu in her rising sign. Her 12th house is mystical Pisces, occupied by retrograde Saturn. For many years she had difficulty understanding her place in the

Birth Chart			
SaR 21:57 Pisces (12)	As 08:52 Ke 26:35 Aries (1)	Taurus (2)	Gemini (3)
Aquarius (11)			Cancer (4)
JuR 29:46 Mo 14:14 Capricorn (10)			Ma 23:33 Leo (5)
Sagittarius (9)	Ve 00:44 Scorpio (8)	Ra 26:35 Libra (7)	Me 12:02 Su 17:05 Virgo (6)

Navamsha

	Me	Mo Ra	Su As
			Ve
SaR			
	Ma Ke		JuR

Today's Transits

Su Me		Ra Sa	As
Ve			JuR
Mo			
Ma	Ke		

Mahadasha Summary

Mo	Wed 07-31-1935
Ma	Tue 07-31-1945
Ra	Wed 07-30-1952
Ju	Fri 07-31-1970
Sa	Thu 07-31-1986
Me	Sat 07-30-2005
Ke	Sat 07-30-2022
Ve	Mon 07-30-2029
Su	Fri 07-30-2049
Mo	Fri 07-30-2055
Ma	Thu 07-30-2065
Ra	Fri 07-29-2072
Ju	Sun 07-30-2090
Sa	Sat 07-31-2106
Me	Mon 07-30-2125

Current Mahadasha

Sa-Ju	Fri 01-17-2003
Me-Me	Sat 07-30-2005
Me-Ke	Thu 12-27-2007
Me-Ve	Tue 12-23-2008
Me-Su	Mon 10-24-2011
Me-Mo	Wed 08-29-2012
Me-Ma	Wed 01-29-2014
Me-Ra	Mon 01-26-2015
Me-Ju	Mon 08-14-2017
Me-Sa	Wed 11-20-2019
Ke-Ke	Sat 07-30-2022
Ke-Ve	Mon 12-26-2022
Ke-Su	Mon 02-26-2024
Ke-Mo	Tue 07-02-2024
Ke-Ma	Fri 01-31-2025

Birth data

Mary
Mon 10-03-1938
18:30:00
Philadelphia, PA
USA
Timezone: 5
Latitude: 39N57'08
Longitude: 75W09'51
Ayan. -23:00:19 Lahiri

Chart 97—Mary

world, since in the midst of people bent on accumulating, she lived a life of natural asceticism. Retrograde Saturn in her 12th house brings a deeply spiritual nature, and since the ruler of her 12th house, Jupiter, is placed in her 10th house of career, only when she dedicated her life to maintaining a spiritual ashram did she feel she had found her place at last.

When you look closely at both of Mary's 10th and 12th houses, you see the 10th ruled by Saturn, which is placed in the 12th house, and the 12th ruled by Jupiter, which is placed in the 10th. This is called an exchange of signs, compounding the connection between these two houses, namely career and spirituality. They go hand in hand. Furthermore, Jupiter is in its house of debilitation in Capricorn, indicating that Mary would get little recognition for her career efforts, which suits her just fine.

Continuing in the same vein, let's take another look at the chart of Pope John Paul II.

Notice that his 12th house is Cancer, ruled by the Moon. That Moon is placed in his 10th house, showing that his career would be permeated with deep spiritual significance. The Pope's Sun is also there, showing that his entire persona would be utilized to this end.

Jupiter sits in his 12th house, and is in its place of exaltation in Cancer. This is another strong indicator of a person deeply immersed in spirituality, and traditionally it is said that this position shows a person who will go to heavenly realms when he dies.

The deep unconscious is another charac-teristic of the 12th house. Let's look again at George Lucas's chart (see Chart 100).

Lucas's 12th house is Pisces, and Jupiter rules that sign. The Jupiter is placed in his 4th house, conjoined by Mars and Rahu. Remember that the 4th house indicates the heart, both physically and emotionally. So we can see from this planetary setup that Lucas receives joy and emotional fulfullment from tapping humanity's primal impulses, the deep unknown (12th house ruler in the 4th). His tendency toward things otherworldly comes from the influence of Rahu in the 4th house. Now glance at his navamsha and notice that with Scorpio rising, his second house ruler, Jupiter, is located in 4th house Aquarius. You'll recall that the 2nd house indicates, among other things, imagination. This confirms our belief that Lucas gets enjoyment by expressing his imagination, and, because he does so in Aquarian ways, it's bound to impact the masses. Remember that Aquarian tendencies are humanitarian oriented.

What Lucas has been able to tap into in his *Star Wars* films is a deep collective unconscious. That is why so many people resonate with his work, and this is one of the characteristics of the 12th house. There have been many stories of people whose lives were actually changed quite dramatically by his *Star Wars* trilogy. That's why the 12th house is called transformative.

What might have fueled his inspiration? The 12th house ruler placed in the 4th has another signification: car accidents. This is further compounded in Lucas's case, since malefic Mars and Rahu conjoin in his 4th

Birth Chart

	Ve 21:50 Ke 22:18 Me 25:21	Su 04:24 Mo 06:48	
Pisces (8)	Aries (9)	Taurus (10)	Gemini (11)

Aquarius (7)			Ju 18:13
			Cancer (12)

Capricorn (6)			As 10:33 Sa 12:10
			Leo (1)

		Ra 22:18	MaR 29:43
Sagittarius (5)	Scorpio (4)	Libra (3)	Virgo (2)

Navamsha

Mo	Ra		
Su			As Sa
Ju	Me	Ve Ke	MaR

Today's Transits

Su Me		Ra Sa	As
Ve			JuR
Mo			
Ma	Ke		

Mahadasha Summary

Su	Tue	10-26-1915
Mo	Tue	10-25-1921
Ma	Mon	10-26-1931
Ra	Wed	10-26-1938
Ju	Thu	10-25-1956
Sa	Wed	10-25-1972
Me	Fri	10-25-1991
Ke	Fri	10-24-2008
Ve	Sun	10-25-2015
Su	Thu	10-25-2035
Mo	Thu	10-24-2041
Ma	Wed	10-25-2051
Ra	Fri	10-25-2058
Ju	Sat	10-24-2076
Sa	Fri	10-24-2092

Current Mahadasha

Me-Ra	Sun	04-22-2001
Me-Ju	Sun	11-09-2003
Me-Sa	Tue	02-14-2006
Ke-Ke	Fri	10-24-2008
Ke-Ve	Mon	03-23-2009
Ke-Su	Sun	05-23-2010
Ke-Mo	Tue	09-28-2010
Ke-Ma	Fri	04-29-2011
Ke-Ra	Sun	09-25-2011
Ke-Ju	Fri	10-12-2012
Ke-Sa	Wed	09-18-2013
Ke-Me	Tue	10-28-2014
Ve-Ve	Sun	10-25-2015
Ve-Su	Sun	02-24-2019
Ve-Mo	Mon	02-24-2020

Birth data

Pope John Paul II

Tue 05-18-1920

12:30:00

Wadowice, POLAND (general)

Poland

Timezone: -2

Latitude: 49N53'00

Longitude: 19E29'00

Ayan. -22:44:53 Lahiri

Chart 98—Pope John Paul II

house of transportation. Rahu was transiting his 4th house at the time of his terrible car accident during his last year in high school, and Lucas's long stay in the hospital gave him enough time to rethink his life, and realize he had a greater purpose to pursue.

What about challenging 12th house issues? Look again at Tonya Harding's chart (Chart 100).

Tonya's 12th house is Taurus, which is ruled by Venus. That Venus is placed in her 5th house. Because the 5th house deals with one's moral character, you can imagine what happens when the ruler of the house of loss is

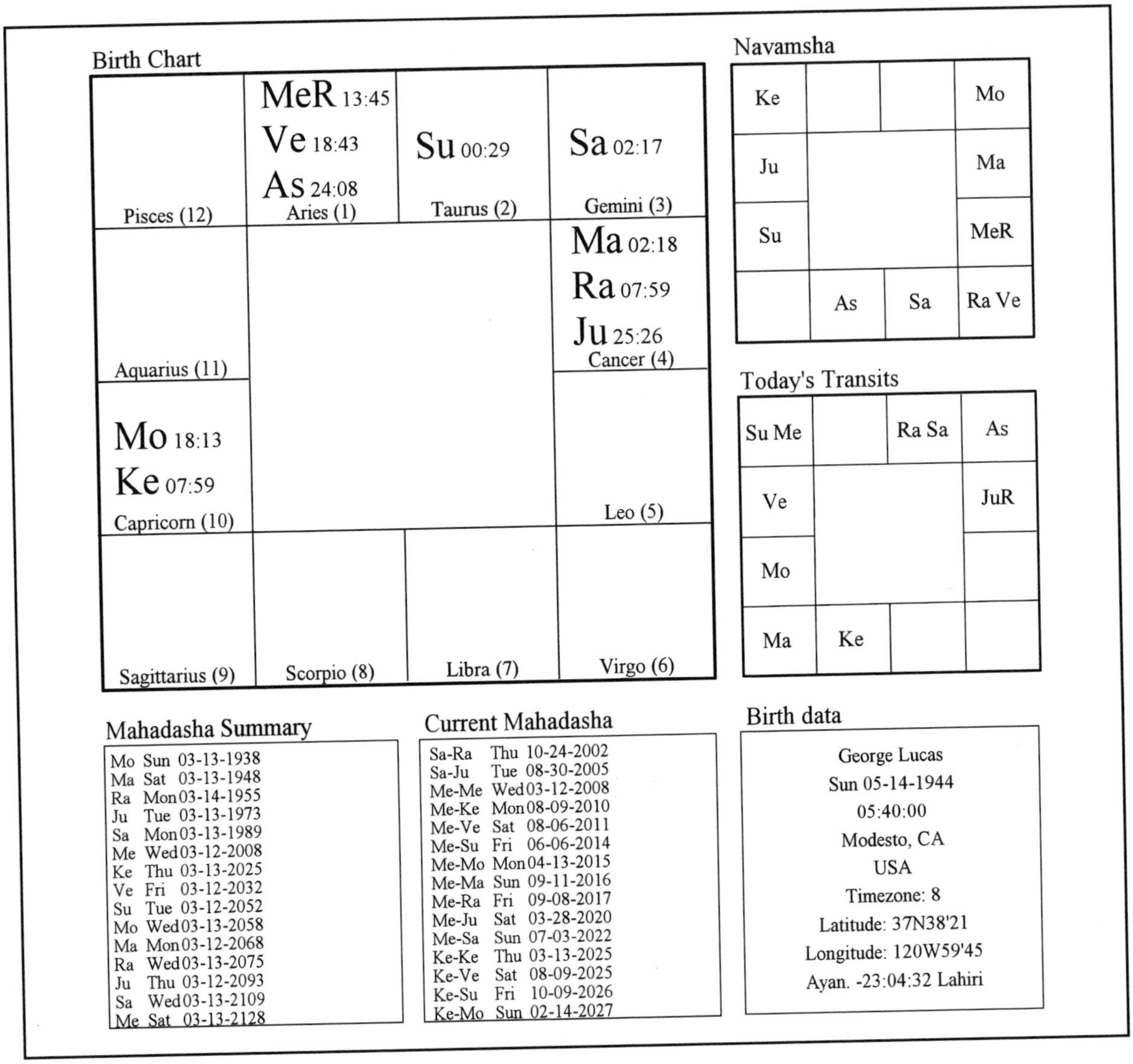

Birth Chart

Pisces (12)	Aries (1) MeR 13:45 Ve 18:43 As 24:08	Taurus (2) Su 00:29	Gemini (3) Sa 02:17
Aquarius (11)			Cancer (4) Ma 02:18 Ra 07:59 Ju 25:26
Capricorn (10) Mo 18:13 Ke 07:59			Leo (5)
Sagittarius (9)	Scorpio (8)	Libra (7)	Virgo (6)

Navamsha

Ke			Mo
Ju			Ma
Su			MeR
	As	Sa	Ra Ve

Today's Transits

Su Me		Ra Sa	As
Ve			JuR
Mo			
Ma	Ke		

Mahadasha Summary

Mo	Sun	03-13-1938
Ma	Sat	03-13-1948
Ra	Mon	03-14-1955
Ju	Tue	03-13-1973
Sa	Mon	03-13-1989
Me	Wed	03-12-2008
Ke	Thu	03-13-2025
Ve	Fri	03-12-2032
Su	Tue	03-12-2052
Mo	Wed	03-12-2058
Ma	Mon	03-12-2068
Ra	Wed	03-13-2075
Ju	Thu	03-12-2093
Sa	Wed	03-13-2109
Me	Sat	03-13-2128

Current Mahadasha

Sa-Ra	Thu	10-24-2002
Sa-Ju	Tue	08-30-2005
Me-Me	Wed	03-12-2008
Me-Ke	Mon	08-09-2010
Me-Ve	Sat	08-06-2011
Me-Su	Fri	06-06-2014
Me-Mo	Mon	04-13-2015
Me-Ma	Sun	09-11-2016
Me-Ra	Fri	09-08-2017
Me-Ju	Sat	03-28-2020
Me-Sa	Sun	07-03-2022
Ke-Ke	Thu	03-13-2025
Ke-Ve	Sat	08-09-2025
Ke-Su	Fri	10-09-2026
Ke-Mo	Sun	02-14-2027

Birth data

George Lucas
Sun 05-14-1944
05:40:00
Modesto, CA
USA
Timezone: 8
Latitude: 37N38'21
Longitude: 120W59'45
Ayan. -23:04:32 Lahiri

Chart 99—George Lucas

located in the 5th (and retrograde). Ethics are not a strong feature for this placement.

This indication is compounded by the ruler of Tonya's 12th house, Venus, placed in conjunction with her debilitated Sun. This shows she doesn't just lack moral character, but she acts on her lack of character as well. Being in the place of debilitation, she would necessarily lack the confidence necessary to be a winner, and would resort to whatever means available to win.

Why does Tonya want to win so badly? Because she feels it is her destiny. That is, it belongs to her. This can be seen by the 10th

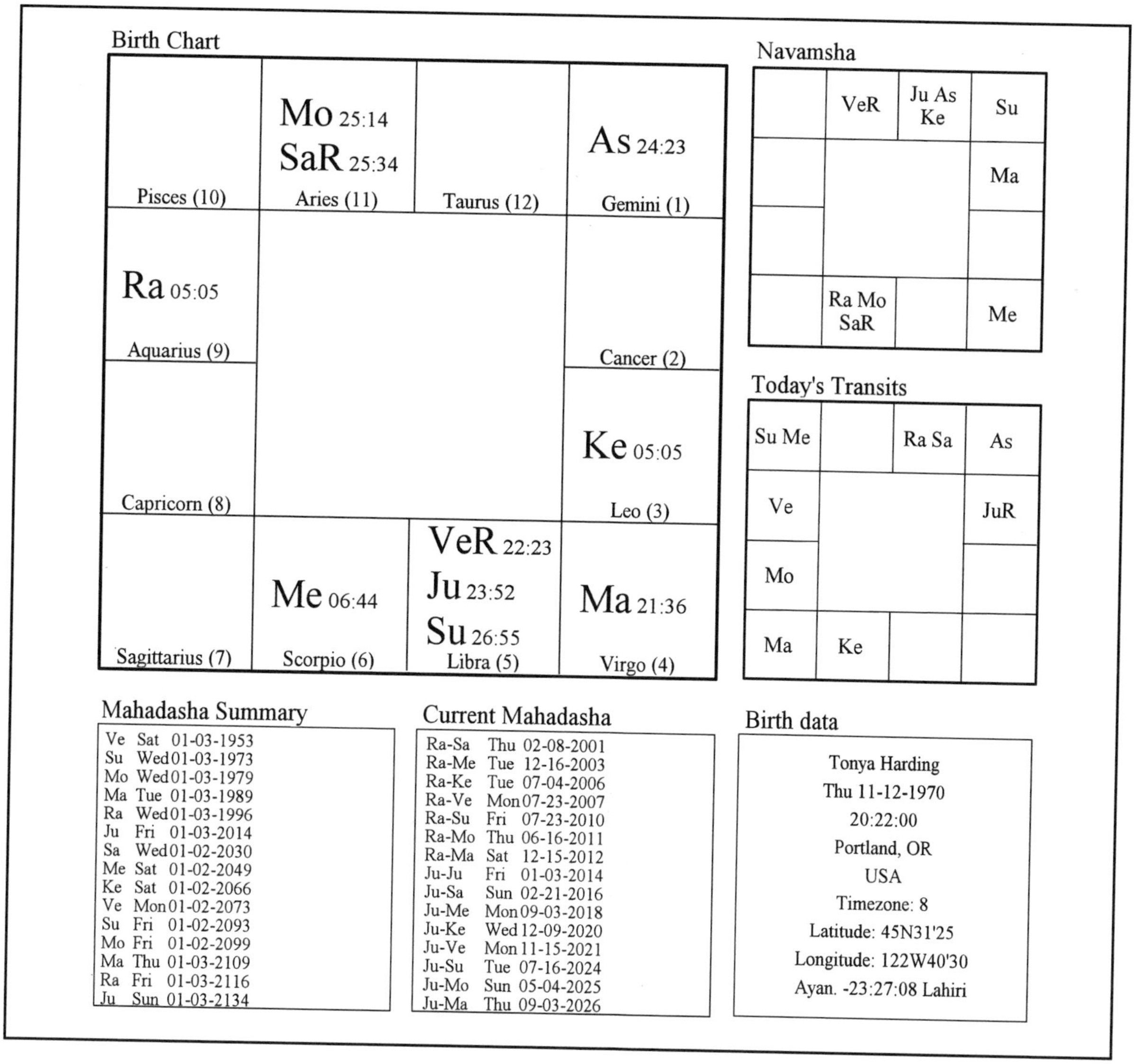

Birth Chart

	Mo 25:14 SaR 25:34		As 24:23
Pisces (10)	Aries (11)	Taurus (12)	Gemini (1)
Ra 05:05			
Aquarius (9)			Cancer (2)
			Ke 05:05
Capricorn (8)			Leo (3)
Me 06:44		VeR 22:23 Ju 23:52 Su 26:55	Ma 21:36
Sagittarius (7)	Scorpio (6)	Libra (5)	Virgo (4)

Navamsha

	VeR	Ju As Ke	Su
			Ma
	Ra Mo SaR		Me

Today's Transits

Su Me		Ra Sa	As
Ve			JuR
Mo			
Ma	Ke		

Mahadasha Summary

```
Ve  Sat 01-03-1953
Su  Wed 01-03-1973
Mo  Wed 01-03-1979
Ma  Tue 01-03-1989
Ra  Wed 01-03-1996
Ju  Fri 01-03-2014
Sa  Wed 01-02-2030
Me  Sat 01-02-2049
Ke  Sat 01-02-2066
Ve  Mon 01-02-2073
Su  Fri 01-02-2093
Mo  Fri 01-02-2099
Ma  Thu 01-03-2109
Ra  Fri 01-03-2116
Ju  Sun 01-03-2134
```

Current Mahadasha

```
Ra-Sa  Thu 02-08-2001
Ra-Me  Tue 12-16-2003
Ra-Ke  Tue 07-04-2006
Ra-Ve  Mon 07-23-2007
Ra-Su  Fri 07-23-2010
Ra-Mo  Thu 06-16-2011
Ra-Ma  Sat 12-15-2012
Ju-Ju  Fri 01-03-2014
Ju-Sa  Sun 02-21-2016
Ju-Me  Mon 09-03-2018
Ju-Ke  Wed 12-09-2020
Ju-Ve  Mon 11-15-2021
Ju-Su  Tue 07-16-2024
Ju-Mo  Sun 05-04-2025
Ju-Ma  Thu 09-03-2026
```

Birth data

Tonya Harding

Thu 11-12-1970

20:22:00

Portland, OR

USA

Timezone: 8

Latitude: 45N31'25

Longitude: 122W40'30

Ayan. -23:27:08 Lahiri

Chart 100—Tonya Harding

house ruler placed in the 5th house. That combination of planets does bring this sense of destiny. But being conjoined with the ruler of her 12th and debilitated Sun, it brought her the limelight in a fashion she didn't expect.

The 12th house also indicates long-distance travel.

Will's 12th house is Cancer, and five planets sit in his 12th house: Venus, Mercury, Sun, Jupiter, and Mars (Chart 101). The first thing he said to me was, "You know what I really want to do? Travel the world and never come back." Can you imagine why? With so many planets bunched in the house of long-distance travel, it must be next to impossible to sit still.

In a chart such as Will's, you can see many challenges. His 1st house ruler (Sun) located in the 12th house affects his confidence and makes him question his self-worth. His 2nd house ruler (Mercury) is in the 12th, affecting his childhood and ability to speak up and be heard. It brings a certain shyness.

Will's 3rd house ruler (Venus) is in his 12th house, which in this case affected his younger brother in a detrimental manner. His 4th house ruler (Mars) placed in the 12th house, the house of its debilitation, indicates a great deal of sorrow for his mother. His 5th house ruler (Jupiter) placed in the 12th indicates that children have become a burden for him. Since Will

Birth Chart

Pisces (8)	Aries (9)	Taurus (10)	Ke 00:55 / Gemini (11)
Aquarius (7)			Ve 06:52 / Me 10:38 / Su 15:18 / Ju 17:15 / Ma 20:18 / Cancer (12)
Capricorn (6)			As 28:04 / Leo (1)
Mo 20:01 / Ra 00:55 / Sagittarius (5)	Scorpio (4)	Sa 21:24 / Libra (3)	Virgo (2)

Navamsha

	Ra Sa		
Ma			
Ju As	Su	Mo Me Ke	Ve

Today's Transits

Su Me		Ra Sa	As
Ve			JuR
Mo			
Ma	Ke		

Mahadasha Summary

Ve	Sat	07-14-1945
Su	Tue	07-13-1965
Mo	Wed	07-14-1971
Ma	Mon	07-13-1981
Ra	Wed	07-13-1988
Ju	Thu	07-13-2006
Sa	Wed	07-13-2022
Me	Sat	07-13-2041
Ke	Sat	07-13-2058
Ve	Mon	07-13-2065
Su	Thu	07-12-2085
Mo	Fri	07-13-2091
Ma	Wed	07-13-2101
Ra	Fri	07-13-2108
Ju	Sat	07-13-2126

Current Mahadasha

Ra-Su	Thu	01-30-2003
Ra-Mo	Thu	12-25-2003
Ra-Ma	Sat	06-25-2005
Ju-Ju	Thu	07-13-2006
Ju-Sa	Sat	08-30-2008
Ju-Me	Mon	03-14-2011
Ju-Ke	Wed	06-19-2013
Ju-Ve	Mon	05-26-2014
Ju-Su	Tue	01-24-2017
Ju-Mo	Sun	11-12-2017
Ju-Ma	Thu	03-14-2019
Ju-Ra	Tue	02-18-2020
Sa-Sa	Wed	07-13-2022
Sa-Me	Wed	07-16-2025
Sa-Ke	Sat	03-25-2028

Birth data

Will
Mon 08-01-1955
09:55:00
Toronto, CANADA (general)
Canada
Timezone: 5
Latitude: 43N40'00
Longitude: 79W25'00
Ayan. -23:14:30 Lahiri

Chart 101—Will

wants to travel and be free so badly, children for him are seen as an obstruction.

Skipping ahead, his 8th, 9th, 10th, and 11th house rulers are also all placed in the 12th house, which affects his health, his father, his career, and his luck, all in a detrimental way. Unfortunately, he has no interest whatsoever in spirituality, which is really how

the placements of these planets could best express themselves.

Now, let's look at Sam, who suffered a stroke, but unlike Will was a spiritually motivated person.

Sam's 12th house, Leo, is ruled by the Sun. That Sun is placed in the 10th house, the house of career. That the 12th house is a house of

Birth Chart			
Ra 08:53 Pisces (7)	Mo 22:59 Aries (8)	Ve 21:24 Taurus (9)	Me 22:08 Su 23:48 Gemini (10)
JuR 14:01 Aquarius (6)			Cancer (11)
Capricorn (5)			Sa 21:54 Leo (12)
Sagittarius (4)	Scorpio (3)	Libra (2)	Ke 08:53 As 10:07 Ma 19:07 Virgo (1)

Navamsha

Ke	As Me	Su	Ma
JuR			Ve
		Sa Mo	Ra

Today's Transits

Su Me		Ra Sa	As
Ve			JuR
Mo			
Ma	Ke		

Mahadasha Summary

Ve	Fri	01-17-1936
Su	Tue	01-17-1956
Mo	Tue	01-16-1962
Ma	Mon	01-17-1972
Ra	Tue	01-16-1979
Ju	Thu	01-16-1997
Sa	Wed	01-16-2013
Me	Fri	01-16-2032
Ke	Fri	01-15-2049
Ve	Sun	01-16-2056
Su	Thu	01-16-2076
Mo	Thu	01-15-2082
Ma	Wed	01-16-2092
Ra	Thu	01-15-2099
Ju	Sat	01-16-2117

Current Mahadasha

Ju-Me	Sun	09-16-2001
Ju-Ke	Tue	12-23-2003
Ju-Ve	Sun	11-28-2004
Ju-Su	Mon	07-30-2007
Ju-Mo	Sat	05-17-2008
Ju-Ma	Wed	09-16-2009
Ju-Ra	Mon	08-23-2010
Sa-Sa	Wed	01-16-2013
Sa-Me	Tue	01-19-2016
Sa-Ke	Fri	09-28-2018
Sa-Ve	Thu	11-07-2019
Sa-Su	Sat	01-07-2023
Sa-Mo	Wed	12-20-2023
Sa-Ma	Sun	07-20-2025
Sa-Ra	Sat	08-29-2026

Birth data

Sam

Sun 07-09-1950

12:00:00

Los Angeles, CA

USA

Timezone: 8

Latitude: 34N03'08

Longitude: 118W14'34

Ayan. -23:09:57 Lahiri

Chart 102—Sam

confinement and hospitalization is appropriate here, since Sam now makes his living by helping severely emotionally challenged people who might otherwise be institutionalized.

Instead, he helps them to integrate into society as much as possible, and trains them to develop the skills necessary for doing so. This came to pass because instead of focusing on his own misfortunes, Sam decided to help others in need. As a result, he is the most uplifting, radiant person you'd ever want to meet.

Now look again at Bruce Lee's chart for a different take on the way that the mysterious aspects of the 12th house can be seen.

Bruce's 12th house is Libra, which is ruled by Venus. That Venus is in the 12th house,

Birth Chart

Ke 14:57 Pisces (5)	**JuR** 14:30 **SaR** 16:27 Aries (6)	Taurus (7)	Gemini (8)
Aquarius (4)			Cancer (9)
Capricorn (3)			Leo (10)
Su 12:12 **As** 13:10 Sagittarius (2)	Scorpio (1)	**Ve** 08:19 **Ma** 11:31 **Mo** 18:22 **Me** 22:14 Libra (12)	**Ra** 14:57 Virgo (11)

Navamsha

Mo	Me	Ra	
Ma			JuR SaR
Ve	Ke	Su As	

Today's Transits

Su Me		Ra Sa	As
Ve			JuR
Mo			
Ma	Ke		

Mahadasha Summary

Ra	Mon	02-09-1925
Ju	Wed	02-10-1943
Sa	Tue	02-10-1959
Me	Thu	02-09-1978
Ke	Thu	02-09-1995
Ve	Sat	02-09-2002
Su	Wed	02-09-2022
Mo	Wed	02-09-2028
Ma	Tue	02-09-2038
Ra	Wed	02-08-2045
Ju	Fri	02-09-2063
Sa	Thu	02-09-2079
Me	Sat	02-08-2098
Ke	Sat	02-09-2115
Ve	Mon	02-09-2122

Current Mahadasha

Ve-Ve	Sat	02-09-2002
Ve-Su	Sat	06-11-2005
Ve-Mo	Sun	06-11-2006
Ve-Ma	Sun	02-10-2008
Ve-Ra	Sat	04-11-2009
Ve-Ju	Tue	04-10-2012
Ve-Sa	Wed	12-10-2014
Ve-Me	Fri	02-09-2018
Ve-Ke	Thu	12-10-2020
Su-Su	Wed	02-09-2022
Su-Mo	Sun	05-29-2022
Su-Ma	Mon	11-28-2022
Su-Ra	Wed	04-05-2023
Su-Ju	Wed	02-28-2024
Su-Sa	Mon	12-16-2024

Birth data

Bruce Lee

Wed 11-27-1940

07:12:00

San Francisco, CA

USA

Timezone: 8

Latitude: 37N46'30

Longitude: 122W25'06

Ayan. -23:01:55 Lahiri

Chart 103—Bruce Lee

along with Mars, Moon, and Mercury. The deeply secret nature of the 12th house had much to do with his success as a martial artist, in much the same way George Lucas was able to pull deep from the 12th house to impact so many.

Lee remains a real mystery, even more than twenty-five years after his death. Even now, many martial arts experts are hard-pressed to explain how he performed certain feats. He was able to hold his fist an inch away from an opponent's chest and by just moving the distance of an inch, throw his opponent across the room: the famous one-inch punch. By pulling deeply from the unknown of the 12th house, he has created and maintained himself as a legend. Interestingly enough, even his demise is masked in secrecy, as a definitive cause of death has never been named. However, because his ruling planet Mars (indicative of the head region) is located in the 12th and opposed by its enemy Saturn, it's quite likely that he died of cerebral edema, as many believe.

Let's close this chapter by looking at an East Indian spiritual teacher's chart to show what a deeply spiritual person's chart looks like (Chart 104). His rising sign is Aries, and the ruler of the rising sign is in the 3rd house.

That three planets occupy his 3rd house speaks to the fact that he was well versed in many aspects of Vedic knowledge, including ayurveda, the classical medical tradition of health and healing. Exalted Jupiter sits in his 4th house, a moksha (liberation) house, and Ketu sits in deeply philosophical Sagittarius in

the 9th house, also a powerful spiritual position.

Now look at his 12th house, Pisces, a deeply mystical sign. Jupiter, the ruler of Pisces, is placed in the 4th house in exaltation, as mentioned. This is a powerful placement for a spiritual aspirant, since both the 4th and 12th houses are connected to liberation, as is Jupiter—and even more so in its place of exaltation.

However, notice that Saturn is located in his 12th house. Saturn in the 12th house made his progress slow and steady, and sometimes filled with tremendous *tapasya* (spiritual austerity). He was a wandering monk, and when he didn't receive enough food he became so hungry that at times he ate dirt. His Moon, which sits all alone in Libra, also indicates that he would pursue a lonely path.

When his Ketu mahadasha began, however, he met a teacher who initiated him into the deepest spiritual truths, and during the time of Ketu he perfected himself. By the time his Venus mahadasha came into power, he had reached his goal.

CLOSING WORDS

Vedic astrology may seem a little overwhelming for Westerners because it presupposes certain Eastern philosophical axioms that might seem quite foreign to many. However, it's not important for you to believe in Eastern thought in order for this system of astrology to work.

There is a story told of the Buddha who likened his teachings to the work of a physician. The physician sees that an arrow has

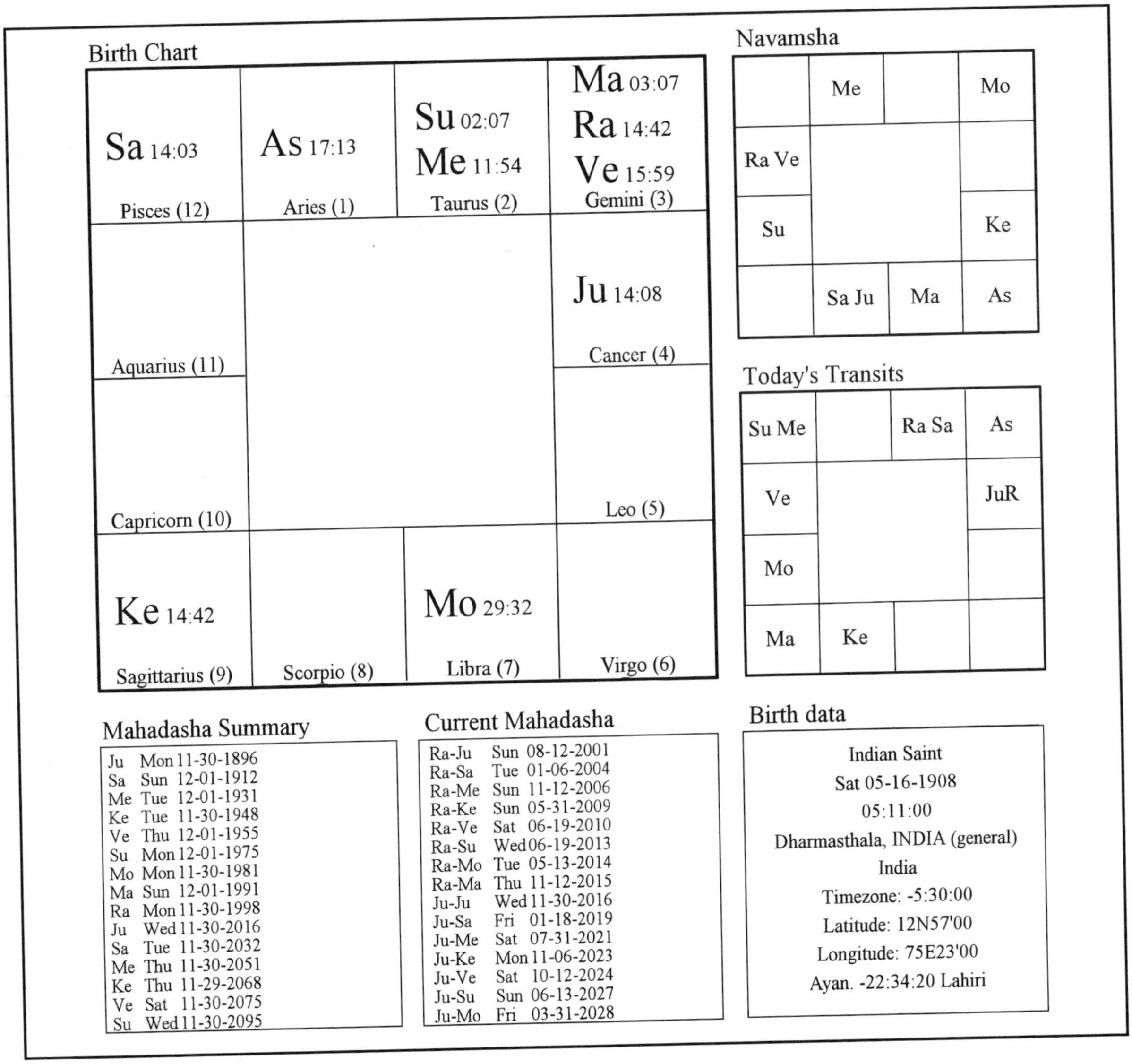

Birth Chart

Sa 14:03	**As** 17:13	**Su** 02:07 **Me** 11:54	**Ma** 03:07 **Ra** 14:42 **Ve** 15:59
Pisces (12)	Aries (1)	Taurus (2)	Gemini (3)
			Ju 14:08
Aquarius (11)			Cancer (4)
Capricorn (10)			Leo (5)
Ke 14:42	**Mo** 29:32		
Sagittarius (9)	Scorpio (8)	Libra (7)	Virgo (6)

Navamsha

	Me		Mo
Ra Ve			
Su			Ke
	Sa Ju	Ma	As

Today's Transits

Su Me		Ra Sa	As
Ve			JuR
Mo			
Ma	Ke		

Mahadasha Summary

Ju	Mon	11-30-1896
Sa	Sun	12-01-1912
Me	Tue	12-01-1931
Ke	Tue	11-30-1948
Ve	Thu	12-01-1955
Su	Mon	12-01-1975
Mo	Mon	11-30-1981
Ma	Sun	12-01-1991
Ra	Mon	11-30-1998
Ju	Wed	11-30-2016
Sa	Tue	11-30-2032
Me	Thu	11-30-2051
Ke	Thu	11-29-2068
Ve	Sat	11-30-2075
Su	Wed	11-30-2095

Current Mahadasha

Ra-Ju	Sun	08-12-2001
Ra-Sa	Tue	01-06-2004
Ra-Me	Sun	11-12-2006
Ra-Ke	Sun	05-31-2009
Ra-Ve	Sat	06-19-2010
Ra-Su	Wed	06-19-2013
Ra-Mo	Tue	05-13-2014
Ra-Ma	Thu	11-12-2015
Ju-Ju	Wed	11-30-2016
Ju-Sa	Fri	01-18-2019
Ju-Me	Sat	07-31-2021
Ju-Ke	Mon	11-06-2023
Ju-Ve	Sat	10-12-2024
Ju-Su	Sun	06-13-2027
Ju-Mo	Fri	03-31-2028

Birth data

Indian Saint

Sat 05-16-1908

05:11:00

Dharmasthala, INDIA (general)

India

Timezone: -5:30:00

Latitude: 12N57'00

Longitude: 75E23'00

Ayan. -22:34:20 Lahiri

Chart 104—Indian Saint

wounded you, and proceeds to extricate the arrow from your body. Instead of letting the physician do his work, you want to know why you got shot, at what angle the arrow entered your body, what type of wood the shaft is made from, and if there are any feathers on the end.

So, it's not so important to understand why Vedic astrology works. Instead, dive in, see for yourself, and let it transform your life.

Remember, what we are seeing in the birth chart is who we were. The habitual patterns in which many of us find ourselves enmeshed were formed in the past for any number of reasons—reasons that don't really matter anymore. So, once you familiarize yourself with your tendencies, keep the ones that serve you, and drop the ones you don't need anymore.

For many of us, carrying around weight from the past is burdensome and needless. Instead of finding excuses for why you can't, bring strength to why you can. Do this by empowering your chart through realigning your purpose to fit your planets. Or use some of the remedial measures we've discussed in this book to give your chart a boost.

The purpose of this book is not to show how superior this system of astrology is to any other. Rather it is to make available in as basic a way as possible a complex and until now greatly inaccessible system that has remarkably practical applications for us in the West. The idea, for instance, that you can live in harmony with your environment rather than need to control and manipulate it is a simple yet far-reaching concept.

If you're familiar with other astrological systems, see what Vedic astrology has to offer, but be careful not to mix apples and oranges. Maintain the integrity of each individual system and look to each for guidance. It can be a mistake to homogenize.

I hope this book has stimulated your interest in this remarkable system of astrology. Although we've touched on just the basics of Vedic astrology, I sincerely hope that you will be able to receive some guidance and support from the information presented. I applaud you for seeking knowledge from the Ancient Teachings because sometimes the door to the future is opened with keys of wisdom from the past. Best of luck on your path.

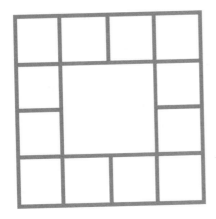

APPENDIX

Vedic Astrology Resources

Charts

Contained within the book is a beginner's version of Parashara's Light, the best Vedic astrology software available, so you can generate your own chart, or the charts of friends and family. See page 264 for more information about this software.

If you don't have access to a computer (or your computer is not compatible with this software), and you would like me to prepare a chart for you (at the cost of $5.00 per chart for shipping and handling), please send the date, place, and time of your birth to me at:

Andrew Bloomfield
1223 Wilshire Blvd. #238
Santa Monica, CA 90403
www.bloomfieldastrology.com

Planetary Mantras

If you would like to obtain a recording of planetary mantras on a CD, you may order from the source listed here. This CD uses mantras slightly different than those depicted in this book, but will produce the same results, nonetheless.

Devi Mandir
5950 Highway 128
Napa, CA 94558
(707) 966-2802
www.shreemaa.org/audio.htm

Vedic Gemstones

King Enterprises
1305 N. "H" Street/PMB 289
Lompac, CA 93436
(805) 736-0449
e-mail: aldawn@earthlink.net

Jyotish Gem Stones
508 N. Second St., Suite 108
Fairfield, IA 52556
(800) 559-5090
www.astrologicalgem.com

Vedic Yagyas (fire ceremonies)

To find out how to have a yagya conducted, contact the Hindu temple closest to you, which you can find at www.mandirnet.org.

Even if there is not a Hindu temple near your home, rituals for planetary purposes can be conducted by Vedic priests on your behalf without your needing to be in attendance.

Contact the main priest or manager of a temple, and let them know the purpose of the yagya. It might be to attract love; because of a legal dispute; for more abundance; to mark the passing away of a close one (yagyas can be performed to ease the soul's journey); to remove obstacles; or for any other purpose, spiritual or mundane.

For an even easier way to order a planetary fire ceremony over the internet, contact:
The M.A. Center
PO Box 613
San Ramon, CA 94583
phone: (510) 537-9417
fax: (510) 889-8585
www.ammachi.org (click on "pujas")
e-mail: puja@ammachi.org

Astro-Locality

To obtain software that shows you the best place to live, or to have an astro-locality print-out sent to you, contact:
Astrolabe
PO Box 1750
Brewster, MA 02631
toll free phone: (800) 843-6682
local: (508) 896-5081
fax: (508) 896-5289
www.alabe.com
e-mail: astrolabe@alabe.com

Vedic Astrologers, Courses, and Books

The American Council of Vedic Astrology
PO Box 2149
Sedona, AZ 86339
(800) 900-6595
www.vedicastrology.org
e-mail: acva@sedone.net

The American Institute of Vedic Studies
PO Box 8357
Santa Fe, NM 87504
(505) 983-9385
Please inquire about their comprehensive correspondence course.

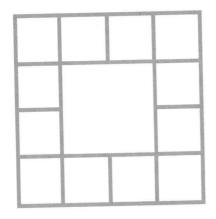

GLOSSARY

ascendant: Also known as the 1st house, this is the zodiac sign rising on the eastern horizon at the moment of your birth. Its qualities and characteristics influence your psycho-physiological makeup.

bhukti: Within the major cycles of the planets (mahadasha), these are smaller periods during which planets exert their influence, and thus flavor, for a time, the overall quality of the mahadasha.

combust: When a planet is situated too close to the Sun (between about 8 and 15 degrees, depending on the planet) it is considered combust. The indications of those planets then become weakened or destroyed.

conjunction: When two or more planets occupy the same house, irrespective of how close they are by degree (though closer degrees have stronger impact), they are considered conjunct.

dusthana: The challenging houses that include the 6th, 8th, and 12th are the dusthana houses. Of these three, the 6th is the least challenging because it is also an upachaya house and can improve over time and with effort.

Ketu: The south node of the Moon is called Ketu. Known as a shadowy influence rather than a planet, this point is determined by where the Moon passes the ecliptic.

kuja dosha: An obstruction to the peaceful enjoyment of married life that occurs when Mars is placed in the 1st, 4th, 7th, 8th, or 12th houses of the natal chart, with a few exceptions (see page 147).

mahadasha: The major cycles of the planets, according to the Vimshottari system, that amplify the planets' tendencies in your chart. These cycles last anywhere from six to twenty years, depending on the planet.

mantra: In the context of Vedic astrology, a powerful Sanskrit sound that activates a particular planetary energy, thereby enhancing its positive influence in your life, or mitigating a troublesome one.

muhurtha: Determining the best date and time to begin an activity.

nakshatra: Vedic astrology divides the zodiac into 27 equal parts, called nakshatras, each representing 13 degrees, 20 minutes of arc. Each is based on the daily course of the Moon and associated with a fixed star or star cluster in the heavens.

navamsha: A method of fine-tuning the prediction of a chart. A ninth harmonic division whereby each sign is divided into 3-degree, 20-minute sections.

opposition: The connection between two or more planets that occurs when they are located in houses 180 degrees from one another. Opposition happens irrespective of how close the planets are by degree (though closer degrees are stronger).

purva punya: Past-life merit, or the lack thereof.

Rahu: The north node of the Moon is called Rahu. Known as a shadowy influence rather than a planet, this point is determined by where the Moon passes the ecliptic.

sandhi: A weak position for a planet that occurs when the planet is located in the very last degree of a sign or within the first degree of the next sign.

square: A challenging aspect that occurs when a planet influences the house 90 degrees (or the 4th house) from itself.

trine: A harmonious aspect that occurs when a planet influences the house 120 degrees (or the 5th house) from itself.

upachaya: Houses that increase over time in their ability to give good results due to your effort and enthusiasm are called upachaya (or improving) houses. These include the 3rd, 6th, 10th, and 11th houses.

vargottama: When a planet is located in the same house in both the natal chart and the navamsha. This indication gives strong emphasis for that planet and its placement, either good or bad.

yagya: A fire ritual performed by Vedic priests to empower a planetary situation, whether to enhance something positive, or help avert something negative.

Aikman, Troy, 180–82, 183

INDEX

About Parashara's Light Vedic Astrology Software

The CD accompanying this book contains a beginner's version of Parashara's Light software, which lets you use the basic chart calculation feature. You can create and view unlimited number of birth charts, and for each one you can generate a one-page printout that contains all the calculations used in the sample charts of the book. When you are ready to access the full range of powerful features of Parashara's Light 6.0, you can easily upgrade to the advanced version. The upgrade details are included on the CD.

Software Installation
1. If you run Windows 98 and you have Norton's SystemWorks 2003, it is advisable to uninstall or disable the CleanSweep component before this installation.
2. Insert the CD-ROM into your CD-ROM drive
3. Autorun will display the installation screen. Choose to install the Parashara's Light software on your hard-disk or to view the demo of the full version.
4. Follow the instructions to finish the software installation

Parashara's Light first edition came out in 1991. Since then, five major updates have followed, turning the program into a powerhouse of interactive calculations. Personalized tutorials introduce a spectrum of Vedic astrology techniques, and personalized reports further support its practical understanding. Above all, the user interface makes the program very easy and intuitive to use, while supporting powerful customization and advanced features when you need them.

Parashara's Light users enjoy access to free technical support and a free subscription to an online Vedic astrology newsletter for ongoing interaction with Vedic astrology experts and for asking questions to keep the learning process active.

Parashara's Light is published by GeoVision Software, Inc., the largest U.S. based Vedic astrology software company, with users in over fifty countries. For over twelve years, the GeoVision Software team, lead by Michiel R. Boender, has been creating award-winning software products based on authentic Vedic astrology techniques and highly accurate astronomical calculations. GeoVision Software, Inc., is exclusively dedicated to the field of Vedic astrology through software development, scientific research, and committed to Vedic astrology education at large.

For any questions regarding installation of the enclosed CD and details about upgrading to the advanced version, please visit the support website www.parashara.com/support.htm. You can also subscribe to the Vedic astrology newsletter at this support site.

If you need assistance with upgrading or have any other questions about the advanced version of Parashara's Light, contact:

GeoVision Software, Inc.
P.O. Box 2152
Fairfield, IA 52556, USA
(800) 459-6847
www.parashara.com/support.htm
e-mail: sales@parashara.com